ANTISEMITISM AND ANTI-ZIONISM

Studies in Migration and Diaspora

Series Editor:
Anne J. Kershen, Queen Mary, University of London, UK

Studies in Migration and Diaspora is a series designed to showcase the interdisciplinary and multidisciplinary nature of research in this important field. Volumes in the series cover local, national and global issues and engage with both historical and contemporary events. The books will appeal to scholars, students and all those engaged in the study of migration and diaspora. Amongst the topics covered are minority ethnic relations, transnational movements and the cultural, social and political implications of moving from 'over there', to 'over here'.

Also in the series:

Cultures in Refuge
Seeking Sanctuary in Modern Australia
Edited by Anna Hayes and Robert Mason
ISBN 978-1-4094-3475-7

Whiteness and Postcolonialism in the Nordic Region
Exceptionalism, Migrant Others and National Identities
Edited by Kristín Loftsdóttir and Lars Jensen
ISBN 978-1-4094-4481-7

European Identity and Culture
Narratives of Transnational Belonging
Edited by Rebecca Friedman and Markus Thiel
ISBN 978-1-4094-3714-7

Inhabiting Borders, Routes Home
Youth, Gender, Asylum
Ala Sirriyeh
ISBN 978-1-4094-4495-4

The Challenges of Diaspora Migration
Interdisciplinary Perspectives on Israel and Germany
Edited by Rainer K. Silbereisen, Peter F. Titzmann and Yossi Shavit
ISBN 978-1-4094-6424-2

Antisemitism and Anti-Zionism

Representation, Cognition and Everyday Talk

RUSI JASPAL
De Montfort University, UK

ASHGATE

Published by
Ashgate Publishing Limited
Wey Court East
Union Road
Farnham
Surrey, GU9 7PT
England

Ashgate Publishing Company
110 Cherry Street
Suite 3-1
Burlington, VT 05401-3818
USA

www.ashgate.com

British Library Cataloguing in Publication Data
A catalogue record for this book is available from the British Library

The Library of Congress has cataloged the printed edition as follows:
Jaspal, Rusi, 1984- author.
Antisemitism and anti-Zionism: representation, cognition, and everyday talk / by Rusi Jaspal.
    pages cm. — (Studies in migration and diaspora)
Includes bibliographical references and index.
ISBN 978-1-4094-5437-3 (hardback : alk. paper) — ISBN 978-1-4094-5438-0 (ebook) — ISBN 978-1-4724-0725-2 (epub) 1. Antisemitism. 2. Antisemitism—Iran. 3. Zionism. 4. Israel—Foreign public opinion, British. 5. Public opinion—Great Britain. 6. Discourse analysis, Narrative—Psychological aspects. I. Title.
 DS145.J34 2014
 305.892'4—dc23

2014012561

ISBN 9781409454373 (hbk)
ISBN 9781409454380 (ebk-PDF)
ISBN 9781472407252 (ebk-ePUB)

Printed in the United Kingdom by Henry Ling Limited,
at the Dorset Press, Dorchester, DT1 1HD

To R.K. and A.D. Jaspal

Contents

Acknowledgements

I would like to begin by thanking the following institutions which have, in one way or another, supported the research activity upon which this book is based: The Center of Israel Studies at the American University, Washington DC, USA; the Iran Media Program at the Annenberg Center for Communication, University of Pennsylvania, USA; and the Association for Israel Studies. I am grateful to the Department of Psychology at Royal Holloway, University of London, UK; the School of Sociology and Social Policy at the University of Nottingham, UK; and the School of Applied Social Sciences, De Montfort University, Leicester, UK, for providing stimulating research environments and for supporting my research over the years.

I thank Professor Joël Kotek and Dr Zsófia Kata Vincze for their immensely helpful attitude to my research into the visual aspects of antisemitism, Dr Andreea Ernst-Vintila for her challenging but constructive criticism on my research into social representations of the Holocaust, and Professor Raphael Cohen-Almagor for inviting me to share my ideas with him and his colleagues at the Middle East Study Group at the University of Hull, which helped crystallise my thinking in this area. I am grateful to Dr Neil Jordan, the senior commissioning editor at Ashgate for his enthusiasm about my idea to write this book, and Dr Anne Kershen, the series editor, for her very helpful and constructive feedback on an earlier version of the book manuscript.

Finally, I must apologise to my family and close friends for neglecting them during the writing of this and other books and thank them for being so patient, understanding and supportive.

Series Editor's Preface

The two nouns which provide the title for this book would appear to refer to recent phenomena, both epithets having emerged in the late nineteenth century; the former denoting hatred of those racially identifiable as Jews, the latter signifying opposition to the establishment, and existence, of a Jewish homeland. Yet, the former has been used by a number of writers and historians, including the author of this book, to describe all forms of 'Jew hatred' since pre-Christian times, most particularly religious antipathy, otherwise defined as anti-Jewishness, whilst anti-Zionism – in the context of hostility to a Jewish nation state – in addition to those to be expected, has been, and still is, manifested by a small minority of ultra-orthodox Jews who believe that a Jewish homeland could only exist with the, still awaited, coming of the Messiah.

However, this is no history book – though the author provides the reader with a commendable historical background to Christian and Muslim 'antisemitism'. This is a volume which provides a highly original, informative and, at times, disturbing, *contemporary* insight into the two designations of the title, and, by deconstructing both, demonstrates how they are, as he explains, 'complex, delineable, yet inter-related social psychological phenomena'. In order to comprehend the social-psychological implications of modern day antisemitism and anti-Zionism, Rusi Jaspal (a chartered psychologist and senior lecturer in psychology) carried out piercing qualitative research amongst two specific groups, young Muslims in Iran and Britain and young Jews in Israel and Britain. He sought to evaluate the psychological motivations of the former and the impact of these on the latter. The interviews with the young people in Iran highlighted the persuasive power of Holocaust denial policy and propaganda. This goes some way towards explaining the mental and emotional imperatives that created the entrenched antisemitic and anti-Zionist views that informed and influenced the interviewees. In an ironic take on history, the young Pakistani Muslims interviewed in Britain, whilst denying they held any antisemitic sentiments, at the same time equated Zionism with Nazism, identifying the residents and advocates of the Jewish state as 'evil'.

In contrast, the Jewish Israelis interviewed considered the two phenomena as formative and interlinked elements of their 'Jewish' identity. However, in the spatial context of Europe and the Middle East, they differentiated between the levels of antisemitism and the threat this posed. These young people had developed defined coping strategies to deal with the phenomena under the microscope, some even at times 'passing' and assuming a non-Zionist identity in order to fend off anti-Zionist attack. Their counterparts in Britain demonstrated the complexity and diversity of being Jewish outside of Israel. As Jaspal clearly illustrates, these diasporic Jews represent secular and religious Jews – the latter ranging from ultra-orthodox to liberal Jews – and pro- and anti-Zionists. As such, their responses to the threat posed by antisemitism and anti-Zionism varied in resonance.

This is a book which explores contemporary issues of international import which have been, in the nature of this book, largely under-researched. Examining the impact of antisemitism and anti-Zionism on young Muslims and young Jews within a psychological framework not only enlarges the breadth of migrant and diaspora studies but, in addition, and most importantly, augments our understanding of the emotional implications of religious and social-political condemnation amongst those who condemn and those who are on the receiving end of that condemnation. Antisemitism may be the longest hatred and anti-Zionism one of the more recent, but anything which increases our awareness of the consequences of those two phenomena and which, as a result, facilitates the eradication of bitterness and loathing is a worthy result. A reading of this book contributes to that understanding and thus should be firmly lodged on the library shelves of those who wish to see improved relations between the proponents and recipients of antisemitism and anti-Zionism.

Anne J Kershen
Queen Mary University of London
Spring 2014

Foreword

Professor Raphael Cohen-Almagor

Antisemitism is a powerful sentiment. It has been a fashionable and successful phenomenon in many parts of the world for generations. Despite many attempts to expose its hideous roots, the underlying ignorance and the brute lies that are spread about Jews, antisemitism has survived all attempts to curb it. It is a resilient and ugly form of racism that has direct implications for Jews throughout the world.

One of the images that are closely associated with Jews is of a person who packs his bag, takes his stick and moves from one place to another. This is the image of the Wandering Jew. Indeed, Jews have been wandering the world, often as they fled from persecution, pogroms and harassment.

In the nineteenth Century, a national movement called Zionism emerged. Its goal was to establish a home for the Jewish people, a place where Jews could live free of antisemitism and violence. After some debate as to where this home should be, the Zionists set their eyes on Palestine as the place that could unite Jews. Understandably, Jews wished to return to the birthplace of their forefathers, to *Eretz* (Land of) Israel. This was the only place on earth to which Jews from different corners of the world feel affinity and connection. The early Zionists recognised that the journey would not be easy, that it would be rife with challenges and obstacles, but they wanted to stop the constant wandering. They wanted to lead their lives as free people, sovereign and independent.

The Zionist idea was to inhabit the land of the Jewish ancestors and to create there a new Jew (Sabra), who is able to lead his life freely, practice his religion and culture with no bigotry and without apology; able to defend himself against antisemitic violence; cultivate his own land, and be productive and social. Zionism demanded a significant personal sacrifice and a radical change in one's life: leaving one's home, one's country; travelling afar to a distant land; often changing one's profession; getting accustomed to a new, rough environment; adopting for many a new language, Hebrew, which at that point in time was confined only to religious studies, not used in one's daily life. Zionism attempted to establish Jewish communal life at the expense of personal bourgeois comfort and the good life of the individual. Collective goals were held superior to individual ambitions. Indeed, Zionism as a revolutionary movement was about individual and social redemption and emancipation, the gathering of exiles, and the creation of a new person, of a new society, in the old land of the Bible. David Ben-Gurion wrote:

> The meaning of the Jewish revolution is contained in one word--independence!
> Independence for the Jewish people in its homeland! Dependence is not

merely political or economic; it is also moral, cultural, and intellectual, and it affects every limb and nerve of the body every conscious and subconscious act. Independence, too, means more than political and economic freedom. It involves also the spiritual, moral, and intellectual realms and, in essence, it is independence in the heart, in sentiment, and in will. From this inner sense of freedom outer forms of independence will develop in our way of life, social organization, relations with other people, and economic structure.[1]

Ben-Gurion further explained that Jewish independence would be shaped further by the conquest of labour and the land, by broadening the range of the Hebrew language and its culture, by perfecting the methods of self-government and self-defence, by creating the framework and conditions for national and political independence and creativity. This was the essence of the Jewish revolution.

Ben-Gurion thought that exile was an insult, that exile ruined Jewish character and life. Exile negated Jewish historical past and Jewish moral mission. Thus, Jews had to return to their homeland and revive the Hebrew language. Ben-Gurion continued the missionary vision of Theodor Herzl, the father of modern political Zionism. Both men understood that Jews would be able to transform into people of character only if they left Europe and migrated to a new land. In *The Jewish State* Herzl wrote: "The Jews have dreamt this kingly dream all through the long nights of their history. 'Next year in Jerusalem' is our old phrase. It is now a question of showing that the dream can be converted into a living reality".[2] The Zionist movement was fortunate to have two giant leaders who had the vision and the courage to pave the way for the significant revolution against immense odds.

In this well-written and well-researched book, Rusi Jaspal rightly asserts that for Theodor Herzl, Zionism offered the only plausible solution to the ominous, lingering problem of antisemitism. Herzl recognised that in exile Jews would continue to face enmity and persecution. Herzl wrote:

> Anti-Semitism increases day by day and hour by hour among the nations; indeed, it is bound to increase, because the causes of its growth continue to exist and cannot be removed. Its remote cause is our loss of the power of assimilation during the Middle Ages; its immediate cause is our excessive production of mediocre intellects, who cannot find an outlet downwards or upwards – that is to say, no wholesome outlet in either direction. When we sink, we become a revolutionary proletariat, the subordinate officers of all revolutionary parties; and at the same time, when we rise, there rises also our terrible power of the purse.[3]

---

1   David Ben-Gurion, "The Imperatives of the Jewish Revolution", http://zionism-israel.com/hdoc/Ben-Gurion_Jewish_revolution.htm

2   Theodor Herzl, The Jewish State (New York: Dover Publications, 1988): 40, http://www.gutenberg.org/files/25282/25282-h/25282-h.htm

3   Ibid., 41.

The Zionist movement has been a successful national, revolutionary movement. In 1948, the goal was achieved when the State of Israel was established. However, the goal of achieving security was not achieved. Antisemitism has not been relaxed. A new racist phenomenon has emerged, anti-Zionism, that has supplemented and bolstered antisemitism. The birth-pangs of the Jewish state were exceptionally painful as the less-than-one-day country was immediately attacked by its neighbours that did not wish to come to terms with its sovereign existence. The Arabs in Palestine did not wish for Zionism to materialise. They did not accept any attempts at compromise over the land as offered by the UN and other intermediaries. The 1947 Partition Plan was rejected *tout court*. Israel's War of Independence is termed *Nakba* (literally "catastrophe") by the Palestinians. The Jewish desire for salvation from violence and constant persecution meant a catastrophe for the Arabs of Palestine.

Since then, Israel's existence has been contested time and again. More wars ensued. Anti-Zionist sentiments intensified. Zionism has been tagged a form of racism. While two of Israel's neighbours conceded to come to terms with the Zionist-Jewish state and signed peace treaties with Israel – first Egypt in 1978 and later Jordan in 1994 – the two other neighbours, Syria and Lebanon, have yet to come to terms with Israel. Peace with the Palestinians remains a desire. More than 60 years after the establishment of the State of Israel, its geographic boundaries are still contested. Israel does not appear on the maps of some of its rivals. Israel is yet to be accepted as a legitimate entity, part and parcel of the Middle East, by many countries, near and far.

Rusi Jaspal's thoughtful and thought-provoking book is intended to provide an understanding of the social and psychological motivations and processes underlying antisemitism and anti-Zionism. It examines these forms of prejudice in two specific case studies, Iranian Muslims and British Pakistani Muslims and the responses to these forms of prejudice among Israelis and British Jews. It also investigates the inter-relations between historical events and their social psychological meanings for groups and individuals. The psychological framework consists of Social Representations Theory, Identity Process Theory and Intergroup Threat Theory.

Combining theory with painstaking empirical analysis, Jaspal shows that the Iranians resort in their publications to a delegitimisation campaign which consists of three inter-dependent components: contesting the legitimacy of Israel; describing the "malevolent" processes whereby the Jewish State was established and is currently maintained; "problem-solving" by demanding the destruction of Israel. By analysing the 2006 International Holocaust Cartoon Contest, designed to deny the Holocaust, Jaspal explains the methods by which Zionism has been transformed into a new form of Nazism. In the crude political cynicism and irony, masterminded by Tehran, the Jews who survived the most comprehensive and vicious campaign to annihilate a people the world has ever known, were said to have "in fact" invented the Holocaust and adopted the ideology of their arch nemesis. By endorsing this contest, Jaspal rightly notes, the Islamic Republic of Iran sought to "normalise" Holocaust denial (that is, antisemitism) as a legitimate means of criticising Israel and Zionism. Jaspal argues that Iranians tend to conflate antisemitism and anti-Zionism. He found similarly strong negative sentiments among British Pakistani Muslims who also mix Holocaust denial, old-fashion bigoted depictions of Jews and unequivocal resentment of the State of Israel.

At the end of his empirical study, Jaspal highlights the general importance of both Jewish ethno-religious and Israeli national identities among the Israeli Jews who were interviewed. Most of them regarded their Jewish and Israeli identities as inextricably entwined, and perceived anti-Zionism as a form of antisemitism. Both forms of prejudice threaten their Jewish and Israeli identities. Jaspal also interviewed British Jews and found that Israeli and British Jews construed anti-Zionism and antisemitism as a fundamentally Muslim, rather than European, phenomenon. Psychologically it is more comfortable, or less disturbing, for people who choose to lead their lives in Europe to associate these forms of prejudice with a religion rather than a continent that has been rife with Christian stern hatred for the Jews for many generations.

Theodor Herzl, who was aware of the malicious continental antisemitism, was a man of vision, a dreamer and a doer. In *The Jewish State*, Herzl wrote:[4]

> But the Jews, once settled in their own State, would probably have no more enemies. As for those who remain behind, since prosperity enfeebles and causes them to diminish, they would soon disappear altogether. I think the Jews will always have sufficient enemies, such as every nation has. But once fixed in their own land, it will no longer be possible for them to scatter all over the world. The diaspora cannot be reborn, unless the civilization of the whole earth should collapse; and such a consummation could be feared by none but foolish men. Our present civilization possesses weapons powerful enough for its self-defence.

For the time being, the vision has been more optimistic than real. Israel still has enemies, and Jews are scattered all over the world. Jews continue to wander, looking for happiness and security. Zionism must find a way to integrate into the Middle East and to garner acceptance especially among the nations surrounding Israel. Then Israel will be more attractive to Jews who may consider making *aliya* (immigrate) to Zion but are cautious not to substitute one form of insecure living with another.

Herzl concluded *The Jewish State* by the following statements:[5]

> We shall live at last as free men on our own soil, and die peacefully in our own homes.
> The world will be freed by our liberty, enriched by our wealth, magnified by our greatness.

---

4   Theodor Herzl, *The Jewish State* http://www.gutenberg.org/files/25282/25282-h/25282-h.htm

5   Theodor Herzl, *The Jewish State* http://www.gutenberg.org/files/25282/25282-h/25282-h.htm

And whatever we attempt there to accomplish for our own welfare, will react powerfully and beneficially for the good of humanity.

Amen!

PART I
Introduction

Chapter 1

Introduction

In the past, the most dangerous antisemites were those who wanted to make the world Judenrein, "free of Jews". Today, the most dangerous antisemites might be those who want to make the world Judenstaatrein, "free of a Jewish state".

Per Ahlmark
Former Deputy Prime Minister of Sweden
11 April 2002

Antisemitism and anti-Zionism are complex, delineable, yet inter-related social psychological phenomena. While antisemitism has been described as an irrational, age-old prejudice (Wistrich, 1991), anti-Zionism is often represented as a legitimate response to a "rogue state" (Corrigan, 2009). Antisemitism and anti-Zionism have been the subject of much discussion among social and political commentators. There are diverse views on them. Not everybody agrees. People rarely admit to being antisemitic but many would readily disclose their opposition to Zionism, an ideology that has acquired negative connotations in many societies. Antisemitism evokes imagery of fascism, extremism, death and genocide, while anti-Zionism evokes imagery of anti-capitalism, anti-racism and minority rights. The former has a malevolent action orientation, while the latter is understood to have a benevolent one. Yet, both antisemitism and anti-Zionism are forms of hostility and prejudice. While antisemitism reflects hostility towards the Jewish people, anti-Zionism essentially constitutes hostility towards the Jewish State. There have been gradual shifts in thematic focus – Jews have been described as excessively cosmopolitan and as insular traditionalists; as weak and effete, as well as mighty and powerful. Moreover, in history, particular groups have been more or less associated with antisemitism – the most aggressive forms of antisemitism were observable among European far-right groups, while today Islamists and many on the political left appear to invoke antisemitic myths in their diatribes against the Jewish State. Despite the multifarious forms that antisemitism has taken in history – including its most recent manifestation in the guise of extreme anti-Zionism – its underlying patterns and action orientation appear to have remained remarkably uniform.

The Necessity of Studying Antisemitism and Anti-Zionism

In history, Jews have suffered unthinkable persecution in their host countries – during medieval times, they were indiscriminately murdered in the European towns in which the blood libel accusation gained traction; in the Russian Empire, thousands of Jews, including young children, were murdered in the violent state-endorsed anti-Jewish pogroms; and during the Nazi regime, at least 6 million Jews were murdered in a systematic attempt to wipe out European Jewry (Dundes, 1991; Gilbert, 1985; Herf, 2006; Klier and Lambroza, 1992). The Holocaust, as the culmination of long-standing European antisemitism, has come to function as a metaphor for the turbulent Jewish history.

Many decades after the Holocaust, overt antisemitism has become disreputable in most circles, but it does manifest itself under newer, subtler guises which bypass the stigma of overt prejudice and racism. Its newer manifestation in the form of anti-Zionism, which is rarely devoid of antisemitic metaphors and imagery, is enthusiastically endorsed by a multitude of actors, groups and organisations – principally left-wing groups and Muslim groups. There is a widespread societal perception that antisemitism is a thing of the past and that it disappeared after the horrors of the Holocaust were revealed to the world. However, this perception is erroneous. Antisemitism lives on. In history, multifarious myths, motifs and representations emerged and contributed to the delegitimisation, demonisation and, many cases, destruction of Jews. In contemporary times, diverse myths, motifs and representations are created, re-created and crystallised in order to delegitimise, demonise and destroy the Jewish State. There appears to be much synergy in representations of the Jewish people and the State of Israel, which can render the delineation of antisemitism and anti-Zionism somewhat difficult. What these forms of prejudice share is a destructive effect upon intergroup relations.

Following the establishment of the State of Israel, the main centre of antisemitism shifted to Arab countries, from which hundreds of thousands of Jews were forced to leave, either through direct expulsion or due to violence and intimidation from their Muslim neighbours (Shulewitz, 2001). In these countries, Jews continue to be openly delegitimised and demonised. Moreover, self-identified anti-Zionist state organisations in the Middle East have perpetrated deadly attacks against Jews, as exemplified by the bombing of a Jewish cultural centre in Buenos Aires, Argentina in 1994. Since 1979, the Islamic Republic of Iran has led the global campaign against Zionism and Iranian officials have not shied away from employing overt antisemitism in their anti-Zionist campaign. Iran's fervent anti-Zionism has induced suspicion, distrust and fear among the Israeli administration (Jaspal and Coyle, 2014). Hostilities have been exacerbated by Iran's nuclear programme, which Israel believes is intended for the development of nuclear weapons to be used against Israel (Pardo, 2007). Tense relations between Iran and Israel have raised fears in the international community over a potential armed conflict between the two countries, and these fears have not necessarily waned after the election of "moderates" in Iran.

Young disaffected Muslims, many of whom were born and raised in European countries, have vented their anger at Israel's perceived treatment of the Palestinians on (non-Israeli) Jews and Jewish institutions in the West. In March 2012, Mohamed Merah, a young man of Algerian descent, shot dead four Jews at a Jewish day school in Toulouse, allegedly because he believed that Israel was responsible for the deaths of innocent Muslims. In France, there have been countless cases of the defacing and burning of synagogues and Jewish cultural centres, physical attacks on Jewish school children and, in 2006, the kidnap, torture and murder of a young Jewish salesman by an antisemitic gang (Golsan, 2010). In Britain, antisemitism is said to be on the rise and spearheaded by Muslim minorities similarly angered by Israel's alleged mistreatment of the Palestinians. The rise in antisemitism is observable all over Europe, as compellingly exemplified by the pages and pages of "antisemitic incidents" which are summarised at the beginning of each issue of *Journal for the Study of Antisemitism* (e.g. Baum & Rosenberg, 2012, 2013).

Antisemitism did not end with the discovery of the Holocaust, but rather it continues to exist and is expressed in diverse ways. It has a complex relationship with anti-Zionism, which is explored in this book. Both forms of prejudice are encouraged and manifested to varying degrees in Arab/Islamic and European countries, respectively. It is difficult to speak of antisemitic/anti-Zionist "tendencies" in specific countries, given that particular social groups within these countries may be more or less committed to these forms of prejudice. This book is intended to provide an understanding of the social and psychological motivations and processes underlying antisemitism and indeed anti-Zionism in order to facilitate positive intergroup relations.

Examining Responses to Antisemitism and Anti-Zionism

Although there has been much debate about antisemitism and anti-Zionism, few scholars have systematically examined the social and psychological repercussions of these forms of hostility for Israeli Jews and diaspora Jews. This can give the impression that these groups do not have a stance on antisemitism and anti-Zionism, and how they respond to these forms of hostility is not entirely clear. In order to facilitate positive intergroup relations, it is necessary to examine such responses, as this will help to construct a fuller picture of the social and psychological outcomes of antisemitism and anti-Zionism.

Despite this lacuna in theory and research, in various accounts of antisemitism and anti-Zionism, there is some cursory insight into reactions from diaspora Jews and Israelis. For instance, in her overview of anti-Zionism on UK university campuses, Klaff (2010) observes that campus anti-Zionism has "resulted in a situation where anti-Semitism is flourishing on UK campuses, causing direct harm to Jewish students and confirming their 'outsider' status" (p. 89). She argues that this has had negative outcomes for social and psychological wellbeing among Jewish students because they may feel compelled to conceal their sense of connection to Israel. It is noteworthy that many Jews construe Israel as a symbol of their Jewish identity (Graham and Boyd, 2010) and, thus, the perceived obligation to conceal their connection to Israel may be psychologically threatening. It is now generally accepted that individuals can derive psychological wellbeing from the manifestation of their ethnic and religious identities and, thus, any hindrance to the construction of a positive ethnic/religious identity can have the reverse effects (Jaspal and

Cinnirella, 2012). Furthermore, Klaff (2010, p. 97) notes that "the demonization of Israel causes Jews to feel emotional pain", particularly when this is coupled with various forms of Holocaust revisionism (see Chapter 2, this volume). Accordingly, Klaff argues that anti-Zionism on campus ought to be regarded as a form of hate speech. However, it must be stated that, although there is some important research into European Jews' responses to antisemitism and anti-Zionism (e.g. Boyd, 2013), there is little qualitative social psychological work on British Jews' responses to these forms of prejudice which can shed light on how their identities may be shaped and how they may attempt to cope with potential threats to identity. This specific research path can provide detailed insight into the social psychological mechanisms underlying responses to antisemitism and anti-Zionism.

In an early paper on identity rejection and identity reawakening, Diller (1980) provided an interesting perspective on US Jews' identities and coping strategies. He discussed Jewish identity rejection, identity ambivalence, secondary emotional reactions and repression and outlined a model for facilitating what he referred to as "Jewish reawakening". He argued that Jews might develop identity rejection when their Jewish identity "is not fully integrated or accepted by the self" (p. 41). Crucially, this may occur when one's Jewish identity is highly stigmatised in a given social context and is perceived as being conducive to negative social and psychological outcomes. Indeed, this response would be expected in an antisemitic context. In such a context, one may be led to believe that one's Jewish identity is incompatible with the dominant cultural, religious or national ethos, thereby facilitating a sense of identity conflict. Under these circumstances, one may opt for the "exit option" (Tajfel, 1975) and repress one's Jewish identity. As part of his four-stage model, Diller suggested that identity-rejecting Jews needed to be exposed to "a different and more satisfying view of their Jewish heritage" (p. 43), highlighting the importance of social representation in identity cognition (see Chapter 4, this volume).

Similarly, scholars before Diller had long argued that some Jews might suffer from "self-hatred" and "negative chauvinism" as a result of the stigma of their Jewish identity (Lewin, 1948). Lewin highlighted that there was an observable tendency for members of marginalised and stigmatised groups to display a degree of hostility towards their ingroups and argued that this was observable in Jewish hostility towards "the Jews as a group, against a particular fraction of the Jews, against his own family, or against himself" (Lewin, 1948, p. 187). He proceeded to argue that such hatred "may be directed against Jewish institutions, Jewish mannerisms, Jewish language, or Jewish ideals" (p. 187). According to Lewin's account, Jewish self-hatred emerged from frustration at Jews' inability to leave their stigmatised ingroup and from their desire to assimilate to the non-Jewish outgroup by accepting the outgroup's negative perceptions of the Jewish ingroup. Although there has been considerable criticism of Lewin's framework, particularly as the concept of self-hatred has been employed in order to stigmatise and even pathologise dissent (Finlay, 2005), it is possible that some individuals come to experience guilt and negative emotions on the basis of their Jewish ethno-religious and/or Israeli ethno-national group memberships and that they may seek to disidentifty with these groups by manifesting what has been described as "self-hatred". This has some overlap with the aforementioned "exit option" described by Tajfel (1975). Similarly, Friesel (2011) argued that Jewish Judeophobia manifested in the guise of anti-Israelism constitutes a "problematic form of Jewish identity" (p. 514), which results from "the intricate balancing act between the influence of the non-Jewish environment and weakening sway of the Jewish heritage" (p. 516).

Friesel's account of contemporary Jews against Israel may also be applicable to Israeli Jews and particularly to the so-called "new historians" in Israel, such as Ilan Pappé (2006, 2007) and Avi Shlaim, (2001, 2009) who have been described as anti-Zionist scholars. However, there are other perspectives that had been offered. Political commentators frequently acknowledge and debate Israel's position in the international community and, more specifically, its political and military actions. Very rarely is the link made between widespread antisemitism and anti-Zionism and the defensiveness manifested by Israel. Some scholars have discussed the notion of Israel's "siege mentality", which refers to the inter-related beliefs that one's ingroup is under siege, that the rest of the world has highly negative intentions towards one's society and that one's society is alone in a unanimously hostile world (Bar-Tal, 2000). It has been noted that when groups, like the Israeli national group, perceive themselves to be existentially threatened by outgroups, they will naturally respond in defensive ways (Jaspal and Yampolsky, 2011). The measures undertaken can seem extreme and disproportionate but are socially and psychologically understandable when viewed in the context of antisemitism and anti-Zionism.

Group members respond to group stigma in diverse ways – some disidentify with the stigmatised group, while others may decide to accentuate their identification with the stigmatised ingroup. It is necessary to examine how Jews and Israelis may be affected by antisemitism and anti-Zionism in order to understand these forms of prejudice in a holistic manner.

Antisemitism and Anti-Zionism: Representation, Cognition and Everyday Talk

This book explores antisemitism, the age-old prejudice, and anti-Zionism, which has been described as a "new antisemitism" (Chesler, 2003; Fischel, 2005), through the analysis of representation, cognition and discourse. The research summarised in this book approaches antisemitism and anti-Zionism from a multi-faceted perspective, examining these forms of prejudice in two specific case studies (Iranian Muslims and British Pakistani Muslims) *and* the responses to these forms of prejudice among Israeli Jews and British Jews. This book marries social psychological theories of representation, cognition and everyday talk in order to provide a complex and fine-grained qualitative account of antisemitism and anti-Zionism among the specific groups that are explored.

This book has three inter-related goals, namely to understand representations and cognitions about Jews and the State of Israel and how these categories feature in people's everyday talk. This is important because it links three important levels of antisemitism and anti-Zionism that have rarely been examined in unison. Much of the existing work on antisemitism tends to be more descriptive than theoretically-oriented (e.g. Chesler, 2003; Fischel, 2005; Wistrich, 1991, 2010) and few are social psychological in focus (though see Cohen, 2009; Cohen et al., 2011). This book constitutes an attempt to redress this imbalance.

There is some research into the distinct ways in which Jews and Israel have been represented in visual art, literature, newspaper media and in others channels of societal information (Lindemann and Levy, 2010a; Wistrich, 1999b). However, the ways in which these categories are anchored to societal phenomena and how they come to represent "tangible" realities are less obvious. The examination of social representations is important because when these representations become politicised and institutionalised, as they are in Iran, for instance, it is likely that laypeople will begin to accept them and potentially act upon them (Baum, 2009b). Similarly, some of the psychological research in the area of antisemitism and, more recently, in the domain of anti-Zionism have outlined specific psychological processes in a linear manner without taking into consideration the important role of social stimuli, such as the social representations, and the pivotal role of social context (e.g. Cohen et al., 2011).

Cognitive accounts of antisemitism and anti-Zionism have considered various facets, many of which are summarised in the next two chapters. However, these forms of prejudice have never been considered in the context of identity processes, namely the processes that underlie the construction of a positive sense of self. This is fundamentally a social cognitive process because it functions principally at the level of thought albeit through interaction with the social world (Jaspal and Breakwell, 2014). Through the lens of Identity Process Theory and other theories from social psychology (see Chapter 4, this volume), this book examines the motivational principles underlying identity construction in order to understand how and why people may manifest antisemitic and anti-Zionist prejudice and how and why people may respond to it in the ways in which they do. This is consistent with emerging research into identity processes and intergroup relations (Jaspal and Yampolsky, 2011; Oren and Bar-Tal, 2014).

The social cognitive approach often ignores or overlooks the fact that complexity, fluidity and, in some cases, contradictions characterise our cognition and everyday discourse. People may manifest views which appear to be contradictory or difficult to decipher unequivocally, perhaps because they are shielded or camouflaged by discursive and rhetorical devices (Potter and Wetherell, 1987). For instance, are individuals, who claim that they are "not racist" but who proceed to make comments that may plausibly be described as racist, racist or not? Often, language is constructed in ways that will shield the individual from stigma and rebuke from others – prejudicial assertions made be offered in ways that appear to be less prejudicial than they are. In addition to exploring representation and cognition, it is important to examine closely the discourse employed by individuals. This can help us to understand the content of their accounts, on the one hand, and how processes of self-presentation may shape their accounts, on the other. A project that ambitiously aims to examine how representation, cognition and everyday talk relate to one another in the context of antisemitism and anti-Zionism requires an equally ambitious, complex and integrative theoretical approach. This book offers such an approach.

Case Studies: Antisemitism and Anti-Zionism among Iranians and British Pakistani Muslims

In this book, it is suggested that, when antisemitism and anti-Zionism are transformed into a systematic ideology and politicised and institutionalised, these forms of hostility can acquire a more dangerous and potentially destructive action orientation. They cease to function solely as cultural or cognitive phenomena, but rather induce and encourage negative patterns of interpersonal and intergroup relations at a large scale. Although there have been numerous studies of antisemitism as a general construct, there has been only scant research into antisemitism and anti-Zionism among Muslim groups (Kressel, 2003). This book focuses upon the institutionalisation and public manifestation of antisemitism and anti-Zionism in the context of the Islamic Republic of Iran, where anti-Zionism, imbued with antisemitic tenets, is a state policy; and in the context of British Pakistani Muslims, who reside in a national context where anti-Zionism has acquired considerable credibility and traction but where the overt expression of antisemitism remains socially stigmatised. The two case studies, selected from many possible others, will provide insight into the diversity and complexity of antisemitism and anti-Zionism, in addition to their unifying tenets. However, these case studies cannot possibly speak for *all* Muslims and there is no intention to do so in this book. Rather, the analysis of these case studies should highlight the convergences, divergences and complexities of antisemitism and anti-Zionism among two under-explored groups.

The Islamic Republic of Iran

The Islamic Republic of Iran espouses an official policy of anti-Zionism, which is frequently punctuated with blatant antisemitism. Unlike most other countries in the Middle East, Iran openly endorses antisemitism, principally in the form of Holocaust denial, which it incorporates into its anti-Zionist program (Litvak, 2006). Küntzel (2010, p. 43) compellingly argues that "no other regime in the world is as anti-Semitic as that of the Mullahs in Tehran" (see also Litvak and Webman, 2010). Shiite Islam, which is the state religion of Iran, has a long history of radical antisemitism. For instance, even until the nineteenth century, there were harsh social restrictions on Iranian Jews, who were, at best, regarded as second-class citizens – they were subjected to pogroms and forced conversions to Shiite Islam and have remained a discreet religious minority in contemporary Iran

(Shahvar, 2009). During the reign of the Pahlavi dynasty (1925–79), Iranian Jews enjoyed a short interval of social prosperity, and the Imperial State of Iran enjoyed diplomatic and strategic relations with Israel (Levy, 1999; Menashri, 1991).

However, from the 1960s Ayatollah Ruhollah Khomeini, the future Supreme Leader of the Islamic Republic, publicly denounced and demonised the Jews, referring to them as *inter alia* "infidels" and "impure creatures" (Khomeini, 1981). The Shah of Iran who was to be deposed in the 1979 Iranian Revolution was referred to as a "Jew in disguise" and a "Zionist agent", accusations which gained traction amid the revolutionary fervour of 1970s Iran. In the immediate aftermath of the 1979 Islamic Revolution, the newly established Islamic Republic severed Iranian-Israeli bilateral relations and withdrew its recognition of Israel (Menashri, 2000). Iran has continuously supported Palestinian sovereignty over the whole of present-day Israel, the West Bank, and Gaza, while periodically calling for the destruction of the Jewish State. It systematically refers to Israel by demeaning terms such the "Zionist regime" and "Occupied Palestine", and positions both Israel and Jews as posing a threat to Iran, Muslims, and the world more generally (Jaspal, 2013a). Iran's clerics and politicians have consistently denounced Israel, questioning its legitimacy as a sovereign state and, at times, calling for its destruction (Takeyh, 2006).

Although the Islamic regime attempts to differentiate between anti-Zionism and antisemitism, the underlying antisemitic agenda frequently surfaces. This is manifested subtly through the interchangeable use of the categories "Jew" and "Zionist" in political discourse (Shahvar, 2006) and, more overtly, through the Iranian regime's blatant denial of the Holocaust (Jahanbegloo, 2007; Litvak, 2006).

It is true that many Middle Eastern countries are deeply anti-Zionist and sometimes overtly antisemitic (Litvak and Webman, 2010). However, there are several important reasons for focusing upon the case study of the Iranian national context, in particular.

- Firstly, the Iranian regime is unique in overtly subscribing to a hybrid anti-Zionist and antisemitic political agenda (Litvak, 2006). Incidentally, this justifies the scholarly consideration of both anti-Zionism and antisemitism in social representations disseminated by the regime.
- Secondly, Iran presents a unique demographic situation, since it constitutes the Muslim country with the highest Jewish population of approximately 25,000–30,000 according to recent estimates (Burke, Maxwell and Shearer, 2012; Sarshar, 2014; Yeroushalmi, 2013). Thus, while Iran's anti-Zionism/antisemitism clearly impinges upon international relations, it also has implications for the Jewish community within its own borders (Küntzel, 2005).
- Thirdly, the Islamic regime is the most vociferous critic of Israel, repeatedly calling for its destruction and for the displacement of its people. Although both "conservative" and "moderate" presidents have been elected in Iran, the official stance on Israel has remained largely the same – a policy of

non-recognition (Katz and Hendel, 2012). It is interesting to consider the social psychological motives potentially underlying anti-Zionism and antisemitism given that Iran has never engaged in military conflict or border or economic disputes with Israel.

- Fourthly, Iran is a context in which overt anti-Zionism is socially normative and expected in the general population – indeed, any recognition or contact with Israel is prohibited. There are several writings on anti-Zionism at the institutional level in Iran (Jaspal, 2013a; Litvak, 2006; Shahvar, 2009). However, in the absence of systematic empirical research into social perceptions among the Iranian general population, it is important to examine how antisemitism and anti-Zionism are regarded and manifested by Iranians themselves and how such representations feature in their everyday thinking and talk.

In addition to the socio-historical research that has examined antisemitism and anti-Zionism in Iran (e.g. Litvak, 2006; Shahvar, 2009), there has been little systematic research into the Iranian media's portrayal of Israel (Jaspal, 2013c; Klein, 2009) and even less empirical research into perceptions of Jews and/or Israel in the Iranian general population (Jaspal, 2011c). Media research is important because it can elucidate the relationship between political and media discourses in Iran, given that there is already considerable knowledge about the Iranian political perspectives on Israel (and, in some cases, Jews) (Shahvar, 2009). Crucially, research into the Iranian media can shed light on how representations of Israel and Jews are disseminated to both the Iranian readership, and in the case of the English-language Iranian Press, how Iran attempts to "export" its ideology beyond its own borders. Even in an overtly anti-Zionist context like Iran, where Holocaust denial is rife, there is a clear desire to avoid overt antisemitic prejudice which is stigmatised in contemporary Western society. Thus, in accordance with the notion of "new antisemitism" (see Chapter 3), Iran tends to refer to the Jewish *state* rather than to the Jewish people. Having considered the motifs and representations that have permeated antisemitic discourses and thinking, one can examine subtle invocations of antisemitic motifs in the media's representations of Israel (see Chapter 5). In other words, close attention to the discursive aspects of media representations is important because this can eludicate *how* Iran represents what it does.

The Iranian media may constitute a source of representations concerning Jews and Israel, but in the absence of major social sciences empirical research into Iranian social attitudes it is difficult to ascertain the clout of the media in shaping social perceptions. As outlined in the next two chapters, there is some emerging social sciences research into Arab and Muslim public perceptions of Jews and Israel, but none which takes a qualitative approach. The research that does exist tends to be quantitative, generating tendencies and, in some cases, statistical patterns in public perception. While this is useful, there is clearly a need to examine qualitative accounts of Jews and Israel in order to provide detailed, nuanced, and contextually sensitive insights into the social psychological aspects of antisemitism and anti-Zionism.

The Pakistani Muslim community in Britain

Following the Second World War and British withdrawal from the Indian subcontinent in 1947, Britain witnessed a large-scale influx of South Asian immigrants, who arrived in the country predominantly in search of employment and economic prosperity. It is often noted that hardship, engendered by poverty and unemployment in the subcontinent, encouraged mass migration to the UK. Hiro (1973, p. 107) observes that for Pakistani immigrants "the economic consideration was the sole motive for migration" and that they did not envisage settlement in the UK or integration into British society (see also Anwar, 1979, who discusses the "myth of return"). Today, British citizens of Pakistani descent constitute a sizeable proportion of the ethnic minority population in the UK – the 2011 UK census recorded approximately 1,125,000 British Pakistanis in England and Wales, and the largest communities are located in London, Birmingham and Bradford. In his overview of the socio-economic status of British Pakistanis, Peach (2005) argues that this group is one of the poorest in the country, after Bangladeshis. Approximately 92 per cent of British Pakistanis are Muslims (UK Census 2011), and research has consistently shown that religious identity is a "core" identity among this population, more so than ethnic, cultural and British national identities (Abbas, 2005; Jaspal, 2011b; Jaspal and Cinnirella, 2013).

The 1989 Rushdie Affair refers to the angry and sometimes violent reaction of many Muslims to Salman Rushdie's book *The Satanic Verses*, which was widely perceived as insulting Islam and particularly the Prophet Mohammed. Since the Rushdie Affair, British Muslims have acquired a negative "hypervisibility" in British society (Abbas, 2005). To many individuals, the angry community response to Rushdie's book, exemplified by a book burning in Bradford in January 1989 and other forms of protest, appeared to illustrate Muslim intolerance and extremism. More recently, Muslims have been associated with Islamist fundamentalism, extremism and even terrorism in both public and media discourses (Cinnirella, 2013; Jaspal and Cinnirella, 2010b). This has been particularly acute after 9/11 and the July 7th attacks in London (Ansari, 2005; Cinnirella, 2013, 2014). Following the Rushdie Affair and with the emergence of second and third generations, British Pakistanis appear to be much more vocal about Muslim suffering and grievances and the Israeli-Palestinian conflict has featured prominently in their thinking (Jikeli, 2013). Indeed, Ansari (2005, p. 162) notes that "Muslim suffering and grievances elsewhere are deeply felt by Muslims in Britain, and influence their attitudes" vis-à-vis key social issues. The State of Israel and the Jewish community are just two issues, upon which many young British Pakistani Muslims have taken a stance.

Many British Pakistani Muslims feel angry about the perceived Israeli subjugation of the Palestinian people and about Israel's military actions in the region (Jikeli, 2013). Such anger is also discernible in some British Muslim institutions. For instance, the Muslim Council of Britain, which is recognised by the UK government, has repeatedly refused to participate in the Holocaust Memorial Day, because it claims that to do so might obscure and shift attention from Israel's treatment of the Palestinians – this decision was emphatically repeated in the aftermath of the 2009 Gaza War (Spencer and Di Palma, 2013). In his qualitative study of perceptions of the Holocaust among many Pakistani Muslims in London, Jikeli (2013) found that a prevalence of doubts, denial and conspiracies about the Holocaust – several respondents believed that 6 million Jews could not have been killed. Crucially, there was a widespread perception that the Holocaust constituted an "excuse" to establish the State of Israel, Thus, as opponents of Israel, there was a psychological incentive for them to deny the Holocaust. In some cases, respondents expressed sympathy and solidarity with the Nazis who perpetrated this act of genocide.

The shared superordinate Muslim identity may encourage individuals to perceive a sense of solidarity with fellow Palestinian Muslims and, thus, a common enmity with the State of Israel (Baum and Nakazawa, 2007). Many commentators on the "new antisemitism" have remarked that its rise can be attributed largely to *Muslim* opposition to the State of Israel, which has resulted in antisemitic acts. For instance, in 2004, 21-year old Asif Hanif from London, UK and 27 year-old Omar Khan Sharif from Derby, UK travelled to Israel to perpetrate suicide bombings in Tel Aviv – Hanif blew himself and three Israelis up and injured 55 others, and Sharif fled the scene after his bomb failed to detonate but was later found dead. In a video recording posted on a Hamas website, Sharif stated that "Muslims are being killed everyday. It is an honour to kill one of those people [Jews]". Such comments were also reiterated by the young French Algerian individual who targeted a Jewish day school in Toulouse.

It is important to consider the sources of information among British Pakistani Muslims in order to understand their perceptions of Israel and Jews. As observed in Chapter 2, Islamic Holy Scripture does appear to contain some anti-Jewish segments, which can easily be re-construed and applied to the contemporary context, thereby providing further credibility to and justification for antisemitism. Furthermore, the British newspaper media is said to be excessively critical of Israel, which is particularly the case for *The Guardian* and, according to some accounts, the BBC (Wistrich, 2011). However, various scholars have noted that British Pakistani Muslims manifest suspicion of the Western media which has "come to be regarded as Western propaganda for consumption by its own public" (Ansari, 2005, p. 162). Similarly, Ahmed (2005) has indicated that British Pakistani Muslims may prefer what is perceived as "Muslim media", which they regard as more balanced and accommodating of their Muslim identity. In empirical research, Jaspal (2011b) has found that, because many British Pakistani Muslims distrust the Western media, this led some disaffected Muslims to explore alternative news outlets such as Iran's government-aligned *The Tehran Times* and *Press TV*. These newspaper outlets are known to be deeply anti-Zionist in representation (see Chapter 5).

Unlike Iranians, British Pakistanis live in a context in which overt antisemitism and extreme anti-Zionism are not socially acceptable, although the British context does appear to accommodate anti-Zionist expression in various social and institutional contexts (Klaff, 2010; Wistrich, 2004). Thus, it may facilitate the development and voicing of anti-Zionism that is punctuated by antisemitism. Given the lack of empirical research in this area, this book explores British Pakistani Muslims' perceptions of and attitudes towards the Jewish people and the State of Israel, alongside those of Iranian Muslims.

Overview of the Book

Antisemitism and anti-Zionism have been passionately debated by historians, political scientists and social scientists (see Chapters 2 and 3). This book makes a social psychological contribution to this debate by providing qualitative insights into antisemitism and anti-Zionism, examining their presence in social representation, individual cognition and everyday talk, and responses to these forms of prejudice by Israeli Jews and British Jews.

Part II of this book approaches antisemitism and anti-Zionism from both historical and social psychological perspectives, investigating the inter-relations between historical events and their social psychological meanings for groups and individuals. Overviews of antisemitism and anti-Zionism are provided in Chapters 2 and 3, respectively. It is argued that the two forms of prejudice are intrinsically related and that in order to gain a better understanding of how antisemitism and anti-Zionism are related, they need to be positioned within a social psychological framework that can accommodate and theorise the distinct levels at which antisemitism and anti-Zionism can function and the distinct ways in which they can be manifested. Accordingly, in Chapter 4, a social psychological framework for examining representation, cognition and everyday talk is outlined. The framework consists of Social Representations Theory, Identity Process Theory and Intergroup Threat Theory and draws upon social psychological theory and research on delegitimisation and dehumanisation. It is argued that a hybrid theoretical approach is necessary for understanding the distinct levels of human interdependence and, crucially, how they relate to one another.

In Part III, empirical insights into social representations of Israel and Jews in Iranian society are provided. This section of the book focuses upon the *sources* of social representations – these sources provide the backdrop against which public perceptions, individual cognitions and everyday discourse may form. This is particularly important in a context in which the media discourses are closely aligned with and stringently regulated by political institutions. In Chapter 5, an empirical qualitative thematic analysis of the Iranian newspaper press is outlined. The chapter focuses upon two government-aligned newspapers and identifies three thematic clusters in habitual reporting on Israel in the Iranian media. It is shown that, although the Iranian newspaper press tends to focus upon the Jewish State, it subtly draws upon antisemitic motifs. In Chapter 6, the Iranian media-led and government-endorsed Holocaust Cartoon Contest, which took place in 2006, is discussed, as a clear example of how antisemitism informs Iranian anti-Zionism. Two hundred and twenty seven cartoons from various countries are analysed using visual thematic analysis and the dominant antisemitic and anti-Zionist themes observable in the cartoons are outlined and discussed in relation to Iran's political agenda and ideology. The overtly antisemitic character of Iranian anti-Zionism is highlighted.

Part IV provides novel empirical insights into the potential antecedents and consequences of antisemitism and anti-Zionism among Iranians and British Pakistani Muslims using qualitative thematic analysis. This section focuses upon individuals' cognition and talk concerning Israel and Jews. In Chapter 7, an interview study with Iranian self-identified political "hardliners" and "reformists" is outlined and the principal themes that summarise their cognitions and perceptions concerning Israel and Jews are highlighted and discussed. It is argued that Iranians appear to differ in their perceptions of Israel and Jews in accordance with both political orientation and identity requirements. However, close attention to individuals' talk highlights the entrenchment of antisemitic myths and representations in their thinking. In Chapter 8, the results of an interview study with British Pakistani Muslims are outlined and discussed, and three themes that summarise their cognitions and perceptions concerning Israel and Jews are highlighted. In this chapter, it is argued that British Pakistani Muslims perceive a strong sense of connection with the Palestinian people and that both Israel and Jews are perceived as posing a threat to their superordinate Muslim identity, a "core" identity in the self-concept. Like Iranians, British Pakistani Muslims also appear to take identity requirements into consideration when thinking and talking about Jews and the Jewish State.

This book constitutes an attempt to provide a holistic and multi-faceted account of antisemitism and anti-Zionism by examining the responses of Israelis and British Jews to these forms of prejudice. In Chapter 9, the results of an interview study with self-identified Israeli Jews are reported. Chapter 10 provides an overview of an interview study with self-identified orthodox, secular and anti-Zionist British Jews. In the concluding chapter, the research presented in this book is summarised and discussed in terms of its theoretical and practical implications in the context of antisemitism and anti-Zionism.

The principal goal in producing this book has been to provide novel insights into antisemitism and anti-Zionism from the perspective a hybrid integrative social psychological framework. Identity Process Theory, Social Representations Theory and Intergroup Threat Theory are concerned primarily with the application of social psychology to the pressing real-world problems functioning at the intrapsychic, interpersonal and intergroup levels of human interdependence. Antisemitism and anti-Zionism are two such problems. It is hoped that the two case studies of Iranians and British Pakistani Muslims will elucidate the complexities, convergences and divergences of antisemitism and anti-Zionism among under-researched groups who manifest these forms of prejudice, and shed light on the social psychology of antisemitism and anti-Zionism. Similarly, it is hoped that the focus on the responses of Israeli Jews and British Jews to the problems of antisemitism and anti-Zionism will pave the way for a more holistic understanding of how these forms of prejudice can shape identity, wellbeing and intergroup relations.

PART II
Antisemitism and Anti-Zionism

Chapter 2

Antisemitism:
Continuities and Discontinuities

Introduction

Antisemitism[1] has a history of several millennia and can plausibly be thought of as one of the most enduring forms of prejudice against any single group. Indeed, Jewish history is fraught with acts of persecution. The Jewish people were exiled from their homeland of Judah during the rule of the Babylonian Empire, which subsequently gave rise to a Jewish diaspora scattered all over the world. In their host countries, in the Christian and Islamic worlds, Jews continued to suffer persecution to varying degrees, and, in some cases, pogroms and even genocide.[2] The study of antisemitism is clearly an important area of research. Despite the immensely insightful contributions made by historians, sociologists, political scientists (Lindemann and Levy, 2010a, 2010b; Perry and Schweitzer, 2002; Wistrich, 1999a, 1996b; Salzborn, 2010; Wittenberg, 2013) and social psychologists (Baum, 2009a; Cohen et al., 2009; Jaspal, 2013a) to the study of this age-old prejudice, antisemitism remains something of an enigma. This chapter introduces the concept of antisemitism and discusses its conceptual and definitional aspects. The continuities and discontinuities of antisemitism are examined across time, space and culture, beginning with a historical overview of antisemitism from antiquity to modern history. Antisemitism in both Christian and Islamic contexts is discussed, and some of the key antisemitic myths, representations and "techniques" are identified. Their trajectory across time, space and culture is charted, as well as their implications for contemporary antisemitism. A series of key social sciences research studies are critically evaluated and their implications for contemporary antisemitism research are outlined.

---

1   Although some scholars differentiate explicitly between anti-Judaism, as a form of religious prejudice, and antisemitism, as a racially-based prejudice (e.g. Cunningham, 2010; Isaac, 2010), here it is employed to encompass both forms of prejudice as there is historical and contemporary slippage between them.

2   It is acknowledged that anti-Jewish persecution was not constant in all of the countries in which Jews resided and that there was periods of positive intergroup relations. In Muslim Spain, for instance, where Jews were said to have been generally treated with tolerance and acceptance (Menocal, 2002), there were instances of brutal anti-Jewish violence, such as the 1066 Granada Massacre which resulted in the deaths of some 4000 Jews (Cohen, 1995; Fernández-Morera, 2003).

Antisemitism: Conceptual Issues

Antisemitism is a slippery concept which has been understood and used in different ways in accordance with time, space and context. The German journalist Wilhelm Marr first used the term "Semitismus" (Semitism) interchangeably with "Judentum" (Jewry) in his pamphlet *Der Sieg des Judenthums über das Germanenthum. Vom nicht confessionellen Standpunkt aus betrachtet* ("The Victory of the Jewish Spirit over the Germanic Spirit. Observed from a non-religious perspective"), published in 1873. In his next pamphlet on German Jewry, "The Way to Victory of the Germanic Spirit over the Jewish Spirit" (1879), Marr employed the term "Antisemitismus" (Antisemitism), in order to denote opposition to what he described as "Jewish domination". Crucially, his use of the term "antisemitism" was intended to highlight the racial, rather than religious, characteristics of Jews and was therefore secular in character. This pamphlet became popular in German society and led to the formation of the *Antisemiten-Liga* (the League of Antisemites), a German organisation which advocated the forced removal of Jews from Germany in order to protect Germany and German culture. The pamphlet and the League of Antisemites helped to introduce the terms "antisemitism" and "antisemite" into the political and cultural lexicon and eventually into everyday language. This referred more explicitly to racial and cultural, rather than purely religious, antipathy to Jews.

Although some scholars have questioned the accuracy of the term given that the Semitic people include Arabs and other ethnic groups, the term has been adopted in several languages, including Romance, Germanic, Slavic and even Turkic languages, to refer to forms of hostility against Jews in particular. Antisemitism has been subjected to considerable debate in the academic world, as scholars have attempted to define its conceptual boundaries and to outline what can and what cannot be legitimately regarded as "antisemitism". In its broadest sense, antisemitism refers to prejudice and hostility towards Jews on the basis of their ethno-cultural and/or religious group membership. Antisemitism attributes to the Jews an exceptional position in the broader social matrix, constructs them as an inferior group and generally excludes them from dominant society (Pauley, 1998). Thus, it also encompasses what some scholars have referred to as "anti-Jewishness" or "anti-Judaism" (e.g. Cunningham, 2010; Isaac, 2010). The distinction between anti-Judaism and antisemitism as religious and racial forms of prejudice, respectively, is useful in historical overviews of antipathy towards Jews (Isaac, 2010) but given their overlap and conflation in contemporary discourses around Jews, the terms appear to be less conceptually delineable.

However, numerous scholars do take issue with this broad definition of antisemitism. From a historical scholarly position, Bernard Lewis (1999) has argued that the term antisemitism should not be used to describe just any hostility towards Jews but rather that it should be reserved for cognition and treatment which construct Jews as a "cosmic evil", the inherent corruptors of all human activity. While hostility can, in principle, reduce if a group is perceived as redeemable, this is not applicable to those groups regarded as a cosmic evil since this is constructed as an immutable, quasi-biological trait. For instance, although medieval Islamic law treated Jews as inferior to Muslims – socially, politically and theologically – Jews continued to be regarded as human beings, as "people of the Book" and, thus, *not* as a cosmic evil. This anti-Jewish prejudice emerged in the context of religion, rather than "race". Similarly, some of the most pivotal figures in modern European antisemitism, such as Wilhelm Marr and Heinrich von Treitschke, appeared to regard Jews as potentially redeemable citizens and, thus, not as a cosmic evil. According to Lewis's conceptualisation of antisemitism, Hitler would, conversely, qualify as an antisemite because, as leader of the Nazi party, he disseminated demonising and dehumanising representations of Jews, whose "reform" was not deemed to be possible due to "racial inferiority" (Gilbert, 1985; Hilberg, 1985).

Many scholars converge in their conceptualisation of antisemitism as a form of racism. Isaac (2010, p. 34) regards it as "a proto-racist set of ideas" and "a collective prejudice with delusional aspects" which "attributes to the Jews, as a collective group, negative traits that are unalterable, the result of hereditary factors". He draws a distinction between antisemitism, which he regards as a form of racism, and anti-Judaism, which conversely constitutes "hostility based on religion" (p. 34). Although Isaac does not discuss the threat component, which is suggested by Lewis's conceptualisation of antisemitism, there is clearly some overlap in their thinking. According to Isaac, antisemitism, as a form of racism, constructs Jewishness as an immutable, quasi-biological trait and, thus, Jews as immutable and beyond reform. Conversely, anti-Judaism, as a form of religious outgroup discrimination, implies that Jews can change and reform provided that they exit their religious group. In the Spanish Inquisition, for instance, Jews and Muslims were afforded the opportunity to renounce their respective religious identities and to convert to Catholicism to avoid expulsion (Roth, 2002). Similarly, in radical Islamism, Jews are not generally viewed as racially inferior to Arabs and are afforded the opportunity for redemption provided that they renounce Judaism and embrace Islam (Wistrich, 2010). However, the language employed to describe Jews sometimes suggests that they are *inherently* inferior to Muslims (Chapters 7 and 8, this volume).

Antisemitism is clearly a very complex form of prejudice, which has permeated time and space. These narrower definitions of antisemitism run the risk of attenuating the gravity of some forms of hostility and discrimination towards Jews due to their Jewishness however this is conceptualised. Furthermore, such narrow definitions of antisemitism can mean that newer, subtler manifestations of Jew-hatred may be overlooked, thereby limiting our ability to identify antisemitic acts when they are committed. There is clearly a need for a definition that facilitates the identification (and even prediction) of antisemitism. Helen Fein (1987, p. 67) provides an apt and inclusive definition of antisemitism which clearly captures the complexity and fluidity of this form of prejudice. She regards it as

> a persisting latent structure of hostile beliefs toward *Jews as a collectivity* manifested in *individuals* as attitudes, and in *culture* as myths, ideology, folklore

and imagery, and in *actions* – social or legal discrimination, political mobilization against the Jews, and collective or state violence – which results in and/or is designed to distance, displace, or destroy Jews as Jews (p. 67, italics in original).

This conceptualisation of antisemitism is useful and insightful in a number of ways. It refers to both religiously- and racially-based prejudice towards Jews. Importantly, antisemitism is implied to have an *action orientation* in that it is intended to produce particular forms of action, both psychological and social. Fein invokes the desired "goal" among antisemites, namely the distancing, displacement and/or destruction of Jewry. This captures the distinct forms that hostility can take. This hostility can be manifested in a deadly, genocidal manner as exemplified by the Holocaust but also in more benign ways – in the Islamic Republic of Iran, for instance, many Jews feel belittled, marginalised and threatened by both the Iranian government and public because of their Jewishness (Jaspal, 2014b). There are likely to be distinct social and psychological "routes" to the goals of distancing, displacement and/or destruction. The most obvious routes include *inter alia* the re-conceptualisation of Jews as animalistic rather than human; Holocaust denial; the isolation of Jews; violence against Jews; and, as outlined by Fein in her definition above, group mobilisation against Jews. Thus, this conceptualisation invites us to consider what antisemites intend to achieve by disseminating particular representations of Jews.

This definition connects various important levels of analysis (which will be discussed in Chapter 4), namely the micro (individual), meso (cultural) and macro (institutional) levels. Fein quite rightly refers to antisemitism as a *latent* yet *persisting* structure of beliefs. It is the complex and dynamic interaction between the individual, cultural and institutional levels which can explain how and why latent or dormant hostile beliefs manage to persist over time and to become quite central to a group's ethos and to an individual's cognitive framework. Fein's definition invites us to think not only about the individual's antisemitic attitudes but also the ways in which these attitudes may be supported or challenged at social and institutional levels. Indeed, social psychology has long argued that the individual's attitude constitutes the product not only of psychological factors but also of social and institutional environment (Bar-Tal, 2000; Moscovici, 1988).

Fein acknowledges that "hostile beliefs" can function and manifest themselves at distinct levels of human interdependence. They may be manifested in the cognitive level of the individual, evoking negative emotions such as anger or disgust, and lead to particular patterns of interpersonal relations, such as avoidance or violence. Such hostile beliefs about Jews have of course been embodied and widely disseminated in age-old antisemitic myths, such as the blood libel, and in antisemitic conspiracy theories, such as that concerning Jewish complicity in the 9/11 terrorist attacks in New York (Gray, 2010; Perry and Schweitzer, 2002). Antisemitism at a cultural level clearly informs and reinforces antisemitism at the individual level, but the relationship is reciprocal – committed antisemites will do all they can to ensure that their cultures continue to accept and convey antisemitic messages. Indeed, Hitler, a committed antisemite, managed to awaken, reinvigorate and crystallise dormant antisemitic beliefs in his national group. As this particular example indicates, antisemitism is most dangerous when it is endorsed, encouraged and manifested at a politico-institutional level. Political groups or institutions may use Jews as scapegoats for political gain by resurrecting extant, though dormant antisemitic myths which they know will gain traction in public consciousness. Once activated in cultural consciousness, antisemitic beliefs can infiltrate the individual's cognitive framework, precipitating patterns of cognition and interpersonal and intergroup relations that are indeed "designed to distance, displace, or destroy Jews as Jews" (Fein, 1987, p. 67). It was of course organised, political antisemitism that culminated in the Holocaust, the most destructive act of genocide against European Jewry perpetrated by institutions, groups *and* individuals alike.

Antisemitism across Time, Space and Medium

Antisemitism is a long-standing and ubiquitous form of prejudice and, thus, any historical overview must be selective. One could write volumes on the history of antisemitism in Germany, France, Poland, Hungary and the many other countries in which Jews have resided. There are now a plethora of insightful studies of antisemitism in distinct geographical contexts, the majority of which have been conducted within the Western world – antisemitism research has focused on many countries in the West (e.g. Dinnerstein, 1994; Jaher, 1994; Vincze, 2013; Wistrich, 1991; Wittenberg, 2013). More recently, scholars of antisemitism have examined novel contexts, such as the Middle East (Jaspal, 2013a; Litvak, 2006; Shahvar, 2009), Latin America (Liwerant, 2011; Milkewitz, 2011; Schvindlerman, 2011) and even Japan, a country with no significant Jewish population (Goodman and Miyazawa, 2000). Distinct communities within nation-states have also been examined in order to understand the spread of antisemitism – such as Muslim minorities in Europe (Jikeli and Allouche-Benayoun, 2013), African Americans (King and Weiner, 2007), and the Muslim minority in India (Kumaraswamy, 2010). Many studies have examined distinct "phases" of antisemitism, such as the pre-Christian era, the Middle Ages, the Enlightenment period, the early twentieth century, and the so-called "new antisemitism". It is also acknowledged that antisemitism may be manifested in a range of distinct media, all of which contribute to crystallising antisemitic representations among members of society – scholars have analysed *inter alia* public opinion (Baum, 2009a; King and Weiner, 2007), media representations (Jaspal, 2013c; Klein, 2009), art and visual representations (Amishai-Maisels, 1999; Kotek, 2009; Vinzce, 2013) religious sources (Lazarus-Yafeh, 1999) and others.

These studies exhibit the ubiquity and persistence of antisemitism across time, space and medium. They have made important strides in elucidating the nature, form and timing of antisemitic outbursts in particular contexts, and have provided vital insights into the *continuities and discontinuities of antisemitism*. Jaspal (2013b) has employed this term to capture the regularities of antisemitism across time, space and medium (i.e. how particular myths and social representations have persisted, albeit modified in accordance with context) and the divergences of emerging antisemitism from previous mythical manifestations (i.e. how particular representations have ceased to exist under novel conditions in favour of others). The analysis of the continuities and discontinuities of antisemitism is eminently important because it enables us to predict how, when and under which social and psychological circumstances particular manifestations of antisemitism can emerge, persist, change and disappear over time. Moreover, it acknowledges that, while in some temporal and cultural contexts, antipathy towards Jews may have focused upon either religion or "race", antisemitism has maintained some consistency in aim and focus. What is striking in the literature on antisemitism is the incredible *consistency* in the basic patterns manifested in antisemitic prejudice (Wistrich, 1991; Lindemann and Levy, 2010b; Perry and Schweitzer, 2008). Long-standing, age-old myths appear to have been re-construed, re-cycled and adapted to suit specific temporal, geographical, cultural, political, religious and ideological contexts so that they can provide an appropriate heuristic lens, serving important sociological and psychological functions (see Chapter 4 on the theoretical approach employed in this book). Although the "methods" of antisemitism may vary in accordance with time, space and medium, the basic tenet of Jewishness as something negative, inferior and evil has clearly persisted, as exemplified by the use of "Jew" as a slur in many languages (Jikeli, 2010) This section focuses upon the vicissitudes of antisemitism from pre-Christian antiquity to the present day, in both Western Christian civilisation and the Islamic world.

Antisemitism in antiquity

There have been many important historical accounts of antisemitism, which have charted its nature and development since the Greco-Roman and pre-Christian eras until the present day (Schwartz, 1999; Perry and Schweitzer, 2002). Schäfer (1998) locates the origins of antisemitism in Egypt's pre-Hellenistic era, and argues that this was the temporal and geographical context in which antisemitic representations began to emerge. In his analysis of Greek and Roman writings on Jews, he describes the focus on Jewish distinctiveness, namely the nature of the Jewish God, Jewish dietary restrictions, the Jewish Holy Sabbath, Jewish sexual customs and the religious practice of circumcision, which served to construct Jews as possessing an "alien culture". Moreover, it has been observed that the Romans generally regarded the Jews as traitorous and rebellious (Perry and Schweitzer, 2002). Focussing upon the destruction of a Jewish temple in Elephantine in 410 BCE and the violent disturbances in Alexandria in 38 CE, Schäfer shows how the aforementioned negative markers of ethnic difference were entwined with threatening characteristics (e.g. impiety and misanthropy) and, thus, led to fear of and hostility towards Jews.

Similarly, Isaac (2010, p. 35) describes in his analysis of Alexandrian texts of the third century BCE a prevalent representation that "the Jews, rather than being God's chosen, were descendants of a group of polluted outcasts, suffering from leprosy and other diseases". Moreover, he highlights that Jews were accused of practicing human sacrifice and cannibalism, which in antiquity served to dehumanise and animalise foreign people (see also Stern, 1974–84). A modified version of this representation was to re-emerge in the Middle Ages with deadly consequences. Conversely, in the Hellenistic, non-Alexandrian era, there was a claim that Jews made no meaningful contribution to civilisation, which decreased their social value. Moreover, in his overview of Roman literature, Isaac (2010) demonstrates the perceived threat of Judaism (often regarded in terms of a "foreign cult") to Roman institutions and to the wellbeing of the state. Seneca, a first century Roman philosopher, and Cleomedes, a Roman astronomer, described Jews as a "most villainous people" and "much lower than reptiles", respectively (Isaac, 2010, p. 38). During this era, antipathy towards Jews appears to have been both religious and ethno-cultural in focus. Despite the clear negativity attributed to Jews in the pre-Christian era, it appears that the overarching representation constructed Jews as wretched and impoverished, rather than as greedy and materialistic, representations which were to emerge and crystallise in the Middle Ages (see Lindemann and Levy, 2010b).

Christendom

Although antisemitism clearly existed in pre-Christian antiquity, Western Christian civilisation is generally thought of as having created a persisting and vicious tradition of religiously-based anti-Jewishness (Wistrich, 1999a). Yet, as Cunningham (2010) observes, there is much debate concerning the historical divide between Christianity and Judaism and the consequential triggers for antisemitism among Christians, with some scholars attributing this to the Crucifixion of Jesus (c. 30 CE), and others to the destruction of the Second Temple in Jerusalem following the Jewish-Roman War (66–70 CE). Cunningham's account of Jewish and Christian antipathy echoes social psychological theorising around intergroup relations (e.g. Stephan and Stephan, 2000; Tajfel, 1982). He argues that, in order to safeguard its own emerging identity, Christendom attacked the respectability and integrity of Judaism through the rhetorical strategies of delegitimisation and dehumanisation. During this time, the charge of deicide against the Jews emerged and was to remain a fundamental tenet of European antisemitism over the next two millennia (Wistrich, 1991). Following the fourth century CE, when Theodosius I made Nicene Christianity the preferred religion of the Roman Empire, the power balance shifted radically in favour of Christianity. This led to an increase in Christian attacks upon synagogues, the curtailment of Jewish rights and privileges and growing marginalisation of Jews in the Empire. Echoing Isaac's (2010) distinction between antisemitism and anti-Judaism, Cunningham (2010, p. 61) argues that hostility towards Jews in early Christianity is better understood as "opposition to Jewish religious tenets and practices" rather than as a racially-based hostility, given that it arose primarily from *religious* intergroup competition in the Roman Empire.

Theologians and other scholars have examined the theological representations from the New Testament which were appropriated by Christians and which gradually came to inform antisemitism in Western Christian civilisation. In the Christian world, Jews were charged with the archcrime of deicide, the killing of the son of God, and were therefore viewed as "the embodiment of evil, a 'criminal people' cursed by God and doomed to wander and suffer tribulation to the end of time" (Perry and Schweitzer, 2002, p. 18; see also Maccoby, 1996). The charge of deicide was unprecedented in the history of religion – in fact, no other religious group has been collectively accused of killing God. This served to attribute to the Jews an exceptional position in the social and historical matrix, depicting them as extraordinarily evil. For centuries, Jews have been charged not only with deicide but also with its ritualistic rehearsal (using Christian children) and with celebrating the death of Christ ever since (Lindemann and Levy, 2010b). Thus, it is easy to see how this accusation could have induced particularly negative representations of Jews as a collectivity and mobilised Christians against them. Indeed, Crossan (1996) has described the charge of deicide in the Gospel as "the matrix for Christian anti-Judaism and eventually for European anti-Semitism" (p.32).

The gospels (John 6:70 and 13:27) describe Judas as a "devil" under the influence of Satan, a representation which is echoed in relation to the Jews in John, 8:43–7. Just as Judas becomes a cultural symbol of greed, criminality and usury, the Jews too were attributed such traits in the Christian world. Indeed, Judas and Jew became synonymous in Christian cultural consciousness (Perry and Schweitzer, 2002). Similarly, there was an intertwinement of the [Jewish] crowd that accepted blame for Jesus's death (as described in Matthew, 27:24–5) and world Jewry to whom Christian antisemites have continued to attribute collective responsibility for the death of Christ (Crossan, 1996). The New Testament's representations of the Jew as deicide, deceitful, evil, satanic, and the Antichrist have been enthusiastically endorsed and reproduced by Christian antisemites for centuries, and have come to form part of the arsenal of contemporary antisemitic motifs.

Many in the Christian world proceeded to develop this arsenal of antisemitic motifs by accusing Jews of desecration of the Host, the ritual murder of Christian children, poisoning wells and spreading disease among Christians, colluding with the mythical Antichrist and attempting to destroy Christendom (Gold, 1988; Wistrich, 1999a). These anti-Jewish representations appeared to consist of two principal elements: firstly, there was an ideological theme of opposing the tenets of Christianity, rooted in the Jews' rejection of Christ ("Jews rejected Christ and hence they desecrate the Host"); and secondly, there was a theme of intergroup competition and conflict between Christianity and Judaism ("Jews wish to destroy Christianity and thus they spread disease among its followers"). These representations were persisting and enduring from the early days of Christianity and were modified and adapted to suit specific temporal and cultural contexts.

Moreover, they were extended in order to foment and crystallise antipathy towards Jews in the general population.

The Middle Ages

The blood libel was one such antisemitic representation which gained considerable traction throughout Western Christian civilisation (Dundes, 1991; Laqueur, 2006). In the Middle Ages, Christians began systematically to accuse Jews of the ritual murder of Christian children and cannibalism. This constituted a re-construal of the accusation of cannibalism which had been present in antiquity. This popular belief was made possible by the existing representation in early Christendom of Jews as an immoral and bloodthirsty group of individuals who were collectively responsible for the spilling of Christ's blood. In the minds of many Christians, Jews were aided and abetted by demonic, satanic forces in their quest to kidnap, torture and murder innocent Christian children to utilise their blood for Jewish religious rituals. As Perry and Schweitzer (2002) observe, medieval Christians provided distinct explanations for this – some claimed that the Jews sacrificed Christian children in ceremonies replicating the crucifixion, while others later asserted that Christian blood was an essential ingredient for matzo, the unleavened bread used for the Jewish Passover.

The blood libel acquired particular popularity in England, where the first cases were reported. In 1144, "William", a young apprentice boy, was found murdered in Norwich, England. Although initially no religious significance was attributed to William's death, some four or five years later the monk Thomas of Monmouth visited Norwich and claimed that the Jews were responsible for the torture and murder of the boy. The monk succeeded in fabricating a myth which was to remain in Christian religious and cultural consciousness for centuries, particularly as many of the alleged victims came to be viewed as Christian martyrs and, in some cases, saints (Göller, 1987; Karl, 1987). Indeed, the blood libel spread rapidly across cultural, geographical and temporal boundaries. This myth was transmitted through religious sermons, chronicles, poems, literature, newspapers, and oral testimonies (Göller, 1987). The charge of ritual murder was reproduced in various English communities: Norwich (1144), Gloucester (1168), Bury St. Edmunds (1181), Bristol (1183), Winchester (1192, 1225, 1235) and Lincoln (1255); as well as in countless communities on the European mainland: Oberwesel, Germany (1287), Rinn, Austria (1462), Trento, Italy (1475), Bösing, Slovakia (1529), Rhodes, Ottoman Empire (1840) and many others.

It appears that the representation of negative Jewish distinctiveness, originating from antiquity, and that of Jewish evil, which emerged in the early Christian era, provided the heuristic tools necessary to believe such a fallacy. Not only would *any* human sacrifice have been completely incompatible with Jewish Holy Scripture (Perry and Schweitzer, 2002) but no compelling evidence was ever provided in support of any of these blood libel cases. Accusations and judgements were often based upon the false testimonies of others, confessions extracted under duress, or simple hearsay. Yet, the consequences for Jews were often horrific. For instance, the blood libel case in Lincoln, England led to the hanging of 12 Jews and to the Crown's confiscation of their property, eventually culminating in the Jews' expulsion from England in 1290, while the alleged killing of a 9-year old boy in Bösing (who, incidentally, was later found alive in Vienna) resulted in the public burning of 30 Jews. Existing anti-Jewish myths and representations were sufficient "evidence" for accusing, condemning and terrorising Jewish communities all over Europe.

It may be tempting to confine the blood libel accusation to the depths of medieval history and to dismiss this as a regrettable aspect of the past but, as Perry and Schweitzer (2002) demonstrate in their detailed historical review of antisemitism, the blood libel accusation has continued to characterise social representations of Jews in modern history. Feldberg (2002) recounts a blood libel case in the small upper New York state town of Massena, which occurred as late as 1928. A four-year-old girl was reported missing by her parents and soon a rumour spread that the local Jewish community had kidnapped the child and drained her blood for a Yom Kippur ritual. The town mayor subsequently ordered a local police officer to question the spiritual head of Massena's Jewish community about ritualistic practices within the Jewish community. Antisemitic sentiment was already observable in the community, which had led to the accusation in the first place but the mayor and state police's actions served to lend credibility to the blood libel accusation. This was not only deeply offensive to the Jewish community but also potentially dangerous, as antisemitic mobs began to mobilise. The child was subsequently found alive and the mayor and state police formally apologised to the Jewish community. The case did not descend into the violence and brutality that had been observable in medieval Europe. However, this event tellingly exhibits the cultural "stickiness" of the blood libel accusation, that is, its ability to transcend cultural, geographical and temporal boundaries in the absence of any evidence whatsoever. Indeed, there were several other such incidents in the US in the twentieth century (Dinnerstein, 1994). Moreover, in Poland, the country in which over 3 million Jews had just been murdered, and just one year after the horrors of the Holocaust were revealed to the world, a blood libel accusation succeeded in mobilising residents of the city of Kielce against the Jews (Gross, 2006). The violent pogrom resulted in the deaths of 40 Jews, many of whom were Holocaust survivors themselves. Not only was the blood libel accusation culturally, geographically and temporally pervasive, it could re-gain ground in communities still coming to terms with the Holocaust.

Antisemitism after the Enlightenment

The Enlightenment, which was characterised by growing secularisation (Israel, 2010), heralded the emancipation of Jews. During this period, there was a gradual shift in focus from charges of deicide, host desecration and human sacrifice to the anchoring of Judaism to imagery of barbarism, cultural primitivism and racial separateness. As Sutcliffe (2010, p. 119) observes, attitudes towards Jews during the Enlightenment era were highly ambivalent, although there was an observable "[h]ostility toward Jewish religious traditionalism". Yet, given the growing prominence of "race" and culture, antipathy towards Jews in this period could plausibly be described as *antisemitism* rather than anti-Judaism. Prominent figures in the Enlightenment movement were overtly antisemitic in their writings, which decisively contributed to antisemitism during this era – French Enlightenment literary figure, historian and philosopher Voltaire, for instance, was said to nurse a "violent hatred of Jews" which to a large degree shaped French public opinion (Meyer, 1963, p. 1177; see also Arnold, 1994). While the focus of medieval antisemitism had been largely upon charges of deicide, ritual murder, the practice of witchcraft and sorcery and the Jewish threat to Christianity, antisemitism during the Enlightment period, though ambivalent and fluctuant, introduced representations of Jewish world domination – more specifically, through control of the international financial system and the media and through the development of revolutionary ideologies (Yadlin, 1999). Thus, the Enlightenment period represented a significant shift from religious anti-Judaism to secular antisemitism.

The theory of an international Jewish conspiracy became the new motif of the era and infiltrated public consciousness. This representation was closely related to a parallel motif of Jews as "greedy, materialistic, conniving Shylocks and unscrupulous financial manipulators" (Perry and Schweitzer, 2002, p. 3), and appeared to modify the medieval myth that Jews sought to destroy Christianity in more secular terms. Yet, many of the secularised antisemitic representations appeared to be underpinned by the anti-Jewish motifs originating from Christian theology. Antisemites already viewed Jews as the embodiment of evil and as inherently self-righteous and self-serving. The emerging representation of an international conspiracy seemed to provide an explanation for the social and economic progress made by European Jewry during the Enlightenment period. According to antisemites, such a conspiracy allowed Jews to optimise their ability to deceive the world and to usurp its resources for ingroup gain.

The representation of the international Jewish conspiracy was crystallised and gained traction following the publication of the notorious forgery, *The Protocols of the Elders of Zion*. The text was written in France in the 1890s by an unknown author but was later published in the Russian Empire in 1903. The Russian secret police is said to have commissioned the text in order to provide justification for the tsarist regime's antisemitic policies and practices, which resulted in a series of anti-Jewish pogroms from 1881 that claimed the lives of thousands of Jews (Perry and Schweitzer, 2002). The *Protocols* purported to describe a meeting of Jewish elders in an ancient Jewish cemetery in Prague, in the Austro-Hungarian Empire, during which the elders allegedly discussed their aim of global Jewish hegemony. The text suggested that Jews would employ a series of devious stratagems, including the subversion of religion, the murder of monarchs and politicians, the instigation of revolutions, class warfare and others. It is noteworthy that the invocation of these stratagems was intended to tap into the beliefs and fears of the general population by invoking real-world events, with which laypeople could identify, and attributing them to the Jews. For instance, in the *Protocols* and in other antisemitic literature that subsequently emerged, such as Adolf Hitler's (1925) *Mein Kampf*, there was a conflation of Jews and Communists and a suggestion that all Jews were necessarily supportive of Communist ideology (Szajkowski, 1972). According to these texts, the overarching Jewish aim, regardless of how it was achieved, was to elevate the global position and power of Judaism vis-à-vis all other religions and civilisations (Cohn, 1966).

The *Protocols* synthesised a number of important antisemitic themes, some of which were clearly observable in medieval antisemitism. Representations of Jews as demonic and satanic, as inherently untrustworthy and conspiratorial, as dangerous and threatening were invoked in the construction of an international Jewish conspiracy that strove for Jewish world hegemony. Crucially, already in print in the Russian Empire from 1903, the text spread rapidly and prolifically around the world – US industrialist antisemite Henry Ford funded the publication of some 500,000 copies of the *Protocols* which were distributed in the US in the 1920s; the Nazis ordered mass publication and distribution of the text and its use in German classrooms from 1933; and, as discussed below, the *Protocols* continue to be referenced and widely distributed in the Middle East. Other texts emerged after the publication (and indeed, the discrediting) of the *Protocols* – Hitler's (1925/2007, p. 174) *Mein Kampf* drew upon the *Protocols* in order to argue that "the whole existence of this people is based on a permanent falsehood", and Henry Ford's (1920) *The International Jew*, which accused Jews of undermining the US through their alleged control of the US press and financial system, included a chapter which aimed to defend the *Protocols* in view of growing doubt concerning its authenticity. Many antisemites have continued to invoke, employ and disseminate the *Protocols* despite the overwhelming evidence and general acceptance that the text constituted a forgery and hoax with no grounding in fact whatsoever.

Despite its discrediting, the antisemitic myths and representations enthusiastically disseminated in the *Protocols* came to inform the social representations of Jews which were constructed, disseminated and encouraged in Europe in the first half of the twentieth century. In modern Europe many Jews had come to occupy sensitive and precarious social positions, such as moneylending and banking, which later rendered them susceptible to criticism, discrimination and scapegoating from outgroups during times of economic turmoil (Gregory, 2001). The antisemitic movements which emerged in Germany and Austria from the 1870s, such as Wilhelm Marr's League of Antisemites, focused principally upon "fantasies of enormous Jewish power, acquired in illegitimate ways, and used with heartless efficiency" (Levy, 2010, p. 123). There was a perception that Jews would go to whatever immoral lengths necessary in order to attain their own goals. Although antisemitism from the Enlightenment era onwards appeared to negativise Jews in apparently novel ways, it was clearly still drawing upon more traditional sources of antisemitic imagery, such as Jewish greed, excessive Jewish influence and immorality (Wieviorka, 2005).

The destructive action orientation of modern antisemitism

Antisemitism from the early twentieth century could be described as possessing an action orientation in that it constructed Jews and Jewishness as posing a threat which required a defensive response from non-Jews. The "appropriate" response varied in accordance with context – while the tsarist regime appeared to turn a blind eye to the sporadic but deadly anti-Jewish pogroms at the turn of the century, Hitler and his collaborators ultimately opted for the systematic annihilation of European Jewry, which later became known as the Holocaust. In order to create a context in which the destruction of European Jewry would eventually be possible, the Nazis readily invoked medieval representations of Jews as host desecrators, demons, ritual murderers and inherently dangerous to Christianity, which they secularised and adapted to the contemporary German context (Wistrich, 1999a). These medieval myths adequately reinforced the Nazis' delegitimising and dehumanising antisemitic agenda. Nazi German stereotypes of Jews evoked Christian religious imagery, and readily made use of the blood libel in order to demonise Jews and mobilise the population against them. Heinrich Himmler, one of the key architects of the Holocaust, was allegedly impressed by the mobilising potential of the blood libel accusation and ordered the Nazi propaganda machine to disseminate this social representation throughout Europe and the Middle East (Perry and Schweitzer, 2002).

Consistent with antisemitic representations in nineteenth century Europe, there was also a theme of Jewish sexual immorality and predation (Vincze, 2013). The Jewish male was represented as racially inferior, yet as a threatening sexual predator prying on Aryan women, while the Jewish female was depicted as an ugly and devious, yet highly fertile, temptress who would lead Aryan men to their demise (as depicted in Hitler's *Mein Kampf*). What rendered Jews so threatening in the eyes of the Nazis was the apparent assimilation of Jews into German society, which rendered them difficult to spot (Burrin, 1999). According to Nazi ideology, the destruction of Jewry constituted an attempt to "save" Germany, but also mankind, from disaster. Similarly, during this era, in Slovak folklore, Jews were represented as strange, guilty and foreign (Krekovičová, 1997), which evoked common Central European social representations of Jews (Herzog, 1994; Rothstein, 1986). In the Polish context, people viewed Jewish characteristics (often deemed to be negative) as more threatening and more immutable than those of other social groups (Kofta and Sedek, 2005). As Perry and Schweitzer (2002, p. 1) highlight, "the Nazis regarded themselves as noble idealists engaged in the biological and spiritual purification of Europe". Their pseudo-biological ideology, which constructed the Aryans as superior and the Jews as subhuman, essentialised, dehumanised and animalised Jews – this created a perception that the allegedly inferior and subhuman traits were "built" into Jews, rendering futile any attempt to "rehabilitate" them. According to the Nazis, Europe could only be "purified" if the Jews were annihilated in their entirety (Spencer, 2010).

What is abundantly clear from the Nazi era (and also from the tsarist regime in Russia) is the destructive force of antisemitism when it is politicised and institutionalised. The destructive action orientation of antisemitism (invoked by Helen Fein) was clearly bolstered and crystallised by *organised and institutionalised political antisemitism*. In her sketch of how antisemitism functioned and accomplished this destructive action orientation in Nazi-administrated Europe, Bergen (2010, p. 198) describes a tripartite system of antisemitism: (i) "antisemitism as ideology" which motivated particular patterns of action against Jews; (ii) "antisemitism in power", that is, how antisemitism might have been shaped as it was institutionalised, legalised and implemented within policy and practice; and (iii) "antisemitism as a product of the Holocaust", referring to the notion that violence against Jews itself produced particular cognitions and emotions (e.g. hatred, resentment) towards the Jews which began during the Holocaust and continued to exist in its aftermath.

The first two components of the system exhibit unequivocally the clout that antisemitism could have when it became a systematic ideology which could be disseminated to the public and when it was legalised and implemented at an institutional level. In Nazi-occupied Europe, its transformation into ideology and its implementation endowed antisemitism with a coherent action orientation, namely the destruction of Jewry. Indeed, as Bergen (2010, p. 201) argues, "power institutionalised Nazi antisemitism and diffused it throughout society in ways that merged its extraordinary force and vehemence with the ordinary, even banal manifestations of everyday life". Through processes of institutionalisation, antisemitic representations came to make sense in everyday life and to be viewed in society as a "natural" response to Jews. Medieval stereotypes of Jews were made to appear reasonable and tangible to laypeople who could now perceive a coherent narrative of the "Jewish threat". The third component highlights the paradoxical force of the Holocaust, the most destructive act of genocide in Jewish history, in perpetuating antisemitism. Indeed, Samuels (2009, p. 2) observes that in Eastern Europe where the local Jewish populations were almost entirely wiped out during the Holocaust, antisemitism has persisted as a "phantom pain syndrome" – no Jews remain but hatred towards them does. Antisemitic beliefs (i.e. that the Jews are evil and that they pose a threat) can function as a heuristic tool for explaining the unexplainable – the systematic murder of 6 million Jews. Moreover, the Holocaust appeared to leave a stigma on Jews, since individuals (including many Jews themselves) came to view them as "eternal victims" who attract suffering (Bergen, 2010, p. 210; see also Bar-On, 2008). This phenomenon has been explained in terms of "secondary antisemitism" which is essentially a "guilt-defensive anti-Semitism" designed to deflect feelings of guilt associated with Jewish suffering (Markovits, 2006).

Many scholars (e.g. Küntzel, 2010; Wistrich, 2010) have argued that, while antisemitism persists in various forms within the West, it is most conspicuous in the social, political and institutional levels in the Islamic world.

Antisemitism in the Islamic world

Antisemitism in the Islamic world has had a distinct trajectory from that of Western Christian civilisation. Richard Breitman (2007) provides an excellent historical overview of Muslim antisemitism, which he contrasts with Christian antisemitism. Although Jews (as well as other non-Muslim groups) undoubtedly faced discrimination in Muslim countries, they were not historically denigrated as an inferior *racial* group (unlike in Nazi-occupied Europe). Antisemitism expressed in racial terms was rare, and the gradual appearance of antisemitic representations (such as the blood libel accusation) can be regarded as a European importation into the Muslim world during the colonial era (Stillman, 2010).

There are diverse academic views on the origins and development of antisemitism in the Islamic world. Some scholars (e.g. Aziz, 2007; Chanes, 2004; Cohen, 2002) have argued that there was no policy or practice of discrimination aimed specifically at Jews and that antisemitism formed part of a more general discrimination towards non-Muslims. Others (e.g. Gerber, 1986; Perry and Schweitzer, 2002; Shahvar, 2009) have argued that discrimination towards Jews in the Islamic world, while qualitatively different from that of the Western Christian civilisation, was much more fervent than that directed against Christians. Most scholars emphasise the qualitative differences between Western/European antisemitism and that of the Islamic world by highlighting that in the latter context Jews were not generally regarded as a "cosmic evil" or as "racially inferior" (Lewis, 1999). There is a suggestion that antipathy towards Jews were religiously motivated and, thus, more akin to "anti-Judaism" than antisemitism. Moreover, it has been argued that, while antisemitism in the Christian world was long-standing and consistent, there were considerable fluctuations in Muslim attitudes towards Jews in accordance with social and political context (Laqueur, 2009; Kramer, 1995).

Some scholars have turned to the examination of *Sharia* (Islamic Law) in order to understand the existence of antisemitism. Under Islamic law, Jews were attributed *dhimmi* status, which meant that they were tolerated and protected as an official minority provided that they accepted a subordinate and inferior status to Muslims (Lazarus-Yafeh, 1999; Poliakov, 1974). In return for toleration and protection, Jews were required to accept Muslim superiority and to pay a special tax known as the *jizya*. There were other social and political restrictions which varied in accordance with jurisdiction – for instance, in some contexts, Jews were required to wear clothing or insignia that clearly distinguished them from Muslims and, in others, they could not serve as witnesses in litigation cases against Muslims (see also Lavarus-Yafeh, 1999). In his historical overview of antisemitism in Iran, Shahvar (2009) argues that Shiite Islam has a long history of radical antisemitism and that the position of Jews in Shiite Iran was more perilous than in Sunni Muslim countries.

Stillman (2010) observes that, although both the Jews and Christians were attributed the *dhimmi* status, Muslims generally regarded Christians as more sincere, less treacherous and less infidel than Jews. However, Goitein (1971, p. 283) notes that, unlike in Christian societies, in Islamic societies antisemitism was generally "local and sporadic, rather than general and endemic". It appears that anti-Jewish sentiment increased and that anti-Jewish stereotypes emerged when Muslims were led to believe that Jews did not act in accordance with their dhimmi (subordinate) status as dictated by Islamic law. Although there were certainly outbreaks of violence against Jews during medieval times (Perry and Schweitzer, 2002), this was not comparable in scale or magnitude to the anti-Jewish pogroms and mass executions observable in medieval Christendom. It is noteworthy that many Jews continued to live in Islamic countries until well into the mid-twentieth century, even after the establishment of the State of Israel (Simon, Laskier and Reguer, 2002).

While antisemitism in Western Christian civilisation (and even in Nazi Germany) clearly drew upon Christian theology in order to substantiate its arguments, Islamic Holy Scripture was relatively ambivalent about Jews and Judaism. Given that Muslims regard the Koran as the verbatim word of God, communicated through the Angel Gabriel, this in turn created ambivalent attitudes towards Jews in the general population. In examining Koranic representations of the Jews, it appears that the Prophet Mohammed held a generally positive attitude towards the Jews during his early stage of his career when he lived in pagan-dominated Mecca. Both Judaism and Christianity were positively evaluated as "ahl al-Kitab" ("people of the Book"), a reference to the monotheistic Abrahamic religions with a revealed scripture, vis-à-vis polytheist traditions that prevailed in Mecca at that time.

However, the Prophet's attitudes towards Jews appeared to worsen when in Medina in 622 he encountered the large, educated Jewish communities from whom he was subjected to ridicule and rejection (Stillman, 2010). The Koranic verses revealed in Medina referred to the Jews as "Yahud" and "Hud" ("Jews") and "alladhina hadu" ("those who are Jewish"), which have negative connotations (Durán and Hachiche, 2001). Furthermore, there are overtly negative verses in the Koran, which *inter alia* anchor Jews to interconfessional tensions and conflict (Sura II:113); represent them as self-righteously believing that only they are beloved of God (Sura II:111); indicate that Jews deliberately distort the meaning of Holy Scripture and therefore invite the wrath of God (Sura IV:46). Similarly, some of the Ahadith (the deeds and sayings which are commonly attributed to the Prophet) depict Jews as dishonest, untrustworthy and malevolent. Perry and Schweitzer (2002, p. 266) argue that the Ahadith are "even more scathing (than the Koran) in attacking the Jews". Jews were depicted as "men whose malice and enmity were aimed at the Apostle of God" (Ibn Hisham, Sira 1, 516), as malicious and self-centred (Al-Waqidi, 363ff). Moreover, the following Hadith, attributed to the Prophet Mohammed but related by Muhammad ibn Ismail al-Bukhari (810–870), has been widely interpreted as evidence of the theological origins of antisemitism in the Islamic world:

> The Day of Judgement will not come about until the Muslims fight against the Jews and the Muslims kill them until the Jews hide behind stones and trees. The stones and trees will say "O Muslims, O Abdullah, there is a Jew behind me,

come and kill him." Only the Gharkad tree would not do that because it is one of the trees of the Jews (Salih Muslim, 41:6985)

This interpretation can be attributed to the fact that some social, religious and political institutions in the Islamic world have cited this Hadith in pronouncements, often in relation to the State of Israel. For instance, the Hamas Charter also includes this Hadith as evidence of the necessity to combat the Jewish State (see Litvak, 1998, for a discussion of the Islamicisation of the Israeli-Palestinian conflict). Moreover, some literature in the Islamic world (e.g. books, stories and poetry) delegitimised and dehumanised Jews as rodents, apes and dogs (Perry and Schweitzer, 2002), although there were no accusations of a Jewish world conspiracy, ritual murder or the poisoning of wells as was observable in European literature (Lewis, 1999). In Islamic theology, representations of Jews and Judaism appear to be ambivalent – sometimes positive and at others highly condemnatory. However, as demonstrated by Hamas's use of the above-cited Hadith, Islamic theology can constitute a source of antisemitic representations for those who wish to delegitimise and demonise the Jewish people.

Kramer (1995) argues that Islamic tradition did not provide the theological or cultural resources for the development of the antisemitic representation of the "Eternal Jew" and that this must have been imported into Islamic contexts from European antisemitism. There was a tenuous representation of the Machiavellian Jew in the Islamic argument of Tahrif which referred to the accusation that Jews had falsified their scripture (Lazarus-Yafeh, 1999), although this accusation was also employed to discredit other religious groups and their texts. Moreover, as observable in the above-cited Hadith (Salih Muslim, 41:6985), Jews were certainly perceived as inviting the wrath of God due to their alleged actions. Modern antisemitic representations of European origin, which emphasised the Machiavellian character of Jews, appeared to complement and extend the subtler theological representations in Islam.

In contrast to the overt anti-Judaism in the Islamic world, it appears that European antisemitic myths first surfaced among Arabic-speaking Christians in Syria who maintained close social, cultural and economic ties with European nations and thereby served as a "bridge" connecting Europe and the Arab world. On the one hand, Arab Christians shared Arab Muslims' contempt and disdain for Jews and, on the other, they were familiar with the negative images of Jews held by Christian European traders and missionaries. Although some European antisemitic representations, such as that of Jews as deicide and that of Jews as a cursed people, were observable among Arab Christians, the blood libel and host desecration accusation and the representation of Jews as an inferior race were generally unknown in the Middle East. The blood libel accusation first appeared in Aleppo, Syria in the 1700s and gained momentum after the notorious Damascus Affair in 1840. This was an incident in which eight prominent Jews in the city of Damascus were accused of murdering a Christian monk for ritualistic purposes

(Florence, 2004). The accused were imprisoned and tortured and several of them died, and the local community pillaged a synagogue in a suburb of the city.

Subsequent to the Damascus Affair, the blood libel accusation lodged itself in cultural consciousness and was more systematically levelled against Jews in Syria, Palestine and Egypt throughout the nineteenth century. In the early twentieth century, the *Protocols of the Elders of Zion* was translated and published in Arabic and began to be cited and publicised by Arab nationalists. Similarly, *Mein Kampf* was translated and published in Beirut in 1935. Despite their discrediting in the Western world, the *Protocols* and *Mein Kampf* have become bestsellers in the Islamic world (Wistrich, 2010), where they are praised and recommended by religious and political leaders alike. Antisemitic literature like the *Protocols* and *Mein Kampf* and also the close political ties between the Arab world and Nazi Germany helped to engender antisemitic social representations in the Arab world, which were to be enduring and fervent (Hirszowicz, 1966). Indeed, antisemitism was so firmly established in Nazi-allied Iraq that on 1st July 1941 Jews were blamed for the fall of the pro-Nazi al-Gaylani regime which had just fled Baghdad and a deadly anti-Jewish pogrom broke out in the capital, claiming the lives of 179 Jews and injuring hundreds more. Though unprecedented in the region, anti-Jewish pogroms were to follow in Egypt, Tripolitania (Libya) and Syria. Through the proliferation of antisemitic literature, the Muslim world has come to accept and internalise many of the discredited antisemitic myths, such as that of the blood libel and that of the "all-powerful and all-controlling Jews", that were subsequently rejected and ridiculed in post-Holocaust Europe (Berenbaum, 2009, p. 6).

Today, the highest levels of antisemitism tend to appear in Arab Muslim nations where between 80 to 85 per cent of the population manifests high levels of antipathy towards Jews. It is noteworthy that Jordan, a nation with no Jewish population and which signed a peace treaty with the State of Israel in 1994, has a 98–100 per cent unfavourability rating (Anti-Defamation League, 2007, 2009). As Perry and Schweitzer (2002, p. 10) note, in many Muslim countries, "antisemitism is pervasive and vicious, routinely employing Christian and Nazi myths, which most westerners now regard as repulsive". Hence, the boundaries of acceptability in many parts of the Muslim world seem to permit the dissemination and encouragement of antisemitism at both institutional and social levels. Government officials and political leaders play an important role in fomenting antisemitic sentiment among Arab and Muslim populations (Simon and Schaler, 2007). Just a cursory glance at newspaper reporting in many Arab and Iranian newspapers clearly demonstrates this – journalists regularly depict ugly caricatures of Jews with hooked noses, hunchbacks and kippas and as animals in order to dehumanise them (see Chapter 6). Moreover, even in Malaysia, a Muslim country with which Israel has had no dispute, the Prime Minister reportedly attributed the fall of the ringgit (the Malaysian currency) to a Jewish conspiracy against Muslims (see Perry and Schweitzer, 2002). In her detailed account of antisemitic imagery in the contemporary Arab-Muslim world, Yadlin (1999) notes that, as in European antisemitism, competing and contradictory accusations are levelled against

Jews, such as the charges of having invented communism and capitalism, and democracy and dictatorship. Moreover, Spencer (2010) argues that antisemitism is quite central to the worldview of political Islamists. As Chapter 3 demonstrates, antisemitism is manifested in a multitude of ways, usually in conjunction with anti-Israeli depictions, but one of the most overt forms of antisemitism which persists in the contemporary world is Holocaust denial.

Holocaust denial

The Holocaust[3] was a programme of systematic, state-organised genocide against European Jewry, which also extended to North African Jews (Gilbert, 1985; Hilberg, 1985; Longerich, 2010; Yahil, 1990). Of the 9 million Jews who resided in Europe, over 6 million were murdered, which almost wiped out the Jewish population of Europe. For the vast majority of human beings, the Holocaust represents an unthinkable crime against humanity, which must be learned about and remembered in future generations so that it can never reoccur. This is exemplified by the number of Holocaust museums and memorials established in the world, as well as the widespread support for Holocaust Memorial Days (Ben-Amos and Bet-El, 1999) and for Holocaust education in schools and colleges (Salmons, 2003; Short, 1994). Jews, both within Israel (Lazar, Litvak-Hirsch and Chaitin, 2008) and in the Diaspora (Blumner, 2006), have been said to regard the Holocaust in terms of a "cultural trauma", which demonstrates its symbolic, psychological and cultural importance for many Jews.

Yet, the ways in which many non-Jewish communities around the world are thinking and feeling about the Holocaust appear to be changing over time – cultural, national and religious identities, pressures and values may distort perceptions of the Holocaust and induce perceptual and affective changes (Rosenfeld, 2011). Holocaust "revisionism" in its various guises – from outright denial to subtle re-construal – has emerged as a cruel weapon of antisemitism in the modern world, designed to delegitimise both the Jewish people and the Jewish State (Lipstadt, 1993). Holocaust revisionism may legitimately be regarded as a form of antisemitism, since this "distorts and denies Jewish history and deprives the Jews of their human dignity by presenting their worst tragedy as a scam", while charging "the Jews with unscrupulous machinations in order to achieve illegitimate and immoral goals, mainly financial extortion" (Litvak, 2006, p. 281). Moreover, Cohen-Almagor (2009) has legitimately referred to Holocaust denial as a form of hate speech.

People tend to associate the Holocaust with human depravity and the human capacity for evil and cruelty (Zimbardo, 2008). Accordingly, Holocaust denial is generally deplored by most rational people and is even illegal in several European

---

3   Although the Holocaust is mainly linked to the genocide of European Jewry, other minority groups, including the Romani people, Slavs, Poles, homosexuals, and the disabled and mentally ill, were also targeted by the Nazi regime (Berenbaum, 1990).

countries (Bazyler, 2006). Yet, Holocaust denial persists. Holocaust "revisionism" (a euphemism for what amounts to Holocaust denial) is manifested in many different forms and just some of its variants are summarised in this chapter. Some people categorically deny that the Holocaust ever occurred, while others re-construe, trivialise or attempt to justify it (Lipstadt, 1993).

A prominent theme in Holocaust revisionism has concerned the death toll in the Holocaust – revisionists have questioned the generally accepted figure of 6 million Jewish victims, claiming that this figure is "exaggerated" or even "impossible" (Litvak and Webman, 2009). The Holocaust may also be used to delegitimise and dehumanise the Jews and the Jewish State by associating them with deception – some revisionists have accused Jews of concocting the "myth" of the Holocaust which serves to construct Jews as an immoral and manipulative people (Rubenstein, 2009). One of the most common accusations in the revisionist repertoire is that the Holocaust was invented in order to justify the creation of the State of Israel, which, in the eyes of some antisemites, dismantles Israel's raison d'être (Perry and Schweitzer, 2002). Similarly, there have even been accusations that Zionist Jews collaborated with the Nazis in the Holocaust in order to create the Jewish State, which serves only to conflate the Jews with their worst tormentors in history. Since the First Palestinian Intifada (uprising), some people have compared Israel's treatment of the Palestinians to the Nazi treatment of Jews and suggested that Israel too is engaged in a programme of genocide against the Palestinians (Litvak and Webman, 2009). This argument can be considered an aspect of Holocaust revisionism because it is intended to reduce the significance of the Nazi Holocaust vis-à-vis Israel's treatment of the Palestinians and to argue that Jews are more evil than the Nazis.

Holocaust revisionism has gained acceptance in some social and political contexts partly because of its expression in pseudo-scientific terms by academics, such as Robert Faurrison, a French professor of literature; Arthur Butz, a US professor of electrical engineering; David Irving, a British journalist and historian and others. Moreover, as discussed in Chapter 3, prominent politicians in the Middle East, such as Syrian President Bashar al-Assad and former Iranian President Mahmoud Ahmadinejad, have publicly denied the Holocaust. Although Holocaust denial in Europe is generally associated with far-right groups on the fringes of politics (Lipstadt, 1993), its distribution in the Islamic world is far greater and the Holocaust is habitually denied in both public and political discourses. Holocaust denial in the Islamic world is often associated with the delegitimisation of the State of Israel in particular (see Chapter 3). In many respects, Holocaust denial evokes some of the antisemitic myths and representations that have been outlined in this chapter. Denial of the Holocaust (and the implicit charge that Jews fabricated this "myth") connects with representations of the Jews as evil, destructive, manipulative, and relentlessly seeking to usurp the world and its resources utilising whatever means necessary. As Porat (1999, p. 325) notes, "denial of the Holocaust depicts the Jews as a sophisticated and powerful organization, capable of talking the entire world into believing a hoax which they invented". Holocaust denial serves to engender a fear that the world and its history are controlled by Jews, echoing the themes of the *Protocols of the Elders of Zion* and thereby fanning the flames of antisemitism. In terms of the "continuities and discontinuities" of antisemitism, Holocaust denial may constitute a relatively novel means of delegitimising the Jews but it reiterates, and performs precisely the same function as, other antisemitic myths and representations that preceded it.

There have been attempts to understand the social and psychological motivations underlying Holocaust revisionism. Holocaust revisionism may be gaining ground in public consciousness partly because it reduces public uncertainty amid suspicion regarding the veracity of the Holocaust narrative and builds upon existing antisemitic prejudice (Benz, 1999). Social psychologists have identified a human need for deriving meaning amid uncertainty (McAdams, 2001) and Holocaust revisionism may constitute a heuristic, sense-making strategy in antisemitic contexts, such as in the many Middle Eastern societies that endorse it. In the case of Germany and other countries that collaborated with the Nazis in perpetrating the Holocaust, there may be a psychological incentive to deny the Holocaust because of wounded national pride and the desire to deflect negativity from the national and ethnic ingroups. Schönbach (1961) coined the term "secondary antisemitism" which refers to the notion that the very presence of Jews reminds non-Jews of the Holocaust and thereby evokes feelings of guilt about it. It is argued that this in turn induces negative feelings and emotions towards Jews, as a form of defence mechanism (Bergmann, 2006). Indeed, there has been some empirical research into secondary antisemitism, which confirms this prediction (Imhoff and Banse, 2009). In recent research into perceptions of the Holocaust among Muslim minorities in Europe (Jikeli and Allouche-Benayoun, 2013), it has been suggested that the Holocaust may be denied to varying degrees because it provides a means of delegitimising Israel which many young Muslims oppose due to its perceived mistreatment of the Palestinians.

In his insightful essay on the relationship between social fantasies of Jews and violence against Jews, Baum (2009b) highlights a number of powerful antisemitic legends that have stood the test of time and crystallised in both the West and the Islamic world:

1. The representation of Jews as eternal wanderers
2. The blood libel representation
3. The representation of a conspiratorial planetary takeover
4. The representation of Jews as money usurers
5. The representation of Jews as devil/ chimera/ subhuman/ biologically determined manifesting a magic/ moral weakness

These antisemitic representations converge in constructing Jewish distinctiveness as inherently destructive to non-Jews. At a basic level, these mythical representations of Jews, which construct them as subhuman and demonic, have served to create negative intergroup attitudes towards Jews in diverse contexts. However, in some contexts, they have done much more than this – they engendered and rationalised an action orientation which permitted unthinkable cruelty towards Jews, including exclusion, pogroms and systematic genocide. Clearly, theory and research need to provide an understanding of the continuities and discontinuities of antisemitism, and its underlying social and psychological mechanisms.

Understanding Antisemitism: Theory and Research

The brief discussion of the continuities and discontinuities of antisemitism in this chapter provides important social and historical insights into this form of prejudice and its development from ancient to modern times. However, as Kressel (2003) notes, there has been relatively less empirical social science research into antisemitism which can shed light on its nature and the motivational processes underlying this form of prejudice, particularly in the Islamic world. Much early social psychological research was conducted in order to understand the social and psychological processes that could have led to the dreadful events of the Holocaust – this included the authoritarian personality (Adorno, Frenkel-Brunswik, Levinson, and Sanford, 1950), obedience to authority (Milgram, 1963), scapegoating (Gregory, 2001), intergroup processes (Brown, 2000; Tajfel, 1982; Tajfel and Turner, 1986) and, more recently, perceived threats from outgroups (Stephan and Stephan, 2000). However, this body of work has not been matched comprehensively by empirical social science research into antisemitism, in particular. Yet, as argued in this chapter, antisemitism constitutes an age-old prejudice that has permeated temporal, cultural and geographical boundaries and, as highlighted in Chapter 1, it continues to pose a significant problem in both the Middle East and the West. Therefore, antisemitism remains well worthy of academic attention.

There have been several correlational survey-based studies, which seek to identify the individual traits that appear to be associated with antisemitism. Frindte, Wettig and Wammetsberger (2005) conducted two studies in Germany that examined antisemitism within the context of authoritarianism and social dominance. They showed that individuals who manifested extreme antisemitic attitudes differed significantly from those who scored low on antisemitism with regard to the extent of authoritarianism, readiness for violence, endorsement of National Socialism and political orientation. They found that authoritarianism was an important predictor of antisemitism. In a unique cross-cultural examination of the social psychological predictors of antisemitism, Dunbar and Simonova (2003) found that the relationship between the right-wing extremism personality and antisemitism was positive and that the degree of manifestation of antisemitic attitudes was similar in both the US and Czech samples, despite the distinct history of intergroup relations between these groups and Jews. Consistent with Gibson and Howard's (2007) assertion, this study suggests that individual personality traits play a more important role in antisemitism than social and environmental factors.

A series of studies over the last few decades have argued that there is a link between particular demographic characteristics and antisemitism. It has been found that male respondents generally manifest greater antisemitism than female respondents (D'Alessio and Stolzenberg, 1991), that unskilled workers are more antisemitic than professionals (Selznick and Steinberg, 1969), that education is negatively correlated with antisemitism (Quinley and Glock, 1979), that younger people are generally less antisemitic than older people (Raab, 1983), and that the higher the concentration of Jews in one's environment, the higher one's level of antisemitism will be (Smith, 1991). In their review of the largely survey-based research into antisemitism, Konig, Scheepers and Falling (2001) identify three principal variables that appear to correlate with antisemitism, namely religion, personality (e.g. authoritarianism) and socio-structural factors (e.g. age, education). While these studies provide an important snapshot of antisemitism in particular temporal, cultural and geographical contexts (admittedly, largely in the US), there are many counter-examples, such as the fact that some of the most antisemitic countries in the world are devoid of a Jewish population (e.g. Anti-Defamation League, 2007, 2009). Furthermore, Weil (1985) examined the effects of education on liberalising attitudes in order to decipher the outcomes for antisemitism. In his cross-cultural research, he found that, while education was positively correlated with liberal attitudes towards Jews in the US and the West, the effect of education on liberal attitudes appeared to be weaker or even reversed in non-liberal democracies or countries with a history of authoritarian government. In addition to demonstrating the tenuous relationship between particular demographic traits and antisemitism and, thus, the simplistic nature of some the existing research, Weil's study provided important insight into the socio-structural predictors of antisemitism.

As demonstrated in this chapter, much social science research points to a correlation between Christian/Muslim religiosity and antisemitism. In their study of Christian antisemitism in the Netherlands, Konig et al. (2000) highlighted that Christian religion was a determinant of both religious *and* secular forms of antisemitism, which in turn exhibited the importance of religious imagery in contemporary secular thinking vis-à-vis Jews. Jaspal (2011c) has conducted survey research into antisemitism among Iranians, which suggests that attitudes towards Jews differ in accordance with political orientation. More specifically, self-identified political "hardliners" scored significantly higher than self-identified political "reformists" on the antisemitism scale. However, *both* hardliners and reformists appeared to manifest more negative attitudes towards Jews than Israel. This preliminary research suggests that the ideas and messages perceived to be associated with specific political identities may gain more or less prominence in accordance with one's own political orientation, but that both hardliner and reformist political orientations appear to incorporate more antisemitic imagery than anti-Zionist imagery. Moreover, a multiple regression analysis indicated that Muslim identity and political trust were significant predictors of antisemitism among Iranians, which suggested that individuals who held trust in the Iranian political regime were more likely to adhere to the "version" of Muslim identity advocated by the regime. Incidentally, this version of Islam can construct Jews as inferior and "impure" (Shahvar, 2009). In a unique and insightful survey study of antisemitism among both Christians and Muslims in North America, Baum (2009a) found that, while personal identity was the strongest predictor of antisemitism among Christians (i.e. the perception that one has personally been mistreated by Jews), *social* identity was the strongest predictor among Muslim respondents (i.e. the perception that one's Muslim ingroup was threatened by Jews). This is likely to be associated with the sorts of messages and representations disseminated at a social level which are subsequently internalised by individuals. Similarly, using religious coping theory, Pargament, Trevino, Mahoney and Silberman (2007) showed that the perception of Jews as desecrators of Christian values, an antisemitic belief, was predicted, in part, by less exposure to messages that challenge representations of desecration.

Accordingly, scholars have sought explanations for antisemitism in theological representations and have claimed that the key to understanding antisemitism lies in Holy Scripture and in representations disseminated in religious contexts. Indeed, analyses of both Christian (Perry and Schweitzer, 2002) and Islamic (Stillman, 2010) Holy Scripture certainly suggest that they constitute important sources of antisemitic representations. Furthermore, they have examined the religious sermons delivered in the Islamic world in order to shed light on the sources of contemporary antisemitism (Litvak, 1998; Shahvar, 2009). The print media has also played an important role – Stillman (2010) has argued that antisemitism (and particularly, the blood libel accusation) crystallised and proliferated as the print media developed in the country. Moreover, the translation, publication and proliferation of key antisemitic texts such as the *Protocols of the Elders of Zion, The International Jew* and *Mein Kampf* around the world have ensured that antisemitic representations remain widely available and continue to be disseminated in all corners of the globe.

Some scholars have examined antisemitism from the perspective of scapegoat theory, which argues that "frustrations attendant to economic downturns produce aggressive impulses that are directed at vulnerable targets, such as minority groups, even when these groups bear no actual or perceived responsibility for economic decline" (Green, Glaser and Rich, 1998, p. 82; see also Gregory, 2001). In their study of authoritarianism and aggression, Doty et al. (1991) found that perceived economic distress was positively associated with antisemitic vandalism, suggesting that individuals used the Jews as scapegoats. Moreover, a report by the Anti-Defamation League cited Russia as a "growing area of concern" and stated that "[w]ith the economic and political instability in the region there has been an increase in political anti-Semitism, with elected Communist Party officials spouting outrageous accusations targeting Jews as scapegoats for Russia's economic, political and social ills" (Anti-Defamation League, 2005).

Some scholars have empirically examined this phenomenon in Russia. In a recent study of Russian antisemitism and scapegoating of Jews, Gibson and

Howard (2007) convincingly argue that, while there is some merit in scapegoat theory in explaining antisemitism, this theory alone provides a rather simplistic snapshot of this form of prejudice. In a longitudinal survey study conducted from 1996 to 2000, they demonstrated that antisemitic prejudice appeared to stem from a complex range of attitudes associated with authoritarianism (an individual trait), rather than from perceptions of economic and political turmoil. Crucially, they argued that "one very important difference between Russia today and the Russia of the past is that powerful and prominent political elites have publicly condemned anti-Semitism and have argued strongly in favour of intergroup tolerance" (p. 218), which may dissuade individuals from scapegoating Jews in times of economic and political turmoil. Similarly, in their study of the scapegoating of Jews in Poland and the Ukraine, Bilewicz and Krzeminski (2010, p. 243) conclude that "[t]he ideological model of scapegoating seems to be a good explanation of anti-Semitism only in countries where Jews are still targets of envious stereotypes". This too attests to the importance of the cultural and ideological milieu within which particular representations of Jews can develop and thrive.

More recently, terror management theorists (Cohen et al., 2009; Cohen et al., 2011) have made important contributions to the study of antisemitism. They have argued that when human beings are reminded of their own mortality, their worldviews acquire salience because they provide a form of psychological protection and that, consequently, in these conditions non-Jews may become hostile towards Jews because Jews represent a challenge to their worldviews. Cohen et al. (2009) argue that Jews may pose both theological and socio-cultural challenges to non-Jews' worldview for the historical reasons outlined earlier in this chapter. In an experimental study, Cohen et al. (2009) demonstrated that participants manifested greater levels of antisemitism in the high mortality condition versus the control condition, suggesting that death anxiety induced higher levels of prejudice towards Jews because of a perceived challenge to one's worldview. Similarly, Greenberg et al. (1990) found that when Christians were encouraged to think about their mortality, their trait ratings of religious ingroup members became more positive while their trait ratings of Jews (a religious outgroup) became more negative. Crucially, Cohen (2009) has found that Jews appear to be uniquely threatening to non-Jews' worldviews – her experimental study showed that mortality salience increased antisemitism scores but not levels of prejudice towards African Americans or Asians, for instance. This has led some scholars to argue that antisemitism should be considered a unique form of prejudice, unlike any other (Wistrich, 2008; see Cinnirella, 2014 for a similar argument in relation to Islamophobia). However, it seems plausible that the key to understanding the apparent uniqueness on antisemitism lies in the myths, messages and representations disseminated at social and institutional levels, which overtly or covertly construct Jews as a particularly menacing group vis-à-vis other outgroups.

Connecting the themes of antisemitism and the Holocaust, Imhoff and Banse (2009) examined the intriguing phenomenon of "secondary antisemitism", which was briefly mentioned earlier in the chapter. In their experimental study at a German university, they found, firstly, that respondents more readily manifested their antisemitic attitudes under a "bogus pipeline", that is, when they were deceived into believing that their "true" attitudes would become apparent to the investigator and that lying was thus futile (see also Cohen et al., 2009) and, secondly, that the acknowledgement of Jewish outgroup suffering due to the German ingroup's past atrocities against the Jews appeared to increase antisemitic prejudice in and of itself. Although they did not fully explain the potential social psychological underpinnings of this increase in prejudice, it is likely that this constitutes a form of coping strategy because knowledge of the ingroup's atrocities against an outgroup could pose a threat to ingroup identity. People may experience negative emotions, such as guilt and disgust, which are aversive for psychological wellbeing.

What this brief review of the social science literature on antisemitism suggests is that (i) there has been a focus either on individual traits or sociological factors, both of which appear to be eminently important explanatory factors in antisemitism, rather than a truly *social psychological* account; (ii) most research has employed survey-based and experimental methods which have yielded quantitative data, rather than qualitative interview research which could provide detailed, nuanced and contextually sensitive qualitative insights into the nature of antisemitism and its underlying social and psychological mechanisms; and (iii) the vast majority of research has focused upon the US and European contexts, rather than in non-Western contexts such as the Middle East and among ethnic and minority groups in the West in which antisemitic prejudice is actually a significant problem. Crucially, the studies converge in showing, in one way or another, the importance of myths, messages and representations in fomenting and establishing antisemitic sentiment in society.

Overview

Antisemitism needs to be defined in ways that can accommodate the fluidity and complexity of this age-old prejudice. An adequate definition of antisemitism will acknowledge its various dimensions, including the distinct levels (psychological, social and institutional) at which it can be manifested, its action orientation (i.e. what it intends to achieve) and its continuities and discontinuities across time, space and medium. In examining the history of antisemitism from antiquity to the present day, it is clear that, while this prejudice has shifted from being conceived in religious to secular terms, many of the underlying myths, messages and representations have been re-construed, re-cycled and adapted to suit specific temporal, geographical, cultural, political, religious and ideological contexts. This is also true of the variants of antisemitism manifested across cultural and geographical frontiers. Antisemitic representations that were peripheral but observable in antiquity, for instance, have re-emerged in subsequent eras as they have acquired relevance to the activities and ethos of specific groups. Although the Nazis generally shunned religion, they did not hesitate to draw upon antisemitic imagery from Christianity. While the specific arguments may have changed across time and space – Jews may be accused of communist sympathies in one context (Rein, 2003) and capitalist sympathies in another (Rubenstein and Naumov, 2001) – what these arguments share is an underlying belief in the "otherness" and subversive character of Jews. It appears that theology has remained an important source of antisemitic social representations, even in supposedly secular contexts. Contemporary antisemitism can, and often does, draw upon and synthesise both religious "anti-Jewishness" and secular forms of antipathy.

Holocaust "revisionism" has come to represent a prominent theme in modern antisemitism – its antecedents and consequences are multifarious. People are motivated to engage in Holocaust denial for a variety of reasons, both social and psychological. Yet, what underlies the revisionist stance on the Holocaust is antisemitism. In discussing its historical, social and psychological aspects of antisemitism, it is evident that this age-old prejudice has gradually developed an action orientation which emphasises the destruction of Jewry. This was of course most conspicuous in the Nazi era. Antisemitism is most likely to acquire such a destructive action orientation when it makes its transition into the ideological and institutional domains – political antisemitism that is institutionalised and state-sanctioned constitutes the most lethal form, largely because it becomes permissible, ubiquitous, normalised and comes to form part of common-sense thinking vis-à-vis the Jewish outgroup. There have been some attempts to examine empirically the nature, antecedents and motivational aspects of antisemitism and these studies converge in demonstrating the importance of examining the social and psychological dimensions of antisemitism, particularly in those contexts in which it remains a pressing problem, such as in the Middle East. The next chapter examines anti-Zionism, which itself may be viewed as an aspect of the continuities and discontinuities of antisemitism.

Chapter 3
Israel and the Emergence of Anti-Zionism and "New Antisemitism"

Introduction

Zionism is a poorly understood ideology. Its underlying philosophy and ideological tenets have been obscured due to the emergence of pervasive negative perceptions of Zionism following the establishment of Israel. These perceptions have intensified in the aftermath of wars as part of the Israeli-Arab conflict. Zionism can be defined as the "movement for national revival and independence of the Jewish people in 'Eretz Yisrael' [the biblical term referring to the Land of Israel]" (Rolef, 1993, p. 343). The ethno-national ideology lays claim to the Land of Israel as the national homeland of the Jewish people and provides both a historical and theological rationale for the establishment of the Jewish State. However, Zionism is understood in a multitude of ways – some recognise its status as an "ethnonational ideology" which posits that "Israel is the expression of the *Jewish* people's right to *national* self-determination" (Beller, 2007, p. 226), while others regard it as an expansionist ideology which aims to extend the borders of Israel and to usurp the land and resources of the Palestinians (and, in some cases, its Arab neighbours) (Corrigan, 2009). Given the multiple representations of Zionism, it becomes increasingly difficult to define *anti*-Zionism – how one defines this naturally depends upon *what* is being opposed. It can refer to the desire for the destruction of the State of Israel, to opposition to perceived Israeli expansionism, or the denial of the Jewish status of Israel, which is the stated policy of the Palestinian leadership (Jaspal and Coyle, 2014). In this book, anti-Zionism is defined as opposition to the ethnonational ideology which highlights the Jewish people's right to national self-determination. This chapter provides a brief historical sketch of the State of Israel and the consequential Israeli-Arab conflict, an overview of anti-Zionist representations and their action orientation and some insight into the debate concerning "new antisemitism".

The Birth of Israel and the Israeli-Arab Conflict

For Theodor Herzl, the father of modern political Zionism, Zionism offered the only plausible solution to the dire, age-old problem of antisemitism (Kornberg, 1993). He recognised that Jews would continue to face enmity from outgroups but firmly believed that a Jewish homeland would provide the Jews with the safety and security that they clearly lacked in the diaspora. Herzl had personally witnessed some of the antisemitism that was described in Chapter 1 and was acutely aware of its destructive action orientation. With the establishment of a Jewish homeland, antisemitism would continue to exist but not in the deadly form in which it had manifested itself in Europe. Gradually, the Jews would be "normalised" as their political status was normalised within their homeland. Although Herzl clearly favoured a Jewish homeland in the Land of Israel, he also contemplated the establishment of a Jewish state in part of Argentina (Herzl, 1895/1946) and discussed the 1903 British proposal of creating a Jewish state in Uganda. After Herzl's death, these proposals were abandoned – the Jewish State was to be established in Palestine. Following the creation of Israel, however, antisemitism persisted and began to be manifested in a distinct guise – through the delegitimisation and demonisation of the Jewish State.

The Israeli-Arab conflict

Following various waves of Jewish immigration to the British Mandate of Palestine, which gave rise to a large Jewish population in the territory (Stillman, 1979), on 29 November 1947, the United Nations General Assembly adopted Resolution 181(II) which recommended the partition of Palestine into Arab and Jewish states. The so-called *Plan of Partition with Economic Union* was accepted by Jewish nationalists but unanimously rejected by the Arabs and soon after the vote civil war broke out (Karsh, 2002). On 14 May 1948, a day before the British Mandate over Palestine ended, Herzl's dream of a Jewish homeland was finally realised when David Ben-Gurion declared "the establishment of a Jewish state in Eretz-Israel, to be known as the State of Israel".[1] The next day, the armies of Syria, Egypt, Transjordan and Iraq, collectively, invaded the newly established State of Israel, which began the 1948 Arab-Israeli War (Bregman, 2000). After almost 10 months of bloody armed conflict which claimed tens of thousands of lives, Israel emerged as the victor, retaining all of the land originally allotted to the Jewish state and capturing 50 per cent of the land allotted to the Arab state. Although the invading Arab nations and the Arab League, more generally, suffered a humiliating defeat, Egypt gained control of the Gaza Strip and Jordan controlled the West Bank (including East Jerusalem and the Holy City). As a result of the conflict, hundreds of thousands of Arabs were either expelled from, or fled, their homes in what had become Israel, giving rise to large Palestinian refugee communities (Karsh, 2011). At the same time, hundreds of thousands of Jews living in the surrounding Arab countries that had invaded Israel suddenly became the target of Arab persecution and reprisal attacks – in the three years following the 1948 War,

---

1   Declaration of the establishment of the State of Israel, 14 May 1948 http://www. mfa.gov.il/mfa/foreignpolicy/peace/guide/pages/declaration%20of%20establishment%20 of%20state%20of%20israel.aspx

some 700,000 Jews from Arab lands were either expelled or voluntarily migrated to Israel (Stillman, 1979).

In 1956 when Egypt nationalised the Suez Canal and closed it to Israeli shipping, Israel (with British and French support) invaded the Sinai Peninsula and captured the Sinai and the Gaza Strip. Under US pressure, Israel agreed to vacate Egyptian territory in return for freedom of navigation in the Straits of Tiran, which the Egyptian authorities granted. While the conflict was viewed as a political failure for Britain and France (Gorst and Johnman, 1996), Israel appeared to win yet another victory against the Arabs, resulting in further Arab humiliation. However, like the 1948 War, the 1956 Suez Crisis had negative implications for Jews in Arab countries – the war led to the expulsion of most of the remaining Jews in Egypt (Laskier, 1995).

On 5 June 1967 Israel launched a surprise attack on Egyptian airfields in response to the mobilisation of Egyptian troops on the Western border and then turned East to engage the Jordanian, Syrian and Iraqi air forces (Bregman, 2000). After six days of armed conflict, Israel successfully defeated the Arab armies and captured the Gaza Strip and the Sinai Peninsula from Egypt, the Golan Heights from Syria, and the West Bank (including East Jerusalem) from Jordan. The surface area of Israel tripled in size and hundreds of thousands of Arabs were now living under Israeli jurisdiction. The Six-Day War, as it came to be known, had major military and political consequences, but it also had cultural and psychological consequences – Israel had gained control of East Jerusalem which it later incorporated into Israeli territory and the Arab world suffered a major blow as it realised that Israel was militarily competent and able to defeat the Arab armies in a swift and co-ordinated manner (Louis and Shlaim, 2012). In 1973 what has become known as the Yom Kippur War was launched by a coalition of Arab countries led by Egypt and Syria, who wished to re-capture the Sinai Peninsula and the Golan Heights, respectively (Bregman, 2000). This was partly an attempt to restore self-confidence in the Arab world, following their military defeats in previous conflicts. Although the war concluded with a military victory for the Israelis, the invading army caught Israel by surprise by embarking upon hostilities on the holiest day of the Jewish calendar. Consequently, some initial military advances were made by the invading Arab armies, which served to ameliorate some of the cultural and psychological trauma that had been caused by previous conflicts. However, both the Sinai and the Golan Heights remained in Israeli hands.

Historians have claimed that Israel's image on the international stage changed radically following the 1967 Six-Day War, because it now came to be perceived as an occupying force, rather than the victim of foreign invasion (Sharon, 2009). In an emerging era of anti-colonialism, this was a deeply problematic position for Israel to occupy and it led to the widespread perception of Israel as a colonising, capitalist force in union with the US. However, attitudes towards Israel did not perpetually remain negative, as Israel did participate in peace negotiations with its Arab neighbours. Indeed, the 1973 Yom Kippur War paved the way for eventual peace negotiations between Israel and Egypt, and the two countries signed an agreement in 1978 which led to Israel's withdrawal from the Sinai and to diplomatic relations between the two countries (Hurwitz and Medad, 2011). Similarly, in 1994, Jordan and Israel signed a peace agreement and established full diplomatic relations (Eisenberg and Caplan, 2003).

Israel's relations with its Arab neighbours have been fraught with conflict ever since its establishment in 1948. In 1982, the Israeli Defence Forces invaded and occupied South Lebanon, following the Palestinian Abu Nidal Organisation's attempt to assassinate Israel's ambassador to the United Kingdom (Fisk, 2001). The aim was to uproot the Palestinian Liberation Organisation which was operating from within Lebanon. During the occupation, Israeli Defence Minister Ariel Sharon was found to be "personally responsible" for a massacre that was perpetrated by Christian militiamen against Palestinian and Lebanese Shiite Muslim civilians in a refugee camp (Eisenberg and Caplan, 1998). This adversely affected Israel's image on the international stage but particularly in the Arab world where Sharon was referred to as "bloodthirsty" and a "butcher". Israel unilaterally withdrew its forces from South Lebanon in 2000, but six years later was again at war with Lebanon after the Iranian-sponsored Lebanese Shiite militant group Hezbollah launched rocket attacks against Israeli targets and crossed into Israeli territory, killing three soldiers and kidnapping two others. Although many Western governments reiterated Israel's right to defend itself against external threats, Western public opinion was generally opposed to Israel's military actions, which were viewed as excessive and heavy-handed. Media reporting and the anti-Israel campaigns which emerged during the conflict overwhelmingly represented Israel as the aggressor and the Lebanese as the victims (see, for example, Dyszynski, 2010).

The Israeli-Palestinian conflict

The crux of the Israeli-Arab conflict is of course the *Israeli-Palestinian* conflict, which has been described as one of the most intractable in the world (Nets-Zehngut and Bar-Tal, 2007). Although originally opposed to the existence of the State of Israel, in the 1993 Oslo Accords the Palestinian Liberation Organisation officially recognised Israel and accepted the proposal of a Palestinian state based on the pre-1967 borders with (East) Jerusalem as its capital. Similarly, Israel, once absolutely opposed to the establishment of a Palestinian state, agreed to negotiate with the Palestinian Liberation Organisation and, subsequently, recognised the newly-founded Palestinian (National) Authority as the sole representative of the Palestinian people.

However, there have been fundamental setbacks between the Israelis and the Palestinians. Having initiated an uprising in 1987, which has come to be known as the First Palestinian Intifada (Alimi, 2007), the Palestinians then began a second Intifada in 2000, which lasted until 2005 (Norman, 2010). This resulted in thousands of deaths on both the Palestinian and Israeli sides, Israeli military incursions and Palestinian suicide bombings, as well as a complete breakdown in peace negotiations. Moreover, the Second Intifada, and particularly the drastic rise in Palestinian suicide bombings in Israeli cities, heralded the Israeli government's decision to construct the Israeli West Bank barrier on occupied Palestinian territory with the aim of separating Palestinians in the West Bank from Jewish communities (both in major West Bank settlements and within Israel's borders). The construction of the West Bank barrier has undoubtedly resulted in a radical decline in suicide bombings in Israel but it has also entailed severe social, political, economic and health consequences for many Palestinians living in the West Bank (Bowman, 2004; Cohen, 2012; Gavrilis, 2004). The separation barrier has brought security, on the one hand, but negative representations of Israel as an "apartheid" state, on the other.

Although the 1993 Oslo Accords (or 1993 Declaration of Principles) established mutual recognition between Israel and the PNA (Brown, 2003), neither a Palestinian state nor peace between the two political entities has resulted from the Accords. Fundamental disagreements remain which impede the two-state solution and peace, leading to uncertainty, mistrust and desperation on both sides. Four of these obstacles are particularly salient in contemporary political debate, namely (i) the status of Jerusalem; (ii) Israeli settlements in the West Bank; (iii) the Palestinian refugee problem; and (iv) Israeli national security.

The first obstacle to peace concerns the status and sovereignty of Jerusalem. As outlined above, in the 1967 Six-Day War, Israel captured East Jerusalem and the West Bank, which had been under direct Jordanian rule since 1948. On 30 July 1980, the Israeli Knesset incorporated the Jerusalem Law into Israel's Basic Laws. The law authorised the annexation of East Jerusalem to Israeli territory and declared that "Jerusalem, complete and united, is the capital of Israel".[2] The PNA regards East Jerusalem (which includes the Old City and, thus, the holiest sites of Judaism) as the capital city of a future independent Palestinian state. The international community does not recognise Israeli sovereignty over East Jerusalem and regards this as occupied Palestinian territory.[3] The PNA refuses to negotiate with Israel until there is a moratorium on Israeli settlement-building in East Jerusalem.

The second, and perhaps most salient, obstacle to peace concerns Israel's settlement policy in the West Bank. Following its capture of the West Bank and East Jerusalem (from Jordan), Gaza and the Sinai Peninsula (from Egypt) and the Golan Heights (from Syria), Israel implemented a policy of Jewish civilian settlement in these territories (Matar, 1981; Shnell and Mishal, 2008). In Israel, these territories were widely represented as being "liberated" from foreign (Arab) control, as contributing to Israel's security, and as strengthening Israel's position in future peace talks (as demonstrated in the Israel-Egypt peace treaty which saw Israel withdraw from the Sinai). Although Israel disengaged from the Gaza Strip and uprooted all 21 Jewish settlements in 2005 (Aronson, 2005; Makovsky, 2005), it has continued to build settlements in the West Bank. Currently, the total Jewish

---

2   Basic Law: Jerusalem – Capital of Israel http://www.mfa.gov.il/MFA/ MFAArchive/1980_1989/Basic%20Law-%20Jerusalem-%20Capital%20of%20Israel

3   United Nations Resolution 478 (1980) http://unispal.un.org/UNISPAL.NSF/0/ DDE590C6FF232007852560DF0065FDDB.

Israeli civilian population of Judea and Samaria (the name that Israel gives to the West Bank) is approximately 350,000. The PNA demands a complete halt to Jewish settlements in both East Jerusalem (its desired capital) and the West Bank before peace talks can resume. However, Israel's separation barrier seems to indicate to the Palestinians that Israel wishes to perpetuate its occupation of the West Bank rather than curtail it (Christison and Christison, 2009). Conversely, Israel believes that the Palestinians deny Israel's right to exist (Bar-Tal and Teichman, 2005). Indeed, it has been found that the PNA repeatedly represents present-day Israel as "Palestinian territory". For instance, the Palestinian Liberation Organisation's logo on the PNA's Mission to the UN website depicts the whole of present-day Israel as Palestinian territory,[4] and various official PNA videos, documentaries, and songs refer to cities in present-day Israel as Palestinian cities.[5] Both the Israelis' physical act of building settlements in East Jerusalem/the West Bank and the Palestinians' symbolic act of representing present-day Israel as Palestine serve to undermine faith in the outgroup's commitment to the two-state solution and, thus, each other's right to exist.

Disagreement regarding the Palestinian "right of return" constitutes a third obstacle to peace. Following the 1948 Israeli-Arab war, thousands of Palestinians were forced to leave their homes in Israel and the Palestinian territories (Karsh, 2011). Today, the Palestinian refugees and their descendants number in the region of approximately 5,000,000.[6] Both the Palestinians and Israelis claim to seek a "just" solution to the Palestinian refugee problem. The PNA and proponents of the Palestinian right of return generally believe that the refugees and their descendants should be permitted to re-settle in the areas that they left (including present-day Israel). However, the Israeli government and opponents of the Palestinian right of return are staunchly opposed to the re-settlement of Palestinian refugees and their descendants within Israel's borders. They claim that this policy would undermine the demographic vitality of the Israeli Jewish population and, consequently, threaten the Jewish character of Israel (Bourhis et al., 1981). They argue that the Palestinian refugees should settle within the borders of their own future independent state. Many critics of the right of return compare the Palestinian refugee problem to the exodus of approximately 1,000,000 Jews from Arab lands between 1948 and the 1970s (Shulewitz, 2001), arguing that the Jews too were forced to leave their homes in Arab/Muslim countries. While the PNA regards the right of return as an "inalienable right", the Israeli government views it as an ambit claim designed to destroy Israel.

---

4   State of Palestine Permanent Observer Mission to the United Nations website http://www.un.int/wcm/content/site/palestine/pid/11543

5   Palestinian Media Watch http://www.palwatch.org/site/modules/videos/pal/videos. aspx?fld_id=latestanddoc_id=5011

6   United Nations Relief and Works Agency for Palestine Refugees in the Near East http://www.unrwa.org/etemplate.php?id=86

Fourthly, the State of Israel is deeply concerned about its national security and the threat of terrorism. National security is viewed as the key to national continuity, and terrorism as an existential threat to it (Jaspal and Yampolsky, 2011). Despite the complete dismantlement of all Jewish settlements and the withdrawal of Israeli troops from the Gaza Strip in 2005, the Hamas regime (which, at the time of writing, governed the Gaza Strip) and its collaborators have fired thousands of rockets into civilian areas in Israeli territory.[7] Hamas never condemns these acts but rather views them as a necessary aspect of its "resistance" strategy (Mishal and Sela, 2000). Since Fatah (which dominates the PNA) was ousted by Hamas from the Gaza Strip, the Israeli government regards it as powerless to curtail Hamas's actions and to guarantee Israel's security. Moreover, it is widely believed in Israel that the PNA makes little attempt to prevent Palestinian terrorism and that it sometimes actively *encourages* it.[8] For instance, President Abbas has been accused of glorifying and sympathising with Palestinian violence against Israel, for example through the naming of public places after Palestinians found guilty of attacks against Israeli civilians, and the PNA's silence on Hamas's rocket attacks from the Gaza Strip.

These obstacles to peace have caused suspicion, at both political and societal levels, concerning the outgroup's "true" intentions. Although both Israel and the PNA claim to adhere to the two-state solution, the actions of the Israeli government and PNA, respectively, seem to indicate a lack of commitment. Indeed, suspicion, mistrust, and despair have repeatedly led to breakdowns in peace negotiations. Crucially, this brief sketch of the major Israeli-Arab military confrontations and "obstacles" to Israeli-Palestinian peace negotiations have provided stimuli for the development of anti-Zionist representations among politicians and laypeople alike. They have been represented, construed and discussed in ways which tend to construct Zionism as an evil and belligerent ideology and, hence, the State of Israel as a "rogue state" based on this ideology. The complexity of the political and military history of Israel tends to be simplified in ways which construct a "need" to confront, and in some cases, dismantle the Jewish State.

Anti-Zionist Representations

While Zionism is regarded by some as a national liberation movement which safeguards and protects the continuity of the Jewish people, it has also been criticised as constituting a racist, colonialist ideology which favours Jews and discriminates against non-Jews (in particular, the Palestinians) (Pappé, 2006, 2007; Shafir, 1999). These perspectives have contributed to anti-Zionism. Conversely, some people

---

7   Israel Defense Forces Blog http://www.idfblog.com/facts-figures/rocket-attacks-toward-israel/

8   *Jerusalem Post* website http://www.jpost.com/Diplomacy-and-Politics/PA-incitement-is-confidence-destroying-measure

consider anti-Zionism to constitute a form of antisemitism, commonly referred to as "new antisemitism" (Chesler, 2003; Sacks, 2002). They argue that anti-Zionism constitutes a means of projecting one's anti-Jewish hostility onto the Jewish State or the "collective Jew". There are two principal strands of contemporary anti-Zionism: firstly, it refers to the growing hostility towards Israel and Jews (who are perceived to be supportive of Israel's actions) in the aftermath of the Second Palestinian Intifada. Such hostility is attributed to left-wing organisations and Muslims, in particular. Secondly, it refers to the persistent anti-Israel bias that is said to exist in the western media, in left-wing intellectual circles and the United Nations. While classic antisemitism focused upon the Jewish people (see Chapter 2), anti-Zionism focuses primarily upon the Jewish State but commonly alludes to the Jewish people. There is often an inter-relation between the alleged focus upon the Jewish State and acts of antisemitism – anti-Zionism, which delegitimises the State of Israel, has been cited as a cause for acts of antisemitism committed against Jewish people in England, France, the US and in the many other countries in which Jews have been victimised.

Anti-Zionism is manifested in a multitude of ways in accordance with social, political and ideological context, but they all converge in their aim to delegitimise the State of Israel. Some organisations and nation-states refuse to use toponym "Israel", preferring the term "Zionist Regime" or "Occupied Palestine" in order to call into question the legitimacy of Israel. This is clearly observable in the Islamic Republic of Iran's stance on Israel (Jaspal, 2013a, 2013c). Others, such as *The Guardian*, tend to represent Israel in a biased manner as a malevolent aggressor in the Israeli-Palestinian conflict (Wistrich, 2011). This section provides a general sketch of some of the dominant anti-Zionist themes that are observable in both Middle Eastern countries, in which anti-Zionism is often an official state policy, and the West, in which anti-Zionism has gained considerable traction since the 1967 Six-Day War, in particular.

As demonstrated in Chapter 2, antisemitism has been characterised by a diverse range of motifs and representations, which construct Jews as villainous, treacherous, bloodthirsty and in other demeaning ways. It is striking to observe the deployment of similar motifs and representations in relation to Israel. While in antiquity Jews were regarded as an "alien" culture, today Israel is often referred to as an "anomaly" in the Middle East (Jaspal, 2013a). Just as Jews were represented as a villainous race throughout their history, the Jewish State is consistently constructed as a villainous state which overtly disregards international law and which is governed by "criminals", as exemplified in a comment made by former London mayor Ken Livingstone.[9] The blood libel accusation which permeated medieval representations of Jews has been deployed in describing Israel's actions – Israeli leaders are frequently depicted as devouring the flesh of Palestinian children (Kotek, 2009), and actual accusations of organ trafficking (of dead Palestinian children) have been levelled against the Jewish State (Wistrich, 2010).

---

9   The Guardian http://www.theguardian.com/politics/2005/mar/04/society.london

The accusation of Jewish world domination frequently surfaces in representations of Israel – while the Nazis accused the Jews of dominating the world, contemporary anti-Zionists level this very accusation against "Zionists" (Jaspal, 2013a).

Islamic countries in the Middle East have undoubtedly become the centre of anti-Zionist representation and activity, given the long-standing and protracted Israeli-Arab conflict. Indeed, various analyses of anti-Zionism in the Middle East have elucidated the scale and intensity of anti-Zionist representation in the public, political and media spheres (Jaspal, 2013c; Litvak, 1998; Webman, 2010; Wistrich, 2010). As Elpeleg (1993) has shown in his excellent biography of Haj Amin al-Husseini, the Grand Mufti of Jerusalem, anti-Zionism can be traced to both Palestinian nationalism (and, more specifically, to the Grand Mufti's collaboration with Nazi Germany), and also to the rise of the Muslim Brotherhood in Egypt in the 1930s. With the establishment of the Jewish State and its numerous military victories against the Arabs, anti-Zionism intensified and began to draw upon antisemitic representations concerning the evil of Jews and historical theological representations concerning the Prophet Muhammed's struggle against the Jews in the early days of Islam. Today, the State of Israel is accused of murdering Palestinian children and stealing their organs, of deliberately attempting to destroy Islam, of instigating political assassinations and natural disasters and of many other malevolent acts against Muslims (Webman, 2010). Anti-Zionist conspiracy theories abound in the Middle East, and are supplemented and supported by frequent references to antisemitic literature such as *The Protocols of the Elders of Zion* (see Chapter 2).

Scholars have cited theological reasons for extreme anti-Zionism in the Middle East, such as the Islamic belief in the dhimmi status of Jews and, hence, the widespread inability to accept a Jewish State on what is perceived as "Muslim land" (Shahvar, 2009). Moreover, given the Islamicisation of the Israeli-Arab conflict, many in the region believe that acceptance of the legitimacy of the State of Israel constitutes an un-Islamic act and is, thus, incompatible with Islamic identity. Wistrich (2010) has noted that many of the Islamist organisations like Hamas, Hezbollah and the Iranian regime that openly espouse anti-Zionism (and, in some cases, antisemitism) as official policy, advocate the total destruction of the State of Israel. It appears that anti-Zionism had become the main thrust of policy in various Arab and Islamic countries in which it is openly and enthusiastically manifested (Wistrich, 2010).

However, it is true that some nations appear to be more anti-Zionist in stance than others and are more overt in their unconditional condemnation of Israel – Britain, for instance, is said to have become "the hub of an assault on Israel's legitimacy" (Wistrich, 2012, p. 538). Anti-Zionism is associated with left-wing political organisations, not only in Britain but in the West more generally. These organisations usually purport to be Marxist, anti-globalist and, crucially, anti-racist (Taguieff, 2010). Yet, these same organisations often employ rhetorical weapons that are no less discriminatory and exclusionary than those used by racists (Wistrich, 2012). Israel is often perceived as a Western, colonial and capitalist creation which oppresses the "native" people of Palestine, suggesting that Israeli

Jews are not "native". The pro-Palestinian and anti-Zionist stance of many of these left-wing organisations means that more often than not a blind eye is turned to any violence perpetrated by Palestinians and Islamists, such as suicide bombings and other atrocities, while any military action taken by the State of Israel is rapidly interpreted as evidence of Israeli "fascism". Following Israel's military responses to the Second Palestinian Intifada (2000–2005) and the Second Lebanon War (2006), anti-Zionist (and, in some cases, overtly antisemitic) representations and images emerged in media, political and public discourses, with a rise in antisemitic attacks in various locations in the West. A common representation in the left-wing repertoire consists of the accusation that Israel functions as an apartheid state, which constructs synergy between the State of Israel and the racist regime in Apartheid South Africa. These motifs construct the State of Israel as a "rogue state" which uniquely disregards human rights in the world and which poses a threat to world peace, and thereby construct a need to destroy the Jewish State.

In Britain, many elite and reputable media outlets appear to endorse anti-Zionist imagery, such as the *London Review of Books* which has consistently represented Israel in unfavourable terms while depicting organisations like Hamas and Hezbollah in more sympathetic terms; and *The Guardian*, which habitually employs biased and inflammatory anti-Zionist language in its coverage of the Israeli-Arab conflict (Wistrich, 2011). Some of the images and political cartoons reproduced in the British media are clearly intended to denigrate Zionism but, in many cases, also verge on antisemitism. For instance, in a political cartoon published in *The Independent* on 27 January 2003 during the height of the Second Palestinian Intifada, Israeli Prime Minister Ariel Sharon was depicted as an ugly and evil-looking naked giant standing in the wreckage of a Palestinian city and consuming the flesh of a Palestinian child. This cartoon was just one of many anti-Zionist political cartoons which echoed the medieval antisemitic blood libel accusation and the representation of Jews as evil and barbaric. While antisemitism may not have been the express aim, the cartoons clearly evoke antisemitic imagery in achieving their anti-Zionist goal (see Chapter 6).

Similarly, prominent UK politicians have manifested support for anti-Zionism, which has served only to legitimise this form of prejudice. For instance, Liberal Democrat Baroness Jenny Tonge publicly expressed sympathy for Palestinian suicide bombings against Israel, stating that "If I had to live in that situation – and I say that advisedly – I might just consider becoming one [a suicide bomber] myself"[10], which served to single out Israel as the root cause of Islamist terrorism. Moreover, she drew a comparison between the Nazi persecution of the Jews in the Warsaw Ghetto and Israel's treatment of the Palestinians, arguing that "You are almost getting a situation like the Warsaw ghetto. People can't get in or out. They can't work. They can't sell anything".[11] In a typical display of anti-Zionism

---

10   BBC News http://news.bbc.co.uk/1/hi/uk/3421669.stm
11   The Guardian http://www.theguardian.com/politics/2003/jun/19/foreignpolicy.israel

with clear antisemitic undertones, Tonge compared Israelis with the Jews' worst tormentors, namely the Nazis, and thereby constructed Israel as an evil entity. Furthermore, recycling the antisemitic representation of Jewish world domination, Tonge appeared to swap the category "Jewish" for "pro-Israeli lobby" in another anti-Zionist statement she made: "The pro-Israeli lobby has got its grips on the western world, its financial grips. I think they've probably got a grip on our party".[12]

There are countless other examples of British political complicity in anti-Zionism: former Mayor of London Ken Livingstone, who claimed that "Israel's own expansion has included ethnic cleansing" as well as the "slaughter and systematic murder of innocent Arabs";[13] the MP George Galloway, who claimed that "despite all the efforts made by the British government, the Zionist movement and the newspapers and news media which are controlled by Zionism" and that "we hate Zionism, we hate Israel, we hate murder and injustice. Israel blasphemes against the Torah by calling itself a Jewish state".[14] His fervent anti-Zionist stance was clearly exemplified by his explanation that "the reason [for not engaging with a question posed by a British-Israeli student during a debate] is simple: no recognition, no normalisation. Just boycott, divestment and sanctions, until the apartheid state is defeated. I never debate with Israelis nor speak to their media. If they want to speak about Palestine – the address is the PLO".[15] These representations, disseminated by prominent political figures and media institutions in the UK, exemplify the general themes of anti-Zionism which are pervasive in the West.

Many "anti-racist" left-wing organisations are committed to anti-Zionism because, in these circles, Zionism is widely regarded as a capitalist, racist, exclusionary, oppressive ideology. This representation is clearly aided by some of the prominent political figures cited above, but its most important boost came in the form of United Nations General Assembly Resolution 3379, passed on 10 November 1975, which "determine[d] that Zionism is a form of racism and racial discrimination".[16] The resolution was voted in 72 to 35 with the support of the Soviet-aligned and Arab and Islamic majority nations. Although the resolution was subsequently revoked in United National General Assembly Resolution 46/86 in 1991, it served to attribute international credibility to the representation that Zionism, the national ideology underlying the State of Israel, constituted a racist doctrine. Opponents of Zionism

---

12   BBC News http://news.bbc.co.uk/1/hi/uk_politics/5366870.stm

13   Anti-Defamation League http://archive.adl.org/special_reports/livingstone/livingstone.html#.UxHaXHlQN6k

14   Totally Jewish news archive http://archive.totallyjewish.com/news/galloway-under-fire-after-tv-slur/

15   The Telegraph blog http://blogs.telegraph.co.uk/news/timstanley/100203777/george-galloway-storms-out-of-a-debate-refusing-to-talk-to-an-israeli-hes-become-an-ideology-on-legs/

16   UN Resolution 3379 entitled "Elimination of all forms of racial discrimination", The General Assembly, United Nations. http://daccess-dds-ny.un.org/doc/RESOLUTION/GEN/NR0/000/92/IMG/NR000092.pdf?OpenElement

would prefer to deny the status of Israel as a *Jewish* state and compel it to absorb the Palestinian refugees from the 1948 war and their descendants. This would effectively amount to the destruction of the State of Israel.

Similarly, the infamous United Nations World Conference against Racism, Racial Discrimination, Xenophobia and Related Intolerances, which took place in Durban, South Africa in 2001, reiterated the representation that Zionism equals racism. The Secretary General of the Arab League referred to Israel's "racist actions" and "Zionist racist practices" against the Palestinians, and proceeded to equate the Palestinians with Jewish Holocaust victims.[17] It therefore facilitated the systematic comparison of Zionism with, and anchoring to, Nazism, as demonstrated by the plethora of anti-Zionist representations that have been observed in a wide range of media. Indeed, in his extensive analysis of Jews and the Jewish State in the Arab and Western media, Kotek (2009) has observed a systematic representation of Israel as the "real" Nazi state, which is responsible for the "Palestinian Holocaust". Clearly, the allegation of "Zionist racism" lies at the heart of the constructed conflation of Zionism and Nazism. It is an elaboration of this original motif. This elaboration has given rise to newspaper images depicting Israeli leaders as Nazis, Israeli soldiers as SS-soldiers, and the Palestinian territories as Nazi concentration camps (Kotek, 2009). Indeed, there is a tendency in left-wing circles to compare Israel to Nazi Germany, and Israel's treatment of the Palestinians to the Nazi genocide of the Jews. Accusations of "ethnic cleansing" and "racial segregation" abound in their discourse. Despite the groundlessness of this assertion, it is invoked, repeated and reiterated.

The representation of Zionism as a racist ideology facilitates the construction of Israel as an apartheid state (Clark, 2012). This is of course intended to establish linkage between contemporary Israel and the racist regime in South Africa which insisted on racial segregation. The construction of Israel as an apartheid regime is inaccurate – Arabs constitute a fifth of the Israeli population; they study and work alongside Israeli Jews; they use the same beaches and public washrooms; there are several Arab representatives in the Israeli Knesset etc. However, the apartheid analogy has existed for decades, and has become particularly prominent following the construction of the Israeli West Bank barrier in 2005. The presence of a physical barrier separating the Palestinian and Jewish communities has provided further impetus for the use of this analogy, because it is cited as "evidence" of segregation. Burke (1984) has argued that "the great danger of an analogy is that a similarity is taken as evidence of an identity. Because two things are found to possess a certain trait in character which our point of view considers notable, we take the common notable trait to indicate identity of character" (p. 97). Anti-Zionists employ such analogies to single Israel out in negative terms and to encourage people to discredit it in ways that other previous regimes (e.g. Apartheid South Africa, Nazi Germany) have understandably been discredited.

---

17   Al-Ahram Weekly Online http://weekly.ahram.org.eg/2001/546/fr2.htm

Despite the inaccuracy of the apartheid representation, it has gained traction and become an anti-Zionist buzzword for delegitimising the State of Israel. It constitutes the focus of the so-called Israel Apartheid Week, an annual series of lectures and events which allegedly aim to "educate people about the nature of Israel as an apartheid system and to build Boycott, Divestment and Sanctions (BDS) campaigns as part of a growing global BDS movement".[18] Thus, users of the apartheid analogy invite us to regard Israel's actions as racist, malevolent and oppressive, rather than as necessary for the safety and security of Israeli cities which have been targeted by Palestinian suicide bombers. This shifts one's attention from security (which is one of the aforementioned obstacles to a peace agreement) onto racism. Crucially, South Africa's apartheid regime was almost unanimously opposed by the world's nations due to its blatant racism and it was eventually defeated. The apartheid allegation in relation to Israel is anti-Zionist in character because it implicitly invites the same outcome for the Jewish State.

While Holocaust denial has been particularly endemic in extreme right-wing political circles and, more recently, in Arab and Islamic contexts (see Chapter 2), anti-Zionists tend to criticise the alleged "use" of the Holocaust by Zionists in order to achieve particular political goals. Although critical debate on representations of the Holocaust in Israeli politics is not necessarily an act of anti-Zionism (see for example Jaspal and Yampolsky, 2011), anti-Zionists sometimes employ or implicitly invoke arguments grounded in Holocaust revisionism. For instance, it has been argued that the Holocaust is exaggerated by Zionists or maliciously invoked in order to induce sympathy among outgroups and to justify political actions. Moreover, as noted above, there is a consistent comparison between the Nazi Holocaust perpetrated against the Jews and Israel's treatment of the Palestinians, which serves to attenuate the Holocaust in which 6 million Jews perished and to demonise the State of Israel for "repeating" the crimes of their worst tormentors (Litvak and Webman, 2009).

Some scholars have noted that anti-Zionism has provided a common platform for various groups opposed to Israel's existence – principally, left-wing organisations and Islamists (Wistrich, 2010, 2012). There are enormous ideological differences between these groups which are simply glossed over in a united front against Zionism and the State of Israel. Collectively, these groups attempt to translate their anti-Zionist representations into anti-Zionist actions.

Anti-Zionism and its Action Orientation

Like antisemitism, anti-Zionism too has an action orientation, which is principally the weakening and destruction of the State of Israel. However, this is sometimes generalised to world Jewry. In extreme cases, self-identified anti-Zionists have

---

18   International Business Times http://www.ibtimes.co.uk/what-israeli-apartheid-week-1438167

targeted world Jewry, wreaking carnage in centres and institutions associated with Jewish communities. For instance, on 19 March 2012 a radicalised Muslim youth went on a shooting rampage at a Jewish day school in Toulouse and shot dead a rabbi and three Jewish children, allegedly because "the Jews have killed our brothers and sisters in Palestine".[19] In a much larger-scale and deadlier attack, a suicide bombing left 85 people dead and hundreds others injured at the Asociación Mutual Israelita Argentina, a Jewish community centre, in Buenos Aires, Argentina on 18 July 1994. The attack targeted the Jewish community centre in particular, most of the victims were Jews and various official enquiries attributed responsibility for the attack to several Hezbollah and Iranian regime officials (Costanza, 2012; Norton, 2007). In short, this was an act of Iranian state-sponsored terrorism directed against Jews.

In addition to these examples of overt antisemitic action orientations of self-proclaimed anti-Zionist individuals and organisations, there are various subtler routes to the action orientation of weakening Israel, the most prominent of which is the economic, political and academic boycott of Israel. Furthermore, many United Nations member states have collectively sought to delegitimise the State of Israel in the form of various anti-Zionist resolutions, such as Resolution 3379, as discussed above. At the public level, there have been attacks against synagogues and Jewish centres, Jewish cemetery desecrations, anti-Jewish diatribes on social networking sites and violent, and in some cases, murderous attacks against Jews.

Many commentators staunchly oppose the boycott of Israel and regard this as a form of anti-Zionism (Klaff, 2010; Newman, 2008). There are a variety of distinct forms of boycott – economic, political, cultural, academic – which all converge in their attempt to cause a severance of ties with the State of Israel, its people and its institutions. The Arab League imposed an official economic and political boycott of Israel in the aftermath of the 1948 War, although many Arab countries had already enforced a policy of boycotting Zionist institutions prior to the establishment of the State of Israel. There have been various changes in the Arabs' approach to the boycott of Israel, with the signing of peace treaties between Israel and Egypt, Jordan and the Palestinian Authority. Today the Arab League's *economic* boycott is applied and enforced to varying degrees. Passport restrictions are more strictly applied throughout the Arab world and in other Muslim-majority countries such as Pakistan, Bangladesh and Malaysia. Most countries in the region do not grant entry to Israeli passport holders or to holders of other passports which bear an Israeli entry stamp or visa. Thus, both economic and political restrictions are in place.

In the West, a number of organisations have advocated an economic boycott of Israeli products. For instance, Boycott, Divestment and Sanctions is a global pro-Palestinian campaign which attempts to exert economic pressure on Israel for it to end its occupation of the West Bank and to grant the Palestinian refugees and their descendants the right to settle in Israel (Barghouti, 2011). Given that the return of

---

19   Euskal Irrati Telebista/Radio Télévision Basque http://www.eitb.com/fr/infos/societe/detail/854031/fusillades-operation-policiere-toulouse/

the Palestinian refugees would result in a non-Jewish majority, this would deprive Israel of its Jewish character and thereby lead to the demise of the Jewish State. Consequently, the organisation can legitimately be described as an anti-Zionist one with an anti-Zionist goal, namely the destruction of Israel. Other organisations like the Palestine Solidary Campaign have constructed an effective economic boycott campaign which aims to isolate and delegitimise Israel. For instance, members have played an important role in encouraging the British people to endorse disinvestment from companies such as Caterpillar, which are said to assist in the occupation of the West Bank, as well as sponsoring the Boycott Israeli Goods campaign which focuses upon Israeli agricultural products and high-tech exports.

The anti-Zionist boycott has been extended to the academic world. In 2002, as Israel was involved in heavy fighting with Palestinian militant organisations in the West Bank, over a hundred British academics, led by Steven and Hilary Rose, published an open letter in *The Guardian* which called for an EU moratorium on research collaboration of any kind with Israeli universities. In 2005 the Association of University Teachers held a council meeting at which they decided to boycott two Israeli universities and to distribute among the thousands of AUT members pro-boycott literature. Various incidents followed – Mona Baker, a lecturer at the former University of Manchester Institute of Science and Technology (now a part of the University of Manchester), dismissed two Israeli academics from the editorial board of an academic journal she edited; in June 2002, Andrew Wilkie, a professor of pathology at Oxford University, rejected an application for a post-doctoral research position that was submitted by a young Israeli scholar on the grounds that that had a "huge problem" with Israel's treatment of the Palestinians.[20] In both cases, investigations took place but neither of these incidents was treated as serious cases of discrimination of the basis of nationality – Mona Baker's actions allegedly did not interfere with her teaching, while Andrew Wilke was briefly suspended and required to take equal-opportunity training.

The umbrella organisation, the Palestinian Call for the Academic and Cultural Boycott of Israel, claimed that "The Israeli academy has contributed, either directly or indirectly, to maintaining, defending or otherwise justifying the military occupation and colonisation of the West Bank and Gaza" (see Fraser, 2005). The University and College Union, which is a merger of the Association of University Teachers and the National Association of Teachers in Higher and Further Education, has repeatedly voted in favour of implementing an academic boycott of Israel and this campaign has received support from prominent scholars, such as Professors Stephen Hawking, Noam Chomsky and Malcolm Levitt. There has been much debate about the appropriateness of an academic boycott with some scholars campaigning for its immediate implementation and others arguing that this would amount to "mixing science and politics" and, thus, contravene university guidelines.

---

20   The Telegraph http://www.telegraph.co.uk/news/worldnews/africaandindianocean/ liberia/1434388/Outrage-as-Oxford-bans-student-for-being-Israeli.html

Although the academic boycott has been debated in a number of countries, Britain has largely spearheaded this campaign perhaps due to its own colonial past, a strong left-wing lobby which is supported by the trade unions and, crucially, support from some Jewish organisations such as the Jews for Justice for Palestinians group (Wistrich, 2011). The involvement of Jewish organisations may appear to falsify the allegation of antisemitism (see Chapter 1). The principal issues brought up by the pro-boycott lobbies include the perceived complicity of Israeli academia with Israel's occupation of the West Bank, the perceived lack of opposition to Israel's occupation of the West Bank among Israeli scholars and the legitimacy of the existence of the State of Israel. Newman (2008, p. 47) notes that "[t]he fact that Israeli universities are the centers of strong social and political criticism of the state, that they are the core of liberal discourse and are the seat of much Israeli-Palestinian research cooperation is totally ignored in this argument". What these events converge in demonstrating is that British university campuses have become an important context for debate and discussion concerning the future of Israel and, in some cases, the legitimacy of the Jewish State itself. The academic boycott, like the economic one, serves only to construct Israel as an apartheid state by treating it in the same way that South Africa was treated during the era of Apartheid. It is implied that, like Apartheid South Africa, Israel should be subjected to disinvestment, boycott and isolation from the international community. There are a number of insightful overviews of the proposed academic boycott in Britain and elsewhere (e.g. Cravatts, 2011; Fraser, 2005; Klaff, 2010; Newman, 2008), which demonstrate unequivocally that the academic boycott of Israel is one of the many actions that are intended to isolate and delegitimise the State of Israel.

Various commentators have pointed to what they have describe as "neo-antisemitism" on university campuses in the West (Beckwith, 2011; Cravatts, 2011; Macshane, 2008; Rosenfeld, 2013). In his analysis of campus antisemitism on US university campuses, Cravatts (2011) has argued that left-wing anti-Zionism is both rife and reliant upon antisemitic motifs and representations, which has caused considerable social and psychological tensions in the academic environment. However, anti-Zionist hostility appears to be more prevalent on UK university campuses than on university campuses in the US and on mainland Europe. Indeed, Klaff (2010, p. 87) has described a "proliferation of anti-Zionist expression on UK university campuses since 2002", that is, the initiation of the debate concerning the academic boycott of Israeli universities. More specifically, Boycott, Divestment and Sanctions and other pro-Palestinian groups have used a number of campaigns on university campuses, which have been deemed as unsettling and offensive by Jewish university students, in particular. This has included: the erection of "apartheid walls" during Israel Apartheid Week, which was intended to crystallise the representation of Israel as a racist, apartheid state; the invitation of political Islamists who refuse to recognise the state of Israel to address university societies (e.g. the Hezbollah representation Ibrahim Mousawi who toured UK campuses in 2008); and the use of explicitly antisemitic myths and motifs, many of which were outlined in Chapter 2, in anti-Zionist speeches (see Klaff, 2010). It appears that the anti-Zionist campus activity has created a situation where implicit antisemitism is also acquiring a degree of acceptability, which has led to feelings of insecurity, otherisation and, in some cases, fear among Jewish university students. Indeed, there have been reports of harassment and discrimination against Jewish students on campus, who are often assumed to be supportive of Israeli policies. This has led to some scholars calling for anti-Zionism on university to be recognised as a hate crime (Klaff, 2010).

Anti-Zionist representations and their unequivocally destructive action orientation create a context in which Israel can be openly delegitimised and demonised, which may itself constitute a hate crime, but also a context in which those who identify with the Jewish State are openly harassed and otherised. This has raised questions about the extent to which anti-Zionism and antisemitism can be delineated.

Empirical Research into Anti-Zionism

As observed, there is considerable debate concerning the conceptual and moral boundaries between antisemitism and anti-Zionism. Recently, social scientists have begun to contribute to this debate by examining anti-Zionism empirically and particularly its relationship with antisemitism. On the whole, the little empirical social science research that has been conducted in this area suggests that antisemitism and anti-Zionism are in fact closely related, although the design of most studies renders it difficult to determine empirically the causal relationship between the two constructs. There is generally a lack of experimental research which would shed light on causality. Nonetheless, there is some emerging evidence that antisemitism at least partially underlies anti-Zionism.

Kaplan and Small (2006) conducted a large survey study of 5000 citizens of ten European countries in which they sought to examine the causal relationship, if any, between antisemitism and anti-Zionism. They demonstrated that the prevalence of those who self-reported antisemitic views significantly increased with participants' degree of anti-Zionist sentiment, even after controlling for other factors. Moreover, their results indicated that those with lower scores on anti-Zionism tended not to harbour antisemitic views, which suggested that it is quite possible to be critical of Israel without being antisemitic. This large-scale, exploratory study demonstrated that there is a relationship between the constructs, but Kaplan and Small did not provide a theoretically-grounded explanation of anti-Zionism and its relationship with antisemitism. Thus, it is difficult to see how and when the two forms of prejudice may converge.

Conversely, in their experimental research into mortality salience and attitudes towards Jews and Israel, Cohen et al. (2009) did position these forms of prejudice within the context of social psychological theory. They reasoned that, because modern sensibilities discourage people from manifesting overt prejudice such as classic antisemitism, individuals would be more likely to channel their prejudice via a more socially acceptable route, namely anti-Zionism. In study 1, they found that antisemitism was positively correlated with anti-Zionism and that individuals appeared to manifest greater levels of anti-Zionism in the bogus pipeline condition, i.e. when they were led to believe that lying would be detected and was thus futile, than in the control condition. The researchers interpreted this result as preliminary evidence that, though individuals regarded anti-Zionism as more socially acceptable than overt antisemitism, they nonetheless recognised the antisemitic undercurrent of their anti-Zionist position. This is an important finding because it is indeed often claimed that anti-Zionism constitutes a more socially acceptable means of manifesting antisemitism. Furthermore, Cohen and colleagues argued that there is likely to be a bi-directional causality between antisemitism and anti-Zionism – antisemites are more likely to express anti-Zionism, while anti-Zionism can also accentuate antisemitism. However, this claim requires further empirical investigation.

Study 3 of their project revealed that in the mortality salience condition participants expressed greater support for punishing Israel (than Russia and India) for human rights transgressions, suggesting a disproportionately punitive attitude towards the Jewish State. Their studies demonstrated that antisemitism and anti-Zionism might feed back into one another due to their bi-directional relationship and, thus, rejected the claim that anti-Zionism is completely unrelated to antisemitism (cf. Klug, 2003). In another experiment examining the underlying antisemitism of anti-Zionist political cartoons, Cohen (2012) found that when participants were led to believe that they would be caught lying they viewed anti-Zionist cartoons as being more justified than in the control condition. In the mortality salience condition, participants viewed the cartoon of an Israeli leader eating the flesh of babies as more justified than in the control condition, although a similar experimental effect was not observed when participants were presented with the cartoon of a *Chinese* leader consuming the flesh of Tibetan babies. She concluded that mortality salience in conjunction with the bogus pipeline induced greater demonisation of Israel than of other countries with a dubious human rights record. Thus, it appears that people do single out Israel vis-à-vis other countries and that they do focus their attention upon the perceived transgressions of Israel more so than those of other countries. Given its close empirical link with anti-Zionism, antisemitism may constitute the explanatory factor.

It has been observed that anti-Zionism appears to be associated with specific groups in society. Frindte et al. (2005) examined the prevalence of anti-Zionism and antisemitism in accordance with people's political orientations. They reasoned that, because it is socially stigmatised to express overt antisemitism in Germany and indeed in many other Western countries, "criticism of Israel and anti-Zionism could represent special forms of substituted communication of anti-Semitic attitudes and, thus, could be described as modern forms or derivations of anti-Semitism" (p. 245). Their survey study indicated that those participants who were politically orientated towards the left were more inclined to voice their anti-Zionist attitudes than political right-wingers, highlighting the social acceptability of anti-Zionism in such political circles. Moreover, they argued that modern German antisemitism could take the form of anti-Zionism or "exaggerated Israel criticism". It is possible that anti-Zionism, or "modern antisemitism", may be manifested in a way that is consistent with the perceived ethos of the particular group – in the case of left-wing individuals in the form of "exaggerated Israel criticism".

There has been limited empirical research into anti-Zionism among ethnic and religious minority groups and in non-Western contexts, although there are some recent exceptions. In a survey study, Baum and Nakazawa (2007) examined antisemitism and anti-Zionism among North American Muslims and Christians. They found that antisemitism and anti-Zionism were moderately correlated and that the main effect of religion on anti-Zionism was significant, while that of ethnicity was not. Their sample included both Arab and non-Arab Muslims and, contrary to expectations, non-Arab Muslims scored higher than Arab Muslims on anti-Zionism, despite the little or non-existent geographical or ethnic commonality with Arab Muslims who have indeed suffered political and military confrontations with Israel. It appears that the shared superordinate Muslim identity united individuals of diverse ethnicities, given that the Israeli-Arab conflict can be construed, at least partly, as a religious conflict through its Islamicisation (Litvak, 1998). In his survey study of antisemitism and anti-Zionism in the Iranian general population, Jaspal (2011c) found that anti-Zionism was predicted by political trust (in the Iranian government) and Iranian national identity, which suggested that individuals who trusted the Iranian regime would adhere to the "version" of Iranian national identity that was disseminated. Crucially, as demonstrated in this book, anti-Zionism is frequently constructed as a necessary tenet of Iranian national identity.

It appears that the causal relationships between antisemitism and anti-Zionism cannot be unequivocally ascertained on the basis of these studies alone, despite their attempts to examine empirically the inter-relations between these forms of prejudice. The key to improving our understanding of these inter-relations may lie in the close examination of individuals' discourses using qualitative analytic methods. Moreover, there is clearly a need to examine the manifestations and motivations of anti-Zionism, as well as its relationship with antisemitism, among those groups that are most associated with this form of prejudice in those contexts in which anti-Zionism is most prevalent. Accordingly, this book explores the case studies of Iranians and British Pakistani Muslims in order to examine the manifestation of antisemitism and anti-Zionism.

Overview

This chapter highlights the multifarious understandings of the political ideology of Zionism and the complexity of anti-Zionism. In this book, it is defined as opposition to the ethnonational ideology which emphasises the Jewish people's right to national self-determination. It is acknowledged that there is considerable debate about the boundaries between anti-Zionism and antisemitism, but there does appear to be a relationship. Anti-Zionism may be caused by underlying antisemitic prejudice, or it may itself induce or exacerbate antisemitism even where antisemitism did not exist before. Moreover, it is plausible to regard anti-

Zionism as an aspect of antisemitic prejudice because of its excessive, negative focus upon the Jewish State and its action orientation to destroy the national symbol of the Jews. To that extent, it can be considered as part of the continuities and discontinuities of antisemitism.

In this chapter, an overview of some of the major events and debates in the Israeli-Arab conflict is provided in order to exhibit the impetus to much contemporary anti-Zionism. There is a widespread perception of negative Israeli/ Zionist might vis-à-vis Arab weakness, which has induced sympathy for the Arab world and hostility towards Israel. Moreover, in the Arab/Muslim world itself, the long history of conflict may have contributed to humiliation, weakened self-confidence and threats to social and psychological wellbeing, inducing hostility towards Israel. In examining some of the anti-Zionist representations which dominate the debate on Israel, it is evident that aspects of the Israeli-Arab conflict and the political obstacles to peace between the Israelis and Palestinians have been offered in support of anti-Zionism. However, these complex aspects are sometimes re-construed in ways that echo the antisemitic myths and motifs outlined in Chapter 2.

This book contributes to existing empirical research into antisemitism and anti-Zionism by examining the case studies of the Islamic Republic of Iran (social representations and public perceptions), and the British Pakistani Muslim community in Britain. It is necessary to examine antisemitism and anti-Zionism in those contexts in which these forms of prejudice are particularly salient, but also in distinct contexts where the boundaries of acceptability may differ. While the Islamic Republic of Iran openly advocates anti-Zionism and sometimes antisemitism, the British context is more ambivalent – it provides social and institutional support for a milder version of anti-Zionism and appears to condone and implicitly encourage anti-Zionism among minority groups, such as the British Pakistani Muslim community.

Chapter 4
A Social Psychological Framework for Examining Representation, Cognition and Everyday Talk

Introduction

Historical and social science overviews of antisemitism and anti-Zionism were provided in Chapters 2 and 3, respectively. The chapters demonstrate that these forms of prejudice have been manifested in channels of societal information (representation), in patterns of thinking, identification, categorisation and emotional experience (cognition), and in the ways in which people communicate (everyday talk). However, the distinct dimensions of representation, cognition and discourse tend to have been examined in isolation from one another, despite the clear linkage between them and the implications that one dimension frequently has for others.

This chapter introduces various social psychological theories which, in unison, can shed light on the inter-relations between representation, cognition and talk. The chapter begins with an overview of (i) Social Representations Theory, which theorises the construction of "common sense" knowledge and its representation in channels of societal information; (ii) Identity Process Theory, which sheds light on how social representations contribute to identity construction, threat and management; and (iii) Intergroup Threat Theory, which describes and examines the nature of threats which can be represented and perceived as being posed by outgroups. This chapter presents a rationale for integrating various levels of analysis – representational, cognitive and discursive – as well as the distinct levels of human interdependence – intrapsychic, interpersonal and intergroup – in order to understand the complex constructs of antisemitism and anti-Zionism, and it provides an integrative theoretical framework for doing so.

Social Representations Theory

Social Representations Theory (Moscovici, 1988, 2000) was designed to theorise how abstract and esoteric ideas are diffused among the public and how they make their transition into societal thinking on a large scale. A social representation is defined as a system of values, ideas and practices regarding a given social object, as well as the elaboration of the social object for the purpose of communicating and behaving. Social representations enable individuals to think and communicate about social phenomena and to evaluate them. Moreover, they implicitly specify "appropriate" ways of behaving in relation to them. For instance, delegitimising social representations of Israel in the Iranian media provide the readership with shared negative imagery of the Jewish State, facilitating cognitions, emotions and social behaviour that result in intergroup tensions (Bar-Tal and Teichman, 2005).

In his analysis of how representations are formed, Moscovici (1988) outlines the processes of anchoring and objectification:

- *Anchoring* reflects the categorisation of unfamiliar objects through their comparison with an existing stock of familiar and culturally accessible objects. For instance, for Iranians to develop an understanding of Israel, it must first be named and imbued with familiar characteristics, which facilitate communication and discussion about it. It has been observed that Iranian Supreme Leader Ayatollah Khomeini frequently linked the Israeli-Palestinian conflict to the Jews' historical "exploitation" of Muslims during the early days of Islam (Shahvar, 2009). This has served to construct Israel unambiguously as the "villain" in the Israeli-Palestinian conflict.
- *Objectification* is the process whereby unfamiliar and abstract objects are transformed into concrete and "objective" common-sense realities. The sub-strategies of objectification include: (i) metaphor use (encouraging us to view something in terms of something else), and (ii) personification (which attributes human characteristics to an abstract phenomenon. For instance, in an analysis of the Iranian media (Jaspal, 2014d) it was found that Israel was frequently referred to in terms of a "cancer". Thus, the country was attributed a concrete "essence" through its metaphorical objectification in terms of a metastatic disease, which engendered a perception that it must be destroyed (in the same way that cancer should be destroyed).

The processes of anchoring and objectification perform both descriptive and evaluative functions by elucidating the "essence" of Israel (i.e. what it is) and its social value (i.e. how it should be evaluated).

Social Representations Theory emphasises that there is a "symbolic space" in which social representations are developed, negotiated and re-configured and that "all human beings hold creative power and agency in their formation and use" (Voelklein and Howarth, 2005, p. 433). Thus, while the media, political institutions and other channels of societal information will clearly influence the genesis and development of social representations, human beings also contribute to the genesis, development and negotiation of representations through interpersonal communication, engagement with social institutions and, importantly, individual identity processes. Thus, in order to gain an understanding of social representations, it is important to examine both media (and other) depictions of Jews and Israel but also the ways in which people talk about them. Social Representations Theory research has employed a wide range of methodological approaches (Breakwell and

Canter, 1993; Vignoles, 2014). In this book, the theory has been used alongside thematic analysis in the interview studies, and alongside critical discourse analysis in the media analytic studies. In order to understand the representational, discursive and cognitive aspects of antisemitism and anti-Zionism and indeed responses to these forms of prejudice, it is necessary to use the theory at multiple levels and from distinct methodological perspectives, all of which can provide distinctive and valuable insights.

Delegitimising and Dehumanising Representations

In contexts of intergroup conflict, social representations may categorise an outgroup primarily on the basis of negative traits in order to deny the humanity of the outgroup and to exclude it from dominant society. This process has been referred to as delegitimisation (Bar-Tal, 2000; Oren and Bar-Tal, 2007). In order for a group to be delegitimised, delegitimising social representations need to form and circulate in society. In theorising delegitimisation, Bar-Tal (2000) has identified a series of ways in which outgroups can be delegitimised:

- *dehumanisation* refers to the attribution of subhuman traits to a group (e.g. demon, monster, Satan);
- *trait characterisation* is the attribution of generally negative characteristics to a group (e.g. liar, aggressor), which elicit a negative evaluation of it;
- *outcasting* constructs groups as violators of pivotal social norms (e.g. murderers, thieves);
- *political labelling* entails the positioning of groups into socially stigmatised political categories (e.g. Nazi, imperialist).

This typology of delegitimisation sheds light on the kinds of social representation that need to emerge in order for a group to be successfully delegitimised. Social representations of outgroups may dehumanise them by anchoring them to animals or non-human entities or by objectifying them through the use of animalistic metaphors. Some political figures in the Western world have anchored Israel to infamous political groups such as the Nazis in order to delegitimise the Jewish State, and have implied that the Jews, despite their trauma during the Holocaust, themselves commit acts comparable to those committed by the Nazis.[1] The process of delegitimisation typically positions the outgroup as posing some kind of threat to the ingroup, and as highlighted in Figure 4.1 (below), this threat can be symbolic, realistic or hybridised.

---

1   The Commentator http://www.thecommentator.com/article/2567/british_member_ of_parliament_claims_liberated_jews_perpetuate_atrocities_compares_mid_east_ conflict_to_holocaust

Threat imagery can be invoked in order to mobilise people against the delegitimised outgroup. Moreover, systematic, institutionalised delegitimisation usually encourages widespread belief in a battle between "good" (represented by the ingroup) and "evil" (epitomised by the delegitimised outgroup). There is a tendency to accentuate the positive characteristics of the ingroup vis-à-vis the negative characteristics of the outgroup, and this clash between "good" and "evil" may be brandished as the underlying cause of intergroup conflict (van Dijk, 1993). Clearly, delegitimisation often evokes cognitions and emotions which may be conducive to full-blown intergroup conflict (Oren and Bar-Tal, 2014). For instance, Bar-Tal (2000) argues that delegitimisation can arouse highly negative emotions of rejection, such as hatred, anger, fear and disgust, which collectively can lead to aggression, violence and even genocide. The Nazi persecution and systematic delegitimisation of the Jews, which culminated in the Holocaust, clearly exemplifies the devastating consequences that delegitimisation can have.

Dehumanisation is a social psychological process which is particularly applicable to cases of antisemitism and anti-Zionism. As Bar-Tal (2000) notes, dehumanisation refers to the attribution of subhuman traits to a group – it divests individuals of the quality of humanness and constructs them primarily as animalistic. There is a long-standing media tendency to represent Jews and, more recently, the State of Israel in a dehumanising manner. Jews and Israelis have been likened to animals in political rhetoric, institutional texts, visual representations and other media. This has undoubtedly contributed to the social acceptability of calling for the destruction of the State of Israel, as is the case in the Islamic Republic of Iran and in other countries.

Kelman (1976, p. 301) has argued that dehumanisation entails the denial of a person's individual and community identities. The denial of individual identity deprives him/her of their status "as an individual, independent and distinguishable from others, capable of making choices" while denial of the community identity denies their membership in "an interconnected network of individuals who care for each other" (Kelman, 1976, p. 301). It is easy to find examples of how Israel and Jews are habitually dehumanised. Jews may be divested of their individual identity while their community identity is conversely accentuated, that is, as a *malevolent* network of individuals who *collusively* care for each other in their *malicious* goals. This dehumanising social representation deprives Jews and Israelis of their capacity to evoke outgroups' compassion, empathy and moral emotions (Bandura, Underwood and Fromson, 1975), which can have negative consequences for intergroup relations and, particularly, for the wellbeing of the dehumanised group.

Delegitimisation, dehumanisation and intergroup threat perceptions are principally social psychological phenomena, which serve intrapsychic, interpersonal and intergroup functions. In order to understand why individuals, groups and institutions may actively create, accept and disseminate delegitimising and dehumanising representations of Jews and Israel, it is necessary to draw upon a multi-level theory that bridges the intrapsychic, interpersonal and intergroup levels – namely, Identity Process Theory.

Identity Process Theory

Identity Process Theory (Breakwell, 1986, 2001; Jaspal and Breakwell, 2014; Jaspal and Cinnirella, 2010a) provides a holistic and integrative framework for examining (i) the structure of identity, namely its content and value dimensions, and the centrality and salience of identity components; (ii) the interaction of social and psychological factors in the production of identity content; and (iii) the inter-relations between the intrapsychic, interpersonal and intergroup levels of human interdependence.

The theory proposes that the structure of self-identity should be conceptualised in terms of its content and value/affect dimensions and that this structure is regulated by two universal processes, namely assimilation–accommodation and evaluation.

- The *assimilation–accommodation* process refers to the absorption of new information in the identity structure (e.g. discovering the existence of antisemitic social representations in one's social context) and the adjustment which takes place in order for it to become part of the structure (e.g. becoming aware of antisemitic social representations and, thus, attenuating one's Jewish identity in order to gain social acceptance).
- The *evaluation* process confers meaning and value on the contents of identity (e.g. coming to view one's Zionist identity in negative terms due to perceived stigma surrounding this identity within a valued ingroup context).

The theory suggests that the two processes of identity are interrelated in that evaluation will affect what is assimilated and how it is accommodated in the identity structure, while assimilation–accommodation provides new elements for the individual to evaluate. Identity processes are in constant operation as the individual navigates through their social world, encountering outgroups, social representations and novel social contexts. Crucially, the processes of identity do not function in a random manner but rather they are guided by a number of motivational principles, referred to as "identity principles". Breakwell (1986, p. 24) argues that "the principles specify the end states which are desirable for identity". Thus, people tend to assimilate, accommodate and evaluate phenomena insofar as they can provide optimal levels of the identity principles. Over several years, Identity Process Theory researchers have identified the following principles of identity:

- The *continuity principle* refers to the human motivation to maintain a sense of temporal continuity;
- The *distinctiveness* refers to the drive to establish and maintain a sense of differentiation from relevant others;
- The *self-efficacy principle* refers to need to maintain feelings of competence and control;
- The *self-esteem principle* refers to the drive to derive a positive self-conception;

- The *belonging principle* refers to the human motivation for deriving feelings of closeness to, and acceptance by, relevant others;
- The *meaning principle* motivates individuals to search for purpose and significance in their existence;
- The *psychological coherence principle* refers to the need for compatibility and coherence between inter-connected identity elements

These principles can be construed at both individual and group levels (Lyons, 1996). Thus, the continuity principle may refer to one's sense of continuity at a psychological, individual level (e.g. believing that one has remained the same person over time and will remain the same in the future), but also at a group level (e.g. believing that one's group has remained the same over time and will remain the same in the future).

Not all of the principles will be constantly salient at any given time but rather it is the social context (and the social representations which are dominant in that social context) which will render particular principles more or less salient. For instance, there appears to be a perception of mutual intergroup threat between Iranians and Israelis, which may in turn render salient the distinctiveness principle (construed at a group level). Conversely, it is conceivable that other principles of identity, such as meaning or psychological coherence, would be relatively less active in this intergroup context.

A core prediction of Identity Process Theory is that if the processes of assimilation-accommodation and evaluation cannot comply with the motivational principles of identity, for whatever reason, identity is threatened and the individual will engage in strategies for coping with the threat. Individuals seek to cope with identity threat because a state of identity threat is aversive for psychological wellbeing. A coping strategy is defined as "any activity, in thought or deed, which has as its goal the removal or modification of a threat to identity" (Breakwell, 1986, p. 78). Coping strategies can function at three levels:

- *Intrapsychic strategies* function at the cognitive and emotional levels and include *inter alia* denial or re-conceptualisation of a threatening stimulus, and compartmentalisation (cognitive separation) of elements which, together, could cause a threat;
- *Interpersonal strategies* aim to modify relationships with other people in order to cope with threat, and include *inter alia* self-isolation from others and "passing" (hiding one's group membership) in interpersonal contact;
- *Intergroup strategies* serve to modify group dynamics, boundaries and relations in order to cope with threat, and include strategically shifting between one's group memberships and engaging in group action (through membership in a pressure group, for instance).

Human beings habitually engage in these strategies as they monitor their identities and attempt to maintain appropriate levels of the identity principles. Within the context of antisemitism and anti-Zionism, it is easy to see how these forms of outgroup prejudice may constitute strategies for coping with identity threat. For instance, by manifesting anti-Zionism the Iranian regime may bolster its image as an assertive, powerful and self-efficacious regime and thereby compensate for threats to its economic control and competence (Jaspal, 2013a). It has been argued that the manifestation of outgroup prejudice can bolster self-esteem among members of the ingroup (Jaspal and Cinnirella, 2010b; Wills, 1981). Conversely, in attempting to cope with the threats to identity associated with perceptions of antisemitism and anti-Zionism, Jews and Zionists may deny that antisemitism is a salient concern and attenuate its social and psychological importance (Shapira, 2006).

Identity Process Theory suggests that identity is the product of both social and psychological processes. Breakwell (1986, 1993, 2001, 2014) has repeatedly acknowledged the role of social representations in determining the content of identity and the value of its components. Social representations determine how individuals assimilate, accommodate and evaluate identity components, what is threatening for identity and how individuals subsequently cope with threat. Both Social Representations Theory and Identity Process Theory acknowledge human agency in people's use and (re-)construal of social representations.

Breakwell (2011, 2014) has modelled the relationship between the individual and social representations in her model of "personalisation". She argues that representations are used and personalised in ways which benefit identity processes. The five components of her personalisation model include:

- *Awareness* – individuals will have varying levels of awareness of a social representation, which can depend upon previous experience, particular personality traits (e.g. shyness; introversion) and group memberships (e.g. being a member of a group that is particularly concerned with a particular social representation). For instance, as highlighted in Chapter 1, many British Pakistanis manifest delegitimising social representations of Israel due to the belief in Israel's mistreatment of Arabs, but many are unaware of the fact that Arabs make up over 20 per cent of the Israeli population and have full citizenship rights in Israel.
- *Understanding* – individuals will differ in their level of understanding of a social representation, which can depend upon social and cognitive factors. For instance, many Iranians are aware of the social representation that the Holocaust constitutes a myth but do not understand the pseudo-scientific arguments presented by Holocaust deniers in order to substantiate this social representation (Litvak and Webman, 2009).
- *Acceptance* – although individuals may have awareness and an understanding of a social representation, they will differ in the degree to which they actually believe it. For instance, Holocaust deniers are generally aware that most people do accept that 6 million Jews were killed in the Holocaust but they do not believe this themselves and declare that this representation of the Holocaust is a "myth". Clearly, some of the coping

strategies described in Identity Process Theory (e.g. denial and negativism) shed light on this aspect of personalisation.

- *Assimilation* – when individuals accept a social representation, it is assimilated to identity, as suggested by the assimilation-accommodation process in Identity Process Theory. Changes take place in identity in order to make room for the social representation and the representation itself undergoes some modification in order to become a part of the identity structure. For instance, Israeli Jews may accept the social representation that the Israeli Jewish ingroup is besieged by hostile (pre-dominantly Arab) outgroups, which in turn may alter their social representation of how they are viewed and treated by the world. This has been referred to as "siege mentality" (Bar-Tal, 2000; see Chapter 1, this volume).
- *Salience* – social representations will vary in their salience for an individual and a group over time. If a group, which is of phenomenological importance to an individual, decides that a social representation is important, it is likely to acquire importance for the individual as well. For instance, since 1979 the Iranian government has systematically represented anti-Zionism as a key tenet of Iranian national identity, and this appears to have rendered anti-Zionist social representations salient for Iranians since that time (Jaspal, 2013a), especially for those who identify strongly with the Iranian national group (Jaspal, 2013c).

The personalisation model integrates social representations and identity processes, because it provides a framework for understanding individual responses to social representations and how these representations may be voiced, accepted or rejected by individuals who are exposed to them. Thus, by examining the social representations that Iranians and British Pakistan Muslims have about Jews and Israel, we can gain greater insight into how these representations are related to identity processes. For instance, the social representation that Israel poses a threat to the Islamic ingroup could plausibly threaten the continuity principle of identity (construed at the group level). A key assumption of Identity Process Theory is that the threatened individual will seek to remove or modify the threat to identity by engaging in coping strategies, which can include outgroup hostility or full-blown intergroup conflict.

Intergroup Threat Theory

Intergroup Threat Theory (Stephan and Stephan, 2000) provides a useful theoretical framework for describing and examining the nature of threats which can be represented and perceived as being posed by particular outgroups. The theory adopts a social psychological approach to threat which argues that whether or not threats have any basis in reality, the perception of threat in and of itself has consequences at both the intergroup and intra-individual levels. The theory draws upon Social Identity Theory (Tajfel and Turner, 1986) and thinking about the inevitability of perceiving threats from other groups due to basic human tendencies towards cautious perceptions of outgroups (Haselton and Buss, 2003).

The theory posits that there are two basic types of threat, both of which revolve around potential harm that an outgroup could inflict on the ingroup, namely realistic and symbolic threats.

- *Realistic threats* are posed by factors which could cause the ingroup physical harm or loss of resources, and can also be represented as individual-level threats causing potential physical or material harm to individual group members as a result of their membership. For instance, the long-standing social representation that Israel seeks to invade and usurp the land and resources of neighbouring countries, including Iran, renders the country a realistic threat in the minds of individuals who accept this representation.
- *Symbolic threats* represent threats to the meaning system(s) of the ingroup, such as challenges to valued ingroup norms and values, and at the individual level of analysis may be associated with loss of face, challenges to self-identity and potential threats to self-esteem (Stephan, Ybarra, and Rios Morrison, 2009). For instance, the social representation that Jews seek to distort Islamic scripture, which has been disseminated by the Iranian authorities, may render the Jews a symbolic threat to Islam.

There has been considerable research into perceptions of realistic threats, largely conducted in the US context. For instance, in a meta-analytic review of intergroup threat and outgroup attitudes, it was suggested that the negative stereotype that Blacks are violent and aggressive might make White Americans fear for their physical well-being and, thus, construe Blacks in terms of a realistic threat (Riek, Mania and Gaertner, 2006). Similarly, given the rise in Islamophobic social representations associating Muslims with terrorist activity reported in many media analyses, it is possible that British Muslims may be construed by sections of the general population as a realistic threat (Cinnirella, 2014).

It is plausible that the perception of group-level threat may also have implications for identity processes at an individual level. The impact of realistic threats for identity processes is likely to depend upon the nature of the realistic threat itself. For instance, the social representation that Israel seeks to cause physical harm to Muslims may severely compromise the (group) continuity principle of identity, since the implication is that the ingroup risks annihilation, thereby, ceasing to exist as a group (see Jaspal and Yampolsky, 2011). On the other hand, the perception that Israel poses threats to the economic well-being of Iranians by supporting and encouraging economic sanctions may threaten the self-efficacy principle of identity, given that Iranians may feel that they lack competence or control over their economy and livelihoods. These observations fit with the argument made by Intergroup Threat Theory researchers that negative stereotypes of an outgroup (for example, as aggressive) are predictive of both perceived realistic and symbolic threats to the ingroup (Stephan, Ybarra and Rios Morrison, 2009).

Symbolic threats, on the other hand, refer to the perceived violation of symbolic self-aspects which are perceived by group members as underlying ingroup identity (e.g. morals, norms, values, standards, beliefs, attitudes, social representation). This type of threat may also ensue from perceived intergroup differences in worldviews (Corenblum and Stephan, 2001). Clearly, some self-aspects are perceived by group members as endowing their group with a sense of distinctiveness from other groups (Simon, 2004). For example, many Iranians believe that their country should have the right to develop nuclear technology for peaceful purposes, and Israel's opposition to this perceived right can challenge this aspect of Iran's distinctiveness from other countries in the region. It is easy to see how this can challenge both self-efficacy (in terms of the agency and autonomy to take decisions relevant to the ingroup) and distinctiveness. Thus, a symbolic threat may be conducive to threats to self-efficacy and distinctiveness. Moreover, like realistic threats, symbolic threats might also jeopardise the perceived continuity of the ingroup. For example, Iranian leaders have publicly stated that Jews seek to alter and misconstrue Islam in order to "contaminate" Islamic teachings (Shahvar, 2009). This is likely to threaten the continuity of ingroup identity given that Jews are depicted as seeking to destroy a key tenet of the ingroup's ethos and collective identity. In other words, Jews are depicted as seeking to install discontinuity in the lives of ingroup members.

In their discussion of Intergroup Threat Theory, Jaspal and Cinnirella (2010b, p 290) have argued that some groups can be positioned "in such a way that they represent a hybridised kind of threat, that combines both realistic (e.g. physical well-being) and symbolic (e.g. cultural) threats to the dominant ethno-national ingroup". Groups that are positioned as posing a *hybridised threat* are deemed to be particularly threatening, which can invite hostile responses from perceivers. Given the interchangeable use of the categories "Jew", "Israel" and "Zionism" and the widespread perception of synergy between these constructs, it is plausible that they are collectively represented and perceived as posing a hybridised threat in at least some contexts.

By reconciling Social Representations Theory, ideas around delegitimisation and dehumanisation, Intergroup Threat Theory and Identity Process Theory, it is possible to understand how particular social representations, disseminated in the media and in other channels of societal information, may challenge identity processes among individuals and lead to particular patterns of cognition and action. Cinnirella (2014) provides a typology of group-level threats (as defined in Intergroup Threat Theory) and how they may map onto individual-level threats (as defined in Identity Process Theory) (see Figure 4.1). Although the focus of Cinnirella's work is on social representations of Muslims in British society (against the backdrop of Islamophobia), this framework can provide a fruitful lens for examining representation, cognition and discourse in the context of antisemitism and anti-Zionism.

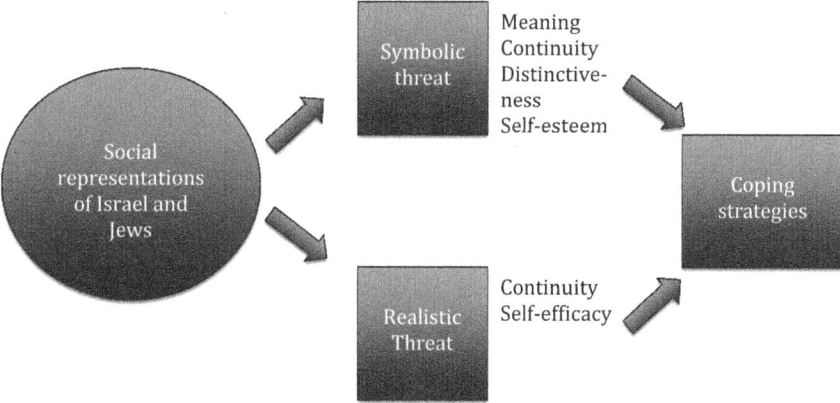

Figure 4.1   The identity principles potentially threatened by social representations of Israel and Jews (adapted from Cinnirella, 2014)

The perception of realistic, symbolic and hybridised threats to the ingroup, reified in social representations, are said to have negative outcomes for intergroup relations (Jaspal and Cinnirella, 2010b; Stephan and Stephan, 2000), while threatened individual identity (in an Identity Process Theory sense) will induce a range of coping strategies which can shape patterns of cognition and intergroup relations. Thus, in aligning these theories, it may be possible to elucidate the reasons underlying individuals' motivations to behave in certain ways in the intergroup setting. Crucially, while Intergroup Threat Theory sheds light upon the nature of threats reflected in media representations and the social representations voiced in individuals' talk, Identity Process Theory provides insight into the potential repercussions of these threats for identity processes, cognition and behaviour.

Overview

This chapter provides an overview of an integrative theoretical framework in which social representations, cognition and everyday talk can be collectively examined. It is argued that identity processes, and particularly the concept of identity threat, can play a pivotal role in elucidating how and why groups and individuals may accept or reject particular social representations of Jews and Israel. It is shown how social representations can form and how they can acquire elements that induce patterns of negative intergroup behaviour. Moreover, the framework demonstrates some of the strategies that may be deployed by individuals in order to cope with identity threat. This integrative framework is useful because it marries various levels of human interdependence – individual, interpersonal and intergroup – thereby providing a holistic approach to the study of antisemitism and anti-Zionism. In the chapters that follow, this integrative framework is invoked and applied to the qualitative data generated by studies of antisemitism and anti-Zionism.

PART III
Textual and Visual Representations of Jews and the Jewish State

Chapter 5

Representing the Jewish State
in the Iranian Press[1]

Introduction

Much existing research into the media in Iran tends to focus on media practices, journalistic tendencies, press censorship and the long-standing anti-Western position of the Iranian media since the Islamic Revolution (Semati, 2008; Sweetser and Brown, 2010). Yet, there have been only cursory observations concerning how the Jewish State and its inhabitants are represented in the Iranian media, which are offered to make general points concerning institutionalised antisemitism and anti-Zionism in Iran (Litvak, 2006; Shahvar, 2009; Takeyh, 2006). As a key source of societal information both for Iranians and potentially for disaffected Muslims in the West, it is important to examine how the Iranian Press discursively constructs Israel and the Jewish people. This is key to understanding how Iran disseminates and exports its anti-Zionist ideology to an international readership in order to broaden its sphere of ideological influence.

After a brief methodological overview of the media study, this chapter provides a fine-grained critical discourse analysis of representations of Israel in two Iranian newspapers, namely *The Tehran Times* and *Press TV*. The following three discursive themes are outlined and discussed: (i) Delegitimising the Jewish State; (ii) The Threat of the Zionist Regime; and (iii) Constructing National Agency in Global Anti-Zionism. This chapter examines (i) how the processes of anchoring and objectification are employed in media discourse in order to generate particular social representations of Israel; (ii) how polemic representations of Israel are consolidated; and (iii) the implications of these representations for intergroup relations.

Methodological overview

The Tehran Times is a daily newspaper published in both print and online formats, which was established by Ayatollah Seyyed Mohammad Beheshti following the

1   This chapter is based upon two previously published articles: Jaspal, R. (2013). Anti-Zionism and the Iranian Press. *Journal for the Study of Antisemitism*, 5(2), 401–25, and Jaspal, R. (2014). Representing the "Zionist Regime": Mass Communication of Anti-Zionism in the English-language Iranian Press. *British Journal of Middle Eastern Studies*, 41(3), 287–305. The content of those articles is used here with the permission of the journals in which they were published.

Islamic Revolution in 1979. According to Behesti, "[t]he Tehran Times is not the newspaper of the government; it must be a loud voice of the Islamic Revolution and the loudspeaker of the oppressed people of the world".[2] Although the newspaper is not state-owned, it aims to disseminate key tenets of the Islamic Revolution and is therefore generally supportive of the Islamic Republic of Iran's ideology. According to its website, *The Tehran Times* "makes a special effort to publish reports on cultural and religious issues", in addition to various other social issues. Although there are no independent data concerning the circulation of the outlet, *The Tehran Times* claims to be "attracting readers from over 80 different countries" and that its website has "over 10,000 visitors each day".

Press TV is a state-owned media outlet, which forms part of the Islamic Republic of Iran Broadcasting Corporation. It was launched in 2007 to "counter" Western news reporting on global issues (in particular, the Middle East). The official vision statement of *Press TV* is described as follows:

> Heeding the often neglected voices and perspectives of a great portion of the world;
> Embracing and building bridges of cultural understanding;
> Encouraging human beings of different nationalities, races and creeds to identify with one another;
> Bringing to light untold and overlooked stories of individuals who have experienced the vitality and versatility of political and cultural divides firsthand.[3]

Like *The Tehran Times*, Press *TV* is similarly conservative in its ideological stance, and has been described as a "mouth-piece" for the Iranian government. Although these outlets attempt to shape public opinion in the West as their target readership, the content of these outlets reflects that of Persian-language newspaper outlets.

Using the keywords "Israel", "Zionist" and "Palestine", the author conducted a search of the online databases for articles published between January 2011 and December 2011. This generated a corpus of 375 articles, all of which were subjected to analysis. The aim of the study was to provide a fine-grained analysis of the discursive aspects of media reporting on Israel, rather than to provide a longitudinal overview of media reporting. The aim was theoretical, focusing on *how* representations are constructed, disseminated and encouraged, rather than purely empirical. A key aim of the study was to examine *habitual* ways of media reporting on Israel, rather than polarised coverage of particularly contentious events (e.g. Lebanon War; Gaza War). Thus, it was deemed appropriate to target a time-frame in which there were no reports of major social or political events concerning Israel/the Israeli-Arab conflict. Although there are frequent skirmishes between the Israeli army and Palestinian militants as well as rocket attacks from

---

2   *The Tehran Times* website, http://tehrantimes.com/nnnnnnnnnabout-ttnnnnnnnnn
3   *Press TV* website http://www.presstv.ir/About.html

Gaza, which often feature in international news coverage, the period covered in the corpus was in fact relatively uneventful.

Critical discourse analysis (van Dijk, 1993) is a language-oriented analytical technique for identifying patterns of meaning within a data set. It aims to integrate discourse, cognition and power, and to bridge the epistemological positions of social constructionism and realism. The technique provides insight into how social reality is constructed in talk and text, acknowledging the possibilities offered by, and potential constraints imposed by, social power relations (van Dijk, 1993). Critical discourse analysis helps reveal the rhetorical strategies for affirming and contesting hegemonic and polemic social representations of Israel and indeed how polemic representations can be elevated to hegemonic position (Jaspal and Yampolsky, 2011).

Delegitimiting the Jewish State

The Islamic Republic of Iran regularly contests the legitimacy of the State of Israel, evidenced by the disparaging ways in which it refers to the Jewish State in political discourse (Jaspal, 2013a; Litvak, 2006; Shahvar, 2009). Articles in the corpus reproduce the anti-Zionist political agenda by contesting the social representation that Israel is a Jewish state:

1. Benyamin Netanyahu's government is facing serious conflicts within the occupied territories as a result of his insistence on the recognition of Israel as a Jewish state ... However, there are serious disagreements about the definitions of the word "Jew" and the expression "Jewish state" inside Israel ... Despite this high level of disagreement, Netanyahu is still adamant about Israel being recognized as a Jewish state[4]

When Prime Minister Ben-Gurion declared the State of Israel in 1948, he explicitly referred to it as a Jewish State (Ben-Gurion, 1948), and indeed the Basic Laws of Israel continue to define the state as a "Jewish and Democratic State"[5]. Pro-Palestinian proponents of the one-state solution tend to contest the Jewish character of the territory, which they view as being occupied by Israel, and instead regard it as Palestine (see Shahvar, 2009). Similarly, in extract 1, there is clear contestation of the notion that Israel should be recognised as a Jewish state. It attributes the "serious conflicts within the occupied territories", which could refer to either the West Bank/Gaza or present-day Israel, to this "insistence" upon being recognised as a Jewish state. Thus, the very existence of the Jewish State is constructed as the root cause of the Israeli-Palestinian conflict, implicitly suggesting that the conflict

---

4   Demos are a sign of the decline of Israel's regional influence, *Tehran Times*, 8 August 2011.

5   The Existing Basic Laws of Israel: Full Texts, The Knesset http://www.knesset. gov.il/description/eng/eng_mimshal_yesod1.htm

would cease to exist if the Jewish State were dismantled. The representation was further challenged through the construction of the terms "Jew" and "Jewish State" as contentious and devoid of consensual interpretation. By contesting the meanings of these terms, the extract denigrated the claim that Israel could possibly constitute a Jewish state, which itself was problematised through its positioning in quotes. The representation that there is a "high level of disagreement" is invoked in order to construct Netanyahu's "insistence on the recognition of Israel as a Jewish state" as inappropriate and perplexing.

Similarly, there was a clear tendency in the corpus to resist social representations of Israeli statehood, by conversely constructing Israel in terms of a "regime":

2. The IAEO [International Atomatic Energy Organisation] chief said that the Zionist regime's agents carried out the terror plot with the help of the US and UK spying agencies[6]
3. The Tel Aviv regime has ordered the Israeli navy to use all possible means to prevent the incoming international aid flotilla from reaching the Gaza Strip[7]
4. Yet Tel Aviv ... continues to accuse the European governments of negligence in backing the Hebrew regime[8]

The category "regime" evokes negative connotations of an authoritarian form of government and, thus, its use here serves to delegitimise Israel. Use of this category was consistent across the whole corpus of articles, although it was characterised differentially in terms of the "Zionist", "Tel Aviv", "Hebrew" or "Israeli" regime. The use of "Zionist regime" in extract 2 seemed to further anchor this "authoritarian regime" to a political ideology which itself has acquired negative connotations (Takeyh, 2006). Indeed, the political ideology of Zionism is frequently represented in negative terms as an "expansionist" colonial ideology (Litvak, 2006), which therefore poses a hybridised threat to surrounding countries.

Extract 3 referred to the "Tel Aviv regime" and thereby constructed the city of Tel Aviv as the centre of the "authoritarian" regime, despite the fact that Jerusalem is the political capital of Israel and the location of the Israeli Knesset (Parliament). This served to distance Israel from the city of Jerusalem, which the Iranian government regards as Islamic territory (Takeyh, 2006). Similarly, the designation of Israel as "the Hebrew regime", as in extract 4, delegitimised the *Jewish* administration of Israel. Indeed, there is a coercive social representation that Palestine is in fact "Muslim land" and that the Jewish population of Israel is illegitimate (Shahvar, 2009).

Articles in the corpus resisted social representations of Israeli statehood through reference to Israelis as "Zionists", rather than as citizens of the State of Israel.

---

6   UK complicity in Iran terrors exposed, *Press TV*, 20 September 2011.
7   Israel navy siege: Gaza-bound French aid ship, *Tehran Times*, 19 July 2011.
8   Unholy peace and Israel's passivity, *Press TV*, 18 September 2011.

5. The Zionists are worried about the grass-roots uprisings in the Middle East[9]

In both political and media discourses, the category "Zionist" was commonly employed to substitute the demonym "Israeli", which served to anchor the seldom-mentioned *people* of Israel to the political ideology of Zionism. It is noteworthy that the articles seldom made reference to the people of Israel. This contributes to the "politicisation" of the *people* of Israel, since their identities as both individuals and citizens of the State of Israel were attenuated vis-à-vis their constructed affiliation and adherence to Zionism. The "politicisation" of the Israeli people foregrounded the "regime", rather than the citizenry, that is, the Israeli people. This served to rhetorically "de-populate" the State of Israel, objectifying the "Zionist entity" as a malevolent "regime" rather than a people consisting of human beings (Klein, 2009).

Iran achieves its aim of delegitimising Israel by anchoring it to social representations of colonialism in political rhetoric. This is particularly evident in the Friday sermons delivered by the upper echelons of the theocratic political establishment (Shahvar, 2009). Similarly, in the corpus, the inhabitants of Israel are represented as (Zionist) colonisers or occupiers:

6. Some American journalists said that these Zionists who come from all over the world should go back to their origins and not stay in Palestine.[10]

As highlighted above, articles in the corpus rarely acknowledge the inhabitants or citizens of Israel. When implicitly acknowledged, as in extract 6, they are anchored to Zionist ideology, which in turn constructs their presence in "Palestine" as a colonial occupation. This extract delegitimises "these Zionists" by representing them as a foreign presence in Palestine "from all over the world", that is, they are not "indigenous" to Palestine and hence have no right to be there. Extract 1 attests to the emerging social representation that the notion of a "Jewish state" is flawed due to the "serious disagreements" concerning the definition of Jewishness. Similarly, this extract implicitly draws on this representation by delegitimising any *Jewish* claim to Israel in the first place – the historical Jewish connection to Israel is simply not acknowledged (Webman, 2010). Conversely, Israelis are constructed as individuals "from all over the world" who "should go back to their origins". Crucially, their *Jewish* origins are not deemed to constitute sufficient cause for settlement in Israel. It is noteworthy that, by naming the territory "Palestine" and resisting social representations of Israeli statehood, articles in the corpus are able to delegitimise Israel rhetorically.

In addition to denying any Jewish connection to Israel, there is a misrepresentation of the demographic distribution of Israel, which serves to

---

9   Iran calls for massive turn out on International Qods Day, *Tehran Times*, 24 August 2011.

10   "West intends to grab MENA resources", *Press TV*, 19 September 2011.

rhetorically racialise the Israeli-Palestinian conflict and further delegitimise the Jewish State:

> 7. How could the Palestinians be called terrorists in their own land when they are fighting a foreign occupation by some Ashkenazi Zionist Jews from Europe?[11]

As in extract 6, the presence of Jews in Israel is represented as a "foreign occupation". Here, the "origins" of these occupiers are said to be "Ashkenazi" and "from Europe". This statement is erroneous given that over 50 per cent of Israelis are in fact of (non-European) Mizrahi or Sephardic background.[12] However, its invocation here contributes to the social representation that Israel constitutes an illegitimate, *racist* occupation of Palestine, due to the implicit anchoring of Israeli occupation to historical *European* colonial policies. There is an implicit racialisation of the Israeli-Palestinian conflict by referring to it as one between Palestinians, the "legitimate" inhabitants of Palestine, and (White) "Ashkenazi Zionist Jews from Europe". Race is strategically deployed to further divide and delineate the inhabitants of Israel (see Richardson, 2004 for an example of how the press deploys the construct of "race" in relation to Islam.). It is against this backdrop of constructed occupation that the article implicitly rationalises Palestinian attacks (against civilians) in Israel. Extract 7 contests the social representation that Palestinian perpetrators of attacks against civilians are terrorists by constructing them as "fighting a foreign occupation ... in their own land". This reflects the common "terrorist versus freedom fighter" dichotomy in political discourse (Halmari, 1993).

Many articles in the corpus referred to an Israeli occupation of Palestinian land, although it was sometimes unclear whether "occupied territory" referred to the West Bank (which indeed is recognised by the UN as an occupation) or to the State of Israel (which the Iranian government regards as "occupied Palestine"). However, the following extract clearly represents the *entire* State of Israel as "occupied Palestine".

> 8. The recent massive demonstrations in occupied Palestine are regarded as public protest against the economic situation and unemployment[13]

Referring to the widespread protests against the rising costs of living in Israel, the extract expressed *Israeli* public protest against a domestic issue as "demonstrations

---

11   Palestinians should not negotiate now!, *Press TV*, 21 September 2011.

12   Central Bureau of Statistics, Government of Israel, Statistical Abstract of Israel 2009, no. 60, Subject 2, Table no. 24 http://www.cbs.gov.il/reader/shnaton/templ_shnaton_e.html?num_tab=st02_24x&CYear=2009

13   Demos are a sign of the decline of Israel's regional influence, *Tehran Times*, 8 August 2011.

in occupied Palestine". The newspapers consistently resisted social representations of statehood and thereby downplayed the existence of the *people* of Israel vis-à-vis the "Zionist regime". When citizens of Israel were mentioned, they tended to be politicised in terms of "Zionists". Yet, this particular article did refer to the popular protests of the *Israeli people*, which acknowledged the reality that Israeli citizens exist, live in Israel and participate in public protests against their government. However, it seemed that this story was covered in accordance with the dominant ideology of the Islamic Republic of Iran, which officially regards the whole State of Israel as "occupied Palestine", by anchoring the Israeli protestors to occupation and colonialism. This represents the people of Israel as occupiers, rather than legitimate citizens.

In addition to the particular categories employed in order to refer to the State of Israel, articles objectified the "regime" in terms of a tangible, malevolent and threatening entity.

9. The regime is a cancerous tumor that will metastasize if even a small part of it remains on Palestinian soil[14]

Political rhetoric in the Islamic Republic tends to construct the State of Israel in terms of a threat to Iran, to Muslims and even to the West (Jaspal, 2013a). Extract 7 evoked imagery of threat by objectifying the State of Israel in terms of a "cancerous tumor". Objectification in this way served to construct what was already represented as an authoritarian regime as a *growing* threat in need of immediate attention. The metaphor of a "cancerous tumor" was effective in creating a sense of mortal threat, on the one hand, since cancerous tumours actively undermine human life, as well as a sense of urgency, given the proclivity of malignant tumours to metastasise, posing a mortal threat to the victim. Incidentally, the extract explicitly employed the verb "metastasize", which forms part of the semantic field of cancer.

Crucially, Israel was constructed in terms of an inanimate, dehumanised entity which threatens its host, namely the Palestinians. Here too stereotypical power differentials between the Israelis and Palestinians were reproduced in order to construct Israel as an authoritarian, malevolent regime, on the one hand, and the Palestinians as the perpetual victims of this mortal threat, on the other. Anchoring Israel to malevolence and threat, and the Palestinians to the position of victimhood, reproduced these stereotypical power relations. Furthermore, the objectification of Israel in terms of an inanimate, yet authoritarian entity represented it as threatening and utterly devoid of humanity. The processes of anchoring and objectification collectively served to encourage some form of action against the "regime". This in turn represents Israel as a hybridised, multi-faceted threat. It has been shown how threat representations can be employed to mobilise groups against outgroups (Bar-Tal, 2000; Oren and Bar-Tal, 2014).

---

14   Recognition of Palestinian state not the final step: Ahmadinejad, *Tehran Times*, 26 August 2011.

In addition to delegitimising Israel, articles in the corpus represent Palestine as indivisible and thereby advocate the destruction of Israel:

10. Ayatollah Khamenei [Supreme Leader of Iran] said, "Our declaration is the freedom of Palestine not the freedom of parts of Palestine".[15]
11. Iranian Foreign Minister Ali Akbar Salehi says Iran believes Palestine cannot be partitioned and Palestinians are entitled to the entirety of the Palestinian territories.[16]

In both extracts 10 and 11, there was an explicit rejection of the two-state solution to the Israeli-Palestinian conflict, which was depicted as inconsistent with "the freedom of Palestine". Articles employed the toponym Palestine in order to construct it as the legitimate state vis-à-vis the delegitimised State of Israel. Furthermore, by constructing the Palestinians as being "entitled to the entirety of the Palestinian territories" rather than to "parts of Palestine", these articles represented the two-state solution to the conflict as unjust and illegitimate. In fact, it depicted the existence of Israel as a *violation* of Palestinian rights, thereby bolstering the threat representation. The delegitimisation of Israel in these articles vis-à-vis the legitimisation of Palestine convincingly contested the two-state solution and served to rationalise the dismantlement of Israel.

The delegitimisation of Israel (as an occupation) was employed in order to *legitimise* all forms of Palestinian violence against Israelis, including extreme genocidal measures:

12. "We advise them (the Zionists) to return to their countries as soon as possible if they want to survive", Naqdi [Basij commander] said.[17]

The rhetorical technique of disseminating a social representation through the quotation of a "socially powerful" source has been referred to as strategic quoting (Jaspal, 2011b). Similarly, extract 12 strategically quoted the commander of Iranian Basij organisation, which is a volunteer paramilitary organisation established by the Supreme Leader in 1979 (Abrahamian, 2008). Like extracts 6 and 7, this one constructed the Jewish inhabitants of Israel as "Zionist" foreigners and suggested that they "return to their countries as soon as possible". Furthermore, the commander was strategically quoted as constructing the *survival* of the Zionists (that is, the Jewish inhabitants of Israel) as conditional upon their departure from Palestine. Articles in the corpus rationalised Palestinian violence against Israelis as legitimate action against an "illegitimate Zionist regime". Extract 12 drew upon this social representation by implicitly threatening "the Zionists" with death if

---

15   Leader rejects two-state solution, *Press TV*, 1 October 2011.

16   Palestine cannot be partitioned: IRI, *Press TV*, 18 September 2011.

17   Netanyahu should get prepared for cage trial: Basij commander, *Tehran Times*, 10 August 2011.

they did not vacate Palestine. In short, the delegitimisation of the State of Israel culminated in implicit threats of genocide against the people of Israel.

Delegitimising social representations, which called for the dismantlement of Israel, accentuated the threatening character of Israel.

Constructing Israel as a Threat

Articles in the corpus systematically constructed Israel as posing a threat. There was a delegitimising social representation that the existence of Israel was supported by a threatening global Zionist conspiracy, which was said to exert influence over the internal affairs of Arab and Muslim countries:

13. Iran's ambassador to Syria has said that Israel is meddling in Syria in an attempt to make up for the collapse of its close allies in the region.[18]
14. The global Zionism wants to target other countries after overthrowing the Syrian government.[19]

In extract 13, Israel was represented as "meddling" in the affairs of Syria, which, at the time of writing, was experiencing violent internal unrest, due to widespread popular opposition to almost five decades of Ba'ath Party rule led by the Al-Assad family (Lesch, 2011). Iran regarded Syria as a close ally and was therefore opposed to regime change in that country, although it did support regime change in several other countries involved in the so-called "Arab Spring" (Bauer and Schiller, 2012; Jaspal, 2014c). Indeed, a sizeable number of articles in the corpus expressed unequivocal support of the Al-Assad government.[20] Consequently, political unrest in Syria was attributed to Israeli "meddling", rather than to the political aspirations of the Syrian people. It was anchored to an "illegitimate" state, rendering the conflict a product of "global Zionism", rather than of popular dissatisfaction with the Syrian political system (Jaspal, 2014c). More specifically, articles constructed the unrest in terms of a malicious "plot" by Israel in order to "make up for the collapse of its close allies", referring to the fall of ex-President Hosni Mobarak in Egypt. Extract 14 explicitly referred to "global Zionism" as plotting to overthrow the Syrian government. Moreover, it constructed "global Zionism" as an active *global* threat by attributing agency to the allegedly ubiquitous ideology, that is, it "*wants* to target other countries". Thus, articles represented the world as an unsafe place due to the existence of Israel and constructed Zionism as the root cause of such unrest.

---

18   "Israel meddling in Syria to compensate for fall of allies", *Tehran Times*, 28 August 2011.

19   "Zionism will not stop with Syria unrest", *Press TV*, 7 October 2011.

20   IRI seeking alliance to protect Syria against U.S. meddling, *Tehran Times*, 10 August 2011.

The Iranian press reiterated the social representation that Israel posed a threat to Iran, Muslims and the world as a whole (Litvak, 2006), and Iran was represented as actively unveiling the global Zionist conspiracy:

15. "Fortunately, all efforts and plots by the U.S. and the Zionist regime have failed and the resistance movement is in a good situation in the region. Iran has played an important role in foiling these conspiracies", Lahoud [former Lebanese president] told Iran's ambassador to Beirut.[21]
16. The move [to hold an international conference in support of Palestinians' rights] has greatly helped thwart the U.S. and Israel plots aimed at creating friction among regional countries.[22]

In both extracts, the "Zionist regime" was implicated, alongside the U.S., in "creating friction among regional countries". These were described as "plots", which evoked imagery of a malevolent conspiracy. Interestingly, articles in the corpus emphasised Iran's role in "foiling these conspiracies". This distanced the statements from Iranian sources but rather to an apparently "objective" third party, namely the former Lebanese president. Similarly, in extract 16, Iran's decision to host an international conference in support of Palestinians rights was said to "thwart" U.S. and Israeli plots. This further accentuated the role of Iran in mitigating the so-called global Zionist conspiracy.

Throughout the corpus, there was a clear emphasis of the "global" character of the Zionist conspiracy. Powerful Western countries, such as Britain and the U.S. were represented as being "dependent on the Zionist lobby":

17. Britain bows to Zionist lobbies. The British government seems to be risking its independence from Zionist lobbies after its recent moves to protect Israeli war crimes suspects from prosecution and boycott a UN anti-racism conference that could lead to the condemnation of the regime.[23]

In extract 17, Britain was said to be subservient to "Zionist lobbies". The metaphor of "bow[ing]" represented the "Zionist lobbies" in regal terms as a "ruler". More specifically, the British government's subservience to Zionism was exemplified by its decisions (i) to withdraw from the UN anti-racism conference, which was regarded by several countries as in fact constituting a co-ordinated smear campaign against the State of Israel, and (ii) to amend legislation which could permit the arrest of former Israeli Minister of Foreign Affairs Tzipi Livni for "war crimes". These controversial decisions and Britain's alleged refusal to condemn the Israeli "regime" were presented as evidence for Britain's subservience to

---

21   'IRI plays important role in foiling evil plots in region': Emile Lahoud, *Tehran Times*, 19 July 2011.

22   *Idem.*

23   Britain bows to Zionist lobbies, *Press TV*, 17 September 2011.

Zionism. The extract problematised the sovereignty of Britain over its internal affairs and politics by highlighting that it was "risking its independence from Zionist lobbies", thereby representing it as *dependent* upon Zionism and not truly an independent, sovereign state.

Similarly, articles in the corpus represented the U.S. as dependent upon Zionism:

18. "US deeply dependent on Zionist lobby"[24]
19. Israel reigns over US polity … It is very clear that news media is quite complacent in this whole situation that is going on with the international bankers and with the Zionist lobby, the very people who control American domestic and foreign policy.[25]

In these extracts, Zionism was said to be in control of "US polity". In extract 19, the metaphor of "reign[ing]" represents Israel (the objectification of global Zionism) in regal terms. Key institutions in the US such as the media and banking sector were represented as being "quite complacent" in the Zionist lobby's alleged control of US polity. Moreover, Zionism was said to exert control over US policy, which resulted in the country's dependence upon Zionism. Collectively, these assertions attested to the social representation of a threatening global Zionist conspiracy, which extended well beyond the geographical boundaries of Israel. This social representation was reproduced in order to explicate implicitly the allegedly pro-Israeli decisions taken by both the US and UK governments. Although several articles in the corpus constructed and disseminated social representations of global Zionist control of world governments, they were reminiscent of longstanding antisemitic social representations of Jewish world domination (Herf, 2006; Shahvar, 2006). In short, by drawing upon antisemitic imagery, several articles represented Zionism as a threat which deprived other countries of their independence.

In fact, there was explicit invocation of *Jewish* control of the "American political scene", highlighting social representational conflation of Zionist *and* Jewish conspiracies:

20. The only visible reason that I can see in the American political scene is the unequivocal control of the one per cent of the population, namely the Zionist Jews (mostly with dual citizenship) in the US, who control the key echelons of power (media, banks and politicians) in the US.[26]
21. Dankof [Mark Dankof, former US Senate candidate]: "There is an issue here that involves Jewish control of the news media, Jewish control of the American political process, disproportionate Jewish control of

24   "US deeply dependent on Zionist lobby", *Press TV*, 3 October 2011.
25   "Israel reigns over US polity", *Press TV*, 7 October 2011.
26   Palestinians should not negotiate now!, *Press TV*, 21 September 2011.

the international banking system ... and an Israel-driven American foreign policy"[27]

Articles in the corpus reproduced antisemitic social representations of Jewish world domination, which were pervasive during the Nazi era and particularly observable in notorious antisemitic Nazi propaganda (see Herf, 2006). Extract 20 represented the Jewish population of the US as Zionists, essentially conflating the two constructs and portraying them as intertwined. The extract provided subordinate, yet superfluous information of little relevance to the report itself, in order to confirm and contribute to negative social representations of the stigmatised Jewish "Other" (van Dijk, 1993). More specifically, it was noted that "Zionist Jews" in the US "mostly" have dual citizenship, evoking imagery of a "split" national loyalty of Zionist Jews. There was a suggestion that, despite their minority status, Jews exerted disproportionately high influence over US affairs, which served to accentuate the social representation that Jews "control the key echelons of power" in the US.

Both extracts 20 and 21 represented Jews as possessing disproportionate institutional control and as abusing this power in order to construct "an Israel-driven American foreign policy". There was an overarching allegation of corruption, since Jews were said to control "media, banks and politicians" – not just to influence but to *control*. Mark Dankof, who was described as a "former US Senate candidate", was strategically quoted as highlighting Jewish control of key US institutions. By accentuating the US identity of the speaker, the article sought to distance the statement from the Iranian ingroup and to attribute it to the US.[28] The technique of strategic quoting might serve to distance these clearly antisemitic remarks from Iran, and construct the Iran-owned outlet as merely showcasing the remarks of a "credible" source. This constituted an important rhetorical strategy given that Iran (and indeed, its media) has been accused of antisemitism, which it denies, claiming that it is anti-Zionist, not antisemitic (Jaspal, 2013a; Litvak, 2006).

In short, articles in the corpus seem to draw upon longstanding antisemitic social representations of Jewish world domination, in order to substantiate polemic representations concerning the threat of a global Zionist conspiracy. In many cases, the representations themselves remained the same – the only apparent difference was the superficial categorical shift from "Jew" to "Zionist". Yet, as exemplified by extracts 20 and 21, antisemitism *did* constitute a feature of Iranian media representations of Israel.

In addition to accentuating the social representation of a threatening global conspiracy, articles in the corpus represented Israel as a threat by anchoring it to terrorism. In this context, anchoring constructed Israel as responsible for

---

27   "Israel reigns over US polity", *Press TV*, 7 October 2011.

28   "IRI plays important role in foiling evil plots in region": Emile Lahoud, *Tehran Times*, 19 July 2011.

domestic "terrorist attacks" in the absence of any legal evidence (Moscovici and Hewstone, 1983):

22. MP Kazem Jalali of the Majlis National Security and Foreign Policy Committee has also said that the assassination was an indiscriminate terrorist operation, adding that the Iranian nation knows that the Zionist regime … is behind these terrorist attacks … The Zionist regime and the U.S. are the axis of terrorism in the world[29]

The article described the assassination of the Iranian nuclear scientist in terms of an "indiscriminate terrorist operation", which represented Israel as a threat with the intention to harm *indiscriminately* the Iranian nation. This performed a "collectivising" function by constructing the assassination of one individual as jeopardising the nation as a whole. Moreover, this event was invoked in order to argue that the Israel formed part of "the axis of terrorism in the world". In short, Israel is represented as *leading* global terrorism.

In the absence of any objective evidence to link Israel to the assassination, the article attributed this accusation to the political figure MP Kazem Jalali, whose membership in a security and foreign policy governmental organisation was emphasised. This was intended to attribute credibility to the speaker, in order to disseminate the social representation of Israel's culpability. This rhetorical technique of disseminating a social representation through the quotation of a "socially powerful" source has been referred to as strategic quoting (Jaspal, 2011b). Indeed, powerful individuals such as politicians and "experts" usually have clout in disseminating social representations (Breakwell, 2001). This polemic representation was further reiterated not only through strategic quoting but also by constructing this knowledge as commonsensical. The Iranian people, that is, the *people* of Iran, were said to be aware of the culpability of Israel. Thus, this polemic representation was hegemonised through its attribution to the general population, rather than to the Iranian government.

Furthermore, even before the trial of the suspect arrested in connection with the assassination, articles in the corpus assured readers of Israel's certain involvement:

23. The trial [of Ali Jamali-Fashi who was accused of assassinating a nuclear physicist] will shed light on the Zionist regime's involvement in terrorist attacks against the Iranian people[30]

Use of the future tense "will", rather than the more tentative auxiliary verb "may", further hegemonised the representation. The extract clearly represented Israel

---

29   Assassination of Iranian academic is a U.S.-Israeli plot: officials, *Tehran Times*, 24 July 2011.

30   Ali-Mohammadi assassin will stand trial today: Tehran prosecutor, *Tehran Times*, 22 August 2011.

as a terrorist entity by constructing its alleged involvement in the assassination as an act of terror *against the Iranian people*, rather than against the Iranian nuclear programme, the government or a particular individual. Thus, the threat was collectivised to the entire nation (Jaspal and Nerlich, 2014). This polemic representation was juxtaposed with and supported by the more established representation (in the Arab world) of Israeli terrorism against the Palestinian *people*:

24. The Zionist regime's terrorist action against the defenseless and innocent Palestinians was an attempt to shift focus away from its internal problems just ahead of the International Qods Day[31]

Extract 24 made clear reference to the hegemonic representation of Palestinian victimhood in order to represent Israel as a terrorist entity. The "de-populated" and dehumanised "Zionist regime" was positioned as the aggressor, while the Palestinians were positioned as their victims. In short, the observations that Israel launched attacks against Iranians *and* the "defenseless and innocent Palestinians" contributed to the overarching social representation that Israel posed a threat. As exemplified by extract 24, articles elaborated this representation by alluding to the reasons allegedly underlying Israel's actions; this was frequently attributed to Israel's desire to "shift focus away from its internal problems". Thus, while the articles represented Israel as a threat and terrorist entity, it was simultaneously implied that Israel was inherently weak and on the verge of destruction due to its "illegitimacy" (Jaspal, 2014d).

In one article, the political ideology of Zionism, which dominated imagery of Israel in Iranian political and media representations, was explicitly anchored to terrorism, further constructing Israel as a threatening terrorist entity:

25. Norway mass killer is pro-Zionist ... Anders Behring Breivik, who killed at least 93 people in a bomb attack and shooting rampage in Norway, has claimed he is pro-Zionist[32]

These outlets very scantily covered the terrorist attacks perpetrated in Norway. As shown in extract 25, these attacks were implicitly attributed to the (irrelevant) political ideology of Zionism. Indeed, van Dijk (1993) discusses the rhetorical strategy of "overcompleteness/irrelevance", whereby newspaper discourse provides subordinate, yet superfluous information of little relevance to the report itself, in order to confirm and contribute to negative social representations of the stigmatised "Other". Breivik has most commonly been associated with extreme right-wing extremism and ultra-nationalism. However, these ideologies were not mentioned in the article. Rather, the role of Zionism was accentuated, which

---

31   Iran denounces Israeli air strikes on Palestinians, *Tehran Times*, 20 August 2011.
32   Norway mass killer, *Tehran Times*, 25 July 2011.

implied that Breivik's adherence to this political ideology might somehow explain his terrorist actions. The categories "terrorist"/"mass killer" and "pro-Zionist" were rhetorically entwined, establishing social representational linkage between them. This contributed to the social representation of Israel as a threatening terrorist entity by normalising the links between the practice of mass killing and the ideology of Zionism. This polemic representation must be examined within the context of existing social representations that Israel has perpetrated deadly attacks against the Palestinians, resulting in "massacres" (Litvak, 2006). In short, Breivik's "pro-Zionist" stance was implicitly constructed as the underlying cause of his terrorist actions.

Constructing National Agency in Global Anti-Zionism

The corpora of newspaper articles clearly attested to the overarching social representation that Israel posed a global threat. Consistent with Identity Process Theory, which argues that human beings respond to threat by deploying coping strategies, there was an emerging social representation in the corpus that the Islamic Republic of Iran would valiantly lead the global anti-Zionism campaign to defeat this threat:

> 26. "Iran sees any act against Hezbollah, Hamas as a threat to its interests ... The world's people should know that today the positions of Hezbollah in Lebanon and Hamas in Palestine are considered as Iran's 'border' with Israel"[33]

In extract 26, the Lebanese Shiite Muslim movement Hezbollah and the Palestinian Islamist organisation Hamas were constructed as being the protégés of Iran, which in turn viewed any act against these organisations as "a threat to its interests". Given that these organisations were pervasively represented as constituting the "Islamic resistance" against Israel (Takeyh, 2006), Iran as their prime supporter was elevated to a position of leadership in this anti-Zionist "struggle". The article proceeded to define the Hamas and Hezbollah "positions" as "Iran's 'border' with Israel", essentially obscuring national boundaries delineating Iran, Lebanon and the Palestinian Territories. Indeed, it has been observed that the Israeli-Arab conflict is Islamicised as a conflict between Zionism and the global Islamic Ummah (Jaspal, 2014d; Litvak, 1998). Despite never having engaged in an armed conflict with the State of Israel, Iran was represented as a primary stakeholder in the conflict and as *leading* the "resistance movement" more commonly associated with Hezbollah and Hamas.

---

33 "IRI sees any act against Hezbollah, Hamas as threat to its interests", *Tehran Times*, 26 August 2011.

Similarly, articles in the corpus represented Iran as leading the *ideological* dimension of the Islamic resistance by organising the International Conference on the Palestinian Intifada, for example:

27. Iran intifada confab to host 70 states. 70 countries are attending[34]

Articles highlighted the centrality of Iran in organising the conference. Extract 27 depicted Iran as leading an increasingly global anti-Zionism, which was implied by the large number of countries attending the conference. This was consistent with the notion that Iran, and its channels of societal information, were keen to construct their anti-Zionist stance as a global and ubiquitous one, shared by many other countries.

This sense of self-inclusion and leadership in a *global* anti-Zionism was juxtaposed with more aggressive social representations of Iran's role in *defeating* Israel:

28. Ayatollah Mahdavi Kani said that Iranian nation has isolated the Zionist regime in the international arena and tightened the noose around it.[35]

According to articles in the corpus, anti-Zionist events such as the International Conference on the Palestinian Intifada and the International Quds Day exemplified how the "Iranian nation has isolated the Zionist regime in the international arena". Extract 28 clearly attributed the isolation of Israel to the efforts of Iran. Crucially, this is constructed as a struggle between the *people* of Iran and an inanimate, inhumane and militarised "Zionist regime" which further popularised anti-Zionism, distancing it from the confines of Iran's political establishment.

Articles in the corpus actively encouraged the social representation that the entire world, not only the Arab world, was becoming increasingly opposed to Zionism:

29. Today Palestine has the support of not only its Arab neighbors but many other countries of the world and Israel has more enemies than it had sixty years back [sic], for example its neighbor Egypt which was an ally till yesterday is now a sworn enemy of the Zionist regime.[36]
30. Governments that allow Zionist embassies to be set up must be reprimand [sic].[37]

---

34   IRI intifada confab to host 70 states, *Press TV*, 27 September 2011.

35   IRI calls for massive turnout on International Qods Day, *Tehran Times*, 24 August 2011.

36   Unholy acts committed in the Holy Land, *Press TV*, 30 September 2011.

37   "Islamic Awakening deposed dictators", *Press TV*, 16 September 2011.

Extract 29 constructed Palestine as a widely supported "state", particularly by its Arab neighbours, while Israel was depicted as gradually losing the allegedly little support it originally had. The extract erroneously highlighted that "Israel has more enemies than it had sixty years back [sic]" and proceeded to cite Egypt as "a sworn enemy of the Zionist regime". It is noteworthy that 60 years ago neither Jordan nor Egypt had diplomatic relations with the State of Israel but, at the time of writing, these countries maintained diplomatic relations. The article appeared to make reference to the popular storming of the Israeli embassy in Cairo in September 2011[38], which was provided as evidence that Egypt was "now a sworn enemy". The provision of inaccurate information was clearly intended to accentuate the Iranian-driven anti-Zionist agenda by demonstrating that anti-Zionism was increasingly pervasive in the world. In addition to the construction of a pervasive global anti-Zionism, articles in the corpus represented any implicit support for Zionism as reproachable, as exemplified by extract 30. This is consistent with the observation that any support for Israel, in whatever guise, is constructed as un-Islamic (Jaspal, 2014d; Litvak, 1998).

The anti-Zionist stance of Iran was optimistically represented as successful in its goal to eradicate Israel:

31. "Some governments proposed the historical tactic of the formation of a Palestinian government in order to buy time for saving the Zionist regime [of Israel]", [Iranian] President Mahmoud Ahmadinejad said. "But this tactic will not be able to save Israel … The Middle East region will not integrate the unseemly patch that is the Zionist regime [of Israel] and will reject it"[39]

In extract 31, the strategic quote from President Mahmoud Ahmadinejad represented the two-state solution to the Israeli-Palestinian conflict as a "historical tactic" of Western governments, rather than as the stated policy of the Palestinian Authority (Parsons, 2005). The Palestinian statehood bid (based on the pre-1967 borders), which was in fact initiated by the Palestinian Authority and opposed by the United States, was thereby represented as part of this tactic. By attributing this to these governments and distancing it from the Palestinian Authority, the internationally recognised representative of the Palestinian people, the extract represented the statehood bid as a malicious attempt to "buy time for saving the Zionist regime". Israel was optimistically represented as being in danger of extinction beyond recourse. It was argued that collective rejection of Israel would lead to its demise:

---

38   Israel seeks calm with Egypt after embassy storming. *The Telegraph*, 11 September 2011.

39   IRI says Middle East will reject Israel, *Press TV*, 25 September 2011.

32. Today, the Zionist regime is at its weakest in history. Therefore, the West including the United States and Europe are offering various plans to protect this fake regime", he [Hossein Sheikholeslam, Secretary of the International Conference on the Palestinian Intifada] added.[40]

33. He [Parliament Speaker Ali Larijani] added, "Now that the ground has been prepared for defending the oppressed Palestinian nation, the Zionist regime is suffering horrendous hallucinations about its existence, so is even scared of its own shadow".[41]

In extract 32, the secretary of the International Conference on the Intifada was strategically quoted as optimistically positioning the "Zionist regime ... at its weakest in history", which represented the Iran's anti-Zionist policy as having its intended effect. Similarly, in extract 33, Israel was metaphorically depicted as "suffering horrendous hallucinations about its existence", which would lead to its demise. This was further accentuated through the metaphorical objectification of Israel being "scared of its own shadow". Similarly, in some articles, this sense of fear has been cited as an explanation for Israel's alleged engagement in "terrorism" against Iran.[42] In short, Iran was represented as being successful and efficacious in its longstanding commitment to "defending" the Palestinians, that is, by advocating a fervent anti-Zionist ideology and exporting it beyond the borders of Iran.

Articles in the corpus legitimised Iran's anti-Zionist policy by constructing Israel as a threat to the Palestinians. However, anti-Zionism was also depicted as an Islamic "duty", particularly as Zionism was said to pose a hybridised threat to Islam, both to the Islamic "worldview" and to the survival of Muslims (Jaspal and Cinnirella, 2010):

34. Israelis burn mosque, Qur'ans ... Numerous copies of the holy Qur'an were also burnt[43]

35. The Israeli regime has demolished a mosque near Tubas in the West Bank ... This is the third mosque demolished by forces of the Israeli regime[44]

36. Sadr [Second Deputy Speaker of the Iranian Parliament] added that the Zionist regime is spending massively to instigate turmoil and insecurity in Muslim Syria[45]

---

40   IRI intifada confab to host 70 states, *Press TV*, 27 September 2011.

41   "Israeli interception of Gaza aid ship, a political ignominy", *Tehran Times*, 20 July 2011.

42   IRI calls for massive turnout on International Qods Day, *Tehran Times*, 24 August 2011.

43   Israelis burn mosque, Qur'ans, *Press TV*, 3 October 2011.

44   Israel razes mosque in West Bank, *Press TV*, 11 October 2011.

45   "Zionism with not stop with Syria unrest", *Press TV*, 7 October 2011.

Extract 34 attributed arson attacks against a mosque to Israelis in general, rather than to any particular subgroup, such as Jewish settlers in the West Bank, for instance. This is analogous to the observation that Western newspapers frequently attribute global terrorism to Muslims in general (Jaspal and Cinnirella, 2010), which can anchor Islam to terrorism (Cinnirella, 2014). In this case, the national category Israeli was anchored to attacks against Islam. Having attributed these attacks to Israelis in general, the article proceeded to explain that the Islamic Qur'an was also burnt. Similarly, extract 35 constructed Israel as a threat to Islam by highlighting a series of Israeli-led demolitions. Use of the verb "raze" in the title of the article constructed this as a complete destruction, further accentuating the threat allegedly posed by the Israel. The acts of burning and destroying Islamic places of worship and the Islamic Holy Book constructed the seldom-mentioned *Israeli people*, as well as their state, as posing a hybridised threat to Islam. Extract 36 depicted Israel as resourceful in its attempt to "instigate turmoil and insecurity" in *Muslim* land. This is consistent with the representation that Israel is malevolent and committed to the destruction of Islam (Klein, 2009). Crucially, this was constructed as *Zionist* aggression against a *Muslim* country, which represented Israel as a threat to Muslims.

Articles explicitly linked the social representation of Israel as a hybridised threat to Islam with the emancipated representation that Muslims should collectively mobilise against Israel:

37. Jalili [Secretary of Iran's Supreme National Security Council] said the liberation of Palestine could serve as the unifying point of Islamic Awakening movements in different countries and could … restore the rights which have been downtrodden by the Zionist regime[46]
38. [Iran's Deputy Defence Minister Vahidi stated that]"It seems as if the second wave of Islamic Awakening in … the fight against the Zionist regime (of Israel) is starting to reveal itself … This awakening will remove all obstacles from its way, and this anti-Zionist wake will take form in other Muslim countries"[47]

Although extract 37 referred to Israeli injustices in the Israeli-Palestinian conflict, the implications of these injustices were generalised to the Islamic Ummah. The extract constructed Israel as deliberately curtailing the rights of the Palestinians, which reiterated the threatening nature of Israel. Social action against the "tyranny" of Israel and, more specifically, "the liberation of Palestine" were represented as the "unifying point of the Islamic Awakening", that is, an ideological tenet linking Islamic Ummah (Jaspal, 2014d). Both extracts 37 and 38 described what has been referred to as the "Arab Spring" as the "Islamic Awakening", that is, they Islamicised the political unrest in Arab countries. In short, there was a sense

---

46   "US deeply dependent on Zionist lobby", *Press TV*, 3 October 2011.
47   Second Islamic Awakening on horizon, *Press TV*, 17 September 2011.

that mobilisation against Israel and commitment to its destruction (implied by the "liberation of Palestine") constituted a pan-Islamic duty. Similarly, in extract 38, anti-Zionism was depicted as central to the Islamic Awakening.

The Ministry of Culture and Islamic Guidance was strategically quoted in order to represent the issue of Palestine as a key *Islamic* concern:

> 39. Iran's Ministry of Culture and Islamic Guidance has released a multimedia CD on Zionism in Tehran ... "Palestine is the main issue of the Islamic world and we could not be indifferent to the 60 years of tyranny perpetrated by the Zionists", Hosseini [the Iranian Culture Minister] mentioned.[48]

In extract 39, anti-Zionism was constructed as a cultural and, more specifically, an *Islamic* concern, given that Iran's Ministry of Culture and Islamic Guidance produced a CD on Zionism. Moreover, the Culture Minister was strategically quoted as referring to Palestine as "the main issue of the Islamic world" and as urging Muslims to stand up for the Palestinian cause. The social representation that Zionism posed a tyrannical threat to the Palestinians and Muslims, more generally, was strategically invoked in order to construct the emancipated representation that anti-Zionism constituted a religious duty. The strategic quote depicts anti-Zionism as a core tenet of Islam.

Several articles in the corpus rhetorically accentuated the anti-Zionist tenet of Islam by highlighting the engagement of Islamic countries in the Israeli-Palestinian conflict:

> 40. Muslim nations are now more determined than ever in their efforts to liberate all of the occupied territories, including occupied holy Qods ... International Qods Day is a day of solidarity with Palestine observed on the last Friday of the holy month of Ramadan.[49]
> 41. Ramadan is one of the means for solidarity among Muslims ... we should remember that the Zionist Regime and the United States are the common enemies of all Muslims.[50]

Since the 1979 Islamic Revolution, Iran has accentuated the Islamic aspect of Iranian identity. Thus, Islam is regarded as a key mobilising tenet of Iranian identity. Accordingly, extract 40 constructed anti-Zionism as a Muslim duty. This process of "liberating" Palestine was optimistically represented as being already under way. In extract 40, the need to "liberate" Palestine was clearly anchored to Islamic duty through the "overcompleteness/irrelevance" rhetorical

---

48   Anti-Zionist multimedia CD released in Tehran, *Tehran Times*, 24 August 2011.

49   Iran calls for massive turnout on International Qods Day, *Tehran Times*, 24 August 2011.

50   Iran calls on Arab cineastes to produce films promoting Islamic unity, *Tehran Times*, 07 August 2011.

strategy; articles constructed the "day of solidarity" as an Islamic duty through its anchoring to the "holy month of Ramadan". Similarly, extract 41 explicitly represented anti-Zionism as an important tenet of Islam by designating Israel as a "common" (shared) enemy of all Muslims. The dictum regarding Muslim solidarity implied the necessity for all Muslims to espouse anti-Zionism in order to maintain a unified Islamic stance. In short, these articles represented anti-Zionism as a necessary religious duty for the global Islamic Ummah.

Overview

This chapter provides an analysis of two Iranian news outlets in order to discern how Iran constructs and "exports" its anti-Zionist ideology and outlines the discursive aspects of the delegitimisation process in textual representations of Israel. Consistent with previous research into Iran's position on Israel, these outlets are unanimous in their negativisation of Israel, which is most frequently referred to in terms of a corrupt and illegitimate "regime", rather than a state (Jaspal, 2013c; Klein, 2009). It is noteworthy that these media outlets provide greater "voice" to members of Iranian politico-religious establishment, who would habitually be afforded minimal space in the mainstream Western press.

Collectively, the results of the analysis point to a rhetorical delegitimisation process, which consists of three inter-dependent components. These include: (i) contesting the legitimacy of the Israel; (ii) describing the malevolent processes whereby the Jewish State was established and is currently maintained; (iii) "problem-solving" by demanding the destruction of Israel. The social representation that the Jewish civilian population constitutes a foreign occupation is consistently employed in order to rationalise acts of violence against the Jewish people. A vast number of articles in the corpus reproduce the social representation that there is a global Zionist conspiracy, which culminated in the establishment of the State of Israel and which continues to support it (Mottale, 2011). It is argued that the category "Jew" has superficially shifted to "Zionist" in the Iranian press, but that the core and structure of this delegitimising social representation remain the same, namely that the Jewish Zionist is cunning and threatening. Articles construct the destruction of the "Zionist regime" as imminent and necessary in order to solve the multiple dangers said to be posed by Israel, including world domination, terrorism against Iran and genocide against the Palestinians. By reproducing these delegitimising representations in the English-language press, Iran exports anti-Zionist ideology to an international readership evoking global sympathy for the destruction of the one and only Jewish State. The next chapter illustrates how anti-Zionism, with a more clearly discernible antisemitic face, unfolds in visual representations.

Chapter 6
Visualising the Holocaust:
Iran's Holocaust Cartoon Contest[1]

Introduction

Political cartoons have long been a vehicle for promoting antisemitism and, more recently, anti-Zionism. In addition to existing work on antisemitic cartoon depictions in Europe (Kotek, 2009; Vincze, 2013), there has been some important research into visual depictions of Jews and Israel in the Middle East (Kotek, 2009; Smith, 2012; Stav, 1999). Long-standing antisemitic myths are often represented in cartoon format in order to shape people's perceptions of Israel – they tend to emphasise the "evil" of Jews and the "conspiratorial" nature of Israel, often conflating the two categories. Such cartoons can validate and promote antisemitism and are sometimes intended to justify draconian measures against Jews and the Jewish State. In addition to exploiting the media as a communicator of its anti-Zionist ideology, the Islamic Republic of Iran makes full use of political cartoons in order to delegitimise and demonise Israel. This was compellingly demonstrated in the Iranian government-endorsed International Holocaust Cartoon Contest in 2006.

As a response to the Danish cartoons controversy in 2005, which depicted the Prophet Mohammed in demeaning ways (Hussain, 2007), the Iranian newspaper *Hamshahri*, which is owned by the Tehran Municipality, sponsored The International Holocaust Cartoon Contest. Submissions to the competition came from a number of countries (see Figure 6.1).

The stated aim of the contest was to denounce "Western hypocrisy on freedom of speech" in reference to the West's response to the Danish Cartoon Controversy. The organisers claimed that the Holocaust Cartoon Contest would challenge the boundaries of the Western notion of freedom of speech by problematising mainstream representations of the Holocaust. Although the stated aim was to reiterate opposition to Zionism and to the State of Israel, the contest clearly exhibited the Iranian regime's antisemitic orientation and its willingness to employ overt antisemitism as a vehicle for promoting its anti-Zionist agenda. Indeed, the contest was endorsed by Iranian officials, including Iran's Culture Ministry.[2]

---

1 This chapter is based upon a previously published article: Jaspal, R. (2014). Delegitimizing Jews and Israel in Iran's International Holocaust Cartoon Contest. *Journal of Modern Jewish Studies*, *13*(2), 167–89. It is used here with the permission of that journal.

2 Anti-Defamation League website http://archive.adl.org/main_arab_world/cartoon_contest.html#.UxI4n3lQN6k.

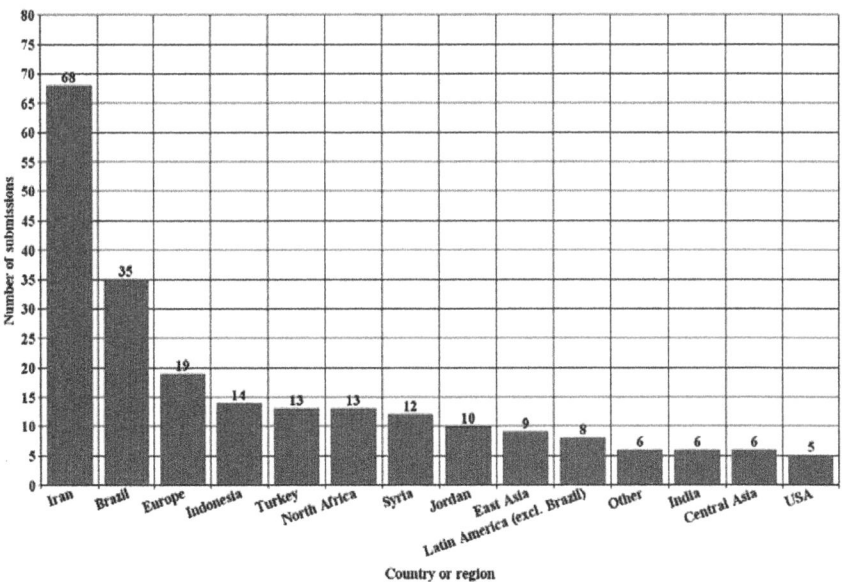

**Figure 6.1		Contributors to the 2006 International Holocaust Cartoon Competition**

Given the social and political importance of the Holocaust Cartoon Contest and the general clout that visual representations can have in shaping public opinion, political views and intergroup relations (Bounegru and Forceville, 2011), this chapter focuses on the 2006 contest as a case study for examining antisemitic and anti-Zionist social representations and patterns of delegitimisation and demonisation in the Islamic Republic. The contest is one of the many ways in which the Iranian regime has sought to disseminate its anti-Zionist ideology (Jaspal, 2013a), but provides unique insight into the overtly antisemitic aspects of this ideology. The chapter begins with a methodological overview of the visual thematic analysis of the cartoons submitted to the contest. Then, the following three superordinate themes, which emerged from the analysis, are outlined and discussed: (i) Constructing the "Evil Jew" and "Bloodthirsty Israel"; (ii) Palestinian Suffering as the 'Real' Holocaust; and (iii) Nazi-Zionism as an International Conspiracy.

Methodological overview

All 227 cartoon submissions to the Holocaust Cartoon Contest are available to download on the Irancartoon Web Gallery website.[3] The 227 cartoons were analysed using qualitative thematic analysis, which has been described as "a method for identifying, analysing and reporting patterns (themes) within data"

3		http://www.irancartoon.ir/gallery/album48

(Braun and Clarke, 2006, p.78). These patterns of meaning are represented as "themes". While thematic analysis has typically been employed in the analysis of textual data (see Part IV of this book), this study applies the method to the analysis of *visual* representations in order to identify social representations of Jews and Israel embodied in cartoons concerning the Holocaust. This approach has been referred to as *visual thematic analysis* (see also Nerlich and Jaspal, 2014).

Thematic analysis was deemed to be advantageous because it can allow the analyst to integrate the micro and macro levels of analysis. For instance, while at the micro level a cartoon may depict a prisoner concentration camp, at a macro level this resonates with imagery of the Holocaust and perhaps genocide, more generally. The aim of the study was to provide a rich thematic description of a relatively small corpus of cartoons, which might elucidate emerging social representations of Jews and Israel. Given the dearth of research into cartoon representations of Jews and Israel, an inductive approach has been adopted whereby the themes are closely linked to the data themselves, and thus data-driven, rather than interpreted through the lens of any pre-existing theory (Patton, 1990).

The analysis focuses upon representations of Jews and Israel in particular, that is, upon (i) the constructed "essence" of Jews and Israel; (ii) their relationships with others (e.g. Palestinians); (iii) historical events associated with Jews and Israel (primarily, the Holocaust). The analytical codes captured the essential qualities of the cartoons, such as *inter alia* the components of each cartoon, its general tone, its potential emotive force, the presence of other groups, and emerging patterns within the data. Subsequently, these codes were collated in order to create overarching themes characterising the corpus of cartoons. Finally, superordinate themes representing the themes derived from the analysis were developed and ordered into a logical and coherent narrative structure. Relevant constructs from Social Representations Theory (such as anchoring and objectification) were drawn upon as a means of theoretically enriching the analysis. All source information regarding the cartoons discussed in the chapter is presented in the footnotes in this chapter.

Constructing the "Evil Jew" and "Bloodthirsty Israel"

Cartoonists construct and conflate images of the "Evil Jew" and "Brutal Israel" in order to construct the social representation that this hybrid "entity" poses a universal threat, that is, to Palestinians, Muslims and the world, more generally.

The cartoons consistently construct Jews in particular as immoral evil beings whose intentions are inherently malevolent. In a cartoon by Abdolhossein Amirizadeh from Iran,[4] the Devil is depicted against a fiery hellish landscape. The figure possesses the physical traits typically attributed to the Devil, such as long and sharp claws, horns, sharp and jagged teeth and pointy ears, but it is also attributed physical traits historically and stereotypically associated with the Jews

---

4   http://www.irancartoon.ir/gallery/album48/Abdolhossein_Amirizadeh_Ira

in antisemitic images, e.g. a long face and a hooked nose (Kotek, 2009; Smith, 2012). The Devil possesses a pitchfork with the Star of David and is depicted as reading a large book entitled "Holocaust" which also displays the Star of David, implying that the Devil is a Jew. Similarly, another cartoon[5] by Majid Salehi from Iran represents a devilish figure brandishing a pitchfork with a menorah, also emphasising the Jewish character of the devilish figure. In two cartoons by Sadik Pala from India, Jews are depicted as parasitical vampire bats, which constituted a prevalent long-standing motif in medieval European antisemitism (Kotek, 2009). In one image,[6] a Jew with sidelocks and a black hat is depicted as a vampire bat with fangs, hanging upside down alongside a real vampire bat. This serves to construct a sense of "natural" solidarity and camaraderie between the vampire Jew and the vampire bat. The vampire Jew foregrounds and presides over Jerusalem – itself represented by a mosque in the background. In the other image,[7] a Jew with sidelocks and a black hat wearing the Star of David is depicted as a vampire with long sharp fangs feeding parasitically on "Palestinian blood". In short, these cartoons anchor Jews to stereotypically evil and parasitic beings.

In addition to embodying evil, Jews are represented as opposing righteousness (Herf, 2006). Alaa Rostam from Syria[8] depicts an obese, menacing-looking Jew with sidelocks wearing a Hasidic black hat on his head and a large weapon on his back. He is represented as drawing a target on the back of an apparently benevolent individual recounting the "truth" of the Holocaust, namely that it never occurred. The constructed aim of the "Evil Jew" is the silencing of this "truth". In another cartoon,[9] Sam Keshmiri from Iran represents a large beast-like figure with sidelocks and a hooked nose next to an angelic child who bleeds, suggesting that the Jewish beast has attacked the child and therefore constitutes the antithesis of the angel, namely evil itself. Similarly, in a caricature by Majid Salehi from Iran,[10] a stereotypically demonic-looking Jew (also with long sidelocks and a hooked nose) who is carrying a briefcase displaying the Israeli flag carries an incapacitated angel tied tightly to his back. In his cartoon,[11] Behnam Bahrami represents an evil devilish figure with red eyes, fangs and pointy ears who is also wearing a Jewish black hat displaying the Star of David. His elongated nose, implicitly attributed to his "lies" about the Holocaust, brutally penetrates a bloodied white dove that was carrying an olive branch. In these cartoons, peace and benevolence (symbolised by the dove and angel, respectively) are brutalised by the hybrid symbol of the "Evil Jew" who is constructed as a threat to peace. These cartoons serve to anchor Judaism to war-mongering.

----

5   http://www.irancartoon.ir/gallery/album48/Majid_Salehi_Iran2

6   http://www.irancartoon.ir/gallery/album48/Sadic_Pala_India_3

7   http://www.irancartoon.ir/gallery/album48/Sadic_Pala_India_2

8   http://www.irancartoon.ir/gallery/album48/Alaa_Rostam_Syria

9   http://www.irancartoon.ir/gallery/album48/Sam_Keshmiri_Iran

10   http://www.irancartoon.ir/gallery/album48/Majid_Salehi_Iran

11   http://www.irancartoon.ir/gallery/album48/Behnam_Bahrami_Iran

Cartoonists make use of existing antisemitic social representations (e.g. that Jews are evil) in order to derogate Israelis (Wistrich, 2005). In a cartoon by Augusto Frank Bier from Brazil,[12] an Israeli soldier on a tank displaying the Star of David is depicted as conversing with the Grim Reaper, the personification of death, who angrily rebukes the Israeli soldier for interfering in "his business", namely death and destruction. Like the "Evil Jew" who causes death and destruction, the State of Israel is depicted as the gasoline which deliberately and callously burns innocent and helpless Lebanese children. This serves to objectify the victim of Jewish-Zionist aggression through the process of personification. Death and destruction are represented as the principal aim of the State of Israel in a cartoon by Carlos Latuff, given that the gasoline bottles displays the flag of Israel and is intended to symbolise the Jewish State.[13] Similarly, in another cartoon by the same artist,[14] former prime minister Ehud Olmert (a personification of the State of Israel) is depicted as a gigantic evil figure towering domineeringly over both Gaza and Lebanon and unleashing devastating bombs single-handedly, causing death and destruction in both territories. In this cartoon, innocent Palestinian and Lebanese civilians are represented as running helplessly for cover from the bombs.

Several cartoonists depict the Palestinian family as the principal and intended victim of Israel, symbolised by the Israeli Defense Forces. For instance, in a cartoon by an anonymous artist from Brazil,[15] a visibly terrified Palestinian family lies embedded within the ground surrounded by Israeli bombs all of which display the Star of David. Their house in the background lies in complete destruction and smoke engulfs the landscape. Furthermore, Miroslaw Hajnos from Poland[16] represents an Israeli soldier as sadistically playing on a seesaw consisting of a plank balanced on a large missile with a terrified Palestinian family. The central theme of the cartoon concerns the sadism of Israel and the enjoyment that its soldiers allegedly derive from terrorising the Palestinians. Consistent with this theme, J Bosco from Brazil produces a cartoon[17] in which an Israeli tank displaying the Star of David as its flag traverses the *Palestinian* landscape (displaying a sign marked "Palestine") and leaves a long trail of human skulls behind it, suggesting the brutality of the Israeli army and the destruction it allegedly leaves behind.

The "Evil Jew" and "Brutal Israel" are depicted as being collectively destructive to Palestine in particular. David Baldinger's cartoon[18] depicts the Star of David (a symbol of both Judaism and Israel) as a shuriken (or throwing star) used to slash and maim Palestine, as suggested by its embedment within a dilapidated wall displaying the Palestinian national flag (symbolising Palestine itself). The

---

12   http://www.irancartoon.ir/gallery/album48/Augusto_Frank_Bier_Brazil_001
13   http://www.irancartoon.ir/gallery/album48/CarlosLatuffBrazil
14   http://www.irancartoon.ir/gallery/album48/CarlosLatuffBrazil2
15   http://www.irancartoon.ir/gallery/album48/Iran3
16   http://www.irancartoon.ir/gallery/album48/Miroslaw_HAJNOS_Poland
17   http://www.irancartoon.ir/gallery/album48/JboscoBrazil_5
18   http://www.irancartoon.ir/gallery/album48/David_Baldinger_usa

wall bleeds and smoke emerges from behind it, suggesting widespread death and destruction in Palestine. Moreover, the consequential suffering of the Palestinians is emphasised (Litvak and Webman, 2009). For instance, in a caricature by Ebrahim Azad from Iran,[19] Palestinians are depicted as being led systematically from a concentration camp (referred to as "Palestine") into an incinerator (caricatured as a Jewish head wearing a black hat with the Star of David). The incinerator excretes human skulls at the other end, which implicitly applies the social representation of the Holocaust to the Palestinian context. In short, the Jewish-Israeli is depicted as perpetrating genocide against the Palestinians. Judaism and Zionism are objectified in terms of violence and deadly phenomena, which provides these religious and political ideologies with a negative psychological tangible essence.

The cartoons construct Israeli brutality as deliberate and calculated (Wistrich, 2005). In a cartoon by Raed Khalil from Syria,[20] grinning, evil-looking Israeli soldiers pose for a photograph next to a dying Palestinian man lying in a pool of blood. The smoke emerging from their weapons suggests that they are responsible for this act of brutality and their grins suggest the calculation and joy with which the act was carried out. The soldiers stand defiantly before the Al-Aqsa Mosque, one of the holiest sites in Islam.

In addition to cartoons depicting the Jew-Zionist as an aggressor against the Palestinians, in particular, often symbolised by a sign "Palestine" or the Palestinian national flag, several images represent the Jew-Zionist as a threat to, or brutaliser of, Muslims more generally. In a cartoon by Djoko Susilo from Indonesia,[21] the Star of David is again depicted as a throwing star which penetrates a crescent (a symbol of Islam) that bleeds. Similarly, images of the victimhood and suffering of Islam and Muslims (implicitly at the hands of the Jew-Zionist) are reiterated in another cartoon[22] of a human eye displaying the crescent (a symbol of Islam) in place of the pupil shedding a single tear. Contributing to the image of an Israeli threat, a cartoon by Raed Khalil from Syria[23] depicts a soldier (wearing the Star of David on his uniform) emerging from a hole and joyfully brandishing his weapon in the vicinity of the Al-Aqsa Mosque, which is barely visible behind explosions, debris and smoke. This serves to attribute the destruction of one of the holiest sites in Islam to the Israeli army. Furthermore, there is an implicit anchoring of the Israeli-Palestinian conflict to historical religious conflict between Jews and Muslims – this has performed an important mobilising function in Arab/Iranian anti-Zionist discourse (Jaspal, 2013a, 2013c; Litvak, 1998).

While Israel is habitually represented as brutalising the Palestinians and threatening Islam, some cartoons depict Israel as posing a threat to the world as a

---

19   http://www.irancartoon.ir/gallery/album48/Ebrahim_Azad_Iran
20   http://www.irancartoon.ir/gallery/album48/Raed_Khalil_Syriaz_2
21   http://www.irancartoon.ir/gallery/album48/Djoko_Susilo_2
22   http://www.irancartoon.ir/gallery/album48/Eliene_Lopez_de_Souza_Brazi
23   http://www.irancartoon.ir/gallery/album48/Raed_Khalil_Syriaz_3

whole (Herf, 2006). For instance, one cartoon[24] depicts the word "Israel" and replaces the final "l" with a large boot trampling on the globe. The globe is represented as falling victim to Israel, an allegedly threatening and brutal entity. Similarly, this threat is reiterated in an image by Nedal Ali Deep from Syria[25] which represents Israel/Jews as an aggressive and malevolent dog with a demonic face barking viciously at a personification of the world, which attempts to appease the vicious dog with a piece of meat (displaying "Palestine"). In short, the ultimate target of the vicious dog (in this context, a metaphor for Jews/Israel) is the whole world, rather than Palestine specifically – Palestine is merely a means of appeasing the Jew-Zionist who allegedly seeks to usurp the world. The construction of the world as the ultimate target serves to crystallise and accentuate the social representation of the Jew-Zionist as posing a threat (as demonstrated in Chapter 5 of this volume).

Palestinian Suffering as the "Real" Holocaust

Cartoonists contest what are regarded in the Islamic Republic as "hegemonic" narratives regarding the Holocaust by constructing the Holocaust as (i) a Jewish "myth" concocted by Jews and Zionists; (ii) a facilitator of brutality against Palestinians; (iii) an event that may have taken place but that caused more harm to the Palestinians than it did to the Jews.

Several images represent the Holocaust as a Jewish invention and Jews as malevolently deceiving the world with this "myth" for strategic gain (Litvak and Webman, 2009). For instance, Homayoun Abdolrahimi from Iran[26] depicts a Jew (wearing the Star of David on his arm) making a public announcement concerning the Holocaust. The Jew is depicted as undergoing the "Pinocchio Effect" (his nose has grown exceptionally long), which suggests that he is deceiving his audience about the Holocaust. Indeed, the length of his nose is intended to reflect the magnitude of the "lie". Indeed, Holocaust deniers typically refer to the Holocaust as one of the "greatest" lies ever perpetrated (Lipstadt, 1993). Similarly, a cartoon by Amir Baghestani from Iran[27] depicts three Jews – one of them creating an Israeli flag by hand; another controlling the world, indicated by the position of the globe at his feet; and the third Jew with a Pinocchio-like nose holding a placard depicting the word "Holocaust". Crucially, the Jew who controls the world "assists" his collaborator who "lies" about the Holocaust by attempting to cut off his long nose with an axe. This cartoon constructs the Jews as deceiving the world but also as possessing a willingness to assist one another in perpetuating the "lie". This echoes social representations of Jewish world domination embodied in antisemitic conspiracy theories (Lindemann and Levy, 2010b). More generally,

---

24   http://www.irancartoon.ir/gallery/album48/khaldoon_gharaibehjordan
25   http://www.irancartoon.ir/gallery/album48/Nedal_Ali_Deep_syria_1
26   http://www.irancartoon.ir/gallery/album48/Homayoun_Abdolrahimi
27   http://www.irancartoon.ir/gallery/album48/Amin_Baghestani_Iran

there is an anchoring of Judaism and Zionism to dishonesty and fraudulent behavior, providing a negative lens for regarding these ideologies.

There is a constructed interplay between Jews and Zionists in concocting the "Holocaust myth". A cartoon by Rahim Taghipour Sedgh Razmi from Iran[28] attributes the "Holocaust myth" to the State of Israel by displaying the word "Holocaust" followed by "Made in Israel". The cartoon constructs this as a Zionist fabrication (Litvak and Webman, 2009). Conversely, in a cartoon by Tallil Abdellatif from Morocco,[29] a smiling *Jew* (wearing a black hat with the Star of David and sidelocks) draws onto his white shirt the vertical blue lines of the Auschwitz concentration camp prisoner uniform, while the world stands behind and observes him gagged. Thus, the Holocaust is represented as a Jewish scam and the world as a helpless bystander (Lipstadt, 1993). Similarly, a cartoon by Hossein Taheri from Iran[30] represents the "Evil Jew" (depicted as an ugly and hairy beast-like figure wearing a Jewish skullcap) as concocting a toxic potion labelled as "Holocaust" by mixing caustic (a chemical which is able to burn organic tissue) and another chemical labelled as "hollow" (referring to the alleged hollowness of the "Holocaust myth"). On the one hand, this constructs the Holocaust as a make-believe Jewish creation and, on the other, as a highly toxic one which poses a hazard. The metaphorical objectification of the Holocaust in terms of a toxic substance serves to delegitimise well-established knowledge concerning the Holocaust and to re-construct it as a damaging hoax.

It is implied in many cartoons that the toxicity of the "Holocaust myth" consists primarily of its facilitation of brutality against the Palestinian people in particular. Maziyar Bizhani from Iran[31] depicts a Jew flying in a hot air balloon with the word "Holocaust" printed across it. From the sky, the Jew aims his rifle at a young Palestinian boy holding a slingshot, which constructs disparity between the alleged power of the Jews (who disseminate the "Holocaust myth") versus that of the Palestinians. Similarly, in another cartoon by Jihad Awrtani from Jordan,[32] a terrified-looking Palestinian man is being beheaded by a large sword with Holocaust written across it, which represents the Holocaust as a (Jewish-Zionist) weapon used against innocent Palestinians. In another contribution,[33] the same cartoonist represents the "t" in "Holocaust" as the crucifix of a Palestinian man wearing a keffiyeh. Each nail used to crucify the Palestinian displays the word "Holocaust". In a cartoon by Sadik Pala from India,[34] a grinning Israeli soldier stands on two book volumes entitled "Holocaust 1" and "Holocaust 2" in order to reach over a wall and fire his rifle at Palestinian civilians. The Israeli soldier is

28   http://www.irancartoon.ir/gallery/album48/Rahim_Taghipour_Sedgh_Razmj
29   http://www.irancartoon.ir/gallery/album48/tALLIL_aBDELLATIF_1
30   http://www.irancartoon.ir/gallery/album48/Hossein_Taheri_Iran
31   http://www.irancartoon.ir/gallery/album48/Maziyar_Bizhani_3_001
32   http://www.irancartoon.ir/gallery/album48/Jihad_AwrtaniJordan_1
33   http://www.irancartoon.ir/gallery/album48/Jihad_AwrtaniJordan
34   http://www.irancartoon.ir/gallery/album48/Sadic_Pala_India_1

depicted as sadistically deriving enjoyment from killing his Palestinian civilian victims. Similarly, in various cartoons by Jaber Asadi from Iran, Israeli soldiers use the Holocaust to defend themselves physically while perpetrating acts of brutality against others. One cartoon[35] depicts a giant Israeli soldier holding a tank in one hand and a Holocaust gravestone as a shield in the other. This suggests that the giant soldier who is indeed potent enough to hold a tank in one hand callously makes use of the "Holocaust myth" for self-defence. In the other cartoon,[36] an Israeli soldier clutches onto a Holocaust gravestone in order to avoid falling from a cliff, which constructs the Holocaust as a lifeline for Israel (and its army). These cartoons, collectively, suggest that the Holocaust is maliciously *utilised* by the Jew-Zionist in order to terrorise the Palestinians and others. The Holocaust is anchored to functionality, rather than to factual history, which depicts it as a "useful", rather than a truthful, narrative.

A number of cartoons construct the Nazi Holocaust as a myth and the "Palestinian Holocaust" as the true one. For instance, Tommy Thomdean[37] from Indonesia depicts the Grim Reaper as reading a book entitled "Holocaust History" which displays the Palestinian flag, rather than a Jewish symbol, suggesting that the "true" Holocaust is the Palestinian one. Crucially, the Palestinian "Holocaust" is implied to be so chilling and devastating that even the Grim Reaper shudders in fear. In a cartoon by Gatto Alessandro from Italy,[38] an empty Auschwitz prisoner uniform is depicted as the wall and window of a prisoner cell in which a sombre-looking Palestinian is imprisoned. Like Taheri's aforementioned cartoon, the empty uniform symbolises the "hollowness" of the Holocaust narrative. Similarly, a cartoon by Carlos Latuff from Brazil[39] depicts a Palestinian man wearing a keffiyeh and an Auschwitz prisoner uniform with a red crescent (symbolising Islam) rather than the Star of David. The prisoner is located within a concentration camp. Crucially, the Palestinian Holocaust is represented as being so severe that it surpasses any act that the Nazis "may" have committed against the Jews. For instance, Abdellah Derkaoui from Morocco[40] represents an Israeli bulldozer as constructing a wall in front of the Al Aqsa Mosque. The wall displays the Auschwitz concentration camp which obscures the Al Aqsa Mosque, suggesting that Israel has itself rendered Palestine a concentration camp much like Auschwitz.

Some cartoonists appear to acknowledge the veracity of Holocaust knowledge but nonetheless construct the Palestinians as suffering the "ongoing" consequences, which allegedly surpass Jewish suffering in the Nazi Holocaust. For instance, in a cartoon by Shiva Sahamifard from Iran,[41] a Jew has been stabbed with a blade

35   http://www.irancartoon.ir/gallery/album48/Jaber_Asadi_Iran
36   http://www.irancartoon.ir/gallery/album48/Jaber_Asadi_Iran_3
37   http://www.irancartoon.ir/gallery/album48/Tommy_Thomdean_Indonesia_5
38   http://www.irancartoon.ir/gallery/album48/Gatto_Alessandro_Italy1
39   http://www.irancartoon.ir/gallery/album48/carlos_Latuff_Brazil
40   http://www.irancartoon.ir/gallery/album48/Abdellah_Derkaoi_Morocco1
41   http://www.irancartoon.ir/gallery/album48/shiva_sahamifard_iran

displaying the Nazi swastika but the blade has passed through the Jew's body and threatens to harm a Palestinian family at the other end. This represents the Palestinians as the innocent victims of the Nazi Holocaust. Similarly, Sidnei Marques from Brazil[42] depicts Hitler as inserting his pistol into the ear of a Jew – the pistol passes through the Jew's skull and poses a danger to an innocent Palestinian man. Galym Boranbayev from Kazakhstan[43] depicts a deceased Jew who has been hanged with a noose displaying the word "Holocaust". However, two Palestinians have in turn been hanged with the sidelocks of the deceased Jew. Similarly, a cartoon by Soheil Setayesh from Iran[44] depicts two books about the Holocaust, one of which has been authored by Hitler (referring to the Nazi Holocaust) and the other by Ariel Sharon, the former prime minister of Israel. This suggests that, despite the Holocaust perpetrated against the Jews, Israel is guilty of perpetrating a "Holocaust" of its own against the Palestinian people. Collectively, these cartoons do acknowledge the Nazi Holocaust but they are intended to attenuate its significance vis-à-vis Palestinian suffering and to construct the Palestinians as innocent ongoing victims of the Holocaust, for which Israel is held responsible (Litvak and Webman, 2009). Incidentally, these cartoons anchor Palestinian suffering to the Nazi Holocaust, in order to provide a lens for considering the extent of Palestinian suffering.

Nazi-Zionism as an International Conspiracy

There is a consistent depiction of Jews and Israelis as Nazis, and of Zionism as overlapping with Nazi ideology (Litvak and Webman, 2009). Cartoonists represent the world as being subservient to the "Nazi-Zionist" ideology due partly to an alleged international conspiracy (involving the US and UK, primarily) and to the constructed power of the "Holocaust myth".

Several cartoonists depict Zionism and Nazism as two sides of the same coin. Choukri Bellahadi from Algeria[45] depicts the flag of Israel, which has been partially peeled off to reveal an underlying Nazi flag (the swastika). This constructs an underlying Nazi ideology as being superficially "camouflaged" by an Israeli flag, thereby representing synergy between the two ideologies. Similarly, a more abstract image by Mohammad Aman from Bahrain[46] represents a falling Star of David which gradually becomes a swastika symbol, suggesting a natural metamorphosis of Zionism into Nazism. Some cartoonists construct the unifying thread between Zionism and Nazism as brutality by depicting lethal instruments.

---

42   http://www.irancartoon.ir/gallery/album48/Sidnei_Marques_Brazil

43   http://www.irancartoon.ir/gallery/album48/Galym

44   http://www.irancartoon.ir/gallery/album48/soheil_setayesh_1

45   http://www.irancartoon.ir/gallery/album48/Choukri_BellahadiAlgeria_1

46   http://www.irancartoon.ir/gallery/album48/Mohammad_Aman_Bahrain

For instance, Alireza Nosrati from Iran[47] depicts a blood-stained axe which displays the symbols of both Nazism (the swastika) and of Zionism (the Star of David). Crucially, the axe is double bevelled – the swastika is displayed on the smaller blade which has less blood on it than the larger blade displaying the Star of David. This suggests that, despite synergy between the ideologies, it is the Zionists who have more blood on their hands than the Nazis.

Cartoonists depict symbolic figures of Nazism and Zionism, particularly Hitler and Sharon, respectively, in order to conflate the two ideological movements. For instance, Maziyar Bizhani from Iran[48] depicts Hitler typically dressed in his Nazi uniform, but his toothbrush moustache is represented as the Star of David, suggesting a form of synergy between Hitler and Zionism. Conversely, in cartoons by Mohammad Aman from Bahrain[49] and Leo Garesia from the USA,[50] former Israeli prime minister Ariel Sharon is represented as a Nazi officer. In Garesi's cartoon, he is depicted as wearing the Star of David on one arm and the Nazi swastika on the other, while displaying the "SS" symbol of the Nazi Schutzstaffel on his collars. Similarly, Aman's cartoon represents Sharon as a ghost-like figure wearing a Jewish skullcap and a Nazi uniform. His uniform displays the SS Totenkopf ("death's head"), which was used by the SS between 1934–45, as well as the Nazi party eagle symbol which, instead of the swastika, displays the Star of David. Wearing a Nazi uniform which also incorporates Zionist symbols, Sharon stands before the flag of Israel. In both cartoons, there is a constructed synergy and hybridity between Nazism and Zionism (Smith, 2012), which is represented as being embodied by Ariel Sharon, himself a personification of Israel. Yet, there is also a more general conflation of Jews and Nazis, as exemplified by a cartoon by Yasin Alkhalil from Syria.[51] He depicts a Jew (stereotypically represented as having a hooked nose and evil grin) holding a large knife and surrounded by a long trail of human skulls leading from the Al Aqsa Mosque. The Jew's reflection in the mirror is Hitler, wearing his military uniform with Nazi swastikas. The well-known atrocities of Hitler and the constructed atrocities of the grinning, knife-wielding Jew in the cartoon are intended to represent Zionism as another form of Nazism. These cartoons anchor Zionism to the Nazi ideology, providing a lens for regarding and evaluating the ideology underlying the State of Israel.

In addition to conflating Nazism and Zionism, some cartoons construct a collaboration between the hybrid Nazi-Zionist alliance, the US and other Western powers (Litvak and Webman, 2009). For example, Jitet Koestana from Indonesia[52] represents a figure with a toothbrush moustache (Hitler), a long beard and sidelocks (the Jew-Zionist) and an Uncle Sam hat (the US). Similarly, a cartoon by Gavimo

---

47 http://www.irancartoon.ir/gallery/album48/Alireza_Nosrati_Iran
48 http://www.irancartoon.ir/gallery/album48/Maziyar_Bizhani_11_001
49 http://www.irancartoon.ir/gallery/album48/Mohammad_Aman_Bahrain
50 http://www.irancartoon.ir/gallery/album48/Leo_Garesia_USA
51 http://www.irancartoon.ir/gallery/album48/Yasin_Alkhalil4
52 http://www.irancartoon.ir/gallery/album48/Jitet_Koestana_Indonesia_3

from Brazil[53] depicts the US flag with 50 stars in the form of the Star of David, which conflates Israel and the US. Reiterating the close relationship between Israel and the US, a cartoon by Esmail Babai[54] depicts an Orthodox Jewish infant (wearing a black hat with sidelocks) asleep in a cot that displays the sign "Made in the US". Moreover, the Jew is covered with a blanket in the form of the UK Union Flag. Crucially, the cot has been placed at the doorstep of Palestine, which implies that the UK and US have played a fundamental role in creating and supporting Zionism/the State of Israel. Cartoonists represent the collaboration between the US, UK and Israel as being a malevolent one, which has resulted in Palestinian suffering. Naji Benji[55] depicts two smiling British and American men restraining a tearful Palestinian as a grinning Jew with sidelocks brands the man with a red hot iron in the form of the Star of David. Thus, the nature of this international collaboration is constructed as sadistic in that the US and UK allegedly facilitate Jewish-Israeli domination and oppression.

The "direction" of influence between Jews/Israel and Western powers is ambiguous with cartoons suggesting different patterns of control and subservience. Gavimo's aforementioned cartoon depiction of the US flag suggests that there is a close relationship between the US and Israel. Conversely, like Babai's cartoon of the Jewish infant delivered to Palestine by the US and the UK, Marcio Leite from Brazil[56] constructs the US as a puppetmaster that controls the strings of an Orthodox Jew with a beard and sidelocks who in turn controls the strings of an Israeli soldier. The Israeli soldier, consistent with the social representation of Israeli brutality, uses his strings to hang a Palestinian. Conversely, Khaldoon Gharaibeh from Jordan[57] represents Jews as controlling the world – Gharaibeh depicts a grinning Jew wearing a black hat with the Star of David playing with a yo-yo in the form of the planet, suggesting Jewish world domination, a social representation that has existed since at least the 1800s (Herf, 2006). This image is similarly presented in the aforementioned cartoon by Gharaibeh which depicts the "l" of "Israel" as a boot crushing the earth. Taken together, the cartoons construct a representation of Jewish-Zionist world domination. Crucially, the "Holocaust myth" is represented as an important means of deceiving the world into subservience to the Jewish-Zionist conspiracy (Lipstadt, 1993). This is depicted in a cartoon by Mohammad Aladwani from Iraq,[58] which represents the world as tearfully sympathising with a Jew crying because of an apparently trivial wound on his finger but as willingly turning its back on a Palestinian with a severed hand. Similarly, in a cartoon by Mostafa Hosseini from Iran[59] the world is indifferent to its severed

---

53   http://www.irancartoon.ir/gallery/album48/Gavimo_Brazil
54   http://www.irancartoon.ir/gallery/album48/Esmail_Babai_Iran
55   http://www.irancartoon.ir/gallery/album48/Naji_Benji_Morocco
56   http://www.irancartoon.ir/gallery/album48/Marcio_Leite_Brazil
57   http://www.irancartoon.ir/gallery/album48/khaldoon_gharaibehjordan_1
58   http://www.irancartoon.ir/gallery/album48/mohammed_aladwani_iraq
59   http://www.irancartoon.ir/gallery/album48/Mosatafa_Hosseini_Iran

arm (Palestine) and instead fixates tearfully on its plastered finger spelling the word "Holocaust". In short, there are different ways of objectifying Jewish and Palestinian suffering, which highlights the differential extent of gravity – the Jewish suffering is objectified in terms of a trivial finger wound, while Palestinian suffering is represented in terms of a severed arm.

Overview

This chapter highlights that, by endorsing the cartoon contest, the Islamic Republic of Iran sought to reiterate its long-standing commitment to anti-Zionism and to export and "internationalise" this ideology. This intention was undoubtedly facilitated by the fact that cartoonists from many non-Muslim countries participated (see Figure 6.1 above), the international publicity that the contest received, and the widespread dissemination of the cartoons on the Internet. Despite the allegedly anti-Zionist intentions of the organisers, the cartoons overtly draw upon long-standing antisemitic themes and motifs, such as (i) ritual murder; (ii) the blood libel; and (iii) Jewish world domination and social representations of Jews as "demonic" and "bloodthirsty", which have been observed in previous research into cartoon depictions of Jews and Israel (see Chapter 2). These themes and descriptions reflect "anti-semyths" originally associated with European antisemitism but which have gradually come to form part of Arab/Muslim discourses on Jews and Israel (Kotek, 2009).

As a response to the Danish cartoon controversy, the International Holocaust Cartoon Contest served several important functions for the Islamic Republic of Iran – maintaining continuity of their politico-ideological agenda and bolstering self-efficacy and distinctiveness in the Muslim world, in particular. Although the organisers of the contest claimed that their aims were anti-Zionist and not antisemitic, this chapter elucidates the overtly antisemitic character of the contest and its cartoons. The cartoons themselves actively draw upon antisemitic imagery – some more overtly than others – in delegitimising Israel and Zionism. They feature a synthesis of "theological, moral, racial, social and political negation", which conflates Jews and Zionists (Stav, 1999, p. 18). Holocaust denial is a core theme in the cartoons, and serves the function of delegitimising the State of Israel and demonising Jews. Although anti-Zionism may well be the "goal" of some cartoonists, the imagery evoked in order to delegitimise Israel and Zionism is quite unambiguously antisemitic.

These satirical cartoons provide their viewers with a distorted, one-sided version of the Israeli-Palestinian conflict and of Jewish history, and may therefore shape viewers' beliefs concerning Jews and Israel in fundamentally negative ways. They are intended to appeal to the Islamic Ummah through the construction of Jewish-Zionist threats to Islam and Muslims. This could contribute to anti-Jewish feeling among Muslims in particular (Jikeli, 2013), while systematic Holocaust denial risks diminishing public understanding of the potential horrors of group prejudice and dehumanisation more generally (Haslam, 2006). By endorsing this contest, the Islamic Republic of Iran sought to "normalise" Holocaust denial (that is, antisemitism) as a legitimate means of criticising Israel and Zionism, creating ideal conditions for negative intergroup relations and social disharmony. The next two chapters examine the ways in which some of the representations identified in Part III of this book may surface in thought and everyday talk.

PART IV
Thinking and Talking about Jews and the Jewish State

Chapter 7

"Death to Israel": Perceptions of Israel and Jews among Iranian Muslims

Introduction

Most research into Iranian antisemitism and anti-Zionism has focused upon the political and institutional level in Iran (Jaspal, 2013a; 2013c; Litvak, 2006; Shahvar, 2009). Some of this research is summarised in Chapter 1. The data presented in this chapter are drawn from an exploratory, qualitative interview study with Iranian men and women. This chapter provides qualitative insights into the social representations held by a group of Iranians concerning Israel and Jews, with a particular focus on the role of identity processes therein. After a brief methodological overview, the following themes are outlined and discussed (i) Anti-Zionism and Iranian National Identity; (ii) Positioning Jews in relation to the Ingroup; (iii) Creating and Elaborating Antisemitic Social Representations; and (iv) Anti-Zionism and Holocaust Revisionism.

Methodological overview

In the summer of 2011, 40 Iranian men and women between the ages of 18 and 28 were invited to participate in an in-depth semi-structured interview study concerning "identity and social attitudes among Iranians". The interview schedule tapped into: (i) self and identity, and particularly religious and national identification; (ii) political trust; (iii) perceptions of Jews and Israelis; and (iv) knowledge of political issues and international relations. The interviews were conducted in Tehran, the capital city of Iran. Of the 40 participants, there were 20 men and 20 women. Twenty-four individuals self-identified as political "reformists" and 16 as "hardliners". The hardline political movement in Iran is known to espouse a strong anti-Zionist position, while the reformist movement appears to take a relatively more pragmatic stance. For instance, in a CNN interview the former reformist president of Iran, Khatami, did denounce the Israeli–Palestinian peace process as "flawed and unjust", but he also stated that the regime in Iran did not "intend to impose our views on others or stand in their [the Palestinians'] way".[1] Moreover, foreign ministry spokesman Hamid Asefi stated that "we respect all decisions taken by the majority of the Palestinians" (see Jaspal, 2013a). This demonstrates the relatively pragmatic stance taken by some reformist politicians

---

[1]   CNN Interactive http://edition.cnn.com/WORLD/9801/07/iran/interview.html

in Iran. It was deemed necessary to recruit participants who identified with either political stance in order to examine the potential relationship between political orientation and social representations of Jews and Israel. The sample could be described as an urban sample because all of the respondents lived in Tehran. They all described themselves as being of Persian ethnic origin, as Shiite Muslim and as very to moderately religious. The sample was relatively educated – 27 participants had completed, or were studying towards, a university degree; 10 participants had completed high school; and only 3 participants had no formal qualifications.

The data were analysed using qualitative thematic analysis, which has been described as "a method for identifying, analysing and reporting patterns (themes) within data" (Braun and Clarke, 2006, p. 78). The study aimed to capture participants' attempts to make sense of their personal and social worlds, with particular foci upon their perceptions of Israel and Jews and of their own identities. Consequently, the analysis adopted a realist, epistemological approach in that participants' talk was viewed as a fairly reliable reflection of their cognitions and representations. The author transcribed the recordings and read the transcripts repeatedly in order to become as intimate as possible with the accounts, and preliminary interpretations were noted in the left margin. These included *inter alia* participants' meaning-making, particular forms of language, and apparent contradictions and patterns within the data. Initial codes aimed to capture, from the analyst's perspective, participants' perceptions of Jews and Israel and their own identities. The right margin was then used to collate these initial codes into potential themes, which captured the essential qualities of the accounts. As highlighted by Braun and Clarke (2006, p. 82), "a theme captures something important about the data in relation to the research question, and represents some level of *patterned* response or meaning within the data set". Themes were developed as part of the data analysis, in order to provide insight into the phenomenological worlds of participants. The list of themes was reviewed rigorously against the data in order to ensure their compatibility and numerous interview extracts were listed against each corresponding theme. At this stage specific interview extracts, which were considered vivid, compelling and representative of the themes, were selected for presentation in this chapter. Finally, four superordinate themes representing the themes derived from participants' accounts were developed and ordered into a logical and coherent narrative structure.

Both the gender and political orientation of each participant are indicated in the extracts below. In the quotations from participants, an ellipsis indicates where material has been excised; and other material within square brackets is clarificatory.

Anti-Zionism and Iranian National Identity

Participants' accounts indicated the gradual development of a national cultural expectation to derogate the State of Israel. They frequently referred to the chant "Death to Israel" which tends to be used alongside "Death to America" in political rallies in Iran (Molavi, 2005). Their accounts provided some insight into the potential motivations underlying anti-Zionism:

> Israel is like the opposite of Iran in a way. It's like everything we are not and we are everything they are not, you know? They are a different kind of people. (Esmail, male, hardliner)

> I'm Iranian so I can't like Israel. It just doesn't fit together. It's an anomaly [...] like being a cat who likes dogs, you know? (Bahar, female, hardliner)

Several individuals highlighted the importance of distinctiveness in determining their social representations of Israel. Esmail described Israel as "the opposite" of Iran and emphasised the *distinct* characteristics of Israel and Iran, respectively. Moreover, he perceived Israelis as "a different kind of people", suggesting insuperable intergroup difference. This removed any possibility of potential solidarity between the two nations but rather constructed them as being fundamentally opposed to one another. This suggested that, for many individuals, Israel represented Iran's "Significant Other", a threatening outgroup which, through intergroup comparisons, provided feelings of distinctiveness (Triandafyllidou, 1998).

Some participants tellingly suggested that it would be incongruous to self-identify as Iranian, on the one hand, and to accept Israel, on the other. Bahar illustrated this incongruence vividly by employing the simile of a cat liking a dog, which was intended to construct imagery of an "unnatural" union. This appeared to suggest that some individuals maintained their anti-Zionist stance in order to safeguard feelings of distinctiveness, on the one hand, and of psychological coherence, on the other. The acceptance of Israel could induce an "anomaly" in identity. Accordingly, most participants attributed negative characteristics to Israel, which is consistent with the notion that it was perceived as Iran's "Significant Other". This frequently culminated in assertions of hatred towards the country, as indicated by Arash's observation:

> If there's no Israel, whom can we all hate? (Arash, male, hardliner)

> I think we've, in Iran, we've come to the point where we need to hate Israel and it would be a surprise if there's suddenly no Israel. Like "where has it gone?" (Maryam, female, reformist)

Crucially, Arash argued that the very existence of Israel provided a target for hatred and that if Israel did not exist Iranians would simply have no outgroup to derogate and to hate. This further demonstrated the importance of distinctiveness as an important motivational principle underlying anti-Zionism, at least partly because of its role in providing a target for outgroup derogation (Triandafyllidou, 1998), itself an important psychological process. As the perceived Significant Other of

Iranians, Israel essentially functioned as a scapegoat for negativity and evil in the world and an external object for directing anger and aggression (Doty et al., 1991).

Yet, there was also a strong indication that by hating Israel participants were simply safeguarding their sense of temporal continuity given the perception of a long-standing intergroup rivalry between Iran and Israel. Maryam highlighted the routineness of anti-Israel hatred in Iran, and argued that it would be "a surprise" (perhaps indicating a rupture between past and present) if Israel no longer existed as a target for outgroup derogation. Indeed, the maintenance of anti-Zionism at the institutional level in Iran has been attributed to the human quest for continuity between past, present and future (Jaspal, 2013a).

Furthermore, anti-Zionism clearly played an important role for self-efficacy, since individuals felt that their vocal anti-Zionist policy symbolised Iran's sovereignty, national integrity and defiance in face of outgroup pressure, namely from "Zionists" and "America":

> Standing up to Israel is what my country is known for and we shouldn't stop this. It sends a good message to the world that we are not the Zionist's slaves or America's slaves. We have control over our own affairs and policies and this is important for our future. (Kianoosh, male, reformist)

"Standing up to Israel" clearly provided some individuals with feelings of pride because they believed that this policy had endowed Iran with the positive reputation of resisting external pressures. This was particularly important in the context of Israel, which has been pervasively represented as a malevolent, yet powerful outgroup in the region (Wistrich, 2010). Given the perception that many countries were unsuccessful in resisting pressure from Israel and the US, individuals derived feelings of distinctiveness from Iran's ability to resist Israel, as well as a strong sense of self-efficacy in maintaining "control over own affairs and policies". Individuals clearly believed that the future of Iran, namely its continuity, depended upon its ability to function as a self-efficacious and distinctive political entity. Thus, anti-Zionism itself constituted a source of *national self-efficacy*, which could be projected to "the world". This was perceived as positive for the ingroup's external image.

In general, anti-Zionism (and by extension, the very existence of Israel) performed important functions for distinctiveness, psychological coherence, self-efficacy and continuity in relation to Iranian national identity. Thus, the abandonment of anti-Zionism could potentially deprive individuals of sources of these principles. However, there was some variation in the ways in which self-reported political orientation shaped perceptions of anti-Zionism among respondents.

Hardliners and the centrality of anti-Zionism

Self-identified political "hardliners" attributed particular importance to Iran's policy of anti-Zionism which they perceived as a cornerstone of Iranian national identity:

As an Iranian, I can't support the Zionist regime even if they have a justification, for Iranians, it is an unacceptable state. (Arash, male, hardliner)

Iranians don't like Israelis. It's a fact. And nothing will change this in this lifetime at least, or ever I think. It's a historical fact. (Mitra, female, hardliner)

What can he [the Iranian president] do? He's in a tricky situation [...] He can only not mention Israel but he can't like acknowledge it, can he? As Iranians, we stand up to Israel, we don't recognise it. We can't. (Golnaz, female, hardliner)

There was a clear perception among hardliners that, as Iranians, they were *unable* to accept or legitimise the State of Israel despite any potential "justification" that the state might have. Arash referred to Israel as an "unacceptable state" while Mitra asserted that "Iranians don't like Israelis". Participants emphasised the immutability of these "tenets" of Iranian national identity through use of the modal verb "can't" and through the depiction of Israeli-Iranian animosity as a "historical fact". Like several hardliners, Mitra perceived animosity towards Israelis as being long-standing and immutable and seemed to resign herself to the "reality" that this would not change. There was no awareness among hardliners of more positive social representations of Israel, which had existed prior to the 1979 Islamic Revolution, when there were in fact full diplomatic relations between the Imperial State of Iran and the State of Israel (Shahvar, 2009). Clearly, anti-Zionist social representations were highly salient in individuals' meaning-making, which led to the essentialisation of Israelis as loathsome and unworthy of acceptance and to the perception that all Iranians unanimously subscribed to the regime's anti-Zionist stance. Respondents appeared to imagine themselves as a "community" united in their national hatred of Israel (Anderson, 1991).

Golnaz sympathetically acknowledged the "tricky situation" of the Iranian president, who by virtue of his "Iranian-ness" was allegedly unable to acknowledge, mention or recognise Israel. She regarded the rejection of Israel as central to the presidential role. There was perceived overlap between the inability of the Iranian president to recognise Israel ("he can't acknowledge it") and that of the Iranian people ("we can't), which served to crystallise the social representation that anti-Zionism constituted a central aspect of Iranian national identity – that is, something that all Iranians ought to accept (Jaspal, 2011c). Interestingly, although not all of the hardline participants personally approved of President Ahmadinejad's political and economic policies, there was unanimous sympathy towards him in the context of his anti-Zionist stance. This suggested that anti-Zionism could perform a unifying function among Iranians, potentially attenuating other political and ideological differences (cf. Baum and Nakazawa, 2007).

Individuals were invited to reflect upon the antecedents of "compulsory" anti-Zionism in Iranian society. The hardliners perceived the State of Israel as posing a threat to the Iranian nation and, particularly, to Iranian sovereignty which served as a justification for "hating" the Jewish State:

> Abbas (male, hardliner): The Jews have always been plotting against us [Muslims] and the Zionists want to attack Iran so what do you expect? That I'll love Israel? I hate it […] They shouldn't exist.

> Interviewer: Why shouldn't Israel exist, in your view?

> Abbas: These sanctions that we have in Iran. People have nothing to eat, no money for rent, nothing to buy in the shop […] The Zionist regime makes these sanctions. Zionists.

> The Zionists won't hesitate for a second to wipe out the Iranian people […] It's in their blood. (Farideh, female, hardliner)

Abbas anchored Zionism to antisemitic social representations of Jewish world domination and, in particular, regarding the Jews' historical desire to destroy Islam (Shahvar, 2009), in order to delegitimise Zionism, the political ideology underlying the State of Israel. Like Abbas, several hardliners regarded historical representations of Jews as evidencing and explaining the alleged misdoings of Zionists. Abbas attributed the crippling economic sanctions imposed on Iran by the international community to "the Zionist regime", which was presented as "evidence" of the "Zionist threat" (Stephan and Stephan, 2000). More specifically, it was argued that Zionists were responsible for the grim social and economic conditions in Iran due to internationally-imposed sanctions. Abbas did not acknowledge the international community's dismay at Iran's nuclear programme but rather accused Zionism of irrationally opposing Iran's "right to nuclear technology" and of pressurising the world into supporting economic sanctions against Iran. The economic sanctions were generally perceived as posing a threat to the national ingroup's self-efficacy, competence and control, which contributed to the threat imagery of Zionism. It is noteworthy that the sanctions were understandably on the minds of most participants as they reflected upon Zionism and Israel, since most of them reported personal experiences of financial hardship related to the sanctions. As Iran's Significant Other, Israel was scapegoated as the principal driving force behind the crippling economic sanctions (Gregory, 2001).

A point frequently made by hardliners in the study was that, just like the Jews who had allegedly attempted to destroy Islam, the Zionists (that is, Israelis) were now engaged in a covert plan to launch an attack against Iran. This was powerfully demonstrated in Farideh's account which suggested that Zionists would be quite willing to annihilate the Iranian people in order to achieve their goals. Given that Zionists were regularly dehumanised and viewed as inhumane and brutal oppressors, the threat representation was rendered all the more credible in the minds of individuals. Although Farideh employed the category "Zionist", her essentialisation of Zionism indicated that the category was being treated like a racial/biological one in much the same way that the category "Jew" has been in antisemitic discourse: "It's in their blood" (see Chapter 2). It was evident from participants' accounts that Israel was perceived as posing both realistic and symbolic threats to the Iranian ingroup, given that participants regarded Zionists as seeking to impose their will on the world and believed that they would go to any lengths (including annihilation) in order to do so. The threat representation jeopardised the perception of group continuity, because individuals felt that there was a risk that the ingroup could come to severe harm at the hands of Zionists (Jaspal and Yampolsky, 2011). In short, anti-Zionist/antisemitic statements of this kind frequently culminated in the assertion that the State of Israel could not and should not be trusted and that a rational response was for Iranians to hate the State of Israel and to reject its legitimacy and existence.

In addition to the realistic threat perceived to be associated with the State of Israel, participants seemed to regard the Jewish State as posing a symbolic threat by curtailing the "legitimate" rights of the Iranian nation:

> What I really hate about Israelis is that they are hypocrites. They have double standards. They have an atomic bomb themselves but they criticise Iran for this [nuclear programme] […] That's not a proper state in my mind. (Nasreen, female, hardliner)

> Basically, they want to say "no" to our nuclear programme because they wish to control Iran, show us they control us and show the world that they control us. The sanctions are their way of controlling us. It makes me sick […] If we don't fight this one to the end, it will be a humiliation for us, as Iranians. (Arash, male, hardliner)

> They say "no" to our nuclear rights and we say "no" to their state. An illegitimate state has no place to rule on these matters, not the Zionist regime. (Faraz, male, hardliner)

Iran's disputed nuclear programme was the example cited in order to demonstrate the alleged "double standards" of Israel and its symbolic threat to Iran. In Nasreen's account, which was by no means atypical of the sample of participants, the characteristic "hypocrite" was attributed to Israelis in general and they were said to have "double standards". The notion that Israel should oppose Iran's nuclear programme, which most participants regarded as being peaceful in intention and nature, was perceived as absurd and hypocritical, due to the widespread belief among participants that "they [Israel] have an atomic bomb themselves". Moreover, for the same reason, several individuals constructed Israel as posing a realistic threat to the region (and especially to Iran). In short, the Iranian respondents believed that Israel was capable of launching a nuclear strike, just as many Israelis believe that Iran is capable of attacking Israel (see Chapter 9).

Arash regarded Israel's obstruction of Iran's nuclear programme *and* its call for economic sanctions against Iran as a means of acquiring, and publicly demonstrating, political "control" of Iran, which was clearly threatening for his sense of (national) self-efficacy as an Iranian: "It makes me sick". There was a perception among many participants that if Iran were to capitulate to Israel's demands for an end to nuclear enrichment there would be an overwhelming sense of defeat, which could further jeopardise feelings of self-efficacy. Faraz appeared to cope with the threat to self-efficacy by delegitimising the State of Israel and observing that, while Israel opposed Iran's right to nuclear technology, Iran opposed Israel's existence. The power and determination to deny Israel's existence appeared to provide some individuals with a boost to self-efficacy, which was otherwise jeopardised by economic sanctions and Israel's overt opposition to Iran's nuclear programme. This may be regarded as a strategy for coping with identity threat (Breakwell, 1986). In short, Israel was perceived as having no right to "criticise" Iran for its nuclear activities and was even viewed as lacking the basic qualities of a "proper state".

Participants proceeded to invoke the qualities of a "proper" or prototypical state and exemplified such a state by referring to the Islamic Republic of Iran, while they delegitimised the State of Israel:

> Iran is a country that has harmed no other country, ever. No invasion of other countries. No bombings. No attacks. Nothing. It is a proper state, as one should be, a proper, an ideal UN member [...] What does Israel do? Break every UN rule, harm other countries, kill women and children in particular and the world doesn't notice. Why is this? (Fardin, male, hardliner)

> A country is not supposed to invade and take over other countries. Iran stays in its own borders. But the Jews just want to take over the whole region, like extend their reach and threaten the region's countries. That includes Iran. Iran is the biggest rival of Israel so I feel proud of Iran. (Faraz, male, hardliner)

Faraz drew upon the social representation of Israel as an invader and occupier of Muslim countries, which is widespread in cultural consciousness in the Middle East (Wistrich, 2010). He referred implicitly to Israel's 1982 invasion of Lebanon and to its subsequent occupation of the country until 2000 in order to exemplify and justify the attribution of the delegitimising characteristics "invader" and "occupier" to the State of Israel. Indeed, participants widely argued that Iran constituted a "proper" state because they believed it had remained within its own borders and never encroached upon foreign territory. By invoking the negative categories "invader" and "occupier", many hardline participants argued that the principal aim of Israel was to threaten and usurp regional countries and ultimately "to take over the whole region", including Iran. This reflected a realistic threat in that Israel was perceived as physically usurping land and the resources of regional countries, on the one hand, and a symbolic threat because individuals regarded Israel as seeking to disseminate its ideology, norms and values in the countries they conquered, on the other hand. This hybridised threat was detrimental to the self-efficacy and continuity principles of identity.

Fardin contrasted Iran and Israel, attributing positive and peaceful characteristics to Iran and malevolent and belligerent traits to Israel. More specifically, he constructed Iran as an "ideal" UN member state which did not encroach upon foreign territory or cause harm to other nations, while accusing Israel of committing acts which called into question its eligibility for UN state membership (see also Jaspal and Coyle, 2014). Thus, by delegitimising the State of Israel in this way, individuals appeared to derive feelings of intergroup distinctiveness and a positive Iranian national identity which had been imbued with positive characteristics. This amounted to a form of downward comparison with Israel, which performed the function of bolstering ingroup Iranian identity vis-à-vis the Israeli outgroup with favourable outcomes for self-esteem (Wills, 1981). As Israel's "biggest rival", Iran was constructed as a defender of peace and freedom in a region which was said to be dominated by "Zionist malevolence". This form of ingroup self-presentation was clearly beneficial for the self-esteem and self-efficacy principles in relation to the national ingroup.

Reformists and the peripherality of anti-Zionism

Self-identified political "reformists" acknowledged the importance of anti-Zionism in Iranian foreign policy since the 1979 Islamic Revolution. However, there was a sense among reformists that the emphasis on anti-Zionism had become more central to the hardliner movement than to Iranian national identity more generally. Although there was some evidence that anti-Zionism could bolster the principles of continuity, distinctiveness and self-efficacy among all Iranians, several reformist individuals viewed anti-Zionism as having little personal relevance to them and denied its centrality to Iranian national identity. This was particularly pertinent in intergroup (hardliner versus reformist) contexts:

> Israel? Let's think about Iran first. Palestinians? Let's think about Iran first. Hezbollah. Iran first. Why do we just get so distracted with Israel, Zionists, Palestinians. It's stupid. (Shabnam, female, reformist)

> I'm not so concerned with Israel. It's the government that wants us to talk and think of Israel, not us, the people. (Massoud, male, reformist)

> I think Ahmadinejad, the majles [parliament], they try to just focus on Israel all the time and they teach us that Israel did this or Israel did that but it's just a distraction […] we Iranians don't care so much about Qods [Jerusalem]. (Kianoosh, male, reformist)

These extracts converge in demonstrating the general disinterest in Israel, anti-Zionism and the Israeli-Palestinian conflict which was observable among many reformists. Shabnam regarded the Israeli-Palestinian conflict and indeed anti-Zionism as a "distraction" from core domestic concerns, such as the economic sanctions that preoccupied many respondents, and argued that the focus on "Israel, Zionists [and] Palestinians" was "stupid". Like other reformists, she believed that Iran should take primacy over outgroup concerns. Crucially, the ingroup was defined in terms of national, rather than religious, identity, which diverges from the emphasis of the Islamic Ummah that has been associated with anti-Zionism (Baum and Nakazawa, 2007; Litvak, 1998).

Similarly, Massoud and Kianoosh explained the "excessive" focus upon Israel and institutionalised anti-Zionism in terms of a governmental desire to distract the Iranian people from domestic concerns, such as the human rights abuses allegedly perpetrated by the hardline Iranian government and the failure of Ahmadinejad's economic policy in the country. In Kianoosh's account, Ahmadinejad (perhaps the personification of Iranian anti-Zionism in cultural consciousness[2]) and the Iranian parliament were said to converge and conspire in their collective desire to distract the Iranian people. There was a clear delineation of the Iranian government, which some reformists perceived to be obsessed by anti-Zionism, and the Iranian people, who "don't care so much about Quds [Jerusalem]". For these respondents, the emphasis on anti-Zionism symbolised the Iranian regime's lack of understanding of, and concern for, the Iranian people.

The Israeli-Palestinian conflict and indeed anti-Zionism were attributed primarily to the *hardline* outgroup and distanced from the (superordinate) Iranian ingroup:

> They [hardliners] give us a bad name and, you know, that is a bad feeling. Why can't we just accept that Jews live there and they live along with Arabs? It's not our issue. They make us all look like the bad guys. We just want peace [...] they [Israel] impose sanctions. (Kamal, male, reformist)

Like Kamal, several reformist participants perceived anti-Zionism as a hardline agenda with which they did not identify. Kamal regarded this hardline agenda as bringing Iran into ill repute on the international stage, particularly as a result of President Ahmadinejad's fervent anti-Zionist stance. This was indicated by his observation that hardliners "give us a bad name" and "make us *all* look like the bad guys". There was a clear desire to differentiate between hardliners and reformists in his account. In addition to jeopardising feelings of acceptance and inclusion from the international community, which threatened the belonging principle of identity, hardline activities also imperilled the self-esteem principle of identity: "that is a bad feeling". In his account, Kamal appeared to acknowledge that there were some "bad guys" namely hardliners but that not all Iranians could be homogenised as anti-Zionists. This delineation of the reformist ingroup from the hardliner outgroup clearly reflected an attempt to deflect the threats to belonging and self-esteem and could thus be regarded as a coping strategy (Breakwell, 1986).

---

2   The   Washington   Post   http://www.washingtonpost.com/wp-dyn/content/ article/2005/10/27/AR2005102702221.html.

Kamal stressed that the Israeli-Palestinian conflict and the existence of the State of Israel were of no concern to Iranians: "it's not our issue". However, like most participants, Kamal did regard Israel as being (indirectly) responsible for the crippling economic sanctions which had been imposed on Iran by the international community. Although he clearly believed the social representation that Israel was responsible for sanctions, Kamal did not appear to identify with anti-Zionism, which he perceived as a hardline agenda and also as a motivator for Israeli aggression (in the form of economic sanctions). While attributing anti-Zionism to the hardline outgroup, Kamal clearly perceived the reformist ingroup as pursuing a peaceful agenda, which was favourable for self-esteem. Thus, the delineation of political ingroup from outgroup enhanced identity processes.

Several participants highlighted their pride at making positive, albeit non-normative, statements regarding Israel:

> For me, it makes me feel quite proud to just say "I'm not against Israel". I like to say it. (Parveen, female, reformist)

> Jahangir (male, reformist): Yes, I'm not anti-Israeli.

> Interviewer: And do you tell anyone else this or?

> Jahangir: I just say it and sometimes my friend is like "shh, be quiet" and I like it, you know. You should speak your mind and be proud to say it.

Parveen and Jahingir explicitly invoked their feelings of pride at contradicting the authority of the Iranian government by making positive and, thus, subversive remarks about the State of Israel. This reflected the strategy of negativism, namely "the state of mind which one is in when one feels a desire or a compulsion to act *against* the requirements or pressures from some external sources [here, the Iranian government]" (Apter, 1983, p. 79). Clearly, some individuals derived a positive sense of self from engaging in this strategy. They appeared to derive pride and satisfaction not because of a personal connection to Israel but rather because of the perceived reactions from others, who clearly recognised and in some cases disapproved of their distinctiveness in this regard. It is noteworthy that distinctiveness need not be positive in order for it to be beneficial for identity processes (Vignoles et al., 2000). Parveen focused upon the act of *saying* that she was not opposed to Israel while Jahangir reported deriving pleasure at the disapproving responses he received from others. For him, this constituted an example of "speaking your mind" which provided him with a positive sense of distinctiveness. Thus, the negativism strategy allowed individuals to manifest opposition to the "norm" disseminated particularly by the hardline outgroup and to derive positive outcomes for identity.

It appeared that the rejection of anti-Zionism constituted a means of carving out a distinctive identity from hardliners. It would be a mistake to claim that this was a systematic tendency among all reformists, since several reformists were inconsistent in their recognition and acceptance of Israel – at times, accepting it and at others, delegitimising it. However, by rejecting "hardline" anti-Zionism, reformists managed to deflect a social representation which they perceived to be associated principally with a political outgroup.

Reformist participants regarded the hardline Iranian government as favouring Arab concerns over Iranian domestic concerns, which was widely attributed to the perceived agenda to further Islamicise the country. It has been observed that intergroup relations between Iranians and Arabs are generally tense and that there is considerable suspicion towards the Arab outgroup due to long-standing intergroup rivalry.[3] Anti-Zionism was regarded as one such "Arab thing", which was irrelevant to Iranian culture:

> This is an Arab thing. They hate Israel because maybe they've got a reason too. Israel has killed Palestinians and they've killed Lebanese people and it's humiliated them. But not us. We are not Arabs. We are Iranians and we don't have any issue with Palestine […] We are not friends [with Israel] but we are not enemies either. (Darioush, male)

Some reformists perceived anti-Zionism as a principally Islamic, rather than Iranian, phenomenon (Litvak, 1998). Although all of the respondents in this study self-identified as Muslims, they differentiated between their Iranian national and Muslim religious identities and reformists, in particular, seemed to view these identities as functioning at distinct levels of abstraction. This is not to suggest that Muslim religious identity constituted a superordinate identity, as has been observed among British Pakistanis, for example (cf. Jacobson, 1997; Jaspal, 2011b). Darioush argued that, while various Arab countries perhaps had cause to oppose the existence of Israel, due to a history of humiliation, war, invasion and killing, the Iranian people had no quarrel with Israel and had no reason to spearhead international anti-Zionism. Participants did appear to accept the social representation that Israel had engaged in atrocities against Arabs – highlighted by Darioush's observation that "Israel has killed Palestinians and they've killed Lebanese people". This could be attributed to the coerciveness and hegemony of this social representation in Iranian society (Shahvar, 2009). However, acceptance of this representation did not appear to induce an anti-Zionist stance.

For Darioush and other reformists, the Israeli-Arab conflict was a foreign issue of little significance to the Iranian national ingroup. Given the salience of Iranian national identity, individuals did not attribute significance to this conflict. Accordingly, participants emphatically differentiated the Iranian ingroup from the Arab outgroup ("We are not Arabs. We are Iranians"). The Iranian-Arab distinction appeared to provide reformist participants with feelings of intergroup distinctiveness. Although Darioush did not claim that Iran and Israel should

---

3   Al Arabiya News http://www.alarabiya.net/articles/2011/10/09/170927.html.

have amicable relations, he nonetheless rejected the social representation of institutionalised anti-Zionism. Thus, some individuals' disidentification with Arabs prompted and indeed justified their disidentification with anti-Zionism and with the Palestinian cause. Their opposition to anti-Zionism seemed to constitute a form of protest against both the hardline outgroup and against Iranian assimilation to the Arab outgroup, which was widely perceived as an Islamicising strategy. It is easy to see how these shifting ingroup-outgroup boundaries bolstered the distinctiveness and self-esteem of the emerging reformist ingroup.

Yet, interestingly, even reformist participants in the study manifested anti-Zionism. The data indicated that reformists engaged in anti-Zionism and accepted anti-Zionist social representations as a form of resistance to colonialism, rather than as a form of Islamic resistance. Thus, their anti-Zionism appeared to perform a distinct function for identity and to have distinct underlying motivations. Israel was perceived as a colonial entity, which interfered with individuals' socialist values:

> I am against Israel but not like the government forces us all to be. The government hates Israel no matter what. I just think they need to give the Palestinians their rights […] The beginning of Israel was colonialism and it's a US-Western creation. It is an extension of America in a way. (Sohrab, male, reformist)

> Israel is the symbol of capitalism […] It is just the rich oppressing the poor. The powerful oppresses the weak. They are just a colonial entity from Europe, and they are trampling on the rights of the innocent Palestinian people. (Noushin, female, reformist)

Several reformist participants described themselves as "intellectuals" whose ideals had underpinned the anti-Shah movement which culminated in the 1979 Revolution. On the one hand, they were keen to differentiate themselves from hardliners and the Islamic Republic of Iran more generally. Yet, on the other hand, they espoused a similarly profound anti-Zionist stance and advocated the dismantlement of the State of Israel. They framed their anti-Zionism not as a form of Islamic resistance, as hardliners tended to do, but rather as resistance against "colonialism" and "capitalism" (Jaspal, 2013d). Indeed, Sohrab accentuated his distinctiveness from "the [hardliner] government" by differentiating the nature of his anti-Zionist stance from that of the government. While the Iranian government's anti-Zionist stance was said to lack reason, *his* opposition to the Jewish State was attributed to Israel's mistreatment of the Palestinians and, more specifically, to their infringement of Palestinian rights. Sohrab and Noushin described Israel as a "US-Western creation" and "the symbol of capitalism", respectively, which was intended to illustrate a left-wing socialist political, rather than religio-national, stance against Zionism (cf. Litvak, 1998).

The anti-colonial ideals, which characterised much Iranian opposition to the West prior to the 1979 Islamic Revolution, was apparent in the accounts of some reformist participants. They anchored the Israeli-Palestinian conflict to colonialism, imperialism and capitalism, objectified by the US, and viewed Israel not as a sovereign state for Jews but rather as a "puppet regime" installed by the capitalist US (Shahvar, 2009). Interestingly, some reformists invoked the 1975 UN General Assembly Resolution (3379) which equated Zionism with racism in order to substantiate the social representation that Zionism posed a (colonial) threat. Noushin and other participants appeared to racialise the Israeli-Palestinian conflict by constructing Israel implicitly as a "white" country established by Europeans for White Europeans, which obscured the reality that over half of the Israeli population consists of Sephardic and Mizrahi Jews.[4]

It was clear that hardliners perceived a hybridised threat emanating from the State of Israel in that it was regarded as imperilling Iran's economic competence, religious and cultural heritage and even the wellbeing of the Iranian people. There was a coercive social representation among hardliners that Israel actively sought to destroy the Islamic Republic possibly through the possession and use of atomic weapons. Conversely, reformists tended to perceive Israel as posing a symbolic threat which ensued from the perception that Israel sought to extend its influence and control throughout the region and thereby curtail the scope, influence, norms and values of the Islamic Republic of Iran. Although anti-Zionism was systematically manifested by hardliners, reformists were much less consistent in their stance vis-à-vis Zionism. Clearly, important identity considerations (e.g. the desire for distinctiveness from the hardline outgroup) overrode ideology.

Positioning Jews in relation to the Ingroup

The Islamic Republic of Iran is home to the largest Jewish community in the Middle East outside of Israel. In view of Iran's official policy of anti-Zionism, which is punctuated by blatant antisemitism (Jaspal, 2013a), there has been some concern about the wellbeing and living conditions of Iranians Jews. These concerns are typically dismissed by the Iranian authorities, who insist upon an unwavering distinction between anti-Zionism and antisemitism and who are keen to demonstrate the "equal rights" of Iranian Jews (Jaspal, 2013a). This section provides insight into how young (Muslim) Iranians perceived Iranian Jews and positioned them in relation to the ingroup.

The young Iranians who participated in this study did manifest antisemitic social representations. Hardline participants tended to be more overt in their condemnation of Jews and, in doing so, they drew heavily upon Shiite Islamic theological representations, many of which could be traced to the political rhetoric of Ayatollah Khomeini. Khomeini's ideology held that, given the "najes" (impure) status of Jews, physical contact and business dealings with them in turn jeopardised

---

4   Central Bureau of Statistics, Government of Israel, Statistical Abstract of Israel 2009, no. 60, Subject 2, Table no. 24 http://www.cbs.gov.il/reader/shnaton/templ_ shnaton_e.html?num_tab=st02_24x&CYear=2009.

the "purity" of Shiite Muslims (Shahvar, 2009). This social representation was clearly observable in the accounts of several hardline participants:

> No, for me, as a Muslim, I can't have anything to do with Jews. In Islam, they are "najes" [impure], inferior and I don't want to jeopardise my relationship with my faith by mixing with Jews […] Islam is pure. (Arash, male, hardliner)

> Islam says that Jews are "najes" [impure] and from their behaviour [in Palestine], they seem to be. (Ehsan, male, hardliner)

Arash and other hardline participants highlighted the centrality of their Muslim identity to their sense of self, which they viewed as forbidding contact with Jews due to their "najes" and "inferior" status according to Shiite Islamic ideology. Ehsan invoked the social representation of Israel's mistreatment of the Palestinians in order to evidence their "najes" status. It was argued that only an impure people could possibly treat others in this way, thereby crystallising a dehumanising social representation of Jews. Similarly, Arash constructed Jews as being inferior to Muslims whose religion he, conversely, described as being "pure". Indeed, this constituted a form of downward comparison, which could bolster ingroup self-esteem and distinctiveness (Jaspal, 2011a; Wills, 1981). There was a juxtaposition between Jewish impurity/inferiority and Islamic purity/superiority. Thus, contact with a "najes" outgroup member was perceived as threatening one's sense of continuity since individuals thought it might jeopardise their relationship with Islam, a valued component of identity.

In addition to citing the "najes" status of Jews, respondents drew upon Islamic theological representations in order to otherise and delegitimise Jews and the Jewish State:

> Israel is an illegal state which should not exist. It has no reason to exist really […] Since the days of the Prophet, the Jews have been deceiving the world and Israel is another example of this, I believe. (Bahar, female, hardliner)

> If we look at history then you can really clearly see that the Jews have been trampling all over Islam since the time of the Prophet and here today you see they are doing the same in Palestine […] They are just doing what they always did. (Mohammad, male, hardliner)

Bahar invoked historical theological representations of Jews as having deceived and undermined the Prophet Mohammad in order to achieve their selfish and malicious aims (Wistrich, 2010). These representations were used to explain the establishment and sustenance of the State of Israel, which Bahar viewed as an "illegal state which should not exist". Drawing upon the antisemitic social representation of Jewish world deception/domination, Bahar contested the legitimacy of the State of Israel. Crucially, *Jewish* deception was constructed as the nucleus of Israel. The Prophet Mohammad, as a personification of Islam, was clearly an important symbol, whose negative experiences with Jews symbolised a broader Jewish theological threat to Islam, for some individuals. This served to construct Jews as posing both a symbolic/theological *and* physical/realistic threat to the Muslim ingroup.

Similarly, Mohammad conflated the early days of Islam and the present day in order to argue that the Jews had consistently been malevolent and threatening, specifically towards Muslims. The routineness of Jewish harm to Muslims was reiterated in the argument that "they are just doing what they always did". The metaphor of "trampling" constructed imagery of contempt and destruction, reinforcing the social representation of Jewish cruelty and ruthlessness. As observed, there was a constructed uniformity between the Jewish threat to Muslims in the early days of Islam and the current threat to Muslims in Palestine. Jewish malevolence and deceit were objectified in terms of the State of Israel. Israel has been represented as the culmination of "Jewish plots" against the Islamic world (Litvak, 2006; Shahvar, 2009). For hardline participants, Shiite Islamic theology provided a principal source of social representations of Jews and Israel, and these representations depicted Jews as posing threats to the Islamic ingroup. Given the hybridised nature of the "Jewish threat", this could be considered a threat to both individual and group levels of the continuity principle of identity (Jaspal and Cinnirella, 2010b).

Just as many reformist participants denied being anti-Zionists, partly as a means of establishing distinctiveness from the hardline outgroup, most individuals in the study categorically denied being antisemitic, although they did acknowledge that antisemitism existed within Iranian society. Despite this desire for positive self-presentation, participants' accounts, both those of reformists and hardliners, did exhibit elements of antisemitic thinking:

> I'm not against Jews at all, you know. They are here and they've always been here [...] You know, there's a long of arrogance in Jews. They think they're the ones who have been chosen by God and that's rubbish [...] Iran was not a Muslim country and everyone converted. They decided to keep their faith. Why? They don't attend Islamic classes and don't even want to know about this. (Ashkan, male, hardliner)

Although Ashkan was keen to dissociate himself from antisemitism by claiming that he was "not against Jews" and by recognising their long-standing connection with Iran, he clearly attributed negative characteristics to Jews as an ethno-religious group. These negative characteristics served to differentiate the Jewish outgroup from the (positive) ingroup (Bar-Tal, 2000). He essentialised Jews as an "arrogant" people due to the Jewish theological belief that they were "chosen" to be in a covenant with God (Frank, 1993), a social representation that he rejected. Individuals in the study seemed to reject this sense of (Jewish) distinctiveness, implied by "chosen-ness", partly because they wished to emphasise the positive distinctiveness of Islam. By recognising the "chosen-ness" of the Jews, some individuals clearly felt that their own sense of positive distinctiveness, on the basis of their Muslim identity, could be subject to jeopardy.

Several participants drew upon common discursive "othering" strategies that have been observed in previous research into talk about immigrants and ethnic minorities (LeCouteur and Augoustinos, 2001; Potter and Wetherell, 1987). For instance, Ashkan constructed Jews as refusing to "integrate" by engaging in a historical self-imposed isolation from other (Muslim) Iranians. More specifically, he highlighted the retention of their Jewish faith (in contrast to Iranians who had converted from Zorastrianism to Islam) as evidencing their "self-imposed isolation" and "negative difference" from other Iranians. Thus, the very notion of Jewish religious distinctiveness seemed to be threatening for some individuals, who appeared to expect religious minorities, such as the Jews, to embrace the Islamic faith. Moreover, in contemporary terms, Ashkan lamented the exemption of Jews from attendance in Islamic religious classes in Iranian public schools and the tendency for Iranian Jewish pupils to decline to attend such classes. The constructed negative valence of Jewish distinctiveness is noteworthy. In short, there was an expectation among some individuals that Iranians Jews ought to relinquish their ethno-religious heritage and assimilate to Muslim Iranian culture, which was represented as the only means of truly integrating in Iranian society. In short, in regards to Iranian Jews, "integration" really meant assimilation (Bowskill, Coyle and Lyons, 2007).

Accordingly, even those individuals who most adamantly denied allegations of antisemitism nonetheless perceived Jews as lacking national authenticity – they were simply not regarded as being "true" Iranians:

> I have no problem with them [Jews] […] but they are not really Iranians are they? They are not true Iranians. Their faith is somewhere else. Their loyalty is somewhere else. (Elham, female, reformist)

Social psychological research highlights the importance of establishing feelings of authenticity in relation to important social identities (Chryssochoou, 2014; Markowe, 1996), especially through "identity validation" from other ingroup members (Jaspal and Cinnirella, 2012). For Elham, Iranian Jews could not be considered Iranian due to their minority Jewish faith. Thus, there was a coercive social representation among participants that Islam was inextricably associated with Iranian-ness, even among those (largely reformist) individuals who lamented the excessive influence of Islam upon Iranian politics. Thus, Iranian national identity and Islamic religious identity appeared to be inter-connected in the minds of young Iranians, which rendered the psychological coherence principle of identity susceptible to threat when the inter-connectedness of these identities was somehow questioned.

It is noteworthy that most participants did regard Iranian Christians as more authentic members of the Iranian national ingroup, which highlighted the particular suspicion held towards Jews. There seemed to be an inability to accept the "Iranian-ness" of Iranian Jews, due to the long-standing social representation of Jewish otherness and questions surrounding the loyalty of Iranian Jews since the establishment of the State of Israel. This suggested that the continuity principle motivated individuals to continue to exclude Iranian Jews from the national ingroup. Like Elham, several individuals perceived Iranian Jews as *disloyal* members of the national ingroup, implying that their Jewish identity interfered with their loyalty to the national ingroup. According to most individuals' accounts, the root cause of Jewish disloyalty to Iran was their supposed affiliation and devotion to the State of Israel:

> They are a bit of an enemy within Iran, like a hidden enemy because they love Israel and even when you hear them talk about Israel, they will never say they're against it. They might say so but you can tell in their voice [...] They will just be very open when they finally get to Israel and forget there's even a country called Iran. They secretly support Israel. It's all very secretive. (Bahman, male, hardliner)

A prevalent social representation among hardliners was that Iranian Jews constituted an "enemy within". Some individuals perceived Iranian Jews as posing a threat due to their invisibility within Iranian society. Thus, while some enemies could be easily identified and stopped, Iranian Jews were said to be hidden within Iranian society and, thus, more threatening.

Bahman attributed the "disloyalty" of Iranian Jews to their covert "love" of Israel, which he evidenced by referring to their supposed proclivity to avoid overt opposition to Israel. More specifically, he appeared to argue that they paid lip service to the Iranian policy of anti-Zionism but upon close scrutiny "you can tell in their voice" that they were not truly opposed to Zionism. There was a perception among participants that the Jews' stated opposition to Israel was insincere and inauthentic. Given the perceived hybridised threat of anti-Zionism and centrality of this policy to Iranian national identity among hardline participants, they tended to regard the "insincerity" of Jewish anti-Zionism as evidence of their "otherness" and as contributing to the "Zionist threat".

Like Bahman, several participants noted that the vast majority of Iranian Jews had emigrated to the State of Israel, which they interpreted as a form of treason or disloyalty towards Iran. There was a perception that the remaining Jews in Iran would also soon leave for Israel. Accordingly, Bahman hypothesised that Iranian Jews would manifest their true national loyalty to the State of Israel upon arrival in the country and "forget" Iran, a country to which they allegedly manifested no commitment. Incidentally, it has been demonstrated that Iranian Jews appear to manifest a strong attachment to their Iranian national identity (Jaspal, 2014b). However, there was widespread suspicion among participants that Iranian Jews were covertly supportive of Israel and that, accordingly, they routinely engaged in acts of espionage against Iran, thereby posing a hybridised threat to the Iranian Muslim majority. It is noteworthy that, in addition to construing the Jewish exodus from Iran as evidence of disloyalty and threat, some participants appeared to express a sense of envy in that they too wished to depart Iran due to the economic conditions in the country, but felt disempowered and helpless.

As alluded to by Bahman, the threat perceived to be associated with Iranian Jews was less conspicuous due to their ability to "blend in":

> The hide their faith and just blend in. They look Iranian, they sound Iranian but they are not really […] I don't really like it when they don't show their religion. (Neda, female, hardliner)

> A guy I knew for years at school – his name was [*mentions an atypical Persian name*] – he had a weird name but we never guessed he is a Jew or anything different from us. He never told us anything. Then one day we hear he's left for Israel and I just thought "What?" He left like he was just waiting for this day. It's like a deceit because you can hide who you are and then when you can, leave us and leave your country […] It made me think about what he thought about Iran maybe. (Shohreh, female, reformist)

There was considerable suspicion surrounding the position and intentions of Jews in Iran. Neda highlighted the alleged ability of Iranian Jews to "just blend in" due to their Iranian appearance and Persian language abilities. It is noteworthy, however, that most Iranian Jews do speak the Persian language as their first language and do not actually speak Hebrew at all (Jaspal, 2014b). However, some individuals' accounts seemed to suggest that their use of the Persian language constituted a deliberate, malicious ploy to "blend in": "they sound Iranian". Moreover, she and others implied that, although Iranians "look Iranian", this too was some form of ploy to give the impression that there are authentic members of the ethno-national ingroup. There was a social representation that Iranian Jews were feigning membership in the Iranian national group, which was underpinned by participants' belief in the national inauthenticity of Iranian Jews.

Several respondents seemed to believe that Iranian Jews deliberately concealed their Jewish ethno-religious heritage in order to gain acceptance and inclusion within Iranian society. Incidentally, this observation served to construct Jewish ethno-religious heritage as a "barrier" to inclusion and acceptance in Iranian society – in short, participants seemed to regard Jewishness as incompatible with Iranian-ness. Iranian Jews were simply not regarded as being authentic members of the ingroup but rather as imposters. It is noteworthy that participants' accounts of Jewish inauthenticity and identity incompatibility echoed Nazi-era social representations of Jews as threatening and invisible imposters who had managed to adopt German customs at a superficial level but who nonetheless remained "foreign" (Herf, 2010).

Like Shohreh, some participants reported feeling misled and, in some cases, betrayed by Iranian Jews who had not disclosed their Jewish ethno-religious heritage. Shohreh recounted her surprise at the discovery that a former school friend was Jewish (rather than Muslim) and that he had emigrated to the State of

Israel. Clearly, what troubled Shohreh was her lack of knowledge about his "true" ethno-religious identity, on the one hand, and his decision to leave Iran for Israel (which many respondents perceived as an enemy state) on the other. Because Jews were generally perceived as posing a threat, there was a sense that ingroup members needed to be aware of Jews and their presence among Muslims in order to identify and halt the threat potentially posed by them. Like other participants in the study, Shohreh believed that her former school friend had deliberately "concealed" his Jewish identity and argued that his subsequent emigration to Israel constituted evidence of his lack of commitment to Iranian national identity, disloyalty and "deceit". Shohreh implied that Iranian Jews willingly deceived Muslims regarding their ethno-religious heritage in order to lead a "comfortable" life in Iran until the opportunity for departure to Israel arose. It appeared that examples of Iranian Jews leaving Iran for Israel had instilled in the minds of some individuals the social representation that Iranian Jews were inherently disloyal to Iran and therefore unworthy of trust or integration/ acceptance in Iranian society. There was a general perception that they posed a hybridised threat to the Iranian ingroup.

The paradox in participants' accounts concerned the desirability of ethno-religious self-disclosure among Iranian Jews. Although some individuals were concerned about the concealment of Jewish ethno-religious heritage among Iranian Jews, there was also a sense that Jewish identity should remain suppressed and silenced in order to protect the position of Shiite Islam in Iran:

> Sara (female, reformist): There are already quite a few synagogues in Iran and most are secret, I think [...] I did see one [...] I don't know. I didn't like it much [...] The Jewish culture is not an Iranian culture really and it can in a way contaminate the Iranian culture, the Shia culture [...] It should be a personal thing at home.

> Interviewer: Should this be the case for all other religions? I mean, Christianity, for instance?

> Sara: No, Christianity is different, I think. They are not the same as Jews.

Sara was one of several individuals who lamented the visibility of Judaism in the Islamic Republic of Iran. Although it was generally acknowledged that Judaism was covertly practiced in Iran, subtle indicators such as "Hebrew writing" on the entrances of small synagogues and "Hebrew singing" in Jewish religious gatherings were nonetheless construed as offensive. The offence lay in the social visibility of Judaism in an officially Shiite Islamic country. Echoing the theme of incompatibility between Iranian-ness and Judaism, Sara argued that because "the Jewish culture is not an Iranian culture" there should be no visible manifestations of Jewish identity. She regarded the manifestation of Jewishness as posing a symbolic threat to both Iran and Shiite Islam given its alleged ability to "contaminate". This perception was consistent with the long-standing religious representation that Judaism, among other religions, is "najes" or impure and therefore liable to cause contamination (Shahvar, 2009). Indeed, this representation was voiced by several, particularly hardline, participants in the study. Yet, Sara was quite clear in identifying Judaism and Jews as posing a particular threat of contamination, and excluded Christianity from the threat representation. Rather, Christianity was neutrally perceived as "different". Most individuals attempted to present themselves as endorsing religious diversity by acknowledging the right of Jews to practice their religion. However, this "right" to religious freedom was modified – Sara and others argued that Judaism ought to constitute "a personal thing at home", rather than be manifested in public space. The confinement of Judaism to private space was generally construed as a legitimate means of limiting the ability of Jews to "contaminate" Iranian and Shiite Islamic norms and values, thereby curtailing threats to the continuity principle of identity.

This desire to confine Judaism to the private sphere stemmed from the perception that Jews, due to the alleged commitment to Zionism and to the State of Israel, would spread Zionist propaganda and, thus, pose a symbolic threat to the Islamic Republic. This itself constituted a paradox given that most reformist participants expressed mistrust of the Islamic theocratic system and a desire for political change in Iran:

> I don't think the Islamic system is the right political system for Iran. A change would be good because it would make me feel I actually have a stake, a role in my own country […] Jews in Iran want to bring the Islamic Republic to an end really. They were the main supporters of the Shah who was a tyrant. (Behzad, male, reformist)

> Iranian leaders are just misleading the people in many ways right now [… .] The Jewish people desire change. They wish to change our country and make it into something that will benefit them, I think. (Darioush, male, reformist)

> I want to see change in this country because I don't trust our leaders at all [… .] As long as they [the Jews] keep it all discreet it's OK. As long as they don't spread their views and religion and ideology in this country, I mean the Zionist ideology. I prefer things to remain the same here. (Tannaz, female, reformist)

The quotes clearly demonstrate individuals' mistrust of the Iranian government, on the one hand, and their resistance to any political change associated with Iranian Jews (or Zionists), on the other. While individuals seemed to support some form of political change, they were fearful that such change could be instigated by Jews. Reformist participants, in particular, manifested their mistrust of the Islamic theocratic system and perceived their leaders as deliberately attempting to mislead the Iranian people in order to serve their own corrupt interests. This social representation was so powerful that many individuals overtly questioned the adequacy and suitability of Islamic theocracy for Iran. Behzad's account implied that a change in Iran's political system could enhance feelings of control and agency and perform an empowering function for the Iranian people, thereby bolstering the self-efficacy principle of identity.

Yet, despite their criticisms of the Islamic political system in Iran, these individuals were deeply suspicious of Jews, whom they accused of attempting to disrupt the Islamic political system. It is noteworthy that when Iranian Jews were perceived as instigating such change this was construed as "disruptive" rather than empowering. Behzad anchored Iranian Jews to the "tyranny" of the former Shah of Iran, who was toppled in the Islamic Revolution which led to the establishment of the Islamic Republic. Thus, the notion that Iranian Jews should wish to "bring the Islamic Republic to an end" was evaluated negatively because it implied that the Jews would also back the Shah's tyranny. Tannaz feared that Jews attempted to "spread their views", which were implied to be incompatible with dominant thinking among Muslims in Iran, "their religion and ideology". Thus, there was a perception that Jews, by virtue of their ethno-religious heritage, were necessarily supportive of Zionist ideology and would attempt to disseminate this ideology, potentially destabilising Iran. Given the perceived incompatibility between the norms, values and social representations attributed to Jewishness and those associated with Iranian-ness, this prospect jeopardised the psychological coherence principle of identity. Moreover, the perceived sense of competition between ingroup and outgroup norms rendered them a symbolic threat to the ingroup.

Interviewees widely argued that, if Iran were to recognise Israel and to re-establish relations with the country, this would be the outcome of *Jewish* lobbying within Iran. This would appear to be a dire over-estimation of Jewish political influence in Iran, given their near invisibility in the country and the fact that they only return one MP to the 290-seat Iranian parliament. However, like Tannaz, most participants were deeply suspicious of Jews because they over-estimated the level of power and control that they might hold within the Islamic Republic, that is, outgroup efficacy was accentuated vis-à-vis ingroup self-efficacy which was attenuated. Thus, despite the potential positive outcomes of internal political change for self-efficacy among disaffected Iranians, the notion that Iranian Jews might exercise their self-efficacy (in instigating such change) was deemed to be unacceptable. The over-estimation of self-efficacy among Iranian Jews seemed to threaten ingroup self-efficacy (Jaspal, 2013a).

Similarly, Darioush lamented the change that Jews were allegedly attempting to instigate in Iran because he, like other interviewees in the study, perceived the Jews as being foreign to Iran and, thus, their attempt to instigate change as external rather than internal. Ingroup and outgroup boundaries were clearly at play here – "our" country would be changed by "them", an outgroup. There was a general desire for continuity, rather than change instigated by Jews. Thus, although political change may well be desirable given the distrust of Iranian leaders, this would only be desirable when initiated from within the country by national ingroup members (i.e. Iranian Muslims).

Creating and Elaborating Antisemitic Social Representations

The previous section described participants' social representations concerning Iranian Jews, which tended to frame Jews in terms of a threat. In order to elaborate upon the threat representation, individuals invoked and modified classic antisemitic motifs, such as those of Jewish deception and Jewish world domination.

Although participants in the study were aware of the social representation of Jewish suffering across distinct historical and geographical contexts, including that of the Holocaust, many of them rejected this representation and argued that a narrative of Jewish suffering had been fabricated by the Jews themselves. This contributed to the antisemitic social representation of Jewish deception of the world:

> They say they have suffered more than anyone in the world […] They are always talking about Jews suffering here, Jews suffering there. I don't think they are suffering so much. It's a lie really […] A Zionist lie. (Neda, female, hardliner)

> Many Jews died in the Holocaust? Many Muslims have also died. Many Iranians died in the "Imposed War" [Iran-Iraq War]. Many Muslims are being killed in Afghanistan, Iraq […] I don't understand the focus on Jews. (Saeed, male, hardliner)

Both Neda and Saeed challenged the social representation of Jewish suffering by arguing that this was a "lie" and, more specifically, that the Holocaust (itself a metaphor for Jewish suffering in history) (Stein, 1978) had been grossly exaggerated. Neda appeared to invoke the repetitiveness of the narrative of Jewish suffering ("Jews suffering here, Jews suffering there"), implicitly arguing that it constituted an attempt to convince people of its validity. Conversely, Saeed elaborated his rejection of the social representation of Jewish suffering by comparing instances of Jewish suffering with those of Muslim and Iranian suffering. He questioned the significance of the Holocaust by focusing upon the number of victims on both sides. Saeed argued that although "many Jews" had died in the Holocaust, "many Muslims" too had died in other conflicts. The argument that innocent Iranians too had been killed in the "Imposed War", which is the term used in Iran to refer to the Iran-Iraq War, constituted an attempt to diminish the social representation of Jewish suffering vis-à-vis Iranian suffering.

Some participants did accept the social representation of Jewish suffering by acknowledging that Jews had suffered more persecution than any other ethno-religious group in history. However, there was a tendency for some interviewees to modify this social representation by depriving the Jews of their victimhood status and arguing that, as an inherently malevolent people, the Jews had inflicted suffering upon themselves:

> Interviewer: Some people would argue that nobody has suffered as much as the Jews have over history. What would be your response to that?

Faraz (male, hardliner): Ask yourself that question. Why do you think they've suffered discrimination everywhere? You can blame one group, another country, another country but the whole world? It's because they lie, they dominate people and they just want to keep the world as slaves, their slaves. In Iran, we know this and we are vigilant.

Faraz deployed the argument that widespread discrimination against Jews over millennia must indicate a shared experience of victimhood among host countries. There was a sense that Jews must have "done something" to merit such uniform treatment at the hands of their host countries. The sheer scale of antisemitic persecution, both geographical and temporal, was strategically interpreted as evidence of Jewish wrongdoing. Faraz denied the victimhood of Jews and instead held them responsible for malevolent acts against their host countries, which he believed had resulted in antisemitic persecution. This served to inculpate Jews, on the one hand, and to implicitly rationalise antisemitism, on the other.

Faraz argued that, while it was possible to "blame one group" for antisemitism, it was unreasonable to charge "the whole world" with irrational antisemitism. Participants were essentially constructing a social representation that the Jews had collectively and perpetually "wronged" the world which had led to (self-inflicted) Jewish suffering. The antisemitic social representation that Jews deceive, control and dominate the world was presented as the key to understanding long-standing antisemitism. Crucially, Faraz drew upon this imagery in explaining and rationalising widespread suspicion of Jews in Iran. In assuming this "knowledgeable" position concerning Jews, Faraz constructed his religio-national ingroup as self-efficacious and, thus, resistant to the negative acts of Jews that had driven the world to antisemitic persecution. More generally, this perhaps bolstered individuals' sense of psychological coherence, since they were able to accept social representations of Jewish malevolence and of Jewish suffering, respectively.

Some individuals invoked antisemitic conspiracy theories, such as the theory that Jews had engineered the 9/11 terror attacks in New York, in order to exemplify the hybridised threat they believed that Jews posed:

I don't have any problems with Israel. I don't really care. It's not a big issue to me […] I think most people know that Jews do have a control and they make things happen. Even September 11th, I saw a documentary that the Jews were not at work that day. Why? They are behind a lot of things that happen in the world […] As long as it doesn't affect me, OK, but it does happen. (Parveen, female, reformist)

Jews in Iran celebrated in their synagogues here and they were caught […] When the Palestinians, the Lebanese are killed, even here they must be celebrating. When they hear Israel has succeeded they are celebrating. When they hear that their plans have worked. (Abbas, male, hardliner)

Both Parveen and Abbas denied any opposition to Israel, and anti-Zionism did not appear to feature prominently in their discourse. Yet, their accounts were underpinned by antisemitic social representations concerning Jewish world control and Jewish atrocities against gentiles. Parveen invoked the conspiracy theory concerning Jewish complicity in the 9/11 terrorist attacks in New York, which suggests that Jewish employees at the World Trade Centre were deliberately absent on the day of the attacks due to prior knowledge of, and complicity in, the attacks. Thus, negative world events, some of which have been attributed to Islamist terrorists such as the 9/11 attacks, were re-attributed to Jews. Social psychologists have long argued that human beings attempt to make sense of a complex world, to reduce uncertainty and to distance negativity from the self by engaging in heuristic processes, such as external attribution (Kelley, 1967). Here, the Jews were scapegoated in order to reduce uncertainty but also to justify the threat representation that many individuals clearly espoused. Like most participants, Parveen attempted to distance herself from the potential accusation of antisemitism by arguing that she personally held no grudges against Jews, but nonetheless accepted the social representation that Jews committed atrocities against non-Jews. This constituted a means of bolstering self-esteem (by deflecting antisemitism) while safeguarding continuity of belief (in Jewish negativity).

Abbas anchored Iranian Jews to the antisemitic social representation of Jewish atrocities, constructing complicity between world Jewry and Iranian Jewry. He modified the polemic social representation concerning Iranian Jewish complicity in Zionism (and anti-Palestinian activities) which was widely disseminated by a hardline weekly Iranian newspaper *Yalesarat* in 2006.[5] The newspaper incorrectly reported that during the 2006 Israel-Lebanon war Iranian Jews celebrated Israeli independence in synagogues in Shiraz, and suggested that Iranian Jews in the city covertly supported Zionism. This caused some unrest in Shiraz, including assaults on synagogues in the city which led to the intervention of the Iranian security forces. Although the newspaper report was subsequently discredited in Iran, Abbas and other participants continued to invoke this polemic social representation in denigrating Iranian Jews and their conduct. Indeed, he argued, more broadly than the original newspaper had, that Iranian Jews celebrated the death of fellow Muslims and the success of Israel within their synagogues. This served to construct Muslim-Jewish intergroup tensions and to accentuate the social representation that Iranian Jews posed a hybridised threat to the ingroup due to their disloyalty.

The perception of disloyalty among Iranian Jews clearly stemmed from antisemitic social representations of Jewish deception. Participants elaborated upon these social representations by referring to *inter alia* the Jewish Banu Qurayza tribe's alleged deception of the Prophet Mohammed, Jewish solidarity against ethno-religious outgroups and the desire for world domination:

---

5   BBC News http://news.bbc.co.uk/1/hi/world/middle_east/5367892.stm

I'm not in favour of the Islamic Republic or the mullahs, you know. They do limit our rights […] How can you expect Jews to be part of an Islamic Republic though? They're not going to be faithful. They will stick to their own kind, Israel which wants to attack Iran. You must keep an eye on them. (Behruz, male, reformist)

Jews have been fooling the world for many centuries. The Prophet was kind and saw good in human beings but was deceived by the Jews […] Jews do this everywhere. Not one place or two. I am talking about everywhere. It's a known fact. (Mitra, female, hardliner)

Respondents widely regarded Iranian Jews as "naturally" bonding with world Jewry and, in particular, with the State of Israel due to their shared Jewish ethno-religious heritage. There was a discernible perception of collusion among world Jewry. Indeed, Mitra attributed to Jews the reputation of "fooling the world for many centuries", thereby constructing this as an essentialised trait associated with the ethno-religious group. The long-standing nature of this negative trait was emphasised through reference to the early days of Islam, in which the Islamic Prophet Mohammed was allegedly "deceived by the Jews". Crucially, the positive characteristics of the Prophet Mohammed ("kind"; "saw good in human beings") were juxtaposed with the negative characteristics of the Jews, which served to reiterate negative social representations of Jews. Mitra invoked the historical social representation of the Jewish Banu Qurayza tribe in Northern Arabia which was defeated by the Muslims led by the Prophet Mohammed (Lewis, 2004). Several individuals drew upon this historical social representation in order to substantiate the argument that world Jewry was inherently deceitful and untrustworthy. This negative trait was constructed as both temporally pervasive ("for many centuries") and geographically ubiquitous ("Not one place or two. I'm talking about everywhere"). It has been observed that Ayatollah Khomeini too drew upon the historical representation of the Banu Qurayza tribe in attempting to justify the dismantlement of the State of Israel (Shahvar, 2009). The invocation of historical social representations was beneficial for the continuity principle of identity, since it safeguarded consistency between past and present and facilitated predictions for the future. It also enhanced the meaning principle of identity, because it allowed individuals to make sense of the present by drawing upon the past.

In participants' accounts, both world Jewry and the State of Israel were perceived as posing a threat, and there was a complex entwining of the contemporary threat popularly perceived to be associated with Israel and the historical representation of Jews undermining Islam. Given the social representation of an Israeli threat ("which wants to attack Iran"), the constructed "natural bond" between Iranian Jewry and Israel rendered the former equally as threatening in the minds of several participants. In view of the "evidence" of the Jews' betrayal of their host countries and the world more generally, Behruz concluded that greater surveillance of the Iranian Jewish community and distrust of their intentions were logical strategies for curbing the threat. More generally, in Mitra's account, it appeared that, because the Jews were historically threatening, there was little reason to doubt that *Iranian* Jews too might pose a threat.

Despite forceful assertions from the Iranian government that it differentiates between Judaism and Zionism, that it honours and respects Judaism and that it opposes only the political ideology of Zionism (see Jaspal, 2013a), there was a systematic conflation of Jews and the State of Israel in most participants' accounts. The conflation of Judaism and Zionism was apparent in their reflections upon how to deal with the "Zionist threat":

> When the Zionists do these things to Muslims, do they think Jews can be safe around the world? If Hezbollah are responsible for the attack on Jews, then it's because of the Zionists. (Esmail, male, hardliner)

> There is a Zionist threat […] If the Zionist Regime continues to meddle in our affairs then Muslims have to protect one another […] You will need to demand answers from Jews here, yes, even here in Iran. (Darioush, male, hardliner)

Several interviewees clearly believed that Jews should be held responsible for the actions of Zionists, and Esmail appeared to endorse reprisals against Jews. The Lebanese Shiite political movement Hezbollah has been accused of perpetrating terrorist attacks against the State of Israel and Jewish targets abroad, such as the bombing of a Jewish cultural centre (la Asociación Mutual Israelita Argentina) in July 1993. Several participants acknowledged that Hezbollah had perpetrated such attacks but justified them by inculpating Zionists and by invoking the threat representation. Individuals implicitly attributed blame to Zionists by arguing that Zionist actions had led to attacks against Jewish civilians. The underlying logic of this argument was that if Zionists were truly concerned with the wellbeing of Jews they would not engage in acts of aggression and violence against Muslims. The attribution of blame in this manner safeguarded the continuity and meaning principles, since individuals were able to justify and make sense of the ingroup's actions while continuing to perceive them as righteous and justifiable.

Yet, although the Israeli-Palestinian conflict was frequently invoked as the basis for attacks against Jewish civilian targets, Darioush viewed Israel's "meddling" in Iran's internal affairs as sufficient cause for harassing the Jewish population in Iran. He perceived Israeli intervention in Iran's affairs, which was frequently exemplified through reference to the assassination of nuclear scientists and the seizure of "Israeli spies" operating in Iran, as evidence of a "Zionist threat", which limited Iran's ability to function as an independent sovereign state. The hybridised threat clearly jeopardised individuals' sense of self-efficacy and continuity on the basis of their national group membership. In order to cope with the threat, there was a perceived need for Muslim solidarity, that is, "to protect one another". This entailed the exclusion of Iranian Jews, who were regarded as silently supporting (and, thus, colluding with Zionists in) Israeli incursions on Iran's sovereignty. Darioush euphemistically suggested that Iranian Muslims "demand answers from

Jews" regarding Israel's actions, which in actual fact constituted a request to hold Iranian Jews *accountable* for Israel's actions. Thus, although there was at times a nominal delineation of the categories "Jew", "Zionist" and "Israel", the roles, responsibilities and inter-relations between these categories were frequently conflated in participants' discourse and thinking.

The conflation of Israel and (Iranian) Jews appeared to perform positive functions for identity and, thus, constituted a strategy for coping with identity threat:

> I always felt sad at Israel's power but Israel is not so powerful […] It's not the super powerful state. In Iran there are also Jews and in our country they cannot control Muslims. Not in the Islamic Republic. (Bahman, male, hardliner)

> Zionism has always seemed like some massive uncontrollable force. A dangerous ideology that we can't do anything about […] We stamp out Zionism in our country. Imam [Khomeini] stamped it out when he killed them in Iran – we had this here too – so they can't dominate us like they do in other countries. (Ashkan, male, hardliner)

Interviewees generally manifested awareness of the social representation of Israel as a powerful and self-efficacious nation-state. There was frequent reference to the "power" and "force" of Israel and its consequential ability to exert control and influence over the world. This appeared to be construed as a threat to the self-efficacy principle of identity – Bahman described his sadness at this perception, while Ashkan lamented his ingroup's inability to curtail Israel's "massive, uncontrollable force". As highlighted by the group vitality framework (Bourhis et al., 1981), the perception that outgroups have greater "vitality" (e.g. control) than the ingroup can constitute a threatening position to occupy (see Jaspal and Sitaridou, 2013). Zionism was clearly perceived as an undesirable, dangerous ideology, which threatened the ingroup's self-efficacy and which, therefore, needed to be defeated. In view of the widespread perception that Israel constituted Iran's Significant Other or "archenemy", the attribution of greater vitality to Israel was immensely threatening for identity among Iranians.

By conflating Zionism and Iranian Jews, some participants appeared to be engaging in a strategy for coping with the threats to self-efficacy associated with Zionism. Although Israel was largely regarded as a "super powerful state", Bahman rejected the validity of this social representation within the context of Iran, where Jews were perceived as powerless and, thus, unable to "control Muslims". Thus, by conflating and homogenising Israel and Iranian Jews, and accentuating the relative powerlessness of Iranian Jews vis-à-vis Iranian Muslims in the Islamic Republic, Bahman seemed to salvage some sense of self-efficacy, that is, the control and competence of his ethno-religious ingroup.

Similarly, while Ashkan perceived Zionism as a "massive, uncontrollable force", he too rejected the validity of this representation within the context of the Islamic Republic and cited the example of Ayatollah Khomeini having "stamped out" Zionism in Iran by identifying and executing Jews with connections to Zionism. Although many individuals clearly perceived Jews, both Iranian Jews and world Jewry, as posing a threat, Jews in Iran were positioned as a relatively weak outgroup in that they were not regarded as able to "dominate us like they do in other countries". Like Bahman, Ashkan emphasised the relative powerlessness of Iranian Jews and Khomeini's "stamping out" of Zionism in the early days of the Islamic Republic in order to bolster his own ingroup's self-efficacy.

There was a tendency for individuals to invoke, elaborate and re-construe antisemitic social representations in order to enhance identity processes and to avert identity threat. Similarly, social representations of the Holocaust could challenge identity and elicit creative strategies for coping with threat.

Anti-Zionism and Holocaust Revisionism

Antisemitic conspiracy theories were observable in participants' accounts, the most noteworthy of which was the social representation that Jews had either fabricated or greatly exaggerated the Holocaust. While scholars have focused largely upon institutional representations of the Holocaust (Jaspal, 2013a, 2014a; Litvak, 2006; Shahvar, 2009), the present study set out to examine how young Iranians themselves thought and talked about the Holocaust.

In some participants' accounts, it was implied that the Holocaust had been fabricated due to a perceived Jewish-Zionist attempt to inhibit a "scientific" debate on the Holocaust:

> I hate Ahmadinejad. I didn't vote for him. I never wanted him. But he came [...] The one thing he did do, and it's courageous, he said to the world "Let's talk about the Holocaust". If Jews have nothing to hide, why hide it? Why do they say "No, we can't discuss this?" Jews in America say it. Zionists say it. (Hooman, male, reformist)

Like Hooman, several participants highlighted their opposition to Ahmadinejad and noted that his policies had caused a destabilisation of the Iranian economy, which constituted a reference to the economic sanctions imposed by the international community. Yet, Hooman commended Ahmadinejad's "courageous" problematisation of the Holocaust and his invitation for critical debate concerning its reality. Statements of this nature suggested that, although there was widespread awareness of the Holocaust, few participants accepted the representation in its entirety and believed that the "truth" had been distorted. Both hardline and reformist participants argued that, regardless of one's personal opinions regarding Ahmadinejad's policies, his ability to "stand up to" the US and Israel by questioning their "version" of the Holocaust was quite admirable. Ahmadinejad's invitation for debate concerning the Holocaust was said to be opposed by Jews and Zionists, suggesting a complicity in seeking to deceive the world about the reality of the event. Hooman clearly believed that Jewish/Zionist opposition to debating the Holocaust attested to a conspiracy.

It is noteworthy that not all participants were so categorical in their rejection of mainstream Holocaust knowledge. Some individuals did appear to accept the social representation but re-constructed it to varying degrees in order to perform particular rhetorical and psychological functions. For instance, by acknowledging the Holocaust explicitly, some individuals were able to deflect potential accusations of antisemitism from the self:

> I do believe the Holocaust happened. Yes. I personally believe this but not all
> Iranians believe it. Still we shouldn't stop people talking about it scientifically
> and analysing the data and looking to see what we misinterpreted and what we
> did correctly. We can know more so Zionists should allow this also. They do not.
> (Noushin, female, reformist)

Although Noushin stated that she did believe that the Holocaust had taken place, she did acknowledge that there was disbelief among Iranians. While this served to position her in opposition to Holocaust deniers, thereby bolstering self-presentation, she nonetheless acknowledged that there was no unanimous agreement regarding Holocaust knowledge. This enabled her, firstly, to argue that there was a need for greater discussion regarding the Holocaust, not necessarily to disprove existing Holocaust knowledge but rather to explore it "scientifically" and, secondly, to criticise the Zionists' alleged tendency to silence debate regarding the Holocaust. Noushin's account represented a subtle means of questioning existing knowledge regarding the Holocaust and of accusing Zionists of maliciously silencing "scientific" debate. This constituted a means of negativising Zionists, the Significant Other, which through processes of downward comparison was favourable for the self-esteem principle of identity (Jaspal, 2011a).

In reflecting upon the potential reasons underlying the Jews'/Zionists' "silencing" of the Holocaust debate, many respondents argued explicitly that the social representation of the Holocaust sustained Israel's existence:

> But I think we need to have a discussion about the Holocaust. If the Holocaust
> has happened as the Jews say, then why don't they allow us to discuss it? I
> feel that Israel's existence is based on what they say about this [the Holocaust].
> (Saeed, male, hardliner)

Although Saeed did not overtly deny the Holocaust, he did indicate there was a need for "a discussion" about it, implicitly suggesting that not all of the facts regarding the Holocaust had been disclosed. This was attributed to the Jews whom Saeed accused of deliberately silencing debate. This demonstrated the tendency for slippage between the categories "Jew" and "Zionist" in participants' accounts. Like Saeed, many participants regarded emotive social representations of the Holocaust as key to Israel's existence. There was a perception among participants that the world had been emotionally blackmailed into accepting the existence of Israel and into condoning its actions. Indeed, there is a social representation in Iranian society that the Holocaust somehow exempts Israel from international criticism (Shahvar, 2009), which itself has led to Holocaust denial. Accordingly, individuals argued that Holocaust representations were invoked in order to silence debate and to justify the "extreme" measures undertaken by the Israeli government. There was a sense that, if the "truth" regarding the Holocaust were disclosed to the world, the State of Israel would lose much of its international support and perhaps even its raison d'être. Thus, some individuals did view the Holocaust as a means of destabilising Israel and thereby removing the threat that it was perceived as posing.

Some participants seemed to differentiate between Jews and Zionists, focusing exclusively upon Zionists as a target for delegitimisation. Similarly, Khosrow accused Zionists of having collaborated with the Nazis in their extermination of Jews:

> Zionism is a branch of fascism. The Zionists collaborated with the Nazis – there is historical evidence. But this has nothing to do with Jews, just the ones who stood up to them […] They [Jews] just suffered the consequences of this. (Khosrow, male, reformist)

Khosrow delegitimised Zionism by anchoring it to fascism, which essentially generalised the negative social representations of fascism that have accumulated over various decades to Zionist ideology (Litvak and Webman, 2009). This served to crystallise linkage between the two ideologies, encouraging individuals to regard and evaluate Zionism through the same negative lens through which fascism is popularly regarded and evaluated. Khosrow and several other participants elaborated on the linkage between Nazism and Zionism by invoking the polemic social representation that Zionists had covertly collaborated with the Nazis in order to create a moral case for the State of Israel (Litvak and Webman, 2009). This polemic social representation has been widely disseminated by Holocaust revisionists in Europe and in the Middle East (Lipstadt, 1993). Crucially, in demonising Zionists, participants indicated that non-Zionist Jews were innocent and themselves had "suffered the consequences of this [Nazi-Zionist alliance]". Khosrow argued that the Nazis did not massacre Zionist Jews but rather those Jews who opposed Zionist ideology, which positioned Zionism in opposition to Judaism. Accordingly, non-Zionist Jews were shielded from the negative social representations attributed to Zionism.

More generally, this constituted a means of problematising social representations of the Holocaust, due primarily to the re-construal and re-attribution of blame. Participants perceived Zionists as the key perpetrators of the Holocaust – the Nazis were conversely represented as the "assassins" sent by the Zionists. This challenged the social representation that Nazis masterminded the Holocaust and, conversely, constructed the representation that Zionism, the ideology that underpins the State of Israel, led to the Holocaust. It may be that some participants were more aware of the sensitivity in world public opinion to antisemitism and the relative acceptability of anti-Zionism, which could have motivated them to craft accounts that nominally delegitimised Zionists, in particular. Yet, as Shahvar (2009) has argued, while a Jew in Tehran may be "tolerated", "once the very same Jew steps into Israel [either physically or metaphorically], he becomes immediately 'a Zionist conspirator', 'an Israeli oppressor', a person who has to be fought with whatever means" (p.103). This was clearly exemplified by the tendency among some participants to shield Jews from negative social representations attributed to Zionism.

The social desirability of shielding Jews, an ethno-religious group, from negative social representations of Zionism, a political category, was observable in several individuals' accounts. However, there was constant slippage between the categories that were employed in order to describe the perpetrators of Holocaust fabrication/ exaggeration. Participants shifted between the categories "Jew" and "Zionist", suggesting that these were interchangeable groups that had collectively engaged in deceit:

> I do think the Holocaust did happen. Yes, people died. 6 million Jews? No, I don't think so. I think that's a lie and it's been successful. The Jews got their state. I'm not against it. But I think this is why they got their country. This is Zionism. They made the world feel bad for them. (Roya, female, reformist)

> I don't have any problem with Jews […] My best friend at university was Jewish […] I can't understand why the Holocaust is so important that countries forbid you to ask questions about this so it seems like the Jews, the Zionists, they are all the same, they want to hide something, I think. (Afsane, female, reformist)

Although some individuals did acknowledge the Holocaust, as Roya did, they nonetheless regarded it as a gross exaggeration in order to elicit the world's sympathy and thereby facilitate Zionist activities. More specifically, the social representation of the Holocaust was perceived as central to Israel's existence. Although participants attributed this social representation to the Jews, the act of deceiving the world and of establishing the Jewish State on the basis of a "lie" was referred to as Zionism. The category "Jew" was attributed to the population, while the category "Zionism" was employed in order to describe the ideological process underlying the establishment of Israel. In short, there was a conflation of these categories. Roya's insistence on Jewish deception of the world served to construct the foundations of Israel as being morally dubious, thereby delegitimising the State of Israel. Superficially, Roya argued that she did not oppose the State of Israel perhaps in order to present herself not as a stakeholder in the debate on Israel and Zionism but rather as a "neutral" actor. Yet, from this apparently neutral position, she was able to denigrate Zionism, Israel and the Jews in a more convincing manner. It is noteworthy that all participants acknowledged and, in most cases, lamented the negative publicity that Iran had acquired due to its anti-Zionist (and, in some cases, antisemitic) activity, given the negative impact that this had had on Iran's international image and, consequently, on participants' self-esteem on the basis of their national group membership. Roya and others clearly wished to deflect such negative publicity from the self and therefore asserted their indifference to the State of Israel.

Similarly, Afsane argued that she in no way opposed the Jews and that she in fact had a close Jewish friend, thereby deflecting potential accusations of antisemitism which may ensue from her subsequent questioning of the reality of the Holocaust. In addition to diminishing the importance of the Holocaust as an attempt to systematically annihilate an entire ethno-religious group, Afsane argued that the sensitivity around "asking questions about" the Holocaust (a euphemism for questioning its reality) must indicate a covert Jewish strategy to "hide something" (namely, the notion that the Holocaust never happened at all). In short, despite prefixing their arguments with discursive disclaimers that they in no way opposed Israel or Jews (Potter and Wetherell, 1987), several participants provided accounts which clearly reflected a demonisation of *both* the Jewish people (who were represented as fabricators of the Holocaust myth) and Zionist ideology.

The tendency to question or deny existing Holocaust knowledge allowed individuals in the study to position themselves as distinctively knowledgeable, which enhanced their sense of distinctiveness. Moreover, the Islamic Republic's distinctively vocal questioning of the Holocaust seemed to bolster feelings of self-efficacy, since individuals believed that this evidenced Iran's independence, autonomy and competence on the international stage. More generally, by questioning the reality of the Holocaust, some individuals were able to derive a sense of meaning by explaining how the Jews, a historically "inferior" people in the minds of many participants, were able to establish and defend the State of Israel.

Overview

This chapter explores social representations of Israel and Jews among a group of Iranian Muslims identified with either a hardline or reformist political orientation. Participants in the study exhibited awareness of antisemitic and anti-Zionist social representations, which they accepted and reproduced insofar as these representations enhanced identity processes. However, the hegemonic social representations that Israel and Jews pose realistic and symbolic threats to the Iranian/Muslim ingroup were unanimously accepted and reproduced by individuals in the sample irrespective of political orientation. This may be attributed to the hegemony and coerciveness of threat representations (in relation to Israel and Jews) in Iranian society.

It is argued that anti-Zionism generally performs positive functions for identity processes among both political hardliners and reformists. The maintenance of an anti-Zionist stance can bolster feelings of distinctiveness from Israel and Zionists, a Significant Other (Triandafyllidou, 1998), and thereby provide a cohesive sense of Iranian national identity. Anti-Zionism may be construed as connecting past, present and future in that this stance provides a sense of continuity in Iranian identity. Moreover, by anchoring the State of Israel to historical representations of Jews, a sense of temporal continuity is established. Thus, anti-Zionism can enhance the continuity principle of identity. Moreover, Iran's vociferous anti-Zionist stance can accentuate feelings of control and competence (in relation to the Iranian ingroup), because individuals feel that Iran is able to make a spirited defence against the potent Israeli outgroup. This can have positive outcomes for the self-efficacy principle. Despite the positive psychological functions performed by anti-Zionism, individuals recognised the *political* functions performed by their anti-Zionist stance. While hardliners clearly perceived this as a central aspect of Iranian national identity and, in some cases, as a tenet of Islamic religious identity, political reformists tended to view anti-Zionism as more peripherally associated with Iranian national identity and as more central to the (outgroup) hardliner "agenda". Thus, anti-Zionism appeared to constitute a stance that divided Iranians in accordance with political orientation. Those reformists who anchored anti-Zionism to political hardliners perceived their own opposition to anti-Zionism as a means of differentiating their political ingroup from the hardline outgroup and of bolstering their intergroup distinctiveness. It appeared that individuals were re-construing anti-Zionism in ways that could enhance identity processes.

The data presented in this chapter challenge the notion that Iranians are anti-Zionist, rather than antisemitic, which is often emphasised by Iranian political leaders (Jaspal, 2013a). It appears that there is a mutual interdependence between social representations of Israel and those concerning Jews – Israel is viewed as a continuation of a historical "Jewish threat", and the Jews as relentlessly supporting Israel in its deeds. Elements of antisemitic thinking were observable in participants' accounts. More specifically, there was considerable conflation between (i) historical representations concerning intergroup relations between the Jews and Muslims in the early days of Islam, and (ii) contemporary social representations concerning European Jewry. There was a geo-cultural conflation of European social representations and "indigenous" Iranian social representations. Individuals systematically drew upon historical antisemitic imagery originating from European contexts) which they married with emerging antisemitic representations from the Iranian and Islamic contexts (e.g. concerning the Jews' alleged support for the deposed Shah of Iran). Holocaust denial was pervasive across respondents, although individuals questioned the Holocaust to varying degrees. While some individuals rejected the reality of the Holocaust outright, others modified elements of the Holocaust in order to question the morality of Jews and Zionists. This demonstrated that Iran's long-standing programme of questioning the Holocaust appears to have infiltrated social representations of this act of genocide among the general population. There was a conflation of social representations of Iranian Jews, world Jewry and Zionists. Although many individuals did differentiate between Jews and Zionists, with the latter being systematically demonised, there was generally a perceived collusion between Iranian Jews and Zionists. Individuals generally held the social representations that Jews were committed to the wellbeing and continuity of the State of Israel and therefore would act in ways that protected Israel even if this meant that their actions undermined Iran. Individuals in the study generally positioned Iranian Jews as "Other" to the national ingroup and, thus, viewed them as posing a threat to the Iranian ingroup, on the one hand, and as a legitimate target for anti-Zionist reprisals, on the other.

Chapter 8
"I'm not Antisemitic but … ": Perceptions of Israel and Jews among British Pakistani Muslims

Introduction

There has been some empirical research into antisemitism and anti-Zionism among Muslim minority groups in Europe, which focuses upon a diverse range of ethnic groups in distinct national contexts (e.g. Jikeli, 2009; Jikeli and Allouche-Benayoun, 2013). Moreover, there is a focus primarily upon Holocaust denial, rather than general perceptions of Jews and the Jewish State. Some of this research is summarised in Chapter 1. The data presented in this chapter are drawn from a qualitative interview study with a group of British Pakistani Muslims. After a brief methodological overview, the following themes are outlined and discussed: (i) "Zionism is evil": Making sense of Zionism; (ii) Defeating the State of Israel; (iii) Deflecting Antisemitism through Compartmentalisation Processes; and (iv) Carving a Space in the Islamic Ummah.

Methodological overview

The data presented in this chapter are drawn from an interview study with British Pakistani Muslim men and women. Like the preceding chapter on perceptions of Israel and Jews among young Iranians, this work had a social psychological focus upon how young British Pakistanis perceive Jews and Israelis and how they cognitively manage social representations of these groups.

Thirty-six British Pakistani Muslim individuals between the ages of 18 and 35 participated in an in-depth interview concerning "identity and social attitudes among British Pakistani Muslims" in the summer of 2012. An adapted version of the interview schedule described in Chapter 7 was used for this study. There were 21 male and 15 female respondents. Fifteen participants were from West London (UK) and the remaining 21 were from the East Midlands (UK). All of the participants described their ethnicity as Pakistani, self-identified as Muslim and regarded themselves as very or moderately religious. Thirty participants had completed, or were studying towards, a university degree; and the remaining 6 had completed high school. Data were analysed using thematic analysis, following the same analytical procedures that were described in Chapter 7.

"Zionism is Evil": Making Sense of Zionism

Participants were invited to reflect on Zionism and to define it on their own terms. Most individuals correctly identified Zionism as the political ideology underlying the State of Israel. There was a coercive social representation that it was a negative and malevolent ideology, with the principal function of oppressing the weak and vulnerable:

> Mohammed (male): Zionism is evil. It's no different from Nazism. It's a form of Nazism, like it has come from Hitler's thinking. The same thing. It's all about being superior, racially superior and they think that about themselves. They just think they're better than everyone, especially Muslims, Palestinians. And they can't get away with thinking that.

> Interviewer: Why do you think that?

> Mohammed: It makes me just so angry, like bad. You know, I feel bad just thinking "they are making out they are better than us?"

Most participants converged in perceiving Zionism as an "evil" ideology, which was frequently anchored to Nazi ideology (Litvak and Webman, 2009). As a complex and poorly understood political ideology, Zionism was perceived by participants through the heuristic lens of Nazism, an ideology which, conversely, is much better understood and more present in social and cultural consciousness (Moscovici, 1988). In anchoring Zionism to Nazism, participants were essentially generalising the pervasively accepted negative characteristics of the fascist ideology to Zionism, in order to construct an understanding of it. In Mohammed's account, Zionism was not only anchored to Nazism, but it was also constructed as constituting a cohesive aspect (or subdomain) of Nazi ideology. Moreover, Zionism was provided with a "human face", not by reference to one of the early Zionist leaders but rather to Adolf Hitler. Thus, through the rhetorical technique of personification, Zionism was objectified as having arisen from "Hitler's thinking" and, thus, interchangeable with Nazism. Hitler himself was regarded as having created Zionism, which implicitly constructed him (and his ideology) as underlying the foundation and sustenance of the State of Israel. This view, though factually incorrect, elucidated individuals' underlying social representation of Zionism. Accordingly, many participants in the study delegitimised the Zionist ideology and regarded it as an ideology that needed to be eradicated in the name of world peace.

   Like Mohammed, several individuals implicitly invoked the notion of the *Jews* as a "chosen people", which was then applied to the notion of Zionism, essentially conflating Jewish theology and Zionist political ideology. Indeed, Mohammed anchored the notion of Jewish "chosenness" to the Nazis' notion of Aryan racial superiority in order to render Jewish "chosenness" meaningful and psychologically tangible. It is noteworthy that many religious groups regard themselves as being somehow "chosen" or singled out by God. Yet, most individuals focused and fixated upon the notion of Jewish "chosenness" in order to demonstrate the racism and Nazi-like characteristics of Zionism. Participants construed the notion of Jewish chosenness as outrageous partly because it conflicted with their belief in the theological superiority of Islam, which was frequently reiterated in interviews. Thus, this notion may have been construed as threatening for self-esteem because it challenged the positive self-conception that individuals derived from their religious identity, and continuity since this jeopardised a long-standing perception of the superiority of their religious ingroup.

As exemplified by Mohammed and Abdul (below), the notion of racial superiority, which was perceived to lie at the heart of Zionist ideology due to its alleged connection with Nazism, was threatening for identity. Participants rejected the social representation of Jewish chosenness because they believed that this implied the superiority of Judaism (and Zionism) over Islam:

> Israelis are not better than Palestinians. Jews are not better than Muslims. Islam is the best religion in the world, the purest. But look at who is getting killed each day. Look at who is living in a nice country and who is living in shit. That is Zionism. (Abdul, male)

Both Mohammed and Abdul highlighted their intense dismay at the social representation that Jews/Zionists might regard themselves as "superior" to Muslims/Palestinians. This was considered the most lamentable aspect of Jewish/Zionist ideology, and Mohammed indicated that Zionists "can't get away with thinking that". As indicated above, Abdul rejected the notion of Jewish "chosenness" by highlighting the superiority and purity of Islam (vis-à-vis Judaism), and invoked the absurdity that "superior" Muslims/Palestinians should be "getting killed each day". This was potentially threatening for individuals' sense of self-esteem and continuity. This implied that Jews/Zionists should be the ones getting killed and "living in shit", given their implicit inferiority. While Abdul attributed the status quo, namely that Muslims/Palestinians are unjustifiably disadvantaged vis-à-vis Jews, to Zionist ideology. Several participants' accounts provided insight into the psychological underpinnings of their intense dismay at the social representation that Jews might regard themselves as superior to other groups. Mohammed, for instance, reported feeling "angry" and "bad" when he thought about the notion of Jewish "chosenness".

Similarly, Abdul reproduced the social representation of Islamic superiority when he argued that "Islam is the best religion in the world, the purest". Thus, the social representation that Jews/Zionists might be superior, or regard themselves as superior, to Muslims seemed to displace a deeply held belief that Islam was a superior religion and that the Jews constituted an inferior people (Shahvar, 2009). Moreover, participants delegitimised Zionist ideology because they believed it empowered Jews politically to pose threats to self-esteem and continuity. Thus, delegitimisation entailed attacking the source of threats to identity and might therefore be considered a form of coping strategy (Breakwell, 1986).

In making sense of Zionism, most participants attributed negative (global) occurrences to this political ideology, in much the same way that Jews have historically been scapegoated for the ills of the world (Lindemann and Levy, 2010b). Although individuals denied being antisemitic, many in fact invoked and adapted antisemitic social representations in order to delegitimise Zionism:

> Samina (female): Zionism, the philosophy of evil. Zionism is evil. All of the heartache in the world, everything that has gone wrong, you can put it all down to Zionism.

> Interviewer: Like what, for example?

> Samina: There is an official version to every story, yeah. And like the Twin Towers, some people reckon it was the Zionists behind that […] they told the Jews not to go to work the day that happened. It's just a big conspiracy, and Zionism is behind it all.

In addition to characterising Zionist ideology as "evil" and "the philosophy of evil", Samina attributed the "heartache in the world" to Zionism. Like Samina, several participants capitalised on the opportunity to distance from their religious ingroup particular accusations popularly levelled against Islamism, such as the social representation that Islamist terrorists were responsible for the September 11th terrorist attacks in New York, which was voiced by the Iranians respondents in Chapter 7. It is understandable that participants should wish to distance these atrocities from their religious ingroup, given their awareness of Islamophobic social representations that have characterised intergroup relations (Cinnirella, 2013). In some cases, belief in conspiracy theories may constitute a means of deflecting stigma and the negative social psychological consequences of Islamophobia. By constructing Zionism as the epitome of evil, participants were able to scapegoat the ideology and, as exemplified by Samina's account, *Jews* for global atrocities (see Gregory, 2001). There was a constructed collusion between Zionists and Jews – a "big conspiracy". The constructed interchangeability between Zionists and Jews served to demonise both categories. Although participants in the study denied antisemitism, they "observed" that Jews had somehow benefited from the actions of Zionists. This suggested that, although the perpetrators of aggression may have been Zionists, the benefactors were Jews. The invocation of antisemitic motifs and the construction of Jews as the benefactors of "Zionist atrocities" served to delegitimise both categories.

There was a potent social representation among participants that Zionism posed a realistic threat, on a global scale:

> It [Zionism] has just crushed humanity and they rule from Tel Aviv. It's a small group of people that have their fingers in a lot of different countries. Like sort of controlling them, controlling us, like puppets, you know. Zionism is evil. It will fall, just like fascism did. It is just a last feature of fascism. (Asma, female)

> I feel so, so pissed off when I think about this. It's like they can do what they want and we can't do anything to stop them. Nothing. They are doing what they please and our hands are tied. That feels bad. It feels really bad personally. (Asad, male)

Like others in the study, Asma anchored Zionism to fascist ideology, which reiterated the constructed link between Zionism and Nazism. In representing Zionism as "evil" and as a threat to humanity, Asma referred to it metaphorically as having "crushed" humanity. Use of the metaphor "crush" suggested violent destruction of humanity in superlative terms. Yet, the act of "crushing" humanity was attributed not only to the ideology of Zionism but to the "small group of people" in Tel Aviv. There was an implicit invocation of antisemitic social representations concerning Jewish world domination, which were applied to an unnamed "small group of people" who "rule from Tel Aviv" and who are the creators of Zionism. Anti-Zionism (here, the characterisation of Zionism as "evil") was thereby entwined with antisemitic imagery. The representation of world domination, which was attributed to Zionists/Jews, may be said to be threatening for the self-efficacy principle of identity, given that the ingroup was said to be "controlled" and, thus, helpless vis-à-vis a threatening outgroup – the Jews who have historically been accused of world domination (Lindemann and Levy, 2010b).

The threat to self-efficacy was clearly discernible in Asad's account, which reflected his anger ("so pissed off") and malaise ("it feels really bad personally") at the lack of the Muslim ingroup's control and competence in face of perceived Zionist aggression. Given that the Zionist outgroup was perceived as having disproportionate clout and efficacy ("they are doing what they please") and that the ingroup was perceived as being helpless in curtailing Zionist outgroup efficacy ("our hands are tied"), self-efficacy may be thought of as threatened. However, there was also a sense of optimism in some participants' accounts. Although some of them lamented the "disproportionate" efficacy of the Zionist outgroup, the anchoring of Zionism to Nazism/fascism allowed individuals optimistically to regard Zionism as a *vincible* movement which "will fall, just like fascism did". This may be viewed as a means of coping with the threat (to self-efficacy) of Zionism since individuals perceive it as a transient and short-lived threat (like Nazism and fascism) and not a perpetual one. Indeed, in some Islamic contexts, Israel is socially represented as an illegitimate entity on "Muslim land", which must eventually be destroyed (Litvak, 1998). This social representation can be beneficial if individuals accept it and believe this goal to be attainable.

Consistent with participants' tendency to anchor Zionism to Nazism/fascism, Maryam objectified Zionism as a "prejudice in the world", which she felt was deliberately obscured and concealed by non-Muslims but revealed by Muslims:

> It's just like a prejudice in the world. You don't see it on BBC or CCN because they are like controlled by Zionists themselves but if you listen to the sermons in mosques, you listen to news in Muslim countries and read Muslim papers, and even like even if you read the Koran, it's all spelt out clearly. Even though it was way before Zionism. The truth is in there. Zionists want to crush Muslims and the world and we are not going to let that happen. (Maryam, female)

The social representation of Zionist world domination was employed to explain the global media's "position" on Zionism. Maryam argued that, given that the Zionists directly controlled the BBC and CCN, it was unsurprising that these influential news outlets should refrain from disclosing the "truth" regarding Zionism, namely that the ideology poses a realistic threat to the Muslim world. Conversely, Islamic sermons, the news in Islamic countries, the Islamic press and the Koran were said to recognise the "truth" of Zionism and its genuine characteristics. Although Maryam avoided overt reference to Jews, she appeared to invoke references to Jews in Islamic scripture in order to argue that Zionism posed a threat. In short, historical threat representations were employed in order to construct and disseminate a contemporary threat representation. This served to glorify Islam and Islamic sources, since Muslims were positioned as being in a particularly knowledgeable position concerning Zionism (vis-à-vis non-Muslims who are "controlled" by Zionists and thus unaware of "the truth"). Indeed, occupation of this knowledgeable position appeared to provide individuals with feelings of self-esteem and distinctiveness, because of the positive self-conception that they derived from "knowing" more than the rest of the world. Respondents generally viewed the majority of the world's population as having been brainwashed by Zionism.

In Maryam's psychological world, this position of knowledge was particularly important because of the perceived threats attributed to Zionism. Many individuals in the study regarded Zionism as curtailing the rights and competence of the Islamic world, which was construed as threatening for the self-efficacy principle of identity. Furthermore, as Maryam's account strikingly exemplified, there was a perception that Zionism posed a realistic threat to Muslims and that it therefore jeopardised the group continuity of Muslims. Like Asma, Maryam also employed the metaphor of "crushing" Muslims, which served to construct Zionism as an aggressive and destructive entity that threatened the very existence of Islam and Muslims. Yet, by constructing a conspiracy theory regarding the BBC and CNN, Maryam was able to make sense of the seemingly anomalous position of the world regarding Israel and thereby safeguard the meaning principle. In times of threat and distress, human beings search for meaning, and conspiracy theories can indeed provide the means for doing so (McAdams, 2001).

There was a hegemonic social representation that the Zionist ideology was malevolent and threatening particularly for the Muslim ingroup, an important component of identity for most British Pakistanis. It appeared that individuals perceived the destruction of the State of Israel as a necessary means of coping with the perceived threat of Zionism.

Defeating the State of Israel

Individuals identified a strong relationship between Zionist ideology and the State of Israel. In view of their unanimous negativisation of Zionism, most individuals openly emphasised the social and political desirability of dismantling the State of Israel. According to participants' accounts, one means of "defeating" Israel was to deny the Jewish character of the country and to support a political system which would be elected by the "native Palestinians", namely Muslim and Christian Palestinians and their descendants, and those Jews who could demonstrate an "indigenous" connection to Palestine. This overtly anti-Zionist stance amounted to a desire for the dismantlement of the Jewish State and for the establishment of a state with a clear (non-Jewish) Palestinian majority.

For most individuals, a basic starting-point was unanimous support for an international boycott of Israeli products:

> Kalim (male): I don't buy Israeli products and I keep an eye on where stuff is made and where companies, like stores and that, are based. I will not buy an Israeli product because I'm not paying a penny towards what they do to Muslims. Their atrocities […] It just feels wrong, like something is wrong, you know. It doesn't feel right.

> Interviewer: What sort of products do you look out for?

> Kalim: Dates, like it was Ramadan and we ended up having dates from Israel. We had them but it just didn't feel right. It felt like it wasn't authentic, you know. Ramadan wasn't the same […] I mean mixing Islam and Israeli dates, that's bad taste really.

> Not a penny of my money is going into a Jew's pocket so he can kill our people […] It's like Gandhi did. If we don't buy, Israel can't survive. (Kamran, male)

Like Kalim, most participants reported avoiding the purchase of Israeli products because there was a perception that this would indirectly support Israel's "atrocities" against Muslims. Driven by the negativised Zionist ideology, Israel was said to actively persecute Palestinians and Muslims and, thus, Israel was perceived as posing a threat to the ingroup. While some participants invoked solely the State of Israel, others conflated Israel and the Jewish people in describing the threat to Muslim group continuity. Kamram observed that his boycott of Israeli products was intended to avoid his money reaching "a Jew's pocket". Despite their frequent slippage between the categories "Zionist" and "Jew", as exemplified in Kamran's account, participants attempted to emphasise their anti-Zionist, rather than antisemitic, stance. Kamran constructed his stance as socially acceptable by anchoring anti-Zionism to Gandhi's struggle against the British Raj in India, which is positively evaluated in cultural consciousness. Indeed, Gandhi is widely regarded as the personification of peaceful struggle. Conversely, both Jews (who "kill our people") and Israel (the objectification of the Jewish people) were viewed as posing a threat to Muslim group continuity. Kamran and other participants perceived the boycott of Israeli products as a means of defeating the State of Israel, which, in view of the perceived threat, appeared to constitute a reasonable response.

Despite the common assertion that the boycott of Israeli products constitutes opposition to Israel's treatment of the Palestinian people (Corrigan, 2009), participants reproduced the social representation of religious conflict between Jews and Muslims, which served as a justification for boycotting Israeli products. Kalim reported that buying Israeli products "felt like something is wrong", suggesting that the continuity principle depended upon a continued boycott of Israeli products. Furthermore, he perceived the notion of purchasing Israeli dates for the Muslim festival of Ramadan as threatening for continuity. He reported that Ramadan "just didn't feel right" due to the presence of *Israeli* dates at a *Muslim* occasion. The threat to continuity ensued from the perception that Ramadan, a holy occasion in the Islamic calendar, was rendered less "authentic" and "not the same", due to the presence of Israeli dates. What may appear a trivial phenomenon to some was perceived as jeopardising the link between past and present for Kalim. There was a constructed incompatibility between the two because of the perceived threat of Israel/Zionism/Judaism to Islam, and the perceived Islamic obligation to oppose Israel.

As former or current university students, most participants in the study were acutely aware of the debate concerning the boycott of Israeli universities in the UK (see Chapter 3). Most individuals supported this proposal and indicated that that the exclusion of Israel from education would contribute fruitfully to the dismantlement of the Jewish State:

> Saira (female): There is no place for Israel in education, like the university boycott is so important. And there is no place for Israel in the global economy. There is no place for Israel on the map. It needs to just disappear and Muslims will be the ones that make that happen at the end of the day.
>
> Interviewer: Why is that?
>
> Saira: America and Europe is too scared to change anything. The big change will come from Muslims, from within the Muslim world [...] The university boycott means they'll lose the intelligence, the educated elite, you know and then they won't be more powerful than Muslims, I think.

As exemplified by Saira's account, individuals questioned the legitimacy of the State of Israel, arguing that there was "no place for Israel on the map" and that it needed to be dismantled. Saira was not alone in expressing the social representation that an academic boycott of Israel constituted a means of inducing its dismantlement. For several participants, the boycott of Israeli universities reflected more than just a desire to support the Palestinian cause. Rather, there was an underlying social representation that the Zionist ideology underpinning the State of Israel was inherently evil and destructive to the world. Thus, the boycott of Israeli universities seemed to reflect a desire to singularly exclude the Jewish State from education and from the "global economy", thereby depriving Israelis of education and economic development. This appeared to reflect a deep-rooted aversion to the State of Israel. The desire for and optimism regarding the destruction of the Jewish State may be connected with the self-efficacy principle. As exemplified by Saira's account, there was a perception that an academic boycott would induce a "brain drain" in Israel, leading to a shortage of "intelligence" and "the educated elite". This in turn would decrease the competence and self-efficacy of the State of Israel, which was perceived as a powerful and threatening state that had defeated its Arab neighbours in a series of armed conflicts (see Chapter 3). Thus, the academic boycott was regarded as an indirect but effective strategy for curtailing outgroup self-efficacy.

In highlighting her avid support for the boycott, Saira expressed her belief that it would be Muslims, rather than "America and Europe", who would instigate change in relation to Israel. Thus, the Muslim ingroup was, conversely, imbued with competence, control and efficacy to bring about change that would defeat the State of Israel. This seemed to suggest a "competing" sense of self-efficacy between the Muslim ingroup and the Israeli outgroup. Indeed, non-Muslim outgroups were regarded as being incapable of instigating such change:

> Us Muslims are the ones you see on the streets protesting and standing up to Israel. Iran. Syria. These are Muslim countries. Not America. (Amir, male)

> You go to anti-Israel protests and it's all Muslims. Some White people but it's mainly just Muslims, you know […] We're the only ones that'll really come out for it, I reckon. If push comes to shove. (Hamid, male)

There was a perceived unity among Muslims in their collective stance on Israel. Amir constructed a common agenda unifying diverse Muslim countries such as Iran and Syria by invoking their commitment to anti-Zionism, which he differentiated from the perceived agenda of the US. He regarded Muslim countries as valiantly "standing up to Israel" which suggested unique and distinctive bravery. Moreover, Hamid attributed the "anti-Israel protests" almost exclusively to the Muslim ingroup, although he acknowledged the participation of "some White people" in them. He too attributed a sense of bravery to the Muslim ingroup by arguing that only they would be willing to oppose Israel "if push comes to shove". The perception of unity among Muslims seemed to provide participants with feelings of self-esteem and self-efficacy, as well as a sense of belonging among like-minded others.

There was a perception that anti-Zionism provided a means of regaining control and of exercising authority against a threatening outgroup:

> I'm not going to just stand for the way they treat Palestinians, Muslims. They have got to be taught a lesson at the end of the day, that if you are going to mess with Muslims, then you're going to get shut down […] If us Muslims aren't going to stand up when it's time, then who will? America? (Hamid, male)

Support for the economic and academic boycott of Israel and for affirmative action against Israel seemed to constitute the product of perceived threat against Muslim group continuity. Participants regarded Israel as posing realistic threats to the wellbeing and survival of Muslims and as posing symbolic threats to the norms, values and traditions associated with Islam. Hamid hypothesised that Israel would be "shut down" due to the threats it posed against Muslims. He clearly perceived a need to defeat Israel due to the threat that he believed Israel posed to ingroup continuity. Yet, despite the perceived threat, it appeared that his belief that Muslims would "stand up [to Israel] when it's time" provided him with a sense of empowerment against the Israeli outgroup. This was constructed as a necessity, given the perceived collusion of Israel and the US, but also as natural solidarity among religious ingroup members. Thus, there were clear benefits for the belonging and self-efficacy principles of identity.

Paradoxically, individuals accentuated anti-Zionism because it provided them with an opportunity to *re-assert* Muslim ingroup self-efficacy:

> Iqbal (male): Only then [when Israel is defeated] will we be able to do the things that are important to us, the things that we want to do and things we need to do. While Israel is there, the Muslim world is like in a tight strait-jacket.
>
> Interviewer: Are all Muslims in a strait-jacket?
>
> Iqbal: Well, Palestinians are Muslims too and they can't lift a finger without Israel. I hate that. I can't describe how angry it makes me.

For some participants, by "defeating" Israel, the Muslim ingroup would be able to realise important actions that were allegedly curtailed by Israel's existence. Iqbal argued that Palestinians, a subgroup within the Islamic Ummah, were unable to govern themselves and to make independent decisions regarding social, economic and religious affairs due to Israeli occupation. Iqbal referred to Israeli occupation and their perceived "control" of Muslims metaphorically as a "tight strait-jacket" which highlighted the perceived severity of Israeli control and reiterated imagery of Zionism (and by extension Israel) as a Nazi, fascist, dictatorial entity. Given the perceived religious solidarity with Palestinians, Iqbal seemed to perceive the lack of control and competence among Palestinians (fellow Muslims) as threatening for his own sense of self-efficacy. He reported feelings of anger and hatred due to this decreased sense of self-efficacy, which indicated that a threat to *ingroup* efficacy also constituted a threat to *personal* self-efficacy. Crucially, participants' accounts suggested that, in order to alleviate and cope with the threat to Muslim ingroup self-efficacy, it would be necessary to defeat the "source" of the threat, namely the State of Israel: "While Israel is there, the Muslim world is like in a tight strait-jacket". Thus, it was implied that only its destruction would "free" the Muslim world from this strait-jacket.

One means of coping with the threat of Israel was optimism regarding its "imminent" destruction. The Arab Spring was prophesied as the "beginning of the end" for Israel:

> With what we're seeing in the Middle East now like the Arab Spring, Muslims are rising up, and it's the beginning of the end for Israel now. (Waqar, male)

> The Arab Spring is all about taking control and Muslims are getting back into control, like they're getting their land back, the control of it. Where does that leave Israel? (Saba, female)

> I think the whole Arab Spring has shown that defeating the State of Israel isn't going to be hard. It's [Israel] going downhill. People are rising up against dictators and Israel is like a dictator. I think it's just a matter of time before people take control of their own countries and their lives and that so they can start making their own decisions. (Mahnoor, female)

Israel's future was anchored to the Arab Spring in order to construct the Jewish State as being on the brink of destruction. Participants in the study appeared to modify and re-construe the social representation of the Arab Spring in order to construct it as central to Israel's demise (see Chapter 5). Given its conceptualisation as a "rogue state" and Zionist ideology as fascism, individuals appeared to position Israel alongside other authoritarian regimes in the Middle East which were being contested by their local populations in the Arab Spring uprisings. There was little appreciation of the democratic character of the State of Israel. The Arab Spring was viewed as evidence of Israel's downfall and, thus, seemed to provide hope that defeating Israel would be an easy task. Indeed, Saira highlighted that the Arab Spring heralded an uncertain future for Israel by asking "where does that leave Israel?" Israel was clearly perceived as a popularly opposed entity which would be defeated purely because "people are rising up against dictators". Moreover, Saba anchored the Arab Spring to the notion of re-acquiring land that rightfully belonged to the Palestinian people, thereby anchoring anti-Zionism to a legitimate struggle for one's "own" land. It was implicitly argued that Palestinians too would re-acquire "their" land from Israel ("a dictator"). There was a strong belief among participants that Muslims were gradually regaining their self-efficacy ("control of their own countries and lives") and that the destruction of the State of Israel would constitute a natural outcome of their re-acquisition of this important principle of identity. Individuals optimistically anticipated the destruction of Israel, which itself seemed to perform positive functions for identity.

The British Pakistani Muslim individuals who participated in this study clearly perceived Zionism as threatening for identity but they exercised their agency over identity in deploying a strategy for successfully coping with this threat. There was an expectation that the Muslim ingroup would ultimately destroy Israel and replace it with a Palestinian state. There was a tension in participants' accounts between an overt anti-Zionism, which respondents proudly accentuated, and a covert antisemitism, which they attenuated through rhetorical and psychological strategies like compartmentalisation.

Deflecting Antisemitism through Compartmentalisation Processes

Although they attempted to avoid overt antisemitism and declared their openness to religious and ethnic diversity, many individuals appeared to draw upon antisemitic social representations in manifesting their anti-Zionist stance. One means of deflecting allegations of antisemitism when manifesting anti-Zionism was to engage in the strategy of compartmentalising the two forms of prejudice, both cognitively and rhetorically:

> Put it this way, I have nothing against Jews. I've got Jewish friends. I know Judaism and they are our cousins, yeah. It's Zionism and this fake state that they've created, that's what I'm against and that's what I go out and protest against […] I don't see why Jews should even have a state. (Ahmed, male)

> Amin (male): Nobody can call me an anti-Jewish person, that's for sure. People say that when I tell them what I think of Israel and that it just needs to disappear but that's does not make me anti-Jewish, does it?

> Interviewer: Why Israel in particular?

> Amin: It's stolen land from the Palestinians. Jews never had their country, did they? What's a Jewish country anyway? Palestine was a country.

Both Ahmed and Amin qualified their anti-Zionist remarks with discursive disclaimers that they had "nothing against Jews" and could not be considered "anti-Jewish" (Potter and Wetherell, 1987). Ahmed further reiterated this point by emphasising that he had Jewish friends, which was intended to distance and discredit the notion that he might be an antisemite. Like Ahmed, several individuals argued that because they had Jewish friends allegations of antisemitism were unfounded, although many of them later proceeded to make antisemitic remarks or stereotypical statements regarding Jews. Furthermore, Ahmed drew upon the shared monotheistic Abrahamic heritage of Judaism and Islam by referring to Jews and Muslims as "cousins" in order to accentuate affinity between the two faith groups and thereby dispel potential allegations of antisemitism. These disclaimers were intended to demonstrate respect and tolerance for Jews and affinity between Muslims and Jews, but closer attention to the content of participants' accounts in fact revealed a lack of tolerance and a perception of insuperable intergroup difference.

Immediately after the discursive disclaimers, Ahmed proceeded to question the validity of Zionism and the authenticity of the State of Israel, which served to delegitimise the Jewish State. Indeed, he manifested opposition to the delegitimised "fake" state. Yet, under further probing, Ahmed, like other participants, revealed that he opposed Zionism because he felt that the Jews' right to their own state was questionable. Similarly, Amin did not accept the notion of a "Jewish country". Thus, this was not necessarily a question concerning the displacement of Palestinians but rather a more fundamental question about the Jews' right to statehood and, consequently, about the legitimacy of the State of Israel. Incidentally, at one point in his interview, Ahmed invoked the establishment of Pakistan (which seceded from British India in 1947 in order to become a homeland for Indian Muslims) and supported statehood for India's Muslims on religious grounds, arguing that Muslims, by virtue of their religious distinctiveness, required a homeland in which they could safely and openly manifest their religious identities without fear of reprisal. Yet, in the context of the *Jewish* State, Ahmed could not see the logic in statehood on the basis of this principle. In short, he modified the social representation of statehood in order to delegitimise Israel, although he endorsed this social representation in the context of Pakistan.

Similarly, Amin rejected the notion of Jewish statehood, arguing that "it just needs to disappear" but denied that these remarks reflected any sense of antisemitism. Participants generally believed that avoidance of the category "Jew" and use of the category "Zionist" positioned them unambiguously in the anti-Zionist, rather than antisemitic, camp (Jaspal, 2013a). By employing the term "Israel" in a systematic manner, individuals believed that their remarks could not be regarded as antisemitic in character. It was evident that, for Amin, the *Jewish identity* of Israel problematised the legitimacy of Israel. He argued that, because they had not possessed a state prior to the establishment of the State of Israel, Jews were simply not entitled to a state of their own. Rather, they were regarded as having "stolen land". This was contrasted with Palestine, which Amin implicitly constructed as a long-standing nation consisting of (non-Jewish) Palestinians. In fact, participants seldom acknowledged that Jews too formed part of the population that inhabited Palestine prior to the establishment of Israel and, like Amin, rejected the notion of a "Jewish country". Thus, the delegitimisation of Israel was founded on the premise that the Jews had no right to the land upon which it was established.

For Abid, his anti-Zionism arose from his outrage at the Jews' alleged occupation of "Muslim land":

I've got nothing against the Jewish religion or anything but this is Muslim land
we're talking about, not Jewish land. What right have the Jews got to be there?
It just proves the point that Jews want to fight Muslims. (Abid, male)

Although Abid qualified his remarks with a disclaimer that he was "not anti-Jewish
or anything", he found it difficult to accept that the Jews should have established
their nation-state on "Muslim land" which he emphatically denied could constitute
"Jewish land". Several participants regarded the Jews as possessing no right to
have their own state in the Middle East. Indeed, it has been argued that there has
been an "Islamicisation" of the Israeli-Palestinian conflict in social and political
discourse, whereby the State of Israel is represented as an anomaly on "Muslim
land" (Litvak, 1998). Individuals accentuated the Islamic character of Palestine
and, thus, the State of Israel was construed as a threat to the continuity principle
of identity. There was a perception that Israel, a Jewish state established on
"Muslim land", created a rupture between past and present and, thus, a negative
and threatening reality for Muslims. For Abid, the Israeli-Palestinian conflict
constituted a religious conflict between Jews and Muslims, with Jews as the
aggressors against Muslims. Indeed, he seemed to perceive the Jews as posing
a realistic threat to the Muslim ingroup because he believed that they wished to
cause harm to Muslims (Stephan and Stephan, 2000). Israel was construed as
sustaining this threat to the Muslim ingroup.

Participants manifested a cynical compartmentalisation of antisemitism and
anti-Zionism by denying any linkage between the two constructs. This provided
an opportunity to negativise Israelis, in particular, without overtly invoking their
Jewish heritage:

Hating Jews is one thing and hating Israelis is another – they've got nothing to
do with each other […] Israelis are a cruel, they're an evil group of people. They
just want to get rich. Look all over the world and you can see them controlling
it all, influencing people, manipulating governments for their own selfish needs
[…] The Koran has warned of their betrayal […] Historically, they have been
involved in murdering kids and innocent people so it's nothing new now, is it?
(Sofia, female)

Sofia acknowledged her "hatred" of Israelis, which she argued had nothing to do
with "hating Jews", thereby deflecting the potential accusation of antisemitism.
Consistent with the social representation that Zionism is evil, participants
constructed Israelis as "cruel" and "evil" in order to rationalise their hatred of
them. Yet, in demonising Israelis, many participants drew upon antisemitic social
representations, such as those of Jewish world domination and Jewish financial
extortion (see Chapter 2). For instance, Sofia argued that Israelis "just want to get
rich", suggesting financial greed, and that they are "controlling it all, influencing
people, manipulating governments for their own selfish needs", suggesting (Jewish)
world domination and a desire to exert excessive influence over outgroups. Thus,

although the category "Israeli" was used overtly, the social representations drawn upon in order to demonise this category appeared to be more pertinent to historical representations of Jews, suggesting an implicit conflation of the categories "Jew" and "Israeli" in the minds of participants.

Like Sofia, Karim and Ali drew upon antisemitic religious/Koranic imagery in order to "demonstrate" the evil of Israelis:

> Muslims are warned about Israelis in the Koran but they will fail and in the Koran it says that even rocks will say "there is one behind me". (Karim, male)

> I've heard this [the historical wrongdoing of Jews] in the mosque [...] it makes sense to me. (Ali, male)

Sofia anchored Israelis to religio-historical representations of Jews in order to provide a religio-historical lens for viewing Israelis. Although the Koran makes no reference to Israelis, there are some verses concerning Jews. Karim erroneously referred to the Koran as a source of information regarding Israelis, although he in fact appeared to make reference to an Islamic hadith (see Chapter 2):

> The Day of Judgement will not come about until the Muslims fight against the Jews and the Muslims kill them until the Jews hide behind stones and trees. The stones and trees will say "O Muslims, O Abdullah, there is a Jew behind me, come and kill him". Only the Gharkad tree would not do that because it is one of the trees of the Jews.[1]

He invoked this religio-historical representation in order to construct religious intergroup conflict between Israelis and Muslims. Moreover, echoing the coping strategy described in the previous theme, some individuals in the study invoked religio-historical representations of this kind in order to reiterate the ingroup's imminent success in defeating Zionism. It was essentially argued that the Muslim ingroup would be victorious over Zionism. This form of anchoring served, firstly, to conflate Jews and Israelis and, secondly, to generalise theologically-based antisemitism to anti-Zionism. Indeed, Ali indicated that he had encountered anti-Zionist social representations within religious contexts, such as his local mosque, which suggested that anti-Zionism was being constructed in Islamic religious terms (Litvak, 1998).

Both the Koran and this particular Hadith make references to Jews, but Karim and others interpreted Koranic and other Islamic assertions regarding the Jews as applicable to Israelis, more generally. The notion that Muslims will be victorious against the Jews on Judgment Day was interpreted as evidence that the State

---

1   Salih Muslim, 41: 6985 http://www.hadithcollection.com/sahihmuslim/169-Sahih%20Muslim%20Book%2041.%20Turmoil%20And%20Portents%20Of%20The%20Last%20Hour/15311-sahih-muslim-book-041-hadith-number-6985.html

of Israel too would fall and cease to exist. Furthermore, in Sofia's above-cited account, there was an implicit allusion to theologically-based antisemitism (largely from Christian sources) which has accused the Jews of blood libels and other ritualistic killings (primarily of children). This antisemitic social representation was employed in order to explain the perceived inclination for Israelis to "murder (Palestinian) children" which constitutes a coercive representation in the Muslim world (Wistrich, 2010). Thus, although participants employed the category "Israelis" in their accounts, it was evident that they were drawing heavily upon antisemitic social representations, suggesting a conflation of the two categories in their minds but a desire to differentiate between them rhetorically.

While some individuals questioned aspects of the Holocaust, others denied it in its entirety (see Chapter 7). Suspicion regarding Holocaust knowledge clearly stemmed from negative social representations of Jews whom individuals accused of "fooling the world":

> The Holocaust, like as we know it now, it's a bit hard to believe the things they come up with. I don't buy it all. A lot of it was just used to justify Israel and what they're doing there. I can't see 6 million people dying under the world's noses. It doesn't make sense to me. (Ali, male)

> The Holocaust is a myth that Jews have just come up with themselves to fool the world. (Afsana, female)

Although Ali categorically rejected any linkage between antisemitism and anti-Zionism and reiterated his "respect" for Jewish people, he did question the reality of the Holocaust as exemplified in his account. In his view, the Holocaust may have taken place but it was being exaggerated and emphasised by Jews/Zionists in order for them to achieve particular political and ideological goals. More specifically, he argued that Holocaust representations were employed to "justify" both the existence of Israel and its actions. He rhetorically supported his denial of the Holocaust by problematising the dominant narrative concerning the Holocaust ("it's a bit hard to believe the things they come up with"), which also served to represent aspects of this narrative as absurd. He considered it impossible that the murder of 6 million Jews could have gone unnoticed by the world's population, and invoked this notion in order to contest existing Holocaust knowledge. Moreover, by presenting a *rationale* for inventing this narrative ("to justify"), Ali offered an inclusive theory which outlined and explained the Holocaust.

Like Ali, several individuals denied aspects of the Holocaust, while reaffirming their commitment to diversity and their respect for Jews. There seemed to be a lack of understanding that Holocaust denial in and of itself constitutes an act of antisemitism, since it "distorts and denies Jewish history and deprives the Jews of their human dignity by presenting their worst tragedy as a scam", while charging "the Jews with unscrupulous machinations in order to achieve illegitimate and immoral goals, mainly financial extortion" (Litvak, 2006, p. 281). While Litvak may have been referring to those contexts in which antisemitism was implicit, in the present study the antisemitic underpinnings of participants' Holocaust denial was abundantly clear. Despite deflecting allegations of antisemitism, participants clearly implicated the Jews in their concoction of an erroneous Holocaust "myth" in order to "fool the world" and to serve their own selfish goals.

Participants in this study were acutely aware of the social desirability of equality and acceptance of minority groups, which appeared to conflict with an underlying antisemitism. Individuals' anti-Zionism appeared to be underpinned by antisemitic social representations, which were invoked despite the widespread desire to conceal antisemitism. Antisemitism and anti-Zionism may have been so pervasive because these forms of prejudice appeared to provide respondents with a sense of belonging within the Islamic Ummah.

Carving a Space in the Islamic Ummah

The semi-structured interviews allowed participants to invoke and describe their perceptions of Jews and Israel. Some issues were not previously envisaged as relevant to participants' sense-making vis-à-vis Israel and Jews. Anti-Zionism appeared to provide a discernible space for young British Pakistanis in the Islamic Ummah, which could enhance feelings of acceptance and inclusion in the religious ingroup (Jacobson, 1997).

Several individuals described negative intergroup relations between Arabs and Pakistanis (see Chapter 7), and complained of the social stigma surrounding their ethnic ingroup membership in contexts involving Arabs. There was a perception that social stigma surrounding their Pakistani ethno-national identity excluded them from the Islamic Ummah:

> I do feel that we as Pakistanis are a bit sidelined by other Muslims, you know […] when I went to Iran, I was surprised that people were a bit disgusted by Pakistanis you know. (Fozia, female)

> I've never felt that accepted by Arabs and that, especially Arab girls. They think they are so bad, like they consider Pakistanis like shit, you know, like slaves and servants and that. (Sajjad, male)

> It [perceived exclusion] can make you like want to hide, you know. Like you're not the same as the rest and like you're an outsider, you shouldn't be there. It feels horrible, you know. (Ayesha, female)

Fozia, a Shiite Muslim, described a pilgrimage to Iran during which she met with Iranian Muslims who held unfavourable attitudes towards Pakistani Muslims, while Sajjad highlighted a perceived lack of acceptance from Arab Muslims (and especially Arab girls). Some participants were aware of a negative social representation of Pakistanis, namely that they were "disgusting", "like shit" and "like slaves and servants" in the eyes of fellow Muslims of non-Pakistani background. This was threatening for the belonging principle of identity among individuals who regarded their religious ingroup as a primary source of belonging. Those individuals who depended on their religious group memberships for feelings of acceptance and inclusion, which has said to be the case for British-born Muslims of Pakistani descent, for instance (Jacobson, 1997), may be particularly susceptible to identity threat when they feel excluded by other Muslims. Identity threat was clearly observable in Ayesha's account, in which she described her desire to "hide" due to the feelings of inauthenticity which ensued from perceived rejection from other Muslims.

Against this backdrop, it was unsurprising that some British Pakistani Muslim individuals appeared to seek feelings of acceptance and inclusion from fellow Muslims of non-Pakistani background. For several participants, the manifestation of anti-Zionism seemed to provide a common platform for self-identification with other members of the religious ingroup, that is, a self-aspect that could bind Muslims:

> There's a lot of fighting even in Islam, Muslims fighting Muslims, killing each other. But one issue that we all fight for is Palestine and, as a Muslim, I can't just sit by and watch Zionists killing Palestinians, Jews taking Muslim land. I think of it as my duty to fight it however I can. (Fatimah, female)

There was tension in many participants' accounts, given that there was a desire to construct Muslims as a unified and cohesive religious group bound by their faith, on the one hand, and a need to acknowledge the discord and conflict exemplified by the Arab Spring and other conflicts, on the other. Yet, the Israeli-Palestinian conflict was said to constitute one core issue around which Muslims of all political persuasions and ethnic backgrounds were united (Litvak, 1998). Fatimah argued that "as a Muslim" she felt compelled to take an anti-Zionist stance, suggesting that this constituted a necessary aspect of Muslim religious group membership ("my duty"). It seemed that, as *Muslims*, individuals felt that they could not tolerate acts of aggression against Palestinians (whom they categorised as fellow Muslims), for instance. Like Fatimah, several participants viewed anti-Zionism as a common concern among all Muslims and thereby contributed to a shared superordinate Islamic identity. This perception was bolstered in the context of the threat representation – respondents regarded Israel and Jews (whom they accused of concealing the "truth" regarding the Holocaust) as posing a realistic threat to the superordinate Muslim ingroup.

Indeed, participants reported forming close and cohesive relationships with other Muslims around the issue of anti-Zionism and support for the Palestinian cause:

> Aijaz (male): I met a lot of good friends in the Palestinian Society [a university group].

Interviewer: Was it the Palestinian Society in particular or have you made friends at other societies too?

Aijaz: Yes but here it was special because it's a cause that us Muslims are all passionate about. We believe in it strongly and it sort of brings us together, you know […] It's like common ground, all the divisions are broken down. That feels good.

There was a sense that relationships built with other Muslims (of various ethnic backgrounds) around anti-Zionism were particularly cohesive and meaningful given the centrality of the issue to individuals' identities (Baum and Nakazawa, 2007). Aijaz indicated that the issue unified groups that might not usually be so cohesive, glossing over potential intergroup differences. His account suggested that this was beneficial for the belonging principle of identity given that this reportedly "feels good". Anti-Zionism contributed to the re-construction and accentuation of a superordinate Islamic identity, which provided sufficient levels of belonging and self-esteem.

Some participants indicated that they felt compelled to take an anti-Zionist stance due to the perceived centrality of anti-Zionism to Islam. In order to accentuate feelings of authenticity (Markowe, 1996), respondents believed that it was necessary to lay claim to an anti-Zionist stance. As indicated by Ali, this was particularly observable in religious contexts, such as religious classes in which the Israeli-Palestinian conflict was discussed:

You couldn't exactly like go to the religious classes and say to them "Oh the Jews are like us and are equal" so you have to follow the line to like fit in […] I wouldn't dream of like saying I accept Israel, not that I do or anything. (Abu, male)

Abu's account highlighted the coerciveness of negative social representations of both Israel and Jews in religious contexts. He regarded antisemitism and anti-Zionism as commonsensical in these contexts and therefore rejected the possibility of expressing any approval of the State of Israel or of Jews, more generally. Furthermore, it was implied that in these contexts Jews were generally considered to be inferior to Muslims, which perhaps constituted a form of downward comparison to enhance the ingroup's self-esteem (Wills, 1981). Like Abu, several participants unanimously invoked the sense of acceptance, inclusion and belonging which ensued from taking an antisemitic and anti-Zionist stance, since acceptance of the social representations disseminated in religious settings essentially allowed individuals to perceive a sense of solidarity. This is consistent with Breakwell's (1993) assertion that social representations are central to the formation and maintenance of a social identity. Similarly, in their research into identity among British Muslim gay men who may feel insecure about their religious group membership, Jaspal and Cinnirella (2014, p. 272) have observed that, for such individuals, acceptance of religious group social representations may constitute "a means of demonstrating, at a psychological level, their affiliation and loyalty to the Muslim in-group, in a context of mounting doubts concerning the authenticity of their religious group membership". Similarly, antisemitic and anti-Zionist social representations may be regarded as important to their religious group membership and therefore not open to contestation if one's religious group membership is to be safeguarded.

Given the perceived centrality of anti-Zionism (and in some cases, antisemitism) to Muslim identity (Baum and Nakazawa, 2007), some individuals regarded their anti-Zionist activities as actively bolstering their Muslim religious identity and as unifying the religious ingroup:

> I was holding a placard saying "Israel is a Nazi state" [at an anti-Israel protest in London] […] To me it was like a duty. As a Muslim, it's a duty and to me it was no different to performing salah. (Qazi, male)

> To me it [anti-Zionism] feels good, like I feel quite proud, like I'm doing my bit. Pakistanis are always like quiet or just moaning about crap things but this is something that has put us on the map, you know, as Muslims. (Sarfraz, male)

Qazi recounted his experience of participating in an anti-Israel rally in London during the Gaza War in 2008 (also known as Operation Cast Lead). In displaying an anti-Zionist placard which read "Israel is a Nazi state", Qazi believed that he was performing his "duty" as a Muslim. By anchoring his anti-Zionist activities to the performance of salah, the practice of formal worship in Islam, Qazi represented anti-Zionism as one of the pillars of Islam and therefore as a fundamental duty that was central to the identification with and practice of the Islam faith. Similarly, Sarfraz construed Zionism as enhancing both his Muslim religious and Pakistani ethnic identities, which in turn provided him with feelings of self-esteem: "it feels good […] I feel quite proud". There was a re-positioning of his Pakistani ethnic ingroup within the Islamic Ummah, which was particularly important for those young British Pakistanis who believed that their ethnic ingroup was excluded from the Ummah due to discrimination from Arabs. Like Sarfraz, several individuals perceived their anti-Zionist activities as exemplifying their commitment to their religious ingroup: "I'm doing my bit". Moreover, anti-Zionism performed positive functions for their Pakistani ethnic identity (a subgroup within their superordinate religious ingroup), since it was perceived as enhancing the reputation, credibility and commitment of Pakistanis "as Muslims". In short, it seemed to endow young British Pakistanis with a space within the Islamic Ummah.

Anti-Zionism, which was imbued and bolstered by antisemitic social representations, provided individuals with feelings of acceptance and inclusion from other Muslims, which crystallised this important social identity and enhanced the belonging principle of identity.

Overview

The data presented in this chapter suggest that the British Pakistani Muslim individuals who participated in this study were firmly committed to anti-Zionism. Individuals accepted and reproduced negative social representations of Zionism, which they anchored to the stigmatised, discredited ideology of Nazism (Litvak and Webman, 2009). The principle of "chosenness", while not unique to Judaism, was also offered in support of the alleged racism and evil of Zionism. The chosenness principle itself was threatening for participants' sense of self-esteem and continuity because of their belief in the superiority of Islam. In reflecting upon negative occurrences in the world, participants scapegoated Zionism, not necessarily as a sense-making strategy but rather as a means of negativising Zionism and thereby rationalising their anti-Zionist position. This in turn enabled individuals to derive feelings of self-esteem from their anti-Zionist position, because there was a perception that they were legitimately opposed to an "evil" ideology. However, some of the motifs invoked in order to delegitimise Zionism, such as that of Jewish world domination, were threatening for the self-efficacy principle of identity.

Although respondents did appear to deflect allegations of antisemitism in various ways, partly because of the social stigma appended to overt racism and prejudice (Nelson, 2002), close attention to their accounts highlighted the antisemitic underpinnings of their thinking in relation to Jews and the Jewish State. There was a perceived conspiratorial collusion between Zionists and Jews, which was explained in reference to historical theological antisemitic representations. There was a constant shift between historical theological representations of Jews and contemporary political representations of Israel. Furthermore, in expressing support for the academic and economic boycotts of Israel, which are often referred to as being anti-Zionist rather than antisemitic in nature, several participants clearly manifested antisemitic social representations. Moreover, there was an observable relationship between anti-Zionism and Holocaust denial, which is consistent with existing research in this area (Jaspal, 2013a, 2014a; Litvak, 2006; Webman, 2010). Holocaust denial was facilitated by the perception of the "evil" and "malice" of Jews and Zionists. The present study demonstrates the importance of examining *how* people talk about antisemitism and anti-Zionism in order to understand these forms of prejudice more holistically.

There was a desire not to compel Israel to enter into peace negotiations with the Palestinians but rather to destroy the Jewish State, highlighting the destructive action orientation of their anti-Zionist stance. Respondents were unable to accept the notion of a Jewish state, although they did see the logic in state-building along ethnic and religious lines in other contexts. This highlighted double standards and the singling out of the Jewish State. In his research into antisemitism and anti-Zionism among Muslims in North America, Baum and Nakazawa (2007) found that Pakistani Muslims appeared to score highly on the antisemitism and anti-Zionism scales. The present study suggests that some British Pakistani Muslims may believe that there is a historical clash between Islam and Judaism, which is currently reflected in the form of the Israeli-Arab conflict, and that Islam must, and eventually will, defeat Israel, a tangible outcome of Jewish self-efficacy (Jaspal, 2013a). The perceived Israeli threats to the Palestinians are generalised to the superordinate Muslim ingroup – the realistic and symbolic threats of Zionism to the ingroup were generalised to the self. Moreover, some individuals appeared to manifest insecurity in relation to the position of Pakistanis within the Islamic Ummah. Given the Islamicisation of anti-Zionism and the social desirability of taking an anti-Israel stance (Litvak, 1998), several individuals appeared to construe this as a means of safeguarding a sense of belonging within the Islamic Ummah. This was cynically perceived as a unifying thread between Pakistani Muslims and Muslims of other ethnic backgrounds. Antisemitism and anti-Zionism appear to constitute responses to threatened identity but their underlying tenets (e.g. Jewish world domination; Zionist oppression; chosenness) may themselves pose threats to particular principles of identity. Yet, in accordance with the predictions of Identity Process Theory, individuals appeared to believe optimistically that Israel could, and would, be destroyed by Muslims, which served as a means of coping with the threat.

PART V
Responding to Antisemitism and Anti-Zionism

Chapter 9
Re-Visiting Siege Mentality: Israeli Responses to Antisemitism and Anti-Zionism[1]

Introduction

This book attests to the phenomenological importance of antisemitism and anti-Zionism among some groups and individuals. This is a long-standing problem with potentially severe ramifications. Israeli Jews are acutely aware of the existence of antisemitism and anti-Zionism. There has been some empirical research into their responses to such forms of prejudice, some of which is summarised in Chapter 1. Based on quantitative survey research, Bar-Tal (2000) has made particularly important social psychological contributions to this area by arguing that Israeli Jews suffer from a "siege mentality" which motivates them to believe that the world is unanimously hostile and united against the Israeli ethno-national ingroup. This chapter re-visits this construct by examining, in two qualitative interview studies, how Israeli Jews respond to antisemitism and anti-Zionism with particular foci upon the implications for identity processes and how they cope with potential threat. This chapter outlines the following themes: (i) Perceived Outgroup Hostility and the Implications for Identity; (ii) Muslim Anti-Zionism as a Continuation of Antisemitism; (iii) Holocaust Denial, Siege and Identity; (iv) Coping with Antisemitism: Re-Establishing Belonging and Self-Esteem.

Methodological overview

The data presented in this chapter are drawn from two qualitative interview studies conducted in the summer of 2010 and the spring of 2012 with two groups of Israeli Jewish individuals. Unlike Part IV of this book, this chapter was characterised by a focus upon how Israeli Jews might respond to antisemitism and anti-Zionism, such as how awareness of antisemitism and anti-Zionism might affect their sense of self and how they might cope with potential threats to identity associated

---

1   Sections of this chapter draw upon a previously published article: Jaspal, R. and Yampolsky, M. (2011). Social representations of the Holocaust and Jewish Israeli identity construction: insights from identity process theory. *Social Identities: Journal for the Study of Race, Nation and Culture*, *17*(2), 201–24. Content from this article is used here with the permission of that journal.

with these forms of prejudice. The principal focus of the study was on the social psychological level, and there was detailed consideration to the social contexts in which individual cognition was embedded.

Forty-three Israeli Jewish men and women between the ages of 18 and 34 participated in an in-depth interview concerning "perceptions of antisemitism and anti-Zionism". The interview schedule tapped into: (i) self-description and identity; (ii) the perceived characteristics of Judaism and Zionism; (iii) experiences of being Jewish/a Zionist in distinct social, cultural and geographical contexts; (iv) experiences and/or perceptions of antisemitism and anti-Zionism; and (v) the implications of these experiences and/or perceptions for identity processes.

There were 20 male and 23 female participants. Twenty participants had a university degree, 10 were completing their military service, and the remaining 13 had completed high school. Participants were recruited from within the Tel Aviv area. A range of ethnic backgrounds were represented in the sample – 27 described themselves as Ashkenazi (European descent), 15 as Mizrahi (Middle Eastern descent) and 1 participant described himself as being of Sephardic (Spanish/North African) descent. All of the participants self-identified as secular Jews. Data were analysed using thematic analysis, following the same analytical procedures that were described in Chapter 7.

Perceived Outgroup Hostility and the Implications for Identity

Individuals generally regarded their Jewish and Israeli identities as being inextricably entwined, in that they perceived Israel as "the one and only Jewish state" and themselves interchangeability as Jews and Israelis. Similarly, there was a perceived causal link between anti-Zionism and antisemitism – individuals attributed hostility towards Israel from outgroups to an underlying antisemitism:

> Our country was built so Jews could call a place "home" and this [Israel] was
> an obvious choice because of our historical, spiritual connection to Israel [
> ...] When people doubt Zionism and say how awful it is, they are really just
> revealing what they think deep down about Jews and that's all. (Dan, male)

Dan accentuated the Jewish character of Israel and reiterated its raison d'être as a Jewish homeland. By accentuating Israel's Jewish underpinnings, Dan was able to argue that anti-Zionism actually constituted a manifestation of antisemitism. He believed that opposition to Israel actually revealed "deep" inner cognitions concerning Jews. Individuals reflected upon the thoughts and feelings evoked by perceived hostility from outgroups towards the State of Israel and to their Israeli national identity. Although most manifested a sense of resilience in face of outgroup hostility, there was an underlying sense of threat to identity in several individuals' accounts:

Sometimes it makes me feel very alone. We are alone in a world that wants to just kill us. Alone in a region surrounded by people who want Jews dead. It is a harsh feeling and I think we Israelis do think of this a lot […] When I went to Europe, I really thought of this even more. Crossing one border to go to another friendly country and everyone is different. There's a different culture there […] they have no idea what we go through. It's a harsh feeling. It makes you wonder what's so wrong with you, your people, that they should do this. (Yiftach, male)

When you see other countries that do such things, you realise that Israel gets a lot of stick. It is singled out for being a Jewish state. It can do nothing right. It's due to our neighbours who hate us for being who we are […] We try but we just can't fit in to this region, no matter what. (David, male)

Yiftach perceived extreme hostility towards both Jews and Israel from neighbouring countries and believed that outgroups "want Jews dead". Like Yiftach, several individuals perceived regional outgroups (namely Arabs and Iranians) as posing a realistic threat to Jews because there was a perception that this wished to cause extreme harm, including death, to Israel due to its status as the Jewish State. It has long been acknowledged in social psychology that human beings actively seek feelings of acceptance and inclusion in relevant social groups (Baumeister and Leary, 1995). Similarly, social groups seek acceptance and inclusion within the broader social matrix. Individuals who perceive valued social groups as being excluded from society may experience similar threats to the belonging principle of identity. This seemed to be true of Yiftach and several other participants in the study. Yiftach indicated that he, as an Israeli, felt "very alone" and elaborated by describing his ethno-national ingroup as being "alone in a world that wants to just kill us" and "alone in a region surrounded by people who want Jews dead". He described this threat to belonging as a "harsh feeling". On the one hand, there was a clear perception of ingroup loneliness, that is, the notion that his ingroup did not belong in a superordinate society or community of nations. On the other hand, there was a perceived realistic threat to the lonesome ingroup from external parties who wished to harm it physically. Indeed, this perception of realistic threat was particularly important because ingroup security has long been a focal concern for Israeli society (Bar-Tal, Jacobson and Klieman, 1998).

Like many respondents in the study, Yiftach appeared to cope with outgroup hostility towards Israel in a relatively resilient manner, although his account did suggest that Israelis experienced threats to the belonging principle due to perceived exclusion, otherisation and threat from hostile outgroups. Interestingly, it was observed that the threat to belonging acquired particular salience when he travelled to Europe and observed positive intergroup relations between European nations, which facilitated an open-border policy between European nation-states. Despite the clear ethnic, cultural and linguistic differences between distinct European nations, Yiftach noted that there was a positive intergroup repertoire, which in turn rendered salient the negative intergroup repertoire characterising relations between Israel and its neighbours. Individuals mulled over possible causes underlying this negative intergroup repertoire and concluded that it was antisemitism that underpinned the anti-Zionist stance of their neighbours. The attribution of anti-Zionism to antisemitism was abundantly evident in David's account – he believed that Israel was "being singled out for being a *Jewish* state". David's account too pointed to a threatened sense of belonging due to consistent otherisation from its neighbours and Israel's futile attempts to "fit into this region".

Given the strong sense of attachment that most individuals attributed to their Israeli national identity, there was a generalisation of group-level threats to the identity principles to the individual level of cognition (Lyons, 1996). Participants expressed intense dismay at the negative outcomes that decades of intergroup conflict with their neighbours and exclusion from the superordinate level had caused for ingroup self-efficacy:

> I feel Israel could have achieved so much. Look where we'd be if we didn't have the whole world, especially the Muslim world, against us, trying to stop us from achieving our potential, blocking any Israeli achievement, refusing to participate against Israeli athletes, blowing up Jewish targets in the world, you see how much time and money we dedicate to [dealing with] Arab terror, it's unthinkable. (Orit, female)

> They (antisemites) have squeezed out all our energy, resources, our everything. They achieve their aim, because even while we are trying to defend ourselves they are draining us […] Look at the Iron Dome. We spend so much catching each Iranian missile.[2] It is draining us slowly. (Ruth, female)

There was a prevalent perception that the State of Israel had been unable to realise its full potential due to several regional countries' steadfast commitment to anti-Zionism, which inhibited "Israeli achievement" in its various forms. Although participants were keen to avoid imagery of Islamophobia in their accounts, they did invoke "the Muslim world", "Arab terror" and "Iranian missiles" in describing the perpetrators of anti-Zionism. Participants invoked Israel's isolation in the domain of competitive sports due to the unwillingness of some nations to compete against Israel and to boycott competitions in which Israel participated. For instance, Arash Miresmaili, the Iranian judoka competitor in the 2004 Summer Olympics, was said to withdraw from the competition in order to avoid having to compete against the Israeli player, Ehud Vaks. He later commented: "Although I have trained for months and was in good shape I refused to fight my Israeli opponent to sympathise with the suffering of the people of Palestine and I do not feel upset at all".[3] Both the

---

2   Here, the participant referred to the notion that the Islamic Republic of Iran supplies both Hezbollah and Hamas with rockets and weapons.

3   *New York Times* website http://www.nytimes.com/2004/08/14/sports/olympics-notebook-iranian-judo-champion-refuses-to-face-israeli.html.

then-mayor of Tehran Mahmoud Ahmadinejad and former president Mohammed Khatami openly congratulated him on his withdrawal. It is noteworthy that, through their engagement with the Israeli media, participants were acutely aware of Iran's anti-Zionist stance in the domain of sport, which they construed as undermining their Israeli national identity.

Most importantly for participants, Israel was said to underachieve due to its necessary preoccupation with security issues which had arisen from anti-Zionism in the region (Bar-Tal, 2000). Orit believed that the State of Israel was compelled to dedicate much of its time, efforts and revenue to limiting "Arab terror" against Israel and "Jewish targets" in the world, which in turn limited the competence and achievement of Israel. Israel was perceived as being obliged to respond to the realistic threat (both to the State of Israel and to Jews abroad) posed by hostile outgroups. Ruth employed the metaphor of antisemites having "*squeezed out* all our energy, resources, our everything" and as "*draining* us" in order to objectify the consequential constraints perceived to be imposed upon ingroup self-efficacy. This suggested a gradual process of elimination which highlighted a perceived realistic threat from hostile outgroups. Indeed, a realistic threat is said to entail threats to the ingroup's resources (Stephan and Stephan, 2000), to which both Orit and Ruth explicitly referred.

Both participants invoked the importance of self-defence which further contributed to the social representation of realistic threat. Ruth exemplified the importance of self-defence by referring to Israel's Iron Dome, which is an air defence system designed to intercept and destroy short-range missiles. Although the Iron Dome is highly effective, it is very expensive to operate – it is estimated that each interceptor missile costs approximately $50,000. Israelis are acutely aware of the social representation of costliness, and within the context of the present study participants construed this as evidence of the strain on Israeli resources. As interviewees contemplated threats to (national) self-efficacy, they invoked the categories "Arab", "Iranian" and "Muslim" in describing the perpetrators of such threats.

Respondents were unanimously supportive of a peace agreement with these groups, despite perceived hostility from them. However, upon close scrutiny the data suggested that Israelis had grown accustomed to the negative intergroup repertoire and that they doubted the prospect of positive intergroup relations with hostile outgroups:

> I don't know, Arab and Israeli, it's not so common to link up, you know. I don't see much hope for this. It's uncomfortable […] The situation is such that I can't imagine what it would be like, as an Israeli, to mix with Iranians, to talk to Iranians. There seems a sort of clash between our civilisations because of politics. With all the threats from them, I mean. (Elad, male)

Elad and others appeared to find it difficult to imagine social and diplomatic relations between Israelis and Arabs and between Israelis and Iranians due to a long history and legacy of negative intergroup relations (see also Jaspal, 2014b). This negative intergroup repertoire appeared to overshadow and obscure the positive intergroup encounters between Israelis and Arabs (Bar-Tal and Teichman, 2005). Elad described this as "uncomfortable" and as a "clash between our civilisations", which suggested that a positive intergroup repertoire could be problematic for the psychological coherence principle of identity. Interestingly, this was also observable among the Iranians who participated in the interview study outlined in Chapter 7 – many of them regarded a positive intergroup repertoire as threatening for psychological coherence. Individuals had come to accept the social representation of realistic threat from hostile outgroups, namely Arabs and Iranians. As Bar-Tal (2000) observes, Israelis are acutely aware of the multiple invasions by Arab armies, the Arab embargo on Israeli products, and decades of Palestinian terrorist attacks against Israeli Jews, which, collectively, have contributed to the social representation that the Israeli ingroup is besieged. Similarly, Israelis are increasingly anxious about the threat perceived to be associated with the Iranian regime, which is suspected to be pursuing a nuclear weapons programme. Consequently, like Elad, many Israelis appeared to have internalised the threat representation, which, as exemplified by Elad's account, was construed as incompatible with the notion of a positive intergroup repertoire with Arabs and Iranians. More specifically, individuals manifested suspicion surrounding the sincerity of hostile outgroups in peace talks, which perhaps rendered the prospect of positive intergroup relations all the more threatening for psychological coherence.

Participants unanimously conceptualised anti-Zionism as opposition to a *Jewish* nation state in the Land of Israel. By extension, there was a social representation among participants that Israeli Jews were "foreign" to the region and not genuinely "Middle Eastern". There was a widespread desire to assert feelings of authenticity, which they felt were jeopardised as a result of this tenet of anti-Zionism:

> They don't think we're true Middle Easterners. They say we're from Europe and we've colonised this place and kicked out the Palestinians but look at me. I am Middle Eastern. I feel Middle Eastern. This is the Middle East. This is where I was born and I really hate it when I hear this. I mean, whatever else, OK, it's a stereotype but me? European? This is absurd. (Hana, female)

Respondents were aware of the social representation that Israel constitutes an example of European colonialism, which is prevalent in the Middle East (Jaspal, 2013a). This was construed as raising questions about the authenticity of Israelis as Middle Easterners and, more generally, regarding the legitimacy of Israel as a nation state within this region. Many Israelis plausibly found this representation fallacious because of the reality that over half of the Israeli Jewish population consists of Sephardic and Mizrahi Jews, that is, Jews of non-European descent. As a Mizrahi Jew herself, Hana rejected the categories "European" and "coloniser" which she believed were commonly attributed to Israelis. Given her self-categorisation as Middle Eastern, she felt that she was incorrectly categorised by hostile outgroups. This seemed to call into question her authenticity as a Middle Easterner, which was threatening for identity (Markowe, 1996). Hana believed that anti-Zionism resulted in the erroneous categorisation of Israelis as "Europeans" and "colonisers", which may be threatening since individuals seek external "validation" of their social identities (Jaspal and Cinnirella, 2012). Incidentally, the lack of outgroup recognition for the State of Israel has contributed to the Israeli siege mentality (Bar-Tal, 2000).

Although perceived anti-Zionism and antisemitism appeared to jeopardise multiple principles of identity, potentially resulting in identity threat, there was a perception that outgroup hostility was a long-standing position to which individuals were culturally accustomed. It appeared that anti-Zionism did have negative implications for identity but it had come to form part of a "routine":

> Generations of Jews were born in a hostile world. We grew up knowing the Arabs hate us, and we have got used to it. Sometimes it does feel bad but not so much. It's just a part of life for us […] If they didn't hate us, it'd be a shock, I'll tell you. My parents told me how strange it was when they went to Jordan. It was like making friends with your biggest enemy all of a sudden. (Sarit, female)

> They are Muslims. What can you expect? Muslims don't like Jews and especially not Jews who are living their own land and controlling their own system. But it's a given. We know this, we've always known it and it's all we've known. Nothing new here. (Oliver, male)

Sarit and Oliver perceived antisemitism as an age-old phenomenon which "generations of Jews" had suffered and which had become an aspect of Jewish existence. Both Sarit and Oliver referred to Arab/Muslim antisemitism as a long-standing prejudice, in particular. They noted that these outgroups were unable to accept the notion of Jewish self-efficacy and political autonomy, objectified by the State of Israel. Although Sarit appeared to construe antisemitism as a threat to self-esteem, which is a predictable outcome of outgroup prejudice (Brown, 2000; Jaspal, 2011a), both she and Oliver invoked the "normality" of Arab/Muslim antisemitism such that they had grown accustomed to it. It could be argued that the perception of outgroup hostility had come to form part of their routine and that it had lost its power to threaten the continuity principle of identity. After all, participants did not perceive outgroup hostility from Arabs/Muslims as unexpected. Oliver referred to this as "nothing new" and made use of the present and present perfect tenses in order to illustrate Jews' long-standing awareness of antisemitism, as well as the centrality of antisemitism to the Jewish experience (Jaspal and Yampolsky, 2011). Conversely, it appeared that, in some cases, reconciliation with hostile outgroups could in fact jeopardise individuals' sense of continuity (see Chapter 7). Sarit illustrated this by referring to her parents' experience of visiting Jordan, a country with which Israel signed a peace agreement after five decades of conflict.

There was a perceived temporal discord in having to view one's "biggest enemy" as a friend, which suggested a potential threat to continuity. Although individuals identified with and endorsed the concept of peaceful and harmonious intergroup relations with hostile outgroups, the perception of antisemitism and anti-Zionism had become potent and enduring and, thus, difficult to change (see Jaspal, 2011a, for an analysis of popular resistance to social change).

There was a perception of antisemitism and anti-Zionism from outgroups, which clearly had unfavourable outcomes for identity in that it could jeopardise the motivational principles of identity. However, it appeared that some respondents were resistant to a change in intergroup relations because this would entail a threat to the continuity principle of identity.

Muslim Anti-Zionism as a Continuation of Antisemitism

Interviewees generally perceived Arab/Muslim anti-Zionism as constituting a continuation of long-standing antisemitism. Indeed, there was a hegemonic social representation that anti-Zionism constituted a subtle, more socially acceptable form of antisemitism (see Chapter 3). The question of hostility from the Muslim world was perceived as posing a particular threat to the Israeli ingroup:

> Ariel (male): There are still people who will show hatred towards Jews in Europe […] they take the opportunity to draw a swastika on Jewish graves or they believe that Jews rule the world but it's not a big problem really. Europeans don't really hate us.

> Interviewer: So is there antisemitism in the world? Does it exist?

> Ariel (male): Yes, the Arabs and Muslims in the world do hate Jews, well, they hate Israel more but they also hate Jews now […] They want to kill Jews, like Iran.

Ariel acknowledged the existence, both historical and contemporary, of antisemitism in Europe, which he exemplified by referring to the desecration of Jewish graves and conspiracy beliefs regarding Jewish world domination. However, he appeared to attenuate the gravity of European antisemitism and argued that Europeans were not antisemitic. Ariel attenuated the importance of these acts of antisemitism vis-à-vis the perceived threat of Arab/Muslim antisemitism, which he regarded as grave and dangerous. Thus, when compared with the perceived threat from Arabs and Muslims, European antisemitism no longer appeared to constitute a serious problem. Indeed, several participants highlighted the centrality of Christianity to historical European antisemitism and believed that, with growing secularism in Europe, antisemitism had gradually decreased in scope and gravity. Conversely, there was a social representation that "radical Islam" which rejected a Jewish presence on "Muslim land" reflected a newer, direr form of antisemitism:

> Anti-Jewish feeling in the, the Middle East, in Muslim countries, is a big, big issue. It's a danger […] Each day there are millions of Muslims who are just praying for Israel to be destroyed so they can create an Islamic state and to do this they will kill Jews. Here in Israel but everywhere because they cannot stand to see Jews having their own state. They cannot stand Jews being in the position that we are in. (Yagel, male)

Yagel felt that the rise in antisemitism "in Muslim countries" was unprecedented, primarily due to the perceived scope and severity of "anti-Jewish feeling". Like Yagel, several individuals anchored anti-Zionism to religious fanaticism by arguing that "millions of Muslims" prayed for the destruction of the State of Israel, which they would subsequently replace with "an Islamic state". Indeed, Shahvar (2009) has highlighted that Israel is widely perceived as a superfluous and undesirable "limb" on the "Muslim body". Moreover, there was a social representation that this would result in a deliberate massacre of Jews due to underlying antisemitism. Yagel reiterated a widespread perception among participants that Muslims were unable to accept the notion of Jewish political autonomy and self-efficacy, objectified by the State of Israel. More generally, respondents believed that Israel safeguarded Jewish group continuity by providing a safe haven for Jews who had historically suffered unthinkable persecution and even genocide. Thus, the perceived desire of Muslims to destroy the State of Israel would almost certainly put Jewish lives at risk. This highlighted the source of the realistic threats perceived by interviewees.

Participants in the study believed that anti-Zionism posed a threat to Jews in general. There was a widespread tendency to conflate the terms "antisemitism" and "anti-Zionism" when discussing social representations of Israel among Muslims. Respondents believed that anti-Zionism constituted a means of expressing underlying antisemitism:

> The creation of Israel has made Jew-hatred less visible than it was but it is still there. It is still beneath this all. We can ask one question: "Why the Jews?" This is the big question, and it all comes back to antisemitism, not anti-Zionism. This is the reason they kill Jews, fire rockets and pursue a nuclear weapons programme […] They value death more than life. (Maya, female)

> For me, it makes more sense for me to just think "oh, it's because we're Jewish" it makes much more sense. It's more meaningful. You can find an explanation for it. Otherwise, I'm lost. I just wonder why they target us, and just us. (Tommy, male)

Like Maya and Tommy, most respondents were convinced that there was an antisemitic basis to anti-Zionism among Muslims. Maya suggested that the creation of Israel had created a novel target for prejudice, which served to obscure antisemitism, rendering

"Jew-hatred less visible than it was". However, she and others attributed this to antisemitism because they believed that anti-Zionism entailed singling out the Jews on the basis of their Jewish ethno-religious identity. Accordingly, Maya interpreted outgroup actions against the State of Israel, such as Hamas's firing of rockets into Israeli territory, as superficially anti-Zionist and fundamentally antisemitic in character. Moreover, she interpreted Iran's nuclear activity as a "nuclear weapons programme" designed to eradicate the State of Israel and its Jewish citizens. In describing Muslim/Arab anti-Zionism, individuals referred to a Muslim struggle against Jews, which they believed to be driven by religious fanaticism, rather than reason. This rendered anti-Zionism a more uncertain, irrational and, thus, threatening form of antisemitism in the minds of participants.

Scholars have offered compelling arguments for considering anti-Zionism a form of antisemitism (see Chapter 3). Many of these arguments appear to be both logical and credible. Similarly, for several individuals in the study, it appeared that the consideration of anti-Zionism as a form of antisemitism provided a psychologically satisfying explanation for a complex and esoteric form of prejudice. Indeed, respondents frequently questioned the logic underlying the international scrutiny of Israel vis-à-vis other countries. For Tommy who questioned the focus on Israel, the notion that anti-Zionism had antisemitic underpinnings appeared to provide an explanation. Due to their awareness of negative social representations of Jews in Islamic religious contexts, the Israeli interviewees appeared to interpret Muslim/Arab anti-Zionism through the heuristic lens of antisemitism. This satisfied the human need for meaning and uncertainty and could therefore be said to safeguard the meaning principle of identity amid potential uncertainty (McAdams, 2001).

The perception of antisemitism was clearly threatening for identity because it jeopardised multiple principles of identity. However, the Israeli interviewees converged in their perception of Israel as a buffer against the threat of antisemitism. Several individuals drew a comparison between Israeli Jews, who were protected by the State of Israel, and diaspora Jews, whom they believed to be at risk:

> Arabs and Muslims are fuelled by anti-Jewish feelings. It's not so much an issue for us in Israel because we are strong. We can defend ourselves and we always have defended ourselves. The problem is for Jews who live in Europe, Iran, the US, everywhere. These are the victims of Muslim terrorism against Jews and Israel. We don't suffer as much as them […] What's the solution? Jews should make aliya. (Dan, male)

> Terrorism against Jews is a global thing now. Not one country but everywhere. And France is the same. Look at France and what happened. It makes me feel unsafe when I travel now, sometimes I just think something could happen […] It's not the local people, it's Arabs, Islamic fanatics, it's people who are willing to give their lives up for this. (Hadar, female)

Dan attributed antisemitism to the Arab and Muslim outgroups, which implied that those countries in which Arabs and Muslims constitute at least a sizeable minority were more likely to have problems with antisemitism. Similarly, Hadar invoked the antisemitic shootings at the Ozar Hatorah School in Toulouse, France, on 19 March 2012, in which a man and three children lost their lives, in order to highlight the perceived threat of terrorism against Jews. More generally, participants reported that countries like the US and the UK were "not the same" because of the infiltration of social representations associated with Arab and Muslim outgroups in these societies, and the growing acceptability of anti-Zionism in these societies (Wistrich, 2010). Given the "global" character of antisemitic terrorism, Hadar reported that she no longer felt safe travelling in Europe, not because of "the local people" but rather because of the threat allegedly posed by Muslim minorities in Europe (Jikeli and Allouche-Benayoun, 2013). There was a social representation that Muslims living in Europe had contributed to growing antisemitism and anti-Zionism in Europe.

Consequently, several individuals highlighted the importance of the State of Israel, which they regarded as a "safe haven" in face of the threat of antisemitism. More specifically, Dan argued that Israelis were "strong" and, thus, able to "defend themselves" against hostile outgroups. This statement enabled individuals to argue that diaspora Jews were, conversely, unable to defend themselves as adequately as Israeli Jews due to their minority status in their host countries. The Jews of "Europe, Iran, the US, everywhere" were collectively perceived as being particularly susceptible to the threat of antisemitic terrorism. Although individuals acknowledged the security threats facing the State of Israel (Bar-Tal, 2000), they believed that Israel was better positioned than other countries to mitigate the threat of terrorism and generally more concerned with the wellbeing of Jews. It appeared that the Israeli interviewees unanimously perceived Israel as a source of self-efficacy, because of its ability to protect and empower its citizens, and as a source of continuity, because it safeguarded the survival of the Jewish people in an uncertain and threatening world. Israel seemed to protect identity at a psychological level. Consequently, individuals in the study converged in the social representation that Israel was a safe haven for Jews. This social representation heralded Dan's recommendation that "Jews should make aliya"[4] in order to safeguard their wellbeing.

> This [antisemitism] is a big issue for Jews in the rest of the world, not people here. We Sabra are soldierly, tough and independent, and this is the reason for Israel. Jews in trouble can find a home in Israel. (Ilan, male)

---

4   The Hebrew term "aliya" (literally "ascent") refers to the immigration of Jews to Israel. It is socially regarded as a commendable act and is a basic principle of Zionism (Shuval, 1998)

Similarly, Ilan regarded antisemitism as "a big issue" for diaspora Jews but not for Israeli Jews. He explained this by pointing to the distinctive character and identity of the Sabra, namely Israeli-born Jews (Almog, 2000). This distinctive identity was based around the perceived military culture and self-efficacy of Israeli-born Jews – traits which Ilan regarded as differentiating Israeli-born Jews from diaspora Jews and which safeguarded their wellbeing and continuity in face of external threats. Indeed, Ilan and most participants reiterated the raison d'être of Israel as a state for "Jews in trouble" where they could find refuge in times of need.

There was widespread acceptance of this social representation of Israel as a safe haven for Jews. However, individuals in the study believed that Muslims deliberately attempted to sabotage Israel's ability to provide a safe haven for Jews and to disrupt this source of identity enhancement among Israelis:

> They [Muslims] try to spread their lies to the whole world and get sympathy and everyone behind them basically just ends up believing it […] Why is England following the campaign that's being led by Muslims? It's because there's a campaign of lies. We all feel powerless to stop it, just no power over this matter at all. (Sarit, female)

As indicated in Sarit's account, there was a social representation that Muslims were actively engaged in a ploy to defame the State of Israel in order to undermine public support of the Jewish State. More specifically, participants argued that Muslims "spread their lies" in their respective host countries to "get sympathy" and that this ploy had had considerable success given that there was growing acceptance of this polemic social representation. Use of the metaphor "campaign" suggested that individuals believed that this constituted a systematic and organised course of action with a specific anti-Zionist goal, namely to undermine the State of Israel. Participants cited England, France and Germany as examples of European countries that were beginning to accept anti-Zionist social representation. On the one hand, this perception of a "Muslim campaign" provided individuals with a heuristic tool to understand global anti-Zionism and to develop an explanation for it, potentially enhancing the meaning principle of identity. On the other hand, this perception appeared to threaten the self-efficacy principle of identity, since several individuals felt "powerless" in face of the campaign perceived to be led by hostile outgroups, and unable to curtail it. Several individuals felt that attempts to curtail this campaign were futile because, consistent with the observed siege mentality of Israeli society (Bar-Tal, 2000), there was a social representation that outgroups were unanimously united in their opposition to the Jewish State. Muslims, however, were perceived as spearheading and encouraging the anti-Zionist campaign in Europe.

Similarly, individuals reflected upon the ease with which governments in Arab and Muslim countries managed to convince their respective peoples of the importance of anti-Zionism and identified their underlying antisemitism as a primary cause for their uncritical acceptance of anti-Zionism:

The government spreads anti-Zionism but they know this is going to be accepted by the people and people will like this message because it's about Jews. Muslims believe they must hate Jews. So there's an implicit problem there. "Jew" has become an important word for them and it makes them just blindly hate us all. (Ariel, male)

In Europe, it was "why do Jews control the world?" and in the Middle East it is "why do Jews have control of our land?" They also believe in the usual antisemitic rubbish but they cannot bear to see us in the Land of Israel. A Muslim cannot bear to see a Jew in this position. (Nora, female)

Like Ariel and Nora, several participants attributed anti-Zionism to the political institutions of Arab and Muslim countries and antisemitism to the general population. There was a sense that the governments of these countries had a selfish political agenda behind their anti-Zionist stance, perhaps to distract their respective peoples from domestic concerns such as human rights, and that they were aware that anti-Zionism would constitute an adequate strategy for popular mobilisation. Ariel perceived anti-Zionism as an effective mobilisation strategy in the Muslim world because he believed that there was a social expectation among Muslims that "they must hate Jews" and that "Jew" had become an important buzzword. There was a social representation that Muslims were inherently and unanimously hostile towards Jews and that they would therefore naturally and uncritically embrace anti-Zionism, as recommended by their governments.

Nora was one of several individuals who elaborated upon the effectiveness of anti-Zionism as a mobilisation strategy. She explained that, while European antisemitism had produced the social representation of Jewish world domination, the Middle East had elaborated this representation by drawing attention to Jewish control of "our land". As highlighted by other participants, Nora believed that Muslims were unable to accept Jewish self-efficacy (objectified by the State of Israel), particularly when this was viewed as undermining the self-efficacy of Muslims: "They cannot bear to see us in the Land of Israel". There was a perception that European antisemitism had informed Muslim anti-Zionism because "they believe in the usual antisemitic rubbish", on the one hand, and because there was an intolerance of Jewish self-efficacy, on the other. In short, participants perceived clear antisemitic underpinnings of anti-Zionism.

Participants converged in their perception of anti-Zionism as a more socially acceptable form of antisemitism. They tended to attribute this primarily to Muslims, both in the Middle East and in Europe, and to perceive this as more threatening than European antisemitism.

Holocaust Denial, Siege and Identity

The centrality of the Holocaust in security perceptions

There is now a body of research that shows the socio-cultural and psychological significance of the Holocaust among Israelis (Bar-On, 2008; Ben-Amos and Bet-El, 1999). Jaspal and Yampolsky (2011) have shown how social representations of the Holocaust can acquire particular salience among Israeli Jews of various ethnic backgrounds due to their participation in collective Israeli social contexts (e.g. the school environment). In these contexts, the Holocaust can come to be conceptualised in terms of a shared loss:

> When you're in the class with all your friends and then they [the teachers] are telling you about the Holocaust there is something that makes you want to just cry, I tell you, not just crying but like a real heartfelt kind of crying. I cried after my classes thinking about how much we have lost. So many Jews died and so I realised that actually, yes, I have lost something too even if my parents were safe in India. We lost so much in the Holocaust. (Moshe, male)

Moshe viewed the communal context of the class environment as being conducive to the perception of the Holocaust as a *shared* loss. It appeared that the shared sense of Israeli identity, which was rendered salient in collective spaces such as the school context, individuals construed the Holocaust as a group-level loss. Interviewees clearly believed that the Holocaust had affected the Jewish ingroup as a whole. Jaspal and Yampolsky (2011) have argued that Israeli Jews may regard the Holocaust as an act of genocide which extends itself into the future and which could be repeated:

> Talking about it like at home, yes, it's sad for us and you feel scared that this could happen in the world because we know that in the world a lot of people have […] tried to kill the Jews. (Sarit, female)

Sarit's account highlighted the centrality of *fear* to her meaning-making vis-à-vis the Holocaust, primarily because this represented an attempt to annihilate the ingroup. Sarit seemed to anchor social representations of the position of Jews in the world to consensually shared hegemonic representations of the Holocaust. This could induce fear of genocide, destruction and annihilation, threatening one's sense of ingroup security (Bar-On, 2008; Bar-Tal and Antebi, 1992; Wistrich, 1999b). The Holocaust was construed as evidence that, after centuries of repeated persecution, the Jews were most destructively targeted by outgroups. Moreover, there was a perception that this could happen again. The Holocaust served as a heuristic lens through which other intergroup conflicts could be regarded, which rendered hostile outgroups all the more threatening for identity (Bar-Tal and Teichman, 2005). In short, the *security* of the ingroup seemed to be perceived as being subject to threat, a feeling which was aggravated by the salience of social representations of the Holocaust (Bar-Tal, 2000).

Some individuals adopted a broad definition of the Holocaust, which included acts of persecution against Jews:

> The Holocaust was not just in Europe or in the concentration camps but there's been a Holocaust for a long time for the Jews, even my grandma when she tells me in Morocco they [Muslims] did a curfew [...] and my uncle was forced to sleep in the cow shit and they degraded him and beat him so badly this is the same thing [...] the Jews were abused by the whole world at different times. (Gilad, male)

Most scholars agree that the Holocaust refers to the specific act of genocide against European Jewry, which was perpetrated by the Nazis and their collaborators (Gilbert, 1985; Salmons, 2003). However, Gilad appeared to conceptualise the Holocaust in much broader terms to encompass antisemitic persecution, in general. This intrapsychic strategy of re-conceptualisation allowed him to position his (Sephardic) ethnic group in relation to the Holocaust. The centrality of the Holocaust in Gilad's meaning-making vis-à-vis antisemitism led him to anchor examples of persecution of this kind to social representations of the Holocaust. He compared antisemitic persecution to the existing stock of familiar and socio-culturally accessible representations associated with the Holocaust, which permeates Jewish Israeli society (Moscovici, 1988). On the one hand, this constituted a means of making sense of antisemitism but, on the other hand, this appeared to induce fear regarding the future. In short, Gilad perceived his ethno-religious ingroup as facing perpetual (security) threats from "the whole world". He elaborated by explaining that various ethno-national groups have engaged in persecutory behaviour against the Jews "at different times" in history (see Bar-Tal and Antebi, 1992). Since the Holocaust was not temporally isolated, it remained a heuristic device to which novel, uncertain situations of persecution and conflict could be anchored (Moscovici, 1988).

It has been observed that Israeli politicians frequently invoke the Holocaust in order to justify and to rationalise Israel's military activities in the Israeli-Arab conflict (Segev, 1992). Similarly, participants invoked the Holocaust as a heuristic lens for understanding the Israeli-Arab conflict:

> I just care about security and if it means to give them [Palestinians] their state then it's good for me [...] We built our country to avoid things like the Holocaust and so we need to keep our country safe to keep Jews safe. (Sara, female)

Sara appeared to endorse the existence of an independent Palestinian state primarily on the basis that this would enhance national security, which was presented as her sole concern. Use of the category "we" indicated acceptance of the social representation that the foundation of Israel constituted a collective ingroup endeavour to ensure that there could be no future repetitions of the Holocaust. Indeed, it has been observed that many Israeli Jews regard the existence of a sovereign Jewish state as essential for the security and survival of Jews in the world (Lazar et al., 2008). The Holocaust seemed to function as a heuristic device for understanding the potential consequences of failing to ensure the safety of Israel, which participants unanimously perceived as a Jewish safe haven. Social representations of current ethno-national ingroup security seem to be anchored to representations of the Holocaust, which functioned as a symbolic warning of the potential consequences of failing to safeguard ethno-national ingroup safety. Participants invoked the Holocaust in order to understand and explain why the establishment of an independent Palestinian state was necessary for ingroup continuity.

Social representations of the Holocaust were clearly central to individuals' meaning-making vis-à-vis Jewish history and the Israeli-Palestinian conflict due partly to the salience of Holocaust representations in Israel (Jaspal and Yampolsky, 2011). These representations surfaced in participants' reflections upon ingroup security, which was viewed as being jeopardised by hostile outgroups (Bar-Tal, 2000). Given the centrality of the Holocaust in participants' meaning-making, they clearly perceived Holocaust denial as a threat to identity.

The threat of Holocaust denial

Given the clear phenomenological importance of the Holocaust in Israeli Jewish cultural consciousness (Bar-On, 2008; Stein, 1978), it was unsurprising that individuals should find Holocaust denial abhorrent and highly threatening for identity. This was clearly observable in individuals' responses to Holocaust denial:

> This [Holocaust denial] goes against everything I believe and stand for, stands against truth. (Anita, female)

> When they deny, they kill another memory. It is taking away our biggest tragedy from us. It is out of our reach. (Yehuda, male)

> When the President of Iran said this, it just made me feel sick because he was trying to change history and change what we know to be true and it felt as if he was managing to do this. (Ofir, male)

Participants' accounts suggested that the perception of Holocaust denial among Arabs and Muslims posed a threat to the continuity principle of identity. Anita indicated that Holocaust denial imposed discontinuity because it contradicted her beliefs and the truth. Similarly, Ofir invoked the Iranian president's denial of the Holocaust in order to exemplify the prevalence of Holocaust denial. This too was threatening for continuity because it was construed as an attempt to "change history" and to alter the truth. Like Anita, Ofir regarded Holocaust denial as introducing discontinuity by replacing truth with fallacy. There was a perception among individuals that Holocaust denial reflected a malicious attempt to take away from the Jewish ingroup "our biggest tragedy" by denying that it had taken place (Litvak, 2006). Yehuda described this metaphorically as "killing another memory", which constructed Holocaust denial as an act of immorality. Holocaust denial was rendered all the more threatening for continuity, because there was a perception among individuals that governments and institutions were succeeding in their campaign to convince the world that the Holocaust constituted a myth.

The perceived efficacy of the campaign of Holocaust denial was threatening for self-efficacy among individuals, since they believed that it was impossible to impact public opinion in the Arab and Muslim worlds due to the prevalence of antisemitism:

> Israel has resources, like money and industry, but it cannot reach the Arab world to educate it and tell it the truth. Not its version but the undeniable truth of the Holocaust. Arabs won't listen. Muslims go to their mosques and there they are brainwashed. Why will they listen to Jews? They just see us as colonists or something. This makes me feel very, very incompetent, as a people we are powerless in this field. (Tal, male)

> I read it [an article about President Ahmadinejad's Holocaust denial] and I just felt helpless. How do I honour the dead? How do I tell these stupid people "my father's uncle and his family died in the Holocaust"? I'm a victim of this, my family is. (Dana, female)

Tal and Dana highlighted their feelings of inability and helplessness in relation to Holocaust denial, because they believed that it was impossible to challenge Holocaust denial among some outgroups. Tal indicated that, while Israel was a self-efficacious and self-sufficient nation-state due to its wealth and industrial development, it lacked the necessary social and political capital to "reach out to the Arab world". This inability to "educate" the Arab world was attributed to prevalent antisemitism in this outgroup context. Tal highlighted the centrality of Muslim religious identity in the Arab world, and the centrality of antisemitism to the Islamic religious institutions of these countries, where individuals were allegedly "brainwashed". Such religious antisemitism rendered any first-hand engagement with the populations of these countries impossible. Similarly, Dana reflected upon her experience of reading an Israeli newspaper article concerning President Ahmadinejad's Holocaust denial, which also evoked feelings of helplessness. More specifically, she felt completely disempowered – she believed it was impossible to "honour the dead" by convincing the Iranian population of the truth that the Holocaust did take place. She highlighted her own victimhood by drawing attention to the fact that her relatives had perished in the Holocaust and that she was, therefore, living testimony to the fact that the Holocaust had occurred. Like Tal, her sense of self-efficacy appeared to be imperilled by her inability to communicate the truth. Tal concluded that "Arabs won't listen", which accentuated the threat to the self-efficacy principle of identity – he, as a member of the Jewish Israeli ingroup, felt incompetent and powerless.

The self-esteem principle seemed to be severely jeopardised as a result of Holocaust denial in the Arab and Muslim world. More specifically, individuals highlighted the feelings of shame that had come to surround discussions of the Holocaust, which was reminiscent of the cultural silence surrounding the Holocaust in post-independence Israel (Bar-On, 2008):

> Well, look when people deny the Holocaust, say "how could Jews be gassed when there were not enough gas chambers" and then they accuse us of lying to create our state, this is a horrific insult. It makes us feel ashamed and almost afraid to talk about the Holocaust. We know it's true but I feel people are thinking I'm hiding behind it. That makes me feel very small. (Maya, female)

On the one hand, many Israeli Jews, and indeed many non-Jews in the world, believe that it is important to discuss the Holocaust and to disseminate knowledge about its antecedents and consequences, in order to avoid genocide in the future (Jikeli and Allouche-Benayoun, 2013; Short, 1994). Yet, some participants experienced feelings of shame when discussing the Holocaust due to their awareness of Holocaust denial. Maya stated that Holocaust denial made her feel insulted, ashamed and disempowered, because she believed that some people accepted the polemic social representation that the Holocaust never occurred. Her observation that this made her "feel very small" suggested that Holocaust denial had negative implications for the self-esteem principle of identity. Like Maya, some individuals felt unable to derive a positive self-conception due to the perception that others accused the Jewish ingroup of lying about the tragedy of the Holocaust. Therefore, as a coping strategy, individuals appeared to avoid discussions of the Holocaust (cf. Bar-On, 2008).

Holocaust denial appeared to induce fear regarding the future among some individuals, who came to perceive Holocaust deniers as inherently evil and irrational people (Jaspal and Yampolsky, 2011). There was a perception that due to their Holocaust denial they were capable of any atrocity:

> This [Holocaust denial] makes me think that the regime [Islamic Republic of Iran] is evil and the people who believe it are evil. How can you see those images on TV, newspapers, in museums, of dead people and dead children and still deny that it happened? People who do it are not human, they are just evil. (Boaz, male)

Boaz appeared to view the Islamic Republic of Iran as "evil" due to its institutionalisation of Holocaust denial. Like Boaz, several participants assumed that Holocaust denial must be widespread in the Iranian general population due to their perception of Iran as a threat. There was a generalisation of Iranian institutionalised representations to the general population. Individuals appeared to attribute the trait of irrationality to Holocaust deniers because of the abundant evidence (i.e. television, media, museums) that the Holocaust did occur and that it caused immense suffering to Jews. Participants regarded people who ignored the abundant evidence which depicts "dead people and dead children" as inhuman and evil – there was a dehumanisation of Holocaust deniers.

Some individuals regarded Holocaust denial as exemplifying hatred against the Jewish people, which could culminate in "another Holocaust":

> To me, the Muslims, when they deny the Holocaust, our biggest tragedy, it just proves that this can happen again and it proves that they would not hesitate to push this agenda forward [...] If Israel is not vigilant, this could be the beginning of the end. (Dan, male)

Although most individuals in the study perceived Israel as a powerful and self-efficacious state which was capable of defending itself from hostile outgroups, there was a perception that Israel must remain vigilant in order to sustain this level of self-defence. For Dan, Holocaust denial represented an attempt to challenge the State of Israel and its ability to function as a safe haven for Jews, because there was a social representation that Holocaust denial was intended to challenge the legitimacy of Israel. He argued that Holocaust denial itself proved that this could happen again, because it symbolised complacency and a loss of cultural memory regarding the actions and events that had ultimately culminated in this act of genocide. Moreover, Dan argued that Holocaust denial shed light on the attitudes and orientations of Holocaust deniers, namely that "they would not hesitate to push this agenda forward", namely to perpetrate genocide against the Jews. Thus, it seemed that some participants perceived Holocaust denial as posing an indirect threat to group continuity among Israeli Jews. It was regarded as contributing to the likelihood of acts of genocide against the Jews.

In view of its perceived threat to Israel, individuals called for group-level action against Holocaust denial in order to minimise its impact:

> What I see [in Iran] is an alliance of people who have evil intentions against the Jewish people, the people of Israel, and we should unite against them all. Every person with a good heart. (Naomi, female)

There was a widespread perception that Holocaust denial should not be ignored because it posed a threat to Jews and provided scope for the repetition of genocide. Like Boaz, Naomi perceived Holocaust deniers as having "evil intentions" and as threatening the Jewish people, which in turn induced a call for people "with a good heart" to unite against Holocaust denial. Naomi included both Jews and non-Jews in this call for mobilisation. Breakwell (1986, p. 142) has argued that individuals will engage in group action in order to "change the social order" for "revising the relative power of groups and devising new ideological systems". Indeed, in this context individuals appeared to call for a revision of the power exercised by hostile outgroups that disseminate antisemitic social representations concerning the Holocaust and to challenge *their* ideological systems. This was perceived as a strategy for eradicating the threat that Holocaust denial clearly posed to identity.

The data indicated unequivocally that the Israeli Jews who participated in this study regarded the Holocaust as an important aspect of their ethno-religious group's history and identity. Thus, Holocaust denial was perceived as a hostile attack against the ethno-religious ingroup and Holocaust deniers as posing a threat to the Jewish ingroup. Participants unanimously regarded Holocaust denial as an aspect of antisemitism, which was threatening for identity (Breakwell, 1986). Accordingly, respondents deployed various strategies for coping with the threat and, as discussed in the next section of this chapter, for re-establishing feelings of belonging and self-esteem

Coping with Antisemitism: Re-Establishing Belonging and Self-Esteem

Israeli Jews are acutely aware of the fundamentally anti-Zionist stance of most Middle Eastern nations. It has been argued that the perception of outgroup hostility, in the forms of both antisemitism and anti-Zionism, can be threatening for identity in a multitude of ways. Individuals in the study exhibited strategies for regaining feelings of belonging and self-esteem, which appeared to be most susceptible to threat.

The perception that Jews and the Jewish State were ostracised by its neighbours resulted in a threatened sense of belonging, partly because of the aforementioned psychological need for both individuals and groups to seek acceptance and inclusion from relevant others and outgroups, respectively (Baumeister and Leary, 1995; Jaspal, 2013a). Accordingly, it appeared that participants re-oriented the national group towards Europe, as an alternative source of belonging:

> Europe, like English people, they are not against Israel but I think they are in a difficult situation where they have lots of Muslims or Arabs in their country and they have to listen to them, their concerns. (David, male)

> The Arabs hate us, they think we are inferior to them […] they are never going to accept us, ever. We have to accept this and move on. Even the Jordanians who are supposed to be our friends display those signs […] The politicians may care, I don't […] Our system, our mentality, it's more European, it's Middle Eastern, European. (Dudi, male)

As outlined earlier, several individuals in the study argued that Europeans were not inherently anti-Zionist but that they been led into a "difficult situation" due to sizeable Muslim minorities in their countries. David attributed anti-Zionism in Europe to "pressure" from Muslims and Arabs who voiced their "concerns" regarding Israel and Jews. Interviewees believed that Britain and other European nations were a "soft touch" in relation to Muslim and Arab immigrants who, conversely, exploited the soft touch approach of their host societies to spread anti-Zionism. Thus, anti-Zionism and antisemitism were distanced from Europeans and attributed to the Muslim outgroup, which was consistent with the threat representation that had developed in relation to Muslims.

Dudi and others appeared to resign themselves to the social representation that Arabs and Muslims would never fully accept the State of Israel due to perceived antisemitism. Dudi exemplified this notion by observing that Jordan, a country with which Israel signed a peace treaty in 1994, continued to be antisemitic, despite this official peace treaty. Participants essentialised Arabs and Muslims as inherently antisemitic and genuinely believed that there was little scope for changing attitudes among these hostile outgroups. Like Dudi, several individuals reported indifference to the perceived antisemitism of their Arab and Muslim neighbours. They coped with perceived antisemitism by positioning their ingroup within the political context of Europe, rather than the Middle East. Dudi argued that Europe was a more suitable "fit" for Israel due to a perceived similarity in political system and "mentality". Moreover, individuals in the study did not generally perceive European to be antisemitic. The re-positioning of the Israeli ethno-national ingroup in the superordinate category European was a common strategy for demonstrating indifference to the exclusion of Israel by its Middle Eastern neighbours, thereby diminishing the threat to belonging. Thus, the positioning of Israel in the European superordinate category appeared to provide feelings of belonging, which compensated for threats to belonging due to the exclusion of Israel by Middle Eastern countries. However, it is recalled that participants also lamented the external categorisation by outgroups as European when Israelis were accused of colonialism in Arab territory. This demonstrated the agency and flexibility of self-categorisation in order to optimise identity processes and to protect identity from threat (Breakwell, 1986, 2010).

It appeared that some participants felt that recent acts of antisemitism had further united Jews in their struggle against outgroup hostility. This too provided a sense of "one-ness" and belonging:

> I never thought about Jews living in Europe or in America, because home has always been Kiryat Gat […] You know, it's a small town […] Hearing about the anti-Jewish shootings in France, that made things change […] I feel that they are going through what we are here […] I felt that we can be stronger than them [antisemites]. (Daphna, female)

Daphna reflected on her reaction to the news of the aforementioned shooting at the Jewish day school in Toulouse. While she had not previously felt much solidarity with diaspora Jews given that her sole focus had been the town in which she had grown up, Daphna reported feeling increased solidarity with diaspora Jews following the shooting. More specifically, this sensitised her to the notion that Jews outside of Israel were facing similar challenges to Israeli Jews, such as terrorism, attacks and killings purely on the basis of their ethno-religious identity. Moreover, there was an emerging social representation among individuals that diaspora Jews were more susceptible to the threat of antisemitism because they lived outside of the State of Israel, a perceived safe haven for Jews. Participants highlighted the increased solidarity and empowerment which they felt in response to attacks against Jews. There was a perception that, collectively, Israeli and diaspora Jews could collectively mitigate the threat of antisemitism and terrorism. This reiterated the group mobilisation strategy for coping with threat, as described by Identity Process Theory.

As alluded to in earlier sections of this chapter, a common strategy for deflecting identity threat associated with outgroup hostility was for Israeli Jews to challenge the legitimacy of outgroups' social representations concerning Jews and the State of Israel:

> Who are they to tell us we are guilty of oppressing the Palestinians? They kill their own people. They don't even allow their people to vote. Iran is a very dark place, it's a place of darkness. (Nora, female)

> Muslims may say that we commit a genocide and when they do all I say is "look within yourselves first". You kill each other in the name of religion, you kill men, women and children, so you are nobody to judge the State of Israel. (Ron, male)

Individuals greatly lamented outgroup criticism from Muslims, which they perceived as hypocritical. Nora rejected the polemic social representation that Israelis oppress the Palestinian people by challenging the legitimacy of the perceived disseminator of this social representation, namely the Islamic Republic of Iran. As noted throughout this book, the Iranian government has been a vocal critic of the Israeli government's treatment of the Palestinians (Jaspal, 2013a). More specifically, Nora challenged the credibility of the Islamic Republic by drawing attention to the social representation that the Iranian authorities "kill their own people" and "don't allow their people to vote". This served to construct the policies and behaviours of the Islamic Republic as even more offensive than the accusations levelled against the State of Israel. Furthermore, by describing Iran as "a place of darkness", Nora imbued Iran with imagery of evil and oppression, thereby de-authorising the Iranian government from making such accusations against Israel.

Similarly, Ron challenged the polemic social representation that Israel is committing genocide against the Palestinian people by challenging the credibility of the perceived disseminator of this representation, namely Muslims, and thus the legitimacy of the representation itself. Ron invoked the notion that Muslims "kill each other in the name of religion" and that this killing is indiscriminate. He drew upon the social representation (hegemonic in the Israeli Jewish context) that militant organisations such as Hamas and Hezbollah kill people indiscriminately and even utilise their own people as "human shields" in order to forward their religious and political agenda (Bar-Tal and Labin, 2001). This too served to deauthorise Muslims, who were homogenised as perpetrators of violence, from making threatening accusations against the State of Israel.

Although most individuals appeared to be resilient in face of anti-Zionism and antisemitism, a contextually sensitive examination of participants' accounts indicated that individuals sometimes utilised interpersonal strategies for deflecting identity threat associated with outgroup hostility. Interviewees appeared to engage in a synthesis of "passing" and shifting between relevant group memberships in order to obscure their Jewish Israeli identities:

> Sometimes I don't tell people straight away that I'm Jewish, an Israeli […] I just think sometimes it's best not to say that so all these stereotypes just come rushing to their head. It's best not to because it doesn't feel good. (Dudi, male)

> We were getting on well, I was having a good time, but I was dreading the question "where are you from?" I just told them my race, I'm a Persian and didn't say more. Not that I'm a Persian Jew […] I just thought it's easier to avoid the topic, a pretty big topic though. (Gili, female)

> I'm Israeli and I'm French […] If I have to talk to a Muslim while I'm in Europe, I'm French. If I'm in England with English guys then I can be Israeli […] I hate the, the break, the break in our relationship. It makes me feel bad. (Adam, male)

Several participants in the study indicated that they sometimes concealed their Jewish and Israeli identities in order to avert confrontations with potential anti-Zionists, which could induce identity threat. In reflecting upon interactions with Muslims in Europe, Dudi reported concealing his Jewish ethno-religious and Israeli national identities because he believed that by mentioning them he could evoke negative "stereotypes" and thus jeopardise emerging relationships with people in this context. Having experienced a rupture in interpersonal relations upon disclosure of his Jewish Israel identity, Dudi reported that this threatened his self-esteem: "it doesn't feel good". Similarly, Adam reported that the disclosure of his Jewish Israel identity could cause a "break in our relationship", which suggested that both the continuity and self-esteem principles were susceptible to threat.

While Dudi reported concealing his Jewish Israeli identity as a strategy for averting threat, some participants reportedly employed more creative strategies such as feigning membership in other social categories or shifting between their ethno-national group memberships. For instance, Gili strategically invoked her Persian Jewish ethnic heritage in order to avoid having to disclose her Israeli national identity to outgroup members. Given her Persian Jewish heritage, her Persian appearance and knowledge of the Persian language, she felt able to "pass" as an Iranian and thereby safeguard her relationship with her interlocutor. Moreover, due to the association of Muslim identity with Iranian identity, Muslim identity would be assumed. As Breakwell (1986, p. 116) has observed, "[p]assing normally refers to the process of gaining access to a group or social category […

] by camouflaging one's group origins". Indeed, Gili and others did camouflage their Jewish Israeli identity in order to avoid identity threat. Adam strategically shifted between his identities and attenuated his Jewish Israeli identity in favour of his French citizenship in order to protect identity in an interaction with a Muslim person, whom he suspected of opposing Israel.

Antisemitism and anti-Zionism clearly posed threats to identity, which in turn induced a multitude of coping strategies. These strategies varied in their level of long-term efficacy – some were clearly short-term strategies designed to protect identity in transient everyday encounters with outgroup members (e.g. passing), while others were intended to encourage some form of social change which would result in favourable social and psychological conditions for Israelis, such as group mobilisation. Yet, all of the strategies shared the same goal – to protect identity processes from threats associated with perceived antisemitism and anti-Zionism.

Overview

This chapter highlights the general importance of both Jewish ethno-religious and Israeli national identities among the Israeli Jews who participated in the study. Most individuals regarded their Jewish and Israeli identities are inextricably entwined, and perceived anti-Zionism as indicative of underlying antisemitism. Moreover, there was a perceived realistic threat from hostile outgroups, echoing the notion of siege mentality (Bar-Tal, 2000). Interviewees invoked social representation that, because anti-Zionism undermined the ideology underlying Israeli national identity, anti-Zionist outgroups essentially wished to destroy the State of Israel. This was particularly threatening because Israel was widely regarded as a Jewish "safe haven" in which Jewish identity could be openly and safely manifested without fear of persecution. Anti-Zionism, therefore, was perceived as being conducive to a lack of safety and security for Jews.

Antisemitism and anti-Zionism were generally construed as threatening for identity, because these forms of hostility jeopardised the principles of self-esteem, self-efficacy and belonging, in particular. Holocaust denial was a particularly threatening form of antisemitism, because it challenged people's sense of self-esteem and continuity over time. Some respondents believed that Holocaust denial was dangerous because they interpreted it as evidence that the Holocaust could reoccur – indeed, this perception has been observed in previous empirical research (Jaspal and Yampolsky, 2011), and appears to be connected to the siege mentality that exists in the Israeli Jewish context. Furthermore, there was a perception that anti-Zionism could challenge one's sense of national authenticity, primarily because anti-Zionism was interpreted as contradicting the Jews' right to a homeland in the Land of Israel, as well as their Middle Eastern identity. Individuals perceived an impoverished sense of self-efficacy because they believed that anti-Zionism had given rise to security threats which in turn required Israelis to dedicate resources to their security, rather than to social and economic development (Bar-Tal,

2000). This highlights that most respondents were keen to end anti-Zionism and intergroup conflict.

Although siege mentality is clearly an important social psychological concern among Israeli Jews (Bar-Tal, 2000), respondents appeared to manifest considerable resilience in face of extreme anti-Zionism and they had developed strategies for coping with the ensuing threats to identity. Most individuals had internalised the social representation that Muslim outgroups were inherently antisemitic, which they construed as "routine" rather than threatening. This suggested the adoption of an acceptance, rather than deflection, strategy. It appears that the continuity principle of identity was no longer susceptible to threat given that participants had "accepted" this representation within their sense of self (Breakwell, 1986). Moreover, respondents appeared to have devised various social psychological strategies for optimising feelings of belonging, self-esteem and self-efficacy. These included re-orienting the Israeli national ingroup towards Europe, where antisemitism was not considered to be as problematic as in the Middle East and where individuals believed that Israel was more accepted. Conversely, Israel's relationship with Middle Eastern countries was attenuated. Consistent with this coping strategy, individuals attributed antisemitism to Muslims, both in the Middle East and in Europe. Thus, there was a tendency for individuals to attenuate European antisemitism rhetorically in order to draw attention to Muslim antisemitism – they were aware of European antisemitism but strategically downplayed its significance. This may be attributed to the human drive to seek acceptance and inclusion creatively and opportunistically so that both individuals and groups can "belong". Respondents frequently challenged the legitimacy of Muslim critics of Israel as a means of deflecting negative social representations and protecting identity from threat.

Some participants reported engaging in the passing strategy in order to avoid anti-Zionism. However, the strategy of passing is unlikely to be psychologically beneficial in the long-term because individuals must derive self-esteem from their group memberships (Tajfel, 1982) and also seek identity validation from relevant others, that is, they need to be recognised as members of their valued social groups (Jaspal and Cinnirella, 2012). Yet, experiences of antisemitism and anti-Zionism problematised identity – this complex situation required a trade-off between avoiding antisemitism/anti-Zionism, on the one hand, and optimising social identity processes, on the other. This may be specific to Israeli Jews given the negative social representations of Israel and Zionism, which have gained ground following the establishment of the Jewish State (see Chapter 3). The next chapter of this book examines responses to antisemitism and anti-Zionism among British Jews, many of whom lay claim to various identities – Jewish, Israeli and British – and charts the relationship between these identities and their perceptions of these forms of prejudice.

Chapter 10

British Jews: Making Sense of Antisemitism and Anti-Zionism

Introduction

Some work on antisemitism and anti-Zionism among British Jews has speculated about the potential wellbeing of British Jews within the specific contexts in which antisemitism and anti-Zionism have arisen. In view of the academic boycott on Israel, this work has focused largely upon the university context (Klaff, 2010). Earlier work has examined upon the notion of the "self-hating" Jew, which is summarised in Chapter 1. This chapter presents the results of two exploratory qualitative interview studies which set out to examine how British Jews conceptualised their Jewishness and their relationship with the State of Israel, and how they perceived and responded to antisemitism and anti-Zionism. Like the other chapters in the book, this work took a social psychological perspective on the interview data and set out to examine the social, rhetorical and psychological aspects of self-identification and perceived outgroup prejudice. In this chapter, the following themes are outlined: (i) Positioning Jewishness and Israel in the Self-Concept; (ii) Setting the Boundaries of Antisemitism and Anti-Zionism; and (iii) Coping with Threatened Identity: Re-Constructing Jewishness and Israel.

Methodological overview

The aim of the present study was to identify the overarching themes in the accounts of a small sample of British Jews and, like the other studies reported in this book, the results are not empirically generalisable to the wider population. Yet, the inclusion of three important subgroups within the British Jewish community, namely Orthodox Jews, secular Jews and anti-Zionist Jews, provided insight into the convergences, divergences and tensions within the heterogeneous British Jewish community. Participants were invited to participate in in-depth interviews concerning "perceptions of antisemitism and anti-Zionism among British Jewry", which took place in the spring of 2013. Individuals who volunteered to participate in the study self-identified as Jewish (which was conceptualised in different ways) and believed that they had an important contribution to make on debates surrounding antisemitism and anti-Zionism. An adapted version of the interview schedule described in Chapter 9 was used for this study.

Forty-seven British Jews participated in the two studies. There were 19 men and 28 women. Thirteen individuals identified as Orthodox Jews; 22 as secular

Jews; and 12 as anti-Zionist Jews. The age range of participants was 18–33 years. For the first study, participants were recruited from within the Jewish community in Golders Green, North London (UK), using a snowball sampling strategy. For the second study, participants were recruited from within the Jewish community in Manchester (UK), also using a snowball sampling strategy. The sample was educated – 40 participants had completed or were studying towards a university degree, and the remaining seven individuals had completed GCSEs/A-levels. Data were analysed using thematic analysis, following the same analytical procedures that were described in Chapter 7.

Assimilating and Accommodating Jewishness and Israel in the Self-Concept

There were distinct social representations of Jewishness and Israel among respondents, and these representations appeared to vary in accordance with their religious and political positions. Many individuals in the study perceived their Jewish identity as central to their self-concept, although Jewishness could be manifested in ethno-cultural and/or religio-spiritual terms (Loewenthal, 2000). For self-identified secular Jews, Jewishness was construed primarily as an ethno-cultural identity:

> Being Jewish for me is, and you should know that this is because I'm more secular than religious [...], well it's spending time with my family on Shabbat, not about *shul* [the synagogue] but respecting the traditions, eating kosher where possible [...] These small things just give me a feeling of where I'm from, where I come from, what my ancestors did, you know [...] It feels good, I suppose. (Josh, secular)

In describing his Jewish identity, Josh cited his adherence to Jewish traditions, such as observance of the Holy Sabbath with family members and adherence to the dietary norms associated with Judaism. Like Josh, several individuals indicated that attending the synagogue was of lesser importance than adherence to Jewish norms and traditions ("respecting the traditions"), which they believed reflected a more secular rather than religious Jewish identity (Sinclair and Milner, 2005). In referring to the "functions" performed by their Jewishness, secular respondents tended to cite psychological constructs, such as inter-generational continuity and lineage, which have come to be associated with *ethnic* identity, in particular (Jaspal and Cinnirella, 2012). For instance, Josh perceived his Jewish identity as providing him with a sense of origin and connection with past generations ("my ancestors"), which has been said to provide ethnic group members with feelings of intergenerational continuity and group-level self-esteem (Jaspal and Cinnirella, 2012). Furthermore, Josh noted that his Jewish identity facilitated a positive self-conception, which suggested that it enhanced the self-esteem principle of identity.

Similarly, as a secular Jew who valued the norms, values, traditions and social representations associated with her Jewishness, Rebecca regarded that State of Israel as an important aspect of her identity:

> Israel is important for any Jew because it is our homeland, in my case, my second homeland. Israel is a spiritual place for some but it's also like a safe haven, I suppose, a place that we can call home […] It's a place where I feel a sense of belonging. (Rebecca, secular)

Like Josh, Rebecca emphasised the ethno-cultural underpinnings of her Jewish identity and her adherence to tradition, rather than spiritual faith. Her Jewishness appeared to provide a sense of connection with past and future generations of Jews, which highlighted the importance of this identity for the continuity principle. Moreover, secular individuals converged in their acceptance of the social representation that "Israel is important for any Jew", both secular and religious, because they construed it as "our homeland" and "a place that we can call home". Incidentally, most individuals highlighted the vicissitudes of Jewish existence in their host countries due to sudden spurts of antisemitic sentiment, which had had negative repercussions for the wellbeing of Jews in the diaspora. In exemplifying and describing these vicissitudes, respondents invoked the social representation of the Holocaust (Stein, 1978). Moreover, persecution against Jews was constructed as a looming and persistent threat, which could re-surface at any given moment due to a long history of antisemitism. While Rebecca acknowledged the "spiritual" value of Israel for more religious Jews, she attached greater importance to the social representation of Israel as a "safe haven" for Jewry. This social representation is also observable in the accounts of Israelis (see Chapter 9). More specifically, awareness of a long history of antisemitism sensitised participants to the practical, real-world importance of Israel. Many individuals did generally manifest a British national identity and indicated a sense of belonging in the national group (Kudenko and Phillips, 2009) – crucially, in Rebecca's case, Britishness was construed as more central to her self-concept than Israel. Yet, Israel was perceived as providing feelings of acceptance, inclusion and belonging – a stable and consistent source of belonging in a world that several respondents perceived to be uncertain for Jews. Israel was objectified as a symbol for Jewishness, be it a religious or an ethno-cultural identity, which could provide a "space" for Jewish continuity by shielding Jews from threats perceived to be associated with hostile outgroups. Self-identification with Israel provided an indirect means of coping with these perceived threats. Israel provided feelings of security, an important principle for many Jews whose experiences have been described in this book, but also group continuity (Jaspal and Yampolsky, 2011).

Orthodox Jews in the study tended to conceptualise their Jewish identity in both spiritual and ethno-cultural terms, although the spiritual component of Jewishness was of particular phenomenological importance. There was a perception among Orthodox Jews that their spirituality *and* ethnicity were intrinsically entwined and inseparable:

> It's a spiritual connection with *HaShem* [God]. It's a sense of community, security, peace within and outside, and we were chosen by *HaShem*. It's really important for me because it gives me a sense of who I am in the world and what my purpose is […] It's a great feeling to be connected to *HaShem*. (Kate, Orthodox)

Kate construed her Jewish identity as symbolising a "spiritual connection with *HaShem*", which highlighted the intrinsic spirituality of her Jewish identity, and as providing "a sense of community", which highlighted the socio-cultural dimension of her Jewishness (see Loewenthal, 2014). The construal of Jewishness as an ethnic identity was similarly observable in Orthodox participants' social representation that they had been chosen by God and that this "chosenness" was transmitted intergenerationally. Like Kate, most Orthodox participants derived a sense of purpose and meaning, feelings of security and inner peace on the basis of their Jewish identity. This suggested that the belonging, meaning and continuity principles of identity were clearly served by identification with Jewishness. Moreover, Kate's observation that "it's a great feeling" to perceive a spiritual connection with God indicated that this was also satisfying for the self-esteem principle of identity. Thus, for Orthodox Jews, Jewishness clearly performed important psychological functions and was most central to their self-concept.

Given its conceptualisation as a Jewish state, Israel performed similarly important functions for identity among Orthodox Jews. Although Jewishness was regarded as primary in the self-concept, Israel was perceived as empowering because it could safeguard and bolster Jewish identity:

> Israel is the Jewish State. It's empowering for any Jew because it's the only country where Jewish customs and identity are enshrined at every level of society. Kosher food, Shabbat, our religious holidays […] Israel is the place where I can be a good Jew and true to *HaShem* and raise my children in a Jewish environment where they can share in it. (Sarah, Orthodox)

Sarah emphasised the Jewish character of Israel, symbolised by the enshrinement of "Jewish customs and identity at every level of society". In Orthodox participants' accounts, the relative ease of manifesting one's Jewish identity in Israel was juxtaposed with the relative obstacles to Jewish identity manifestation in British society, for instance (Valins, 2003). Sarah cited Israel's observance of Jewish dietary requirements, the Holy Sabbath and Jewish religious holidays as examples of the inherently Jewish character of the country. Like Sarah, several Orthodox individuals in the study implied that Israel was more conducive to a Jewish lifestyle than other national contexts, which led them to view Israel as empowering for Jews. This suggested that the self-efficacy principle of identity was bolstered by identification with the State of Israel. It was construed as providing feelings of control and competence in relation to one's religious life, which might not be possible if Israel did not exist. The stated goal of many of the Orthodox Jews who participated in this study was to "be a good Jew and [to be] true to *HaShem*" as indicated by Sarah. Israel was generally perceived as facilitating this goal and was therefore regarded as positive and beneficial for identity processes. Given the psychological importance of being "true to *HaShem*" and "a good Jew", Israel, a facilitator of Jewish identity and adherence to the tenets of Judaism, appeared to bolster the self-esteem principle of identity. It was indirectly conducive to a positive self-conception (Gecas, 1982). It is noteworthy that several Orthodox Jews feared that Jewish norms, values and customs were slowly losing ground among younger generations of the Jewish community (Valins, 2003). Conversely, Israel was perceived as providing a "space" for a Jewish socialisation, thereby protecting group continuity at a more symbolic level.

For some interviewees and particularly those who identified as "anti-Zionist Jews", Jewish identity appeared to be of lesser phenomenological importance than other social identities, such as their British national identity and their political group membership. This was clearly manifested in Jason's account:

> Being Jewish isn't really up there in my list of priorities. To be honest, it's more like a position I'll take if I need to. I have strong political views, you know, and sometimes it sort of helps out to be Jewish or to be able to say it (laughs), you know, at times […] Sometimes it's kind of like a license in a way to say what you've got to say. (Jason, anti-Zionist)

Although Jason self-identified as Jewish, which was indeed one of the criteria for participation in this study, he clearly attributed less importance to his Jewish identity than to his political identity. He referred to his Jewishness as not "up there in my list of priorities" suggesting that it reflected a subordinate, rather than psychologically central, identity. Indeed, some participants appeared to *acknowledge* their Jewish heritage without really perceiving a strong psychological "attachment" to it. Jason tellingly referred to his Jewish identity as a "position" he could take in particular social contexts in order to perform rhetorical tasks. Later in his interview, he referred to political debates concerning the Israeli-Palestinian conflict and to the "utility" of his Jewish identity in defending his political and ideological position vis-à-vis the conflict. For Jason, his position as a Jewish individual allowed him to make particular statements and to avoid criticisms and allegations to which he believed a non-Jew might normally be susceptible. For instance, several participants acknowledged that there was considerable sensitivity around criticism of the State of Israel in the context of the Israeli-Palestinian conflict and that critics of Israel had often been accused of antisemitism. Conversely, Jason felt that he could bolster the socialist political cause, which he wholeheartedly supported, without having to face the stigma associated with antisemitism, because of his own Jewish heritage. Indeed, he conceptualised his Jewish identity as a "kind of licence" and a privileged position to make controversial statements and to immunise him from stigma. Thus, his Jewish identity appeared to perform rhetorical and discursive, rather than psychological, functions for Jason, who in other circumstances attached little or no importance to this component of his self-concept. Crucially, this suggests a distinct psychological (and rhetorical) motive for disidentification from Jewishness from the one suggested by Diller (1980), who attributes disidentification to repression. It appears that individuals are resourceful in managing their identities and in exploring their situational benefits.

Similarly, it has been observed that Jews who oppose Zionism may be referred to as "self-hating Jews" (Lewin, 1948). Indeed, Finlay (2005, p. 202) has argued that "the term is often used rhetorically to discount Jews who differ in their life-styles, interests or political positions from their accusers, and that such misapplications of the concept result from essentialized and normative definitions of Jewish identity". The term can perform a delegitimising function by labelling others as "treacherous and pathological" (p. 217). "Self-hating Jews" are positioned as ingroup "Black Sheep" because they are viewed as deviating from the ingroup norm (here, commitment to Zionism) which may adversely affect the social image of the ingroup (Marques, Abrams, Páez, and Hogg, 2001). Both Jason and Harry (below) were aware of the social representation of the "self-hating Jew", which was threatening for identity. Harry responded to this accusation by attributing importance to his Jewish identity, which he delineated from the State of Israel. This allowed him to protect his identity while continuing to disidentify with the State of Israel:

> To me, Israel is a pariah state, you know. As a Jew, I don't want to tarnish my Jewish background which I'm very proud of […] and the idea of Israel is just totally out of sync with my socialist and democratic values. And I speak for many, many Jews and, no, we don't hate ourselves or our faith. We just cannot support the idea of Zionism and a state just for Jews who believe in this particular thing […] What about us Jews? Don't we have a voice? (Harry, anti-Zionist)

Like Harry, some individuals in the study felt that negative social representations of Israel had adversely impacted social representations of Judaism and led some people to assume that Jews unanimously supported Israel. They attempted to safeguard positive images of Judaism, on the one hand, and to preserve membership within the Jewish ingroup by deflecting accusations of being "self-hating Jews", on the other. Given that many individuals derived self-esteem on the basis of their Jewish identity ("I'm very proud"), this group membership was important and, thus, the "self-hating Jew" label was threatening for the belonging and self-esteem principles of identity. Individuals struggled to retain acceptance and inclusion in the group by attempting to evade the "self-hating Jew" label. Yet, given the close link between Jewishness and Israel in the minds of many respondents, both Jewish and non-Jewish, anti-Zionist Jews did clearly face some ostracisation on the basis of their opposition to the State of Israel.

Harry and other respondents appeared to oppose Zionism because they perceived the ethos of Israel as being at odds with "socialist and democratic values", which were of primary importance particularly for those individuals who manifested an anti-Zionist stance. A left-wing socialist identity was often regarded as requiring an anti-Zionist stance because of the perceived right-wing orientation of Zionism. Anti-

Zionism was perceived as central to this political identity. Thus, in order to safeguard the psychological coherence principle of identity, individuals believed that it was necessary to oppose Zionism – they attempted to align their individual identity with their important political identity. Consequently, Harry reproduced the polemic social representation that Israel is a "pariah state" which contravenes global norms and therefore stands as an outcaste in the international community (see Chapter 3). He rejected the ideology of Zionism and the social representation that Israel constitutes a Jewish state ("a state for just Jews"). This stance can also be attributed to the desire to protect his Jewish identity, since he believed that identification with Israel might "tarnish" his Jewishness, but also his socialist political orientation which seemed incompatible with Zionism. There was a perceived conflict between these identities.

There was a desire among some respondents to construct a social identity around their Jewishness (conceived as a religio-spiritual and/ or ethno-cultural identity) and their anti-Zionist stance. Indeed, Harry and Jason asserted that there were many Jews who were staunchly opposed to the State of Israel despite their Jewish heritage, and wished to emphasise the existence of this anti-Zionist subgroup within the Jewish diaspora. This appeared to perform the function of safeguarding acceptance, inclusion and belonging within the Jewish ingroup by decreasing the image of a "Black Sheep" and promoting the representation of anti-Zionist Jews as a substantial minority within the Jewish community. Moreover, some participants clearly attempted to safeguard positive social representations of Jews by highlighting their disidentification with the State of Israel, thereby suggesting that there was not uncritical acceptance of Zionism within the diverse Jewish community.

These data demonstrate the diverse meanings and social representations attributed to Jewishness and the State of Israel, and that Jewish and Zionist identities can vary in their importance in accordance with the social and ideological milieu. Regardless of their position vis-à-vis Jewishness and Israel, the interviewees unanimously took a stance on antisemitism and anti-Zionism which they viewed as relevant, in one way or another, to all Jews.

Setting the Boundaries of Antisemitism and Anti-Zionism

The data suggested that people's social representations of antisemitism and anti-Zionism differed in accordance with their self-categorisation as secular, Orthodox or anti-Zionist Jews. Secular Jews acknowledged the long history of antisemitism in Europe, but perceived antisemitism as having transformed from a European phenomenon into a primarily *Muslim* phenomenon:

> The old antisemitism was before a thing of Christians that just believed the that Jews had killed Christ, that they committed the ultimate act of evil […] Europeans who believe that Jews want to loot Europe or skinheads. Nowadays what you have now is you have actually a dangerous, hidden kind of antisemitism. That's

> Muslims that say "oh, I'm a minority", yet they desecrate our graves, beat up our children, throw bricks through Jewish homes and what have you. (Neil, secular)

Neil made a temporal distinction between "old antisemitism" and a more recent "hidden kind of antisemitism". He exemplified old antisemitism by citing the historical motifs that Jews committed deicide and that they extorted money from their host countries and which he attributed primarily to Christian ideology (see Chapter 2). Like Neil, most secular respondents perceived antisemitism as having declined radically within the European context and any antisemitism that was observable among Europeans was attributed to "skinheads", a stigmatised subgroup. It is noteworthy that individuals tended to attenuate the significance of "European antisemitism" in order to highlight the "greater" significance of "Muslim antisemitism" (as observed among Israeli Jews in Chapter 9). In other contexts, there was acknowledgement of antisemitism in Europe, both Western and Eastern Europe, but individuals seemed to regard this as considerably less problematic than antisemitism from Muslims. Indeed, Neil and other participants regarded the new emerging *Muslim* antisemitism as posing a "dangerous" threat to Jewry, which he exemplified by referring to Jewish grave desecration, vandalism and violence against children (Iganski and Kosmin, 2003). Neil perceived this form of antisemitism as dangerous because of its allegedly "hidden" nature – he regarded it as being less socially conspicuous largely because antisemitic acts were perpetrated by a minority group rather than by the majority group. Individuals construed the minority status of Muslim antisemites as shielding them from public scrutiny:

> Muslims these days they'll just get away with murder. They can break the boundaries, the law, bit by bit and then a lot, like even say some pretty aggressive things about Jews, Israel, whoever isn't in their camp and nobody seemed to bat an eyelid. (Sue, secular)

Like Neil, Sue attributed contemporary antisemitism and anti-Zionism to Muslims. She believed that Muslims were able to engage in antisemitic behaviour with considerable ease: "they'll just get away with murder", due to their minority status. Several individuals invoked the culture of political correctness in Britain (Hughes, 2010), which they believed had inadvertently accentuated antisemitism due to the "sensitivity" with which Islam and Muslims were treated by the dominant British majority. Sue's remark that Muslims had considerable latitude in manifesting overt antisemitism stemmed from an emerging social representation that Britain's political correctness was out of control and had engendered negative outcomes for British Jews. Political correctness was generally said to be conducive to political and social paralysis in relation to curtailing the "aggression" of Muslims towards non-Muslim outgroups. Like Sue, several individuals perceived this as threatening because they regarded attempts to curtail Muslim antisemitism as futile – in Sue's view, there was little awareness or acknowledgement of Muslim antisemitism and, thus, no collective attempt to curtail it.

Unlike the Orthodox participants in the study, self-identified secular respondents regarded anti-Zionism as more threatening for identity than antisemitism, primarily because anti-Zionism was generally regarded as the *expression* of a covert underlying antisemitism:

> Neil (secular): Antisemitism is really just a thing of the past. Somebody who doesn't like Jews is basically just an idiot. A racist idiot. It doesn't affect me at all […] Anti-Israeli sentiment, now this is a big problem. A serious one. Because it undermines the very symbol of who we are in a way that doesn't really get criticised much, and nobody seems to care when Israel is being totally demonised.

> Interviewer: How does this make you feel?

> Neil: It's an important part of my heritage, my life and I'd say my future as well. And as a Zionist myself, a proud Zionist, it does kind of me feel, I'd say, undermined […] I fear sometimes that if these people get there way, will I have a home in the future? A place to bring my children up where we can be who we are?

Like several secular Jews in the study, Neil perceived overt antisemitism (in the traditional sense of the term) to be quite rare, which was generally attributed to the culture of political correctness that heavily stigmatises overt racism: "Someone who doesn't like Jews is basically just an idiot". However, anti-Zionism was clearly perceived as having replaced *overt* antisemitism. These forms of prejudice were often conflated by secular participants who regarded anti-Zionism as a more socially acceptable "face" of antisemitism (see Chapter 3). Close attention to participants' accounts revealed that anti-Zionism (namely, advocating the destruction of the Jewish State) was perceived as an attempt to deprive Jews of a homeland, thereby depriving them of their future and self-efficacy.

Secular individuals converged in their description of anti-Zionism as a dire threat to Jewish identity due to its attack upon an important "symbol of who we are". Like Neil, many respondents construed Israel as an objectification of Jewishness, that is, a symbolic aspect of this ethno-religious identity. Moreover, Neil believed that the social acceptability of anti-Zionism and the lack of public concern surrounding this form of "demonisation" rendered it a particularly threatening phenomenon. While there was confidence among Jews that overt antisemitism was had been dealt with by the authorities, several participants feared that anti-Zionism was acquiring greater social traction due partly to Muslim influence and sympathy towards the Palestinian cause, thereby jeopardising the future of Jews. This suggested that the continuity principle of identity was susceptible to threat due to the uncertain future which individuals believed to lie ahead.

In reflecting upon his feelings about anti-Zionism, Neil offered an account which suggested that anti-Zionism threatened his sense of continuity due to the centrality of Israel to his sense of self. This was analogous to the threat that perceived antisemitism posed to Orthodox Jews for whom their Jewish faith was the most central component of the self. In view of his construal of Zionism as an important component of his heritage, life and future, and the pride and self-esteem which he derived from his Zionist identity, *anti*-Zionism threatened the psychological thread connecting past, present and future. He felt that this undermined an important and enduring aspect of the self. For many participants in the study, the State of Israel performed an empowering function and provided individuals with feelings of control, competence and self-efficacy, because it was perceived as providing a secure future for Jews in a seemingly hostile world (Bar-Tal, 2000). Anti-Zionism was regarded as jeopardising this source of self-efficacy because it disrupted the perception of a secure future for oneself ("a home in the future") and for future generations of Jews ("a place to bring my children up where we can be who we are"):

> Anti-Zionism is quite debilitating for us as a people. It sucks out the autonomy of Jews, I mean, our ability to act independently, politically independently, I mean. (Benjamin, secular)

Benjamin powerfully illustrated the threat that anti-Zionism could pose to the self-efficacy principle of identity by describing it as "debilitating" for the Jewish people. Given that the State of Israel symbolised Jewish self-efficacy, perceived anti-Zionism (which participants regarded as an attempt to destroy Israel, rather than to merely criticise it) constituted an obstacle to deriving sufficient levels of self-efficacy. More specifically, Benjamin and other individuals in the study argued that anti-Zionism aimed to deprive the Jews of political autonomy and independence and to cause them to become dependent upon outgroups. It is easy to see why this would be threatening for Jews who regard Israel as the objectification of Jewish self-determination and self-efficacy. Some individuals anchored this scenario to the historical "exile" of the Jews and their statelessness for 2000 years, in order to highlight the extent of the threat to self-efficacy (Funkenstein, 1993). Indeed, to allow anti-Zionism to achieve its goals would was regarded as synonymous with self-destruction. Thus, for the secular individuals who participated in this study, the perception of anti-Zionism was clearly threatening for the continuity and self-efficacy principles of identity.

Orthodox participants tended to invoke the Holocaust when thinking about antisemitism because this was perceived as a metaphor for Jewish history (Stein, 1978). However, the conceptual boundaries of the Holocaust were often broadened in order to elucidate the threat which was perceived to be posed by Muslim antisemites, in particular (Jaspal and Yampolsky, 2011). Indeed, individuals regarded Muslims as the principal driving force behind contemporary antisemitism:

> The Holocaust is a major part of our historical journey as Jews. It happened to us all […] 21st century antisemitism is a, well generally a Muslim thing. That is not to say that all Muslims are antisemites. I have many Muslim friends myself who accept my Jewish faith and they respect it but there does seem to be a view in Muslim community that it's OK to hate Jews and OK to say it because of the

conflict in Israel. Perhaps in the faith there is something that's interpreted that way. Nowadays it's a Muslim rather than Christian thing. (David, Orthodox)

They [Muslims] think it's OK to say that Israel is all evil incarnate. When they talk of Israel what they really mean is that Jews, the people who built the State of Israel, are evil [...] They're saying that we, the Jewish people, have no right to claim that land because we're not Muslims. (Kate, Orthodox)

Like the secular interviewees, Orthodox individuals regarded contemporary antisemitism as a fundamentally "Muslim thing". David invoked the notion that it had become socially acceptable within the Muslim community to "hate Jews" and to make derogatory statements regarding Judaism. Although most participants acknowledged that not *all* Muslims were necessarily antisemitic and that there was variation in attitudes towards Jews, there was a perception that antisemitism was widespread within the Muslim community and that Islamic teaching had been (mis-) used to fuel antisemitism within the Muslim community. Like Neil, David appeared to regard antisemitism as having shifted from being a Christian to a Muslim phenomenon. The invocation of antisemitism appeared to evoke imagery of Islam in the minds of participants. Similarly, Kate focused upon Muslim anti-Zionism, which she believed to symbolise an underlying antisemitism, a perception which was widespread among respondents. Like Kate, several individuals viewed use of the term "Israel" as a euphemism for the Jewish people in the discourse of outgroups, largely because they themselves perceived Israel as an objectification of the Jewish people. Thus, the demonisation of Israel was said to reflect a demonisation of Jews "who [had] built the State of Israel". Kate argued that Muslims were more inclined to express antisemitism than other groups (due to the perception of Israel as "Muslim land"), and that this provided them with latitude in manifesting anti-Zionism and antisemitism in an overt and unrepentant manner. It was evident that antisemitism (and anti-Zionism which was interpreted as antisemitic in essence) was threatening for self-esteem, because it constructed a negative image of Jewishness which was central to the Orthodox participants' self-concept.

Like Kate, several Orthodox respondents perceived anti-Zionism as threatening because it challenged an important symbol of Jewish identity. However, some Orthodox respondents differentiated between antisemitism (prejudice towards Jews and Judaism) and anti-Zionism (prejudice towards Israel and Zionism):

Isaac (Orthodox): Israel is meaningful for us all as Jews but our faith is much more valuable and important. Israel is a symbol of our faith. When people criticise Israel, they criticise people, oppose Israel, the government, this is a symbol of Jews, not so bad. But when they criticise Jews and commit acts against Jews, this is our faith and our connection with our faith.

Interviewer: How does this make you feel?

Isaac: Well, bad, very bad. It deprives you of your dignity and singles you out just
because of something about yourself you hold close to your heart. It undermines
who I am, not just a symbol like Israel.

Although most participants, both Orthodox and secular, acknowledged the
importance of Israel as an element of their identity, because it symbolised their
Jewish faith as indicated by Isaac, Jewish faith was a more central aspect of identity
among the Orthodox (Valins, 2003). Isaac distinguished between anti-Zionism
and antisemitism and highlighted the distinct psychological impact that each
form of prejudice could have. When juxtaposed with antisemitism, he perceived
anti-Zionism as "not so bad" because it was directed towards a government and
"a symbol of Jews", rather than explicitly towards Jews themselves. Conversely,
Isaac perceived antisemitism as more threatening due to its overt focus upon "our
faith and our connection with our faith" which were clearly central to his identity as
an Orthodox Jew. This was threatening for the self-esteem principle as exemplified
by Isaac's observation that this made him feel "very bad" and deprived him of his
dignity. Moreover, this resulted in negative distinctiveness, given that it "singles
you out" negatively on the basis of a central aspect of identity, namely Jewish faith.
The Orthodox Jews' accounts suggested that perceived antisemitism could also
threaten the continuity principle of identity because it undermined individuals'
sense of self-construal and thereby disrupted the psychological thread between
past and present. Crucially, there was a perception among participants that, while
disidentification with the State of Israel may be possible, disidentification with their
Jewish faith was impossible because it entailed a negative re-construal of the self-
concept. Thus, it was deemed important to maintain a positive image of Jewishness,
an enduring aspect of the self-concept among Orthodox Jews.

Like Orthodox and secular Jews, even anti-Zionist Jews who participated in
the study took a stance on antisemitism, which many of them defined in terms
of non-Jews' erroneous assumptions and generalisations regarding the political
orientation of Jews. More specifically, individuals believed that the assumption
that all Jews unanimously and uncritically supported Zionism, Israel and Israel's
policies was antisemitic in nature, because it negatively stereotyped Jews on the
basis of their heritage:

It's the assumptions, the stupid assumptions. Basically you're Jewish and
therefore you must be a Zionist. You must support every move Israel makes
[…] It's like they just attach something to me that isn't mine, it isn't really me
but they think it is. For me, this is antisemitism […] People just assuming things
about you because of who you are. (Sally, anti-Zionist)

Given that Sally defined herself as an anti-Zionist Jew, erroneous assumptions
regarding her stance on the Israeli-Palestinian conflict was particularly threatening
for her identity. She clearly perceived herself, and wished to be recognised, as an
anti-Zionist and, thus, the ascription of a Zionist identity by outgroups deprived her

of the "identity validation" that is so fundamental to identity construction (Jaspal and Cinnirella, 2012). In short, individuals seek recognition of the identities that they value and wish to manifest socially.

Some individuals were aware of an outgroup assumption that Jews "support every move Israel makes" due to their Jewish identity and, given the unambiguously anti-Zionist stance of some participants, this assumed link between Judaism and Zionism was perceived as erroneous and offensive. Sally and other anti-Zionist participants were deeply opposed to Zionism, which rendered outgroups' ascription of a Zionist identity as threatening for their self-image. This would not be beneficial for their sense of continuity or self-esteem, primarily because of the stigma surrounding Zionism in the minds of these individuals. Moreover, respondents indicated that the non-Jews' assumptions concerning Jews' attachment to the State of Israel could threaten their sense of belonging within the British national ingroup, because identification with Israel was regarded as being incompatible with a British national identity. They expressed their awareness of negative social representations concerning the position of Zionism in contemporary British society, which in turn could lead to non-Jews automatically excluding and marginalising them on the basis of their Jewish heritage.

Although Sally cited this as an example of antisemitism, neither she nor other participants regarded antisemitism as a serious social problem in British society. There was some acknowledgement of the existence of antisemitism but anti-Zionist Jews tended to dismiss this either as a relatively rare occurrence or as something "fabricated" by Zionists in order to achieve particular goals. In any case, antisemitism was clearly delineated from anti-Zionism:

> I see antisemitism, which is hatred and violence against Jews and hatred of the Jewish faith, and anti-Zionism as two separate things. They are not the same thing at all and it's misleading to suggest otherwise […] I'm a Jew. I don't agree with the concept of Israel as a Jewish State. And I think Zionists, yes Zionists, have basically got to stop using antisemitism as their buzzword. (Joe, anti-Zionist)

Joe made a clear distinction between Judaism and Zionism, which allowed him to distinguish clearly between antisemitism and anti-Zionism. He rejected linkage between the two constructs, and argued that conflation of the two constructs was "misleading". Like Joe, several anti-Zionist participants themselves identified as Jewish, which in turn "evidenced" the possibility of being Jewish and anti-Zionist at the same time. Indeed, Joe expressed disagreement with "the concept of Israel as a Jewish State", which reflected his anti-Zionist position. Moreover, at an intergroup level, Joe delineated his Jewish ethno-religious ingroup from the Zionist outgroup, and implicitly attributed negative characteristics (e.g. dishonesty) to this outgroup. (Such rhetoric was reminiscent of the emerging intergroup boundaries between Iranians in the reformist and hardline political camps, as outlined in Chapter 7.) Joe argued that the accusation of antisemitism was strategically employed by Zionists "as their buzzword" in order to pursue their political and ideological agenda. In short, as a Jew, Joe perceived antisemitism as a concern for him and for his ethno-religious ingroup, but he believed that anti-Zionists had appropriated this concern in order to defeat anti-Zionism, a qualitatively distinct construct in Joe's opinion.

It was deemed necessary to examine the potential antecedents of anti-Zionism among Jews, in order to understand why individuals had come to compartmentalise Judaism and Zionism and why they rejected any linkage between antisemitism and anti-Zionism, despite the hegemonic social representation among many Jews that antisemitism and anti-Zionism are indeed related. Interestingly, for individuals who self-identified as anti-Zionist Jews, anti-Zionism appeared to perform positive functions for identity:

> As a campaigner, I'm very proud of the work we do in defence of human rights. This is all in the name of human rights. Our anti-Zionism cause is an empowering one. It is an empowering feeling to know that you are helping the Palestinians regain their rights, their legitimate rights. (Mike, anti-Zionist)

> I grew up in a Jewish and mainly Zionist area and I don't know I suppose my views it's something that sets me apart from other Jews, others in my community and I'm proud to be different, well, in this way at least […] I'm part of the Jews for Justice for Palestinians and I feel very pleased and happy to be in this group because, well because, we're like-minded and we understand each other. Most Jews don't understand us. (Richard, anti-Zionist)

For Mike, his anti-Zionist work symbolised his defence of human rights which provided him with feelings of pride and self-esteem – he was able to derive a positive self-conception on the basis of what he regarded as humanitarian work. Indeed, anti-Zionism was perceived as a necessary stance in order to protect human rights because there was a pervasive belief that Zionism undermined the human rights of Palestinians and illegitimately favoured Jews. Interestingly, some respondents described feelings of guilt in response to the perceived suffering of the Palestinians, which conversely undermined a positive self-conception. Given that some individuals described anti-Zionism as being "all in the name of human rights", disidentification with Zionism mitigated those feelings of guilt which impeded self-esteem. Conversely, the perception of working towards a positively valued phenomenon such as human rights bolstered the self-esteem principle. Similarly, Richard's account suggested that anti-Zionism enhanced feelings of *positive distinctiveness*. More specifically, Richard described growing up in a context in which Zionism was unanimously valued and embraced by other Jews and, thus, his anti-Zionism provided him with a means of differentiating himself from others within his social milieu ("others within my community"). Given that these individuals reported feeling "proud to be different" on the basis of their anti-Zionism, it is easy to see why they might embrace this stance (Vignoles et al., 2000).

As clearly exemplified by Mike's account, there was a perception of competence and control derived from anti-Zionism because some individuals believed that this empowered them to assist the Palestinians in acquiring their human rights, "their legitimate rights" which were allegedly threatened by Zionism. Given the perception of empowerment vis-à-vis this important cause, anti-Zionism appeared to have positive outcomes for the self-efficacy principle of identity. As Richard indicated, anti-Zionist Jews were not stand-alone figures but rather had come to think, function and achieve collective goals in terms of a distinctive social group (Tajfel, 1982; Tajfel and Turner, 1986), which conceivably bolstered the self-efficacy principle. Individuals felt empowered because they worked collaboratively and cohesively as a social group (Breakwell, 1986). This in turn elucidated a further "benefit" for identity – individuals clearly believed that their anti-Zionist group membership (in Richard's case, in the Jews for Justice for Palestinians pressure group) provided them with feelings of acceptance and inclusion which were habitually curtailed within their Jewish ethno-religious ingroup. Richard attributed his threatened sense of belonging in the Jewish community to the notion that most Jews self-identified with Zionism. Thus, he believed that his rejection of Zionism essentially positioned him outside of the Jewish community. Indeed, there is a tension between belonging and uniformity among group members, on the one hand, and interpersonal distinctiveness, on the other, which is referred to as "optimal distinctiveness" in social psychology (Brewer, 1991). It appeared that, like Richard, some individuals opted for enhanced interpersonal distinctiveness from ingroup members on the basis of their anti-Zionist position. Richard appeared to compensate for the decreased sense of belonging by focusing upon his membership in the Jews for Justice for Palestinians pressure group which he had joined. Unlike the mainstream Jewish community, the pressure group provided access to and communication with "like-minded" individuals with whom he perceived a mutual understanding. Indeed, this was conductive to feelings of acceptance and inclusion and, thus, bolstered an otherwise threatened sense of belonging.

Coping with Threatened Identity: Re-Constructing Jewishness and Israel

For secular and Orthodox respondents in this study, both antisemitism and anti-Zionism were regarded as threatening, albeit to varying degrees, while the self-identified anti-Zionist participants generally *valued* anti-Zionism and construed antisemitism either as a non-issue or as a stereotypical perception of Jews as inherently supportive of Israel. The data suggested that identity processes, threat and coping played an important role in individuals' meaning-making vis-à-vis Jewishness, Zionism and the State of Israel.

Individual and interpersonal strategies for coping with threat

Participants were unanimously aware of negative social representations of Zionism in British society, which secular and Orthodox individuals tended to attribute to negative media reporting on Israel and pro-Palestinian stakeholders and which anti-

Zionist participants attributed to Israel's policies and actions. Individuals may have less social psychological incentive to identify with social entities and groups which are socially stigmatised (Tajfel, 1982), because of the negative outcomes that this can have for the self-esteem principle of identity (Gecas, 1982). Yet, the State of Israel did constitute an important aspect of identity for many secular and Orthodox participants. Thus, some individuals avoided manifesting publicly a connection with Israel, although they did *privately* perceive an attachment to it:

> I know what makes British people tick about Israel and what they've sort of been led to think and so I just don't mention Israel. I don't even go there. I just steer clear from this whole situation because there is a clash there. That way, I feel I can be British when it's important and Jewish when it's important. (Keiran, secular)

Keiran identified a "clash" between his British and Zionist identities because of the negative social representations of Zionism in British society. He attributed these social representations to "what they've sort of been led to think", which constituted a reference to negative media and political representations of Israel in Britain. As a result of the existence of such negative social representations, Keiran resorted to attenuating his Zionist identity in both public and private contexts in order to perceive himself and to present himself as a British national group member. There was a compartmentalisation of these identities in order to avert the "clash" between them – Keiran reporting "be[ing] British when it's important and Jewish when it's important", shifting between his group memberships in accordance with context and social importance (Jaspal, 2011b). The strategy of compartmentalisation ensured that phenomenologically important elements of his identity (i.e. Britishness and attachment to Israel) could be retained but activated in accordance with social context.

For secular and Orthodox participants, perceived antisemitism and anti-Zionism could induce threats to the self-esteem principle because individuals felt unable to derive a positive self-conception on the basis of two components of identity which were, in one way or another, phenomenologically important. Like Keiran, some individuals attempted to deflect the threat to self-esteem, which ensued from perceived disapproval from others, by concealing their support for Zionism in interpersonal communication:

> Isaac (secular): Sometimes I do sort of find myself giving in and just going along with the typical discussion of Israel […] I remember, once at a Christmas do, conversation somehow turned to Israel and someone basically turned around and said that Israel uses, no misuses, the Holocaust just to get what it wants and, and I, I mean, to push stuff through and I just sat there and agreed, to my eternal shame […] Looking back, it was an antisemitic and anti-Zionist remark.
>
> Interviewer: And how does this make you feel looking back?

Isaac: It wasn't upsetting at the time. If anything I blended in. I was one of the crowd and it actually felt good not to be the odd one out supporting "the oppressor".

Some individuals appeared to engage in transient denial of their Jewish identity, which constitutes an intrapsychic coping strategy, and in "passing", an interpersonal coping strategy (Breakwell, 1986). Isaac reflected upon his experience of a Christmas party during which his colleagues criticised Israel's "misuse" of the Holocaust in order to elicit sympathy from the international community and to perform particular acts. Although he habitually disagreed with this view and referred to it as "an antisemitic and anti-Zionist remark", Isaac reported assimilating his stance to that of his colleagues in order to avoid "excessive" distinctiveness from his colleagues and to risk their disapproval (Brewer, 1991). In short, Isaac agreed with his colleagues and participated in their condemnation of Israel. There was a sense that this process functioned at an intrapsychic level, as a form of transient assimilation to others' social representations, as it induced no psychological conflict at the time, as well as at an interpersonal level, enacted through communication with others.

Isaac engaged in the interpersonal strategy of passing by "gaining exit from the threatening position [here, Zionism] through deceit" and entered "a new interpersonal network" on false premises (Breakwell, 1986, p. 116). This facilitated a sense of inclusion and acceptance, thereby enhancing the belonging principle of identity, protecting it from threat: "I blended in. I was one of the crowd". Moreover, by passing himself off as an anti-Zionist, Isaac was able to protect his sense of self-esteem because disclosure of his attachment to Israel, could have exposed him as an ingroup "Black Sheep" (Marques, Yzerbyt and Leyens, 1988). Indeed, Isaac noted that "it actually felt good" because he avoided positioning himself alongside "the oppressor", a negatively evaluated social category. Although in retrospect Isaac felt ashamed of having passed himself off as an anti-Zionist and "betrayed" his Jewish ingroup to a certain degree, at the time passing protected his identity from threat and bolstered his psychological wellbeing.

Individuals felt under increasing pressure to manifest an anti-Zionist stance despite their attachment to Israel. This was regarded as necessary in order to maintain a sense of belonging in the British national group due to their awareness of negative social representations of Israel in British society (Wistrich, 2011):

It's become quite difficult, in the last few years especially I think. I just feel like I'm gagged a bit and it shouldn't be this way in the country, in a country of freedom and moderation […] It's changed how I see Britain in a way because we are really gagged about Israel, Jews I mean. We can't say out loud what we think […] I feel a bit forced [to oppose Israel] if I want to fit in. (Natalie, secular)

There was a perception among some secular and Orthodox Jews that it had become difficult for Jews to openly identify with the State of Israel due to fear of disapproval from non-Jewish co-nationals. Indeed, individuals believed that overt self-identification with Israel might jeopardise their acceptance and inclusion in the national group, thereby threatening the belonging principle of identity. Indeed, most individuals attached importance to Britishness and wished to be accepted and included within the national group. Yet, Natalie described the stigma in Britain surrounding overt self-identification with Israel in terms of feeling "gagged" and "silenced". Crucially, she believed that such social censorship of attachment to Israel was aimed at British Jews, in particular. Like Natalie, several participants felt that their sense of belonging in the national group was potentially jeopardised by overt self-identification with Israel and public recognition of their attachment to the country. This presented a dilemma because both elements of identity (Britishness and attachment to Israel) were important for the self-concept. There was a reported tendency to conceal their Zionist stance and, as exemplified by Isaac's account, to oppose Zionism in public domains despite the inconsistency of this public stance with their private stance. Although this was transiently successful as a coping strategy, individuals' awareness of the discordance between their public and private stances could induce a sense of conflict and, thus, threatened psychological coherence (Jaspal and Cinnirella, 2010a).

More generally, awareness of negative social representations of Israel in British society and the perceived need to conceal one's attachment to Israel induced a re-construal of Britishness among some individuals. For instance, Natalie observed a negative change in the British national context in that she perceived Britain as having transformed from "a country of freedom and moderation" into a context in "we can't say out loud what we think" (see Wistrich, 2004). The perception of such negative change targeting her ethno-religious ingroup, in particular, could be threatening for the continuity principle of identity, because it induced a negative change in thinking about an important element of identity, namely Britishness. Moreover, it appeared that some individuals felt alienated by the emergence of negative social representations of Israel in British society, potentially jeopardising their attachment to Britishness.

Similarly, given their awareness of the delegitimisation of the State of Israel and of the conflation of Judaism and Zionism in social and political discourse in Britain, there was an observable tendency among Orthodox Jews to compartmentalise, at a psychological level, their Jewish and Zionist identities:

> The constant diatribes against Israel, sometimes it can make me feel quite bad even about being Jewish, a Jew. Can you imagine that? For many, Judaism and the Holy Land are so entwined that you basically, you can't separate them out. Because of all the pressure you know, they are two distinct, separate things […] The way I see it, if there's no Israel, I'm still Jewish. We Jews have had our faith without a state for 2000 years. However, If I'm not Jewish, I'm nothing. (Aaron, Orthodox)

> Jerusalem, Yirushalayim, is an important part of my Jewish faith and my Jewish identity. I try not to think about it too much but […] it's almost as if it's not the same as the divided Jerusalem, politically charged Jerusalem that's on people's

minds. I have my own Jerusalem in my mind which is different from the one that everyone castigates the Jews for. (Dovid, Orthodox)

There was agreement among several participants that the Land of Israel constituted an important component of their Jewish identities because of its historical, religious and spiritual significance. Thus, anti-Zionism (referred to as "constant diatribes against Israel") could negatively impact self-esteem in relation to their Jewish identity. Indeed, Aaron observed that it could make him "feel quite bad about being Jewish" partly because of his awareness of the social representation among non-Jews that Jews unanimously and uncritically supported Israel and its actions. Although individuals like Aaron perceived the connection between Jewish identity and the Holy Land as entwined and natural, which rendered them inseparable in the minds of many Jews, there was a tendency among some Orthodox Jews to distance themselves from Israel in order to "shield" their Jewish identity from stigma. Aaron noted that "because of all the pressure" from hostile outgroups, his Jewish identity and the Holy Land had been separated out in his mind so that they now constituted "two distinct, separate things".

Human beings are resilient and agentive in their construction and maintenance of identity (Breakwell, 1986, 2010), and Aaron quite clearly demonstrated a creative approach to maintaining and protecting his identity by compartmentalising his Jewish identity and his attachment to the Land of Israel. In order for the assimilation-accommodation process of identity to function in this way, he revised the content of identity and the salience of its elements and reasoned that he could remain Jewish, clearly a very important element of his identity, in the absence of Israel. He invoked the historical social representation that Jews had indeed been in exile for two millennia prior to the establishment of Israel as evidence of this possibility. Conversely, he noted, that loss of his Jewish faith would deprive his life of meaning ("If I'm not Jewish, I'm nothing") (Silberman, 2005). Thus, Aaron's account demonstrated a clear compartmentalisation of his Jewish and Zionist identities in that a connection between them was no longer necessary for realisation of his Jewish identity, an important component in the hierarchy of elements in his identity.

Dovid, also an Orthodox Jew, manifested a similar strategy for protecting his identity. He reported attempting to suppress imagery of Jerusalem when thinking about his Jewish faith because of the apparent conflict that this induced in view of negative social representations of Israel among hostile outgroups. However, it was evident that Jerusalem, which he referred to by the biblical Hebrew toponym Yirushayalim, did possess an important position in his identity as a Jew. Dovid engaged in the creative strategy of re-conceptualising Jerusalem in order to compartmentalise his Jewish and Zionist identities. More specifically, he retained in his mind a purely spiritual and biblical construction of Jerusalem, which was free of any association with the negative social representations of Israel disseminated by hostile outgroups, and suppressed the "politically charged Jerusalem" which posed threats to his self-esteem as a Jew. This protected his self-esteem and his sense of belonging because it provided a buffer against the perceived disapproval from non-Jews.

There was strong indication in the data that British Jews might perceive a sense of incongruence between Britishness and Zionism, which could induce threats to psychological coherence, in addition to the other principles of identity. The self-identified anti-Zionist participants in this study also reported feelings of incongruence between Israel and their self-image (and particularly, their political beliefs which contributed to their self-image). This rendered salient the psychological coherence principle of identity:

> Israel conflicts with my beliefs, deeply held political beliefs. I believe in people having basic human rights and these are human rights, not just Jews' rights. Israel has a policy of favouring Jews only and not other religions […] I have a belief in human rights but Israel seems to disregard these basic rights. I don't understand the logic of a state for Jews, based on race. For me, it's unreal in a democratic society […] I can't really accept a capitalist US province in the name of Judaism, so I'm a Jew against Israel. (Sandy, anti-Zionist)

Sandy noted that the ethos of Israel was inconsistent with her "deeply held political beliefs", namely her socialist political orientation, and with the hegemonic representation that all individuals are entitled to human rights regardless of ethnic origin. Conversely, Israel was perceived as "favouring Jews only" and as contravening "basic [human] rights". Sandy perceived Israel as a "racist" state which was incompatible with democratic norms, rendering it "unreal in a democratic society". Conversely, there was perceived disjuncture between her political orientation and the perceived ethos of Israel, which rendered salient the psychological coherence principle of identity. Moreover, Sandy believed that Zionism (conceived primarily as a capitalist ideology) was incompatible with her Jewish identity. Indeed, as a Jewish socialist, she felt unable to accept the notion of a "capitalist US province in the name of Judaism". There was a perception among some individuals that Jewishness was "misused" in the name of Zionism.

Thus, in Sandy's account, there appeared to be conflicts between various identities – her Jewish identity and Zionism, on the one hand, and her political identity and Zionism (metaphorically objectified in terms of "capitalism"), on the other. In order to minimise and avert threats to psychological coherence, Sandy accentuated her Jewish and political identities, which she regarded as compatible, while rejecting Zionism as an unacceptable ideology. In a similar vein, Israel was perceived not as an objectification of Jewishness, as in the accounts of secular and Orthodox participants, but rather as a "capitalist US province". In short, Sandy sought to re-establish and re-affirm her Jewish identity by representing herself as "a Jew against Israel" thereby highlighting the possibility of self-identification with both Jewishness *and* anti-Zionism.

Like other participants in the study, Paul too perceived Zionism as jeopardising the position of Jews in British society and, more specifically, as inhibiting their acceptance and inclusion by the non-Jewish British majority. This could induce a degree of defensiveness in relation to British national identity, as individuals strove to manifest and demonstrate their Britishness:

> Paul (anti-Zionist): I suppose growing up Jewish, going to a Jewish school, having parents from quite a religious Zionist background, I did grow up wondering about who I am and my place in society and that […] I almost felt a bit kind of, I don't know if defensive is the right word? Yes, slightly defensive.

> Interviewer: Defensive about what?

> Paul: You know, am I being stereotyped for being Jewish or […] is person X saying Y because I'm Jewish. I guess I didn't feel 100% accepted as British.

Like Paul, several individuals in the study highlighted the tensions between their British national and Jewish ethno-religious identities because of the perceived divergences between these identities and their respective social representations (Jaspal and Cinnirella, 2010a). Paul identified his Jewish upbringing, his Jewish education and the religious Zionist stance of his parents as contributing to uncertainty in his British national identity. He believed that non-Jews questioned his Britishness, partly because of the assumed link between Jewishness and Zionism. This was highlighted in his tendency to interpret others' actions and intentions as threatening, that is, as resulting in his exclusion on the basis of his Jewishness. Paul felt unsure about how he fitted into British national society because the aforementioned factors seemed to be incongruous with British national identity (cf. Kudenko and Phillips, 2010). Some individuals did acknowledge a state of defensiveness which resulted from the perceived incongruity between British national and Jewish ethno-religious identities, in that they sought to assert their Britishness and to demonstrate to others the authenticity of their British national identity. For Paul and other participants, Zionism was regarded as being inconsistent with Britishness, which was rendered salient in stereotypes of Jews as unanimously and uncritically accepting Zionism. These perceptions of incongruity jeopardised individuals' sense of Britishness.

It appeared that the insecurities and uncertainties in relation to Britishness (induced by the perceived incoherence between their British national and Jewish ethno-religious identities) might underlie individuals' anti-Zionism (cf. Lewin, 1948). It is plausible that Paul sought to distance himself from "problematic" aspects of his Jewish upbringing and identity, namely the familial commitment to Zionism, by disidentifying with Israel and by adopting an overtly anti-Zionist stance. Some individuals came to "feel" more British by expressing anti-Zionism:

> One of the cornerstones of being British is freedom and of course equality regardless of race and that just is not something that Zionism advocates […] Opposing Zionism is actually a very British position to take in my view. (Marcel, anti-Zionist)

Marcel's social representation of Britishness consisted of the notions of freedom and equality, which justified his strong attachment to his British national identity. Essentially, he argued that he self-identified with this national category partly because it mapped onto his self-perception as somebody who valued freedom and equality "regardless of race". Conversely, his social representation of Zionism consisted of imagery of *in*equality and lack of freedom, which naturally rendered his British national identity and the endorsement of Zionism as incongruous and potentially threatening for psychological coherence. Consequently, for Marcel, self-identification with Britishness *required* a rejection of Zionism, because the endorsement of equality and freedom meant that it was necessary to reject an ideology opposed to these notions. This echoed the perception among both British Pakistani and Iranian Muslim participants in this study that anti-Zionism constituted a central tenet of their Muslim identities and must therefore be manifested in order to construct an *authentic* Muslim identity (see also Jaspal, 2013a). In the case of some anti-Zionist British Jews, anti-Zionism was regarded as an important tenet of Britishness.

Joining pressure groups for defending Israel/Zionism

While those Jews who clearly valued a sense of belonging in the national group favoured deflection and interpersonal strategies in order to maintain feelings and acceptance and inclusion in Britain, some secular individuals in the study engaged in a group-level strategy for defending their attachment to Israel and for defending identity from threat. They derived positive social and psychological outcomes from participating in a pro-Zionist pressure group:

> Joining StandWithUs[1] [a non-profit pro-Israel education and advocacy organisation and pressure group] really did wonders for me. For a while, I was just thinking: who am I? What does Israel mean to me as a Jew? How can I deal with what other people are saying, you know, most people who are opposed to the Jewish homeland? How do I make a real change to Jews? […] These were all things that really got to me and got me thinking about my future and with StandWithUs I feel the future of Israel is secure. (Rebecca, secular)

The group-level strategy of group mobilisation and participation in pressure groups enabled some individuals to combat the threats that antisemitism and anti-Zionism posed to identity. Rebecca highlighted that her awareness of anti-Zionism had raised questions surrounding her identity as a Jew and how she ought to respond to anti-Zionism from non-Jews. It appeared that anti-Zionism had induced uncertainty vis-à-vis her Jewish and Zionist identities because of the increasing stigma surrounding these group memberships in British society. Her participation in StandWithUs appeared to perform positive functions for her identity. It reduced the uncertainty

---

1   StandWithUs UK http://www.standwithus.co.il/uk-3/.

that had been induced by anti-Zionism by providing responses to the questions that anti-Zionism had raised for her identity. More specifically, StandWithUs appeared to bolster the self-efficacy and continuity principles of identity, because the actions of the group induced feelings of security concerning Israel's future, providing both a sense of ingroup control and competence but also a psychological thread between present and future. Furthermore, given that anti-Zionism was perceived as indirectly threatening the security of Israel, an important component of identity for many individuals (Bar-Tal, 2000), participation in the pro-Israel pressure group re-established feelings of security.

Attachment to the State of Israel had jeopardised individuals' sense of inclusion and acceptance, thereby posing threats to the belonging principle of identity. For these individuals, membership in a pro-Israel pressure group could mitigate the threat to belonging:

> You know, I was quite a committed socialist but I just feel totally thrown out of the party because they just went on and on about Israel and as a Jewish person the reality is I do support Israel as a Jewish homeland, just like many other states were created for Muslims or for Christians and here we have the one and only Jewish state […] So the Socialist Party wasn't for me because I was not for them, as a supporter of Israel. (Keiran, secular)

Participants pointed to their various social group memberships, such as their Jewish ethno-religious and political group memberships. There was a perception among some individuals that they had been ostracised from particular social groups due to outgroup hostility to either their Jewish or Zionist identities. For instance, Keiran reported feeling excluded from socialist political circles because of his attachment to Israel, which he believed to be natural "as a Jewish person". More specifically, he believed that this social representation was central to his Jewish identity but clearly incompatible with the socialist political organisation of which he was a "committed" member. It appeared that his ethno-religious and political identities were represented by other members of his political circle as being incompatible, which had negative outcomes for Keiran's sense of psychological coherence. Crucially, this perception of incoherence was rendered salient by other people; it did not originate from a psychological level (see Jaspal, 2011b for a discussion of how relevant others can induce a perception that one's identities are not compatible). Thus, Keiran came to believe that, "as a supporter of Israel", a stance which he believed to be central to his Jewish identity, he would not be accepted by and included in the Socialist Party, which led to his departure from the group. Clearly, his Jewish and Zionist identities featured more prominently in his self-concept, which induced the need to take a stance on the incompatibilities between his ethno-religious and political identities. Like several other participants, Keiran came to derive feelings of acceptance and inclusion from alternative group memberships, namely the Jewish community and a pro-Israel organisation that he subsequently joined. This curbed the threats to belonging induced by his exclusion from the Socialist Party, clearly an important group membership on the basis of his political identity.

Through their participation in pro-Israel pressure groups, some individuals appeared to develop creative intrapsychic strategies for averting identity threat, such as re-considering the characteristics associated with the categories Israel and Zionism:

> When sceptics talk about Israel, they just seem to think that Israelis just break international rules and oppress Palestinians and wage war and what have you. I like to remember that Israel is a leader in technology, charity, supporting other countries. It is winning the battle on cancer. It makes enormous contributions to science and technology. This is something I'm proud of, as a Jew and as a British person. (Adam, secular)

> Zionism has given us voice and power to do great things. Jews are a very brainy people. We have made great strides in science for example. (Jim, secular)

While interviewees were acutely aware of negative social representations of Israel as a belligerent "rogue state" that ignored international norms and oppressed the Palestinian people, most secular and Orthodox individuals either attenuated or rejected these representations in favour of more positive ones. Adam, for instance, attributed these social representations to "sceptics", and constructed them as the product of anti-Zionist stakeholders with a particular agenda. This served to discredit these social representations, thereby attenuating their importance for meaning-making vis-à-vis Israel. Conversely, Adam accentuated positive social representations of Israel as "a leader in technology, charity, [and] supporting other countries" and made observations regarding Israel's "enormous contributions" to health, science and technology and particularly the field of cancer research. Moreover, Jim re-conceptualised Zionism as an ideology which had facilitated "great strides in science" through the political autonomy and agency that it gave Jews, "a very brainy people". He attenuated the negative representations of Zionism by highlighting its positive side which he believed had resulted in benefits for humankind.

As Adam's account demonstrated, Israel's leadership role provided some individuals with feelings of pride and a positive self-conception "as a Jew and as a British person". More specifically, as a Jew, Adam felt able to lay claim to the achievements and accomplishments of the State of Israel because of the perceived connection and inseparability of Israel and Judaism. Moreover, there was a perception that Britishness naturally valued charity, public health and science and technology, which in turn contributed to a positive social representation of Israel from the perspective of Britishness. On the one hand, this established linkage between British and Zionist identities and, on the other, it embellished social imagery of Israel, facilitating its assimilation-accommodation and positive evaluation as a component of identity. Crucially, individuals provided positive accounts of their involvement in pro-Israel pressure groups because they believed that these group contexts exposed them to alternative, more positive social representations of Israel and Zionism, to which they felt they had no access due to a perceived media and political bias against Israel. Given that Israel constituted an important component of identity, participants naturally sought positive representations of this identity element and distanced themselves from negative representations.

Having acquired awareness of positive social representations of Israel and Zionism, many individuals deemed it necessary to disseminate these positive social representations beyond the confines of their pressure group and to challenge alternative, more negative social representations of Israel, which they believed to permeate British society (Wistrich, 2011):

> It's my duty as a Jew and a Zionist to show the world the truth about Israel and I wish to crush the Islamist, leftist propaganda that demonises the Jewish State. Our work does this and we are making big and good changes in the world, I think […] The Muslim community is hard to influence but slowly we are showing people that we won't just sit back and watch blatant antisemitism grow. (Michael, secular)

> Since I joined [the pressure group], I can honestly say that I've never felt downgraded or delegitimised or whatever you want to call it […] It's made me realise that we know and that's what matters and we can support one another […] We all know that our group and our activities are having a good, strong impact on society and on society's, I guess, perspective on Israel […] I'm really proud of this campaign and I feel good about it and of course proud of us and our work. (Vicky, secular)

As outlined earlier in this chapter and in Chapter 9, Israel was widely perceived as a Jewish safe haven and as a context in which Jews could safely and openly manifest their Jewish identities, amid uncertainty about the position and safety of Jews in the world. Dismayed by the perceived coerciveness of anti-Zionism in the world, Michael regarded the pro-Israel pressure group, of which he was a member, as enabling him to "show the world the truth about Israel". This clearly performed an empowering function for individuals in the study, and benefited the self-efficacy principle of identity. Michael felt able to fulfil his "duty as a Jewish man and a Zionist", two important components of his identity.

Like Michael, several respondents interpreted anti-Zionism as an intergroup struggle between Jews and hostile outgroups, such as Islamists and left-wing political groups. Michael's membership in a pro-Israel pressure group enabled him to challenge anti-Zionist outgroups and their "demonising" social representations of Israel. Moreover, this membership enabled him to implement what he construed as necessary social change. Even in face of the apparent futility of attempting to change negative social representations of Jews and Israel (among the Muslim community, for instance), Michael felt that he was doing *something* to mitigate anti-Zionism by retaining active membership in the pro-Israel pressure group. Participants viewed pro-Israel group mobilisation as contributing positively to the mitigation of anti-Zionism and antisemitism, which were collectively threatening for identity.

Participation in pressure groups was intended to improve social representations of Israel, an important component of identity, and thereby bolster the self-esteem principle of identity. Individuals derived a positive self-conception on the basis of their pressure group membership, as exemplified by Vicky's account. Moreover, her group membership essentially shielded her from the negative social representations disseminated by hostile outgroups, which might habitually lead to decreased self-esteem. It is noteworthy that the secular and Orthodox participants in this study did identify strongly with their Jewishness and the State of Israel and, thus, antisemitism and anti-Zionism were construed as threatening for self-esteem. For Vicky, her pressure group membership facilitated a re-focusing upon the mutual support that members could provide to one another, rather than the negative social representations disseminated by outgroups. Vicky derived pride and self-esteem from the knowledge that their group activities were performing positive functions for their Jewish and Zionist identities. This perception was echoed in Michael's account. Thus, the ingroup's "campaign" to improve social representations of Israel constituted an important source of self-esteem for Vicky and others, suggesting that their pressure group membership protected them from threat.

It is noteworthy that, through participation in pro-Israel pressure groups, some individuals regarded the challenging of anti-Zionism as their "duty" as Jews, that is, as an act that was central to their identity as Jews. It appeared that the link between Jewishness and Israel had been reiterated within the context of pro-Israel pressure groups, as individuals widely reported having been further sensitised to this link during their participation in the group. For many respondents, the link between Jewishness and Israel was construed as natural, given the ethno-religious underpinnings of the establishment of the State of Israel. However, they believed that dominant social representations of Israel in British society had caused a weakening of the perceived link between Jewishness and Israel. This could be attributed to the trepidation of some individuals at the notion of acknowledging their Zionist identities in British society. Yet, participation in pro-Israel pressure groups empowered some individuals to challenge negative social representations of Israel, not by attenuating their importance as suggested by the accounts of Adam and Jim, but by actively and forcefully challenging the authority of anti-Zionists to criticise the State of Israel.

> I've come to deal with this because I just think to myself "how dare you criticize Israel?" when you endorse horrendous things yourself? It is incredible as far as I'm concerned. What would you know about peace and freedom? (Catherine, secular)

> We are one and we know that we must stand together when we are faced with antisemitism […] Together we know the Torah, we know Scripture. What antisemites say is not so important to us in that we do, we can see through their lies […] We come together when need be. (Aaron, Orthodox)

Both membership in pressure groups (as was the case for many secular informants) and close affiliation to religious circles (as was the case for Orthodox Jews in the study) enabled some individuals to reject and counteract negative social representations disseminated by hostile outgroups (Breakwell, 2001). Catherine described how her strong and cohesive Jewish identity and her involvement in her local synagogue had provided her with feelings of solidarity with other Jews, allowing her to challenge the authority and legitimacy of outgroups who disseminate anti-Zionist and antisemitic social representations. Similarly, Aaron focused on the sense of solidarity which he felt enabled Jews to challenge the legitimacy and validity of antisemitism ("we can see through their lies"). Individuals felt able to immerse themselves in scripture which provided a buffer against antisemitism, depriving it of its power to threaten identity.

The threats to self-esteem, belonging and continuity associated with negative social representations were deflected through the process of rejecting the social representations themselves. Catherine questioned the legitimacy of the assertions of anti-Zionists by arguing that Muslim anti-Zionists had no right to criticise the State of Israel given the human rights records of Muslim countries. This essentially de-authorised Muslim anti-Zionists from criticising Israel's stance on "peace and freedom", since they themselves allegedly had no experience in this domain. The outright rejection of dominant social representations echoes the interpersonal strategy of negativism, which refers to "the state of mind which one is in when one feels a desire or a compulsion to act *against* the requirements or pressure from some external source" (Apter, 1983, p. 79). In short, individuals were able to protect their identity by counteracting such "pressures" from hostile external sources.

Overview

This chapter highlights the diverse conceptualisations of Jewish identity among British Jews, which appear to differ in accordance with one's orientation as Orthodox, secular or anti-Zionist. While Orthodox Jews conceptualised their Jewishness in religio-spiritual terms, secular Jews construed their Jewish identity in ethno-cultural terms. The self-identified anti-Zionist Jews manifested a more ambivalent relationship to their Jewishness – they all acknowledged Jewish "origins" but perceived this identity in different ways. Some of them manifested a close attachment to their Jewish identity in religio-spiritual terms, but delineated this unequivocally from Zionism, while others viewed their Jewishness as a nominal identity of little phenomenological importance.

Secular and Orthodox Jews acknowledged the threat of antisemitism and anti-Zionism but, like the Israeli Jews whose accounts were described in Chapter 9, they construed these forms of prejudice as a fundamentally Muslim, rather than European, phenomenon. While the Orthodox viewed antisemitism as more threatening than anti-Zionism, both had a negative effect upon them because of the centrality of Jewish spirituality and the symbolic importance appended to Israel, as the Jewish State. Conversely, secular Jews regarded anti-Zionism as more threatening for identity, because the destruction of Israel was perceived as debilitating for the

Jewish people, regardless of how they construed their Jewishness. In particular, anti-Zionism was regarded as challenging the self-efficacy and continuity principles of identity. The self-identified anti-Zionist Jews who participated in this study appeared to make strategic rhetorical use of their Jewish identity in order to challenge Zionism without facing accusations of antisemitism. Indeed, their Jewish origins provided a "safe position" for the manifestation of anti-Zionism.

In explaining the origins of their anti-Zionism, it is useful to invoke tenets of Identity Process Theory – individuals appeared to derive feelings of positive distinctiveness on the basis of their anti-Zionist position, given the widespread stigma appended to Zionism and to the State of Israel in the West. Moreover, there was some evidence that negative emotions, such as guilt, and the desire for supporting "human rights" induced an anti-Zionist stance. Crucially, individuals felt that anti-Zionism was consistent with their left-wing political orientation, which was a "core" identity for many anti-Zionist Jews. This safeguarded the psychological coherence principle of identity. Thus, anti-Zionism may be considered an identity-enhancing strategy. Similarly, secular and Orthodox individuals attempted to cope with the threat of antisemitism and anti-Zionism by engaging in various coping strategies. Some attenuated the public manifestation of their Zionist identity and confined this identity to private spheres, which allowed them to avoid encountering antisemitism and anti-Zionism in the public sphere. A similar strategy manifested by respondents included the passing strategy, as discussed in Chapter 9, whereby individuals denied their Jewish origins in order to safeguard a positive identity. Participants reported compartmentalising their Jewish and Zionist identities in order to shield their Jewish identity from the stigma that they believed to be associated with Zionism. A long-term strategy manifested by many secular participants, in particular, was their decision to join and actively participate in pro-Israel pressure groups, which provided a "safe" social and psychological space for manifesting their Zionist identity and an attachment to the State of Israel. This allowed them to re-construe the meanings of their identity in positive ways and to de-construct the social stigma appended to Zionism and Israel. Although antisemitism and anti-Zionism was clearly threatening for many of the British Jews who participated in this study, there is no doubt that many of them had developed creative and resilient strategies for curtailing the negative social and psychological effects of these forms of prejudice.

PART VI
Conclusion

Chapter 11

Antisemitism and Anti-Zionism:
Putting the Pieces Together

This book has focused upon two contexts in which antisemitism and anti-Zionism are pressing concerns: the Islamic Republic of Iran, which has an overtly anti-Zionist state policy, punctuated by blatant antisemitism; and among British Pakistani Muslims, many of whom are increasingly concerned about the Israeli-Arab conflict and angered by Israel's perceived treatment of the Palestinians. Moreover, it has focused on two contexts in which the consequences of antisemitism and anti-Zionism are harshly felt, namely among Israeli Jews and British Jews. In examining antisemitism and anti-Zionism, one could have studied many other contexts, groups and communities. However, these case studies drawn from radically distinct contexts provide useful insights into the more general motivations, antecedents and consequences of antisemitism and anti-Zionism.

Much previous research has focused on the manifestation of anti-Zionism and antisemitism at the institutional level in Iran and, in the absence of empirical research into public opinion, it has been difficult to ascertain how Iranians may think and feel about Jews and Israel. Given that Iran has an authoritarian press system and that the press media tend to represent the official government position, scholars have speculated that "it is likely that ordinary Iranians [...] do believe the propaganda that they are served" (Litvak, 2006, p. 280). Moreover, it has often been argued that antisemitism is on the rise in Europe due partly to the anger felt by young Muslims. However, previous researchers have provided only partial insights into how members of Muslim communities in Europe may think and feel about Jews, focusing, for instance, on perceptions of the Holocaust (e.g. Jikeli and Allouche-Benayoun, 2013). The perspectives of Israeli Jews and Jews in the diaspora have seldom been examined in accounts of antisemitism and anti-Zionism, which has resulted in a partial snapshot of these forms of prejudice. This book makes a novel contribution to existing theory and research by examining how Iranians and British Pakistani Muslims think and feel about Jews and Israel, and how Israeli Jews and British Jews think and feel about antisemitism and anti-Zionism, using qualitative methods which provide detailed, nuanced, and contextually sensitive empirical insights. These insights suggest that there are three principal areas in which the findings of this research can be positioned: in representation, cognition and everyday talk.

In this book, it is suggested that the Iranian press systematically delegitimises Israel by constructing social representations that challenge the legitimacy of the Jewish State. It has been shown that channels of societal information, such as the Iranian press and the government-endorsed Holocaust Cartoon Contest, delegitimise Israel (and Jews) through three main processes. The first component of the delegitimisation process entails the problematisation of Israel's right to exist and is manifested in the guise of questioning the Jewish character of Israel. Furthermore, there is widespread negativisation of Israel through the use of demeaning terms such as "regime", "fake" and "illegitimate". Although there is a general "silencing" of the civilian population of Israel, when the Israeli Jewish people *are* mentioned, they are habitually denigrated in terms of "foreigners" and "occupiers" due to their "European", non-Palestinian origins. This reflects Bar-Tal's (1990) notion of *trait characterisation*, that is, the attribution of negative characteristics to the outgroup and their consequential "otherisation". The social representation that the Israeli civilian population is in fact a foreign occupation is consistently employed in order to rationalise acts of violence against the Israeli people (Bar-Tal, 1990). It is noteworthy that Iranians and British Pakistanis readily invoked this social representation in interviews *and* that the Israelis and Jews who participated in interviews expressed awareness of this delegitimising social representation. This suggests that the representation has proliferated and gained traction in society (Moscovici, 1988).

The second component of the delegitimisation process entails the construction of social representations regarding the "origins" of Israel, that is, the circumstances underlying its establishment and maintenance. There is a coercive social representation of a global Zionist conspiracy, which is said to culminate in the establishment of the State of Israel. Moreover, it was implicitly suggested that this conspiracy was the "force" underlying the sustenance of the State of Israel (Mottale, 2011). In fact, many of Israel's allies, including the U.S., are represented as lacking political independence but rather as being wholly dependent on the "Zionist lobby". Put simply, Zionism was represented in terms of an international conspiracy involving multiple nations, all of which are at the mercy of the Zionists. The social representation of a global Zionist conspiracy and the notion that this conspiracy actively threatens the world are in fact rooted in well-established historical representations concerning Jewish world domination and the allegedly inherent malevolence of the Jews, as highlighted in Chapter 2. It seems that the category "Jew" has superficially shifted to "Zionist" in public discourse, but the core and structure of this delegitimising social representation remain the same: the Jewish Zionist is cunning and threatening. These social representations collectively exemplify Bar-Tal's notion of *outcasting*, whereby the outgroup is represented as violating pivotal norms. "Global Zionism" is entirely negativised through its anchoring to malevolence and evil and its objectification in terms of violent "unrest" (in Muslim countries, such as Syria). Moreover, the delegitimising metaphors of "plot" and "meddling" are frequently employed in order to describe Zionist actions. Similarly, the representation of a global Zionist conspiracy was conflated with that of a Jewish world conspiracy in many of the cartoons submitted to the Holocaust Cartoon Contest. While channels of societal information invoked implicitly antisemitic imagery in constructing anti-

Zionist representations, the interviewees more readily drew upon overt antisemitism in their delegitimisation of Israel.

The third component of the delegitimisation process entails "problem-solving", that is, how the threat posed by the "fake", "illegitimate", yet highly threatening enemy may plausibly be eliminated. Anti-Zionist circles construct the destruction of the "Zionist regime" as imminent and necessary in order to solve the multiple dangers said to be posed by Israel, including world domination, terrorism and genocide against the Palestinians. As Bar-Tal (1990) argues, delegitimisation has a behavioural implication for the delegitimising group in that "it implies that the delegitimized group does not deserve human treatment and therefore harming it is justified" (p. 66). Thus, draconian and potentially violent measures are constructed as being acceptable and even necessary for dealing with the "Zionist Other". Given the multifarious threats allegedly posed by the Zionist enemy, which stretch well beyond the boundaries of the Muslim world, anti-Zionism is constructed as becoming an increasingly pervasive and logical *global* response. This is exemplified by the constructed "victimhood" of Western nations which are at the mercy of the Zionist conspiracy. Islam is represented as *leading* the "global" campaign against the global Zionist conspiracy, which constructs Islam as benevolent (vis-à-vis the allegedly malevolent "Zionist regime") and one which is self-efficacious in its campaign against Zionism. There is an optimistic construction of the success of global anti-Zionism. There is a representation of a withering Zionist regime and the Zionists are portrayed as fearful of their imminent demise. It is noteworthy that the problem solving component of delegitimisation was keenly invoked in interviews with both Iranians and British Pakistanis, who optimistically argued that the Jewish State would be destroyed by the Islamic Ummah.

The link between social representation and social cognition is of crucial importance (van Dijk, 1993). Bernard Lewis (2003, p. 93) has argued that "Israel serves as a useful stand-in for complaints about the economic privation and political repression under which most Muslim peoples [in the Middle East] live" and that anti-Zionism may constitute a means of "deflecting the resulting anger". Moreover, it has been argued that media representational strategies may impact the motivational principles of identity (Jaspal and Cinnirella, 2010b). This stance may help to establish (i) a sense of belonging in the Islamic world, (ii) feelings of self-efficacy vis-à-vis Israel (and the Jews) and (iii) a sense of continuity over time. Indeed, it is easy to see how the channels of societal representation construct Israel as a *common* concern for the Islamic Ummah, promoting feelings of ingroup belonging and self-efficacy (competence and control).

Individuals readily invoke and accept representations which enhance their own identity. Delegitimising social representations of Israel indicate that the Jewish State possesses negative characteristics, which, through processes of downward comparison, can provide individuals with feelings of self-esteem (Wills, 1981). Through self-comparison with their "Significant Other", Iranians and British Pakistani Muslim may come to feel far superior (Jaspal, 2013a). The external attribution of both domestic and international problems, such as the Arab Spring, to the "malevolence" of the State of Israel, that is, scapegoating, can enhance meaning-making. It provides an immediate explanation for negative occurrences, which may have positive outcomes for a collective sense of meaning (McAdams, 2001). The identification of Israel as a scapegoat may well provide individuals with feelings of acceptance, inclusion and belonging in the broader Muslim East/ Arab world, where anti-Zionism is normative. Indeed, anti-Zionism is said to constitute a common platform in the Islamic world, potentially bridging otherwise irreconcilable sectarian divisions (Takeyh, 2006). The social representation that Muslims *direct* global anti-Zionism and will bring about the demise of the State of Israel, which is frequently reproduced in Iranian news outlets, could accentuate feelings of competence, control and self-efficacy at the institutional level. Thus, these media representational practices seem to have positive social psychological outcomes for Iranian and British Pakistani Muslims, due to the shared superordinate religious identity (Baum and Nakazawa, 2007).

Delegitimising anti-Zionist representations may deprive Israel and its citizens of humanness and of the ability to evoke empathy and compassion (Bar-Tal, 1990; Kelman, 1976). The anti-Zionist ideology of Iran is endowed with a thin, superficial veil of acceptability by drawing upon historical social representations that construct Israel as (i) an inhumane regime that oppresses and threatens, and (ii) the product of a global Zionist/Jewish conspiracy which mercilessly controls the world. These delegitimising social representations are intended to arouse negative emotions of rejection, such as hatred, anger, fear and disgust, which can be conducive to popular acceptance of harm, violence and even genocide against the delegitimised target (Bar-Tal, 1990). This action orientation is further crystallised in the cartoons exposed and publicised in the overtly antisemitic Iranian government-endorsed Holocaust Cartoon Contest.

Important historical accounts demonstrate that Iranian antisemitism is historically associated with Shiite Muslim ideology (Litvak, 2006; Shahvar, 2009). The evidence presented in this book suggests that the maintenance of the former Supreme Leader Khomeini's overt antisemitic and anti-Zionist ideology may constitute a means of safeguarding the continuity principle amid important social and political change in Iran (Abrahamian, 2008; Ansari, 2006). It is noteworthy that concessions have needed to be made in the regime's policy and ideology, highlighting the potential for threats to continuity. The former Iranian president Khatami's term demonstrated that a gradual acceptance and accommodation of Israel within the Iranian identity structure might be possible, without necessarily threatening continuity (Jaspal, 2013a). This could be facilitated by decreasing the salience of historical representations of Khomeini's antisemitism and by reiterating the continued support of the Palestinians. However, his successor former president Ahmadinejad's adamant resurrection of *dormant* historical representations condemning Jews and Israel meant that any change in ideological position may be construed in terms of a threat. Indeed, the "Jewish threat" to continuity is actively accentuated by the regime and echoed by the Iranian respondents who participated in the interview study. The Iranian authorities attempt to motivate Iranians to oppose the "Zionist regime" in order to counteract what they conceptualise as a threat to Iran's continuity as a great nation. In the interviews, self-identified political hardliners consistently did oppose Israel.

In examining the interview data generated in studies with Iranian political hardliners and reformists, it is evident that antisemitic and anti-Zionist social representations are accepted and manifested in order to bolster the principled operation of identity processes in the ways predicted by Identity Process Theory (Breakwell, 1986). The delegitimisation of Israel appeared to enhance the distinctiveness, self-esteem, continuity and psychological coherence principles of identity from the perspective of Iranian national identity. Clearly, this was an important incentive for manifesting anti-Zionist prejudice. When one re-visits the data generated from the analysis of Iranian media and visual representations, it becomes clear how and why members of the Iranian general population may view Israel in these terms and how and why they may derive feelings of distinctiveness, self-esteem, continuity and coherence from its delegitimisation. Incidentally, even the substantive social representations that were identified in the Iranian press were reproduced and accepted by many of the Iranians and British Pakistanis who participated in the interview studies. This demonstrates the "stickiness" of these social representations and their ability to transcend cultural and geographical boundaries as they proliferate and enter everyday thinking and talk (Breakwell, 2014).

Among British Pakistanis, the establishment of the Jewish State on "Muslim lands" was construed as a chronic threat to Muslim ingroup identity. Moreover, the perceived moral transgressions of Israel against the Palestinian people constituted a continuous psychological threat, accentuated by the reality of Israel's consistent victories in military conflicts with neighbouring Arab states since 1948 (Gilbert, 1998). Anti-Zionism can constitute a strategy for coping with threat. Crucially, self-identification functions primarily at the superordinate level of Muslim identity, which renders transgressions against fellow Muslims in the Palestinian territories threatening for identity among British Pakistani Muslims. Anti-Zionism and antisemitism appeared to be construed as facilitating access to, and a sense of belonging in, the Muslim Ummah amid uncertainty about their acceptance and inclusion by other Muslim groups. This appeared to induce a hyper-affiliation to the stance and ideology perceived to be associated with "Muslim authenticity" (see Jaspal and Cinnirella, 2014). Accordingly, individuals reproduced the social representation that the Jewish State would be destroyed and that Muslims would regain control of Palestine. For many individuals, Israel exists in the present so that the Muslim ingroup can eventually recapture "Muslim land" in the future in a dramatic display of ingroup control and competence. Thus, anti-Zionism was used opportunistically for the enhancement of identity.

Although there is clearly a psychological incentive for bolstering the principled operation of identity processes, as demonstrated in Chapter 7, close attention to participants' accounts also indicated that individuals may be constructing particular relationships with Israel and Jews for strategic purposes. For instance, the self-identified reformist participants appeared to distance themselves and their political ingroup from the hardline outgroup by rhetorically rejecting anti-Zionism. Identity plays a central role here – in particular, political identity. In order to sustain and crystallise their reformist political identity, self-identified reformists may rhetorically reject anti-Zionism and even *identify* with Israel. Apparent contradictions in participants' accounts suggested that a discursive rhetorical approach could shed light on their antecedents (Potter and Wetherell, 1987).

There appears to be a tension between cognition and talk. On the one hand, there is a clear link between antisemitism and anti-Zionism, because anti-Zionism is frequently bolstered and substantiated by antisemitic myths and representations. Individuals are seldom able to discriminate between the categories "Israeli" and "Jew". For instance, the Iranians and British Pakistani Muslims who participated in the studies described in this book often assumed widespread Jewish endorsement of Israel's policies and therefore held Jews responsible for Israel's actions. They frequently conflated the history of intergroup relations between Jews and Muslims *and* the contemporary Israeli-Arab conflict. They used long-standing antisemitic myths of Jewish world domination in order to explain the establishment and sustenance of Israel, and the mythical blood libel in order to make sense of Israel's alleged atrocities against the Palestinians. Yet, there was a conscious attempt, particularly in interviews with British Pakistani Muslims, to avoid overt antisemitism, that is, to separate out antisemitism and anti-Zionism in their talk. Individuals attempted to do this by using discursive disclaimers such as the one that is used in the title of Chapter 8; they rejected the accusation of antisemitism by claiming to have Jewish friends and "nothing against Jews"; and sometimes referred to the Jews as the "cousins" of Muslims. The apparent inconsistency between these discursive tendencies and the use of antisemitic representations in manifesting anti-Zionism can only suggest that self-presentation competes with cognition. Individuals think what they think, but try to talk about their thoughts in ways that will be deemed socially acceptable.

Although the relationship between anti-Zionism and antisemitism has been debated, there is little doubt that anti-Zionism has, at least in part, given rise to antisemitic acts (see Chapter 1). Moreover, particularly in Middle Eastern anti-Zionism but also in the West, there is often an interchangeable use of the categories "Zionism", "Israel" and "Jew", which serves to blur the boundaries between these groups and categories. Many anti-Zionist organisations, groups and individuals adamantly deny antisemitism, but close attention to their discourse often reveals an antisemitic undercurrent as the semantic boundaries between the aforementioned categories are blurred. In addition to the linguistics of anti-Zionism, much contemporary anti-Zionism is often manifested in ways that render it reminiscent of, if not indistinguishable from, antisemitism. The themes and representations invoked bear much resemblance to age-old antisemitism. When considering the continuities and discontinuities of antisemitism, as in Chapter 2, two key questions emerge: Is anti-Zionism just another form of antisemitism? Is it a continuation of antisemitism, albeit with a more socially acceptable façade?

Many prominent scholars have convincingly argued that anti-Zionism *does* in fact constitute a form of antisemitism, principally because it tends to single out the Jewish State and deprives the Jews of their right to national self-determination (e.g. Cohen et al., 2009; Litvak, 2006; Matas, 2005; Shahvar, 2009). Harkin (2002) has posited that "Israel is the state of the Jews. Zionism is the belief that the Jews should have a state. To defame Israel is to defame the Jews. To wish it never existed, or would cease to exist, is to wish to destroy the Jews". It is acknowledged that legitimate, balanced criticism of aspects of Israeli political policy does not necessarily reflect antisemitism (Cohen et al., 2009). Accordingly, Sharansky (2004) has proposed the "3-D test" to determine whether anti-Zionism is antisemitic – the 3 Ds include demonisation, delegitimisation and double standards in relation to Israel. Conversely, others have taken the position that anti-Zionism – no matter what variety – cannot legitimately be regarded as antisemitic. For instance, Klug (2003) has argued that hostility towards Israel "is not a new form of antisemitism; it is a function of a deep and bitter political conflict", and that the "underlying hostility towards it [Israel] in the region is not hostility towards the state *as* Jewish but *as* European interloper or as American client or as non-Arab and non-Muslim – and in addition, *as* oppressor". On the basis of the evidence presented in this book, one could plausibly take issue with Klug's position, because what offended both the Iranian and British Pakistani Muslims who participated in this study was the notion that Israel, a Jewish homeland, had been established on what was perceived to be "Muslim land". Thus, *Jewish* control of *Muslim* land was perceived as abhorrent. Notions of Israel as a "European interloper" or "American client" were quite peripheral to this key social representation. Moreover, regardless of the antecedents of anti-Zionism, i.e. whether or not it is antisemitic in character, it certainly appears to give rise to antisemitism, both in cognition and in action (Litvak and Webman, 2010).

Scholars have argued that "new antisemitism" constitutes a newer version of Jew-hatred, which is habitually manifested in the guise of anti-Zionism. Fischel (2005, p. 228) writes that in Europe this is associated with "leftists, vociferously opposed to the policies of Israel, and right-wing antisemites, committed to the destruction of Israel, [who] were joined by millions of Muslims, including Arabs, who immigrated to Europe [...] and who brought with them their hatred of Israel in particular and of Jews in general". This amalgamation of anti-Zionism and antisemitism is most conspicuous in the interviews conducted with Iranians and British Pakistanis, and are manifested in accounts of historical intergroup relations between Jews and Muslims (Livtak and Webman, 2010). There were observable antisemitic diatribes in the form of theological allusions to Jews, grounded in several, arguably misunderstood, Koranic verses and other Islamic theological sources such as "Ahadith" (Kessler, 2003).

The term "new antisemitism" is perhaps somewhat misleading. It suggests that anti-Zionism is something exceptional in the repertoire of antisemitic motifs. However, as this book clearly demonstrates, antisemitism has always been characterised by diverse motifs and representations, sometimes contradictory but consistently negativising and demonising. This is what has led to discussions about the continuities and discontinuities of antisemitism (Jaspal, 2013b). Anti-Zionism, though focused on the Jewish State rather than the Jewish people in principle, appears to constitute just one of the many forms in which antisemitism has been manifested in history. Thus, it is troubling that anti-Zionism does appear to be socially acceptable in many contexts. While it is a state policy and, thus, the *only* acceptable stance on Israel in the Islamic Republic of Iran (Jaspal, 2013a), it is increasingly acceptable in the UK context where it is cynically associated with anti-racism, anti-colonialism and anti-capitalism (Wistrich, 2004, 2011). Anti-Zionism is also widely associated with peace, freedom and human rights. More specifically, it seems to be the optimal position if one wishes to support Palestinian rights. It is of course entirely possible to opt for the two-state solution and, thus, to support both the Palestinians' right to statehood as well as that of the Jews. However, the academic and economic boycott of Israel, of which the vast majority of interviewees expressed acute awareness, does not appear to be conducive to peaceful and harmonious intergroup relations – neither does the unanimous endorsement of the boycott that was expressed by respondents.

Indeed, in the interviews conducted with Israelis and British Jews, as our two case studies of responses to antisemitism and anti-Zionism, there was a coercive representation that anti-Zionism amounted to antisemitism and that both (inter-related) forms of prejudice were threatening for identity. Individuals associated the problem of antisemitism with Muslims, in particular, and appeared to construe this outgroup as particularly threatening (Stephan and Stephan, 2000). The notion of siege mentality was observable among Israeli Jews and identity threat was visible in the accounts of British Jews (Bar-Tal, 2000). However, there was a strong sense of resilience among both groups, as individuals sought to protect their identities from threat and to adjust to social contexts in which they believed that antisemitism and anti-Zionism were pervasive. Respondents described a number of coping strategies with varying levels of long-term efficacy. In making sense of the development of antisemitism and anti-Zionism, many Israeli and British Jews identified the Muslim outgroup as a posing a threat. Furthermore, the notion of coping sheds light on a particular group of Jews (and possibly, Israelis) who have been the subject of much debate in academic studies of Jewry, namely anti-Zionist Jews and Jews who oppose the State of Israel. Like the reformist Iranians whose perceptions and experiences were described in Chapter 7, anti-Zionist Jews appeared to construct Israel in ways that favoured and bolstered their own political identities which took primacy over their ethno-religious identities.

Some Implications

In examining the theoretical implications of the research presented in this book, it is useful to recall some of the empirical research into antisemitism and anti-Zionism that was summarised in Chapters 2 and 3, respectively. The principal theoretical approaches to social psychological research into antisemitism and anti-Zionism have included terror management theory, scapegoating theory, social identity theory and the authoritarian personality. Terror management theorists argue that antisemitism and anti-Zionism may function as a means of reducing the terror that ensues from one's awareness of one's own mortality, and recent empirical research appears to support this hypothesis. Scapegoating theory highlights the human tendency to blame vulnerable outgroups for social, political and economic upheaval. The authoritarian personality suggests that "hierarchical, authoritarian, exploitative" parent-child relationships can later induce an authoritarian personality in adulthood (Adorno et al., 1950, p. 482), thereby crystallising an antisemitic orientation in the individual. All of these approaches have considerable merit in explaining antisemitism and anti-Zionism. Over the years, they have generated much empirical support. It is true that some individuals have personality traits, such as authoritarianism, that render them more or less disposed to outgroup derogation. It is true that awareness of one's mortality is threatening and that it can induce defensive responses, usually directed towards outgroups with a distinct worldview from our own. It is also true that groups direct their frustration at vulnerable groups in times of crisis in order to obscure and conceal their own shortcomings and failures. These perspectives are all valid and make a contribution, but alone their explanation can only be partial. This is why an integrative approach that examines representation, cognition and everyday talk is so important.

This book takes a more holistic approach to antisemitism and anti-Zionism. In this book, threat is a core construct. It can be defined in two principal ways. Intergroup Threat Theory describes the nature of threats that can be constructed and perceived – realistic or symbolic. This is useful in identifying and describing group-level threats. Conversely, Identity Process Theory provides a more complex social psychological approach to threat, arguing that it occurs when identity processes cannot comply with the principles of self-esteem, continuity, distinctiveness and so on. As the model presented in Chapter 3 tentatively indicates, realistic and symbolic threats may affect particular identity principles and potentially induce identity threat. This book views identity threat as a key means of understanding antisemitism and anti-Zionism, since it is assumed that threat will evoke defensive responses such as outgroup prejudice (Jaspal and Cinnirella, 2010b). The data presented in this book suggest that Iranians and British Pakistani Muslims may manifest antisemitism and anti-Zionism as means of enhancing ingroup identity in an *a priori* manner, and as a means of coping with existing threats to identity. However, antisemitism and anti-Zionism may in turn render identity susceptible to threat due to the social representations that may emerge as part of one's anti-Zionist/antisemitic stance (e.g. the representation that the Israeli Jewish outgroup seeks to destroy the Muslim ingroup). It is noteworthy that threat also plays a prominent role in explaining Israeli and British Jews' perceptions of Muslims – contemporary antisemitism/anti-Zionism was almost exclusively attributed to Muslims. Threat allows for different predictions from those that are offered by many other researchers of antisemitism and anti-Zionism. It is true that antisemitism is an age-old prejudice that has plagued the world for thousands of years. However, the threat-focussed approach does not suggest that antisemitism and anti-Zionism are in any way unique or "inevitable" (cf. Wistrich, 1991). Antisemitism and anti-Zionism will arise when these forms of prejudice are represented as being beneficial for identity processes. Crucially, in some contexts, such as the ones described in this book, they are indeed actively encouraged by governments, institutions and the media. This is why the level of representation must form part of any social psychological account of antisemitism and anti-Zionism.

In linking social representations and social action, it seems appropriate to recall that "[w]hen people believe firmly that they are on the side of good and are working to make the world a better place, they often feel justified in using strong measures against the seemingly evil forces that oppose them" (Baumeister, 1997, p. 377). Crucially, social representations that construct Israel as a malevolent, oppressive, terrorist "regime" antithetical to the values of Islam and which construct mobilisation against Israel as a necessary duty for "good" Muslims are dangerous. They encourage acts of violence against those individuals perceived to be associated with Israel, namely Jews. Kelman (1976) states that dehumanisation serves to deprive individuals of agentic and collective aspects of humanness, which can result in their failure to evoke compassion among perpetrators of abuse and violence. Accordingly, dehumanised victims are seldom shown any mercy. Thus, dehumanising and demonising social representations may serve to construct Israelis and Jews as a legitimate target for discrimination, abuse and physical violence. The implications for intergroup relations could be devastating. This in turn is likely to encourage defensive responses from both the Israeli government and diaspora Jews (Bar-Tal and Antebi, 1992).

Antisemitism and anti-Zionism are worrying phenomena in both the British Pakistani and Iranian contexts. Britain is a diverse and relatively tolerant country, in which overt prejudice and discrimination are socially stigmatised and, in most cases, outlawed. Anti-Zionism presents a new set of challenges, especially as it infiltrates social, economic, educational and other contexts in which diverse communities co-exist. It is not yet considered a form of hate speech, though it seems to fit the criteria for being considered in those terms (Klaff, 2010). It is perceived in antisemitic terms by many Jews, although many anti-Zionists deny that their intentions are antisemitic in nature, and this ignites tensions between groups and communities. Many of the Israeli and British Jews who participated in the interview studies manifested unfavourable attitudes towards Muslims, whom they held responsible for the perceived rise in antisemitism and anti-Zionism. Research with other British ethno-religious minorities groups shows that minority intergroup tensions can arise, persist and threaten social harmony, as they are ignored in favour of majority-minority relations (Jaspal, 2013e). Overt anti-Zionism can easily metamorphose into antisemitism, as demonstrated in this book, igniting the flames of intergroup tension and conflict. Iran is a perhaps a more pressing context. The Iranian government has actively crushed the self-efficacy of internal Iranian Jews, who are subjected to scrutiny and forbidden from exhibiting any support for the Jewish State, a crime potentially punishable by death (Jaspal, 2014b). It is argued that the regime's ability to influence and control Jews in Iran enhances their own self-efficacy. This constitutes a worrying reality, in a country with tens of thousands of remaining Jews and amid the "war of words" characterising Iranian-Israeli relations. This book is testimony to the importance of exploring antisemitism and anti-Zionism, their continuities and discontinuities, their convergences and divergences and, crucially, their antecedents and consequences. It is testimony to the importance of considering the potential impact of prejudice for those who are targeted. It is testimony to our collective responsibility – as researchers, policy makers, community leaders and community members – to facilitate the basic social and psychological conditions necessary for positive intergroup relations so that diversity and identities can be celebrated, rather than threatened.

References

Abbas, T. (ed.) (2005). *Muslim Britain: communities under pressure*. London: Zed Books.

Abrahamian, E. (2008). *A history of modern Iran*. Cambridge: Cambridge University Press.

Adorno, T.W., Frenkel-Brunswik, E., Levinson, D.J., and Sanford, R.N. (1950). *The authoritarian personality*. New York: Harper and Row.

Ahmed, T.S. (2005). Reading between the lines – Muslims and the media. In T. Abbas (ed.), *Muslim Britain: communities under pressure* (pp.109–26). London: Zed Books.

Alimi, E. (2007) *Israeli politics and the first Palestinian intifada: political opportunities, framing processes and contentious politics*. London: Routledge.

Almog, O. (2000). *The Sabra: the creation of the new Jew*. Berkeley and Los Angeles, CA: University of California Press.

Amishai-Maisels, Z. (1999). The demonization of the "Other" in the visual arts. In R.S. Wistrich (ed.), *Demonizing the other: anti-semitism, racism and xenophobia* (pp.44–72). Amsterdam: Harwood Academic Publishers.

Anderson, B. (1991). *Imagined communities: reflections on the origin and spread of nationalism*. London: Verso.

Ansari, H. (2005). Attitudes towards jihad, martyrdom and terrorism among British Muslims. In T. Abbas (ed.), *Muslim Britain: communities under pressure* (pp.144–63). London: Zed Books.

Ansari, A. (2006). *Iran, Islam & democracy – the politics of managing change*. London: RIIA.

Anti-Defamation League (ADL) (2005). Anti-Defamation League, "Europe and the Former Soviet Union", in *ADL 1998 Annual Report*, http://www.adl.org/ annual report/1998/inter europe.asp (accessed 6 July 2010).

Anti-Defamation League (ADL). (2007). Attitudes Toward Jews and the Middle East in Five European Countries. http://www.adl.org/anti_semitism/European_ Attitudes_Survey_May_2007.pdf (accessed June 15, 2009).

Anti-Defamation League (ADL) (2009). Attitudes toward Jews in seven European countries. http://www.adl.org/PresRele/ASInt_13/5465_13.htm (accessed 19 June 2010).

Anwar, M. (1979). *The myth of return: Pakistanis in Britain*. London: Heinneman Educational Books.

Apter, B. (1983). Negativism and the sense of identity. In G.M. Breakwell (ed.), *Threatened identities* (pp. 75–90). Chichester: John-Wiley & Sons.

Arnold, A. (1994). Tainted greatness: the case of Voltaire's anti-semitism: the testimony of the correspondence. *Neohelicon*, 21(2), 357–67.

Aronson, G. (2005). Issues arising from the implementation of Israel's disengagement from the Gaza Strip. *Journal of Palestine Studies, 34*(4), 49–63.

Aziz, H. (2007). Anti-Semitism among Muslims. In T. Abbas (ed.), *Islamic political radicalism: a European perspective* (pp.71–82). Edinburgh: Edinburgh University Press.

Bandura, A., Underwood, B. and Fromson, M.E. (1975). Disinhibition of aggression through diffusion of responsibility and dehumanization of victims. *Journal of Personality and Social Psychology, 9*, 253–69

Barghouti, O. (2011). *Boycott, divestment, sanctions: the global struggles for Palestinian rights.* Chicago, IL: Haymarket Books.

Bar-On, D. (2008). *The others within us: constructing Jewish-Israeli identity.* Cambridge: Cambridge University Press.

Bar-Tal, D. (1990). Causes and consequences of delegitimization: models of conflict and ethnocentrism. *Journal of Social Issues, 46*(1), 65–81.

Bar-Tal, D. (2000). *Shared beliefs in a society.* London: Sage.

Bar-Tal, D., and Antebi, D. (1992). Siege mentality in Israel. *International Journal of Intercultural Relations, 16*, 251–75.

Bar-Tal, D., Jacobson, D. and Klieman, A. (eds) (1998). *Security concerns: insights from the Israeli experience.* Stamford, CT: JAI.

Bar-Tal, D. and Labin, D. (2001). The effect of a major event on stereotyping: terrorist attacks in Israel and Israeli adolescents' perceptions of Palestinians, Jordanians and Arabs. *European Journal of Social Psychology, 31*(3), 265–80.

Bar-Tal, D. and Teichman, Y. (2005). *Stereotypes and prejudice in conflict: representations of Arabs in Israeli Jewish society.* Cambridge: Cambridge University Press.

Bauer, M. and Schiller, T. (2012). The Arab Spring in 2012. *CAP Perspectives, 1*, 1–3.

Baum, S.K. (2009a). Christian and Muslim anti-Semitic beliefs. *Journal of Contemporary Religion,* 24(2), 137–56

Baum, S.K. (2009b). When fairy tales kill. *Journal for the Study of Antisemitism, 1*(2), 187–208

Baum, S.K. and Nakazawa, M. (2007). Anti-Semitism versus anti-Israeli sentiment. *Journal of Religion & Society, 9*, 1–8.

Baum, S.K. and Rosenberg, N.E. (2012). Antisemitic incidents from around the world: January–June 2012. *Journal for the Study of Antisemitism, 4*(1), 9–26.

Baum, S.K. and Rosenberg, N.E. (2013). Antisemitic incidents from around the world: January–June 2013. *Journal for the Study of Antisemitism, 5*(1), 5–20.

Baumeister, R.F (1997). *Evil: inside human violence and cruelty.* New York: Freeman.

Baumeister, R.F. and Leary, M.R. (1995). The need to belong: desire for interpersonal attachments as a fundamental human motivation. *Psychological Bulletin, 117*, 497–529.

Bazyler, M.L. (2006). Holocaust denial laws and other legislation criminalizing promotion of Nazism. Paper presented at Yad Vashem Museum, Jerusalem, Israel, December 25, 2006.

Beckwith, L. (2011). Antisemitism at the University of California. *Journal for the Study of Antisemitism*, *4*(2), 443–62.

Beller, S. (2007). *Antisemitism: a very short introduction*. Oxford: Oxford University Press.

Ben-Amos, A. and Bet-El, I. (1999). Holocaust Day and Memorial Day in Israeli schools: ceremonies, education and history. *Israel Studies*, 4, 258–84.

Ben-Gurion, D. (1948). Declaration of establishment of State of Israel. Speech delivered to the Jewish People's Council on May 14, 1948. http://www.mfa.gov.il/mfa/foreignpolicy/peace/guide/pages/declaration%20of%20establishment%20of%20state%20of%20israel.aspx (retrieved 10 June 2011).

Benz, W. (1999). The motivations and impact of contemporary Holocaust denial in Germany. In R.S Wistrich (ed.), *Demonizing the other: Anti-semitism, racism and xenophobia* (p.335–48). Amsterdam: Harwood Academic Publishers.

Berenbaum, M. (ed.) (1990). *A mosaic of victims – non-Jews persecuted and murdered by the Nazis*. New York: New York University Press.

Berenbaum, M. (2009). A new journal on antisemitism. *Journal for the Study of Antisemitism*, *1*(1), 5–8.

Bergen, D.L. (2010). Antisemitism in the Nazi era. In A.S. Lindemann and R.S. Levy (eds), *Antisemitism: A history* (pp.196–211). Oxford: Oxford University Press.

Bergmann, W. (2006). Anti-Semitic attitudes in Europe: A comparative perspective. *Journal of Social Issues,* *64*(2), 343–62.

Bilewicz, M. and Krzeminski, I. (2010). Anti-Semitism in Poland and Ukraine: the belief in Jewish control as a mechanism of scapegoating. *International Journal of Conflict and Violence*, 4(2), 234–43.

Blumner, N. (2006). The Holocaust as stark reminder: ethno-national identity, diaspora and the ideological process(es) of memory. Paper presented at the Annual Meeting of the American Sociological Association, 10 August 2006, Montreal Convention Center, Montreal, Quebec, Canada.

Bounegru, L. and Forceville, C. (2011). Metaphors in editorial cartoons representing the global financial crisis. *Visual Communication*, *10*, 209–25.

Bourhis, R.Y., Giles, H. and Rosenthal, D. (1981) Notes on the construction of a 'Subjective Vitality Questionnaire' for ethnolinguistic groups. *Journal of Multilingual and Multicultural Development*, 2, 145–55.

Bowman, G. (2004). About a wall. *Social Analysis: The International Journal of Social and Cultural Practice*, *48*(1), 149–55

Bowskill, M., Lyons, E. and Coyle, A. (2007). The rhetoric of acculturation: when integration means assimilation. *British Journal of Social Psychology*, *46*(4), 793–813.

Boyd, J. (2013). Jewish life in Europe: impending catastrophe, or imminent renaissance? The Institute for Jewish Policy Research Report, November 2013.

http://www.jpr.org.uk/documents/Jewish%20life%20in%20Europe%20-%20
Impending%20catastrophe%20or%20imminent%20renaissance.pdf (retrieved
4 October 2013).

Braun, V. and Clarke, V. (2006). Using thematic analysis in psychology. *Qualitative Research in Psychology*, *3*, 77–101.

Breakwell, G.M. (1986). *Coping with threatened identities*. London: Methuen.

Breakwell, G.M. (1993). Social representations and social identity. *Papers on Social Representations*, *2*(3), 1–20.

Breakwell, G.M. (2001). Social representational constraints upon identity processes. In K. Deaux and G. Philogène (eds), *Representations of the social: bridging theoretical traditions* (pp. 271–84). Oxford: Blackwell.

Breakwell, G.M. (2010). Resisting representations and identity processes. *Papers on Social Representations*, *19*, 6.1–6.11.

Breakwell, G.M. (2014). Identity and social representations. In R. Jaspal and G.M. Breakwell (eds), *Identity process theory: identity, social action and social change* (pp.118–34). Cambridge: Cambridge University Press.

Breakwell, G.M. and Canter, D. (1993). *Empirical approaches to social representations*. Oxford: Oxford University Press.

Bregman, A. (2000). *Israel's wars: a history since 1947*. London: Routledge.

Breitman (2007). Muslim Anti-Semitism: Historical Background. *Current Psychology*, *26*(3), 213–22.

Brewer, M.B. (1991). The social self: on being the same and different at the same time. *Personality and Social Psychology Bulletin*, *17*, 475–82.

Brown, R. (2000). Social identity theory: past achievements, current problems and future challenges. *European Journal of Social Psychology*, *30*, 745–78.

Brown, N.J. (2003). *Palestinian politics after the Oslo accords*. Cambridge: Cambridge University Press.

Burke, K. (1984). *Permanence and change: an anatomy of purpose*. Berkeley, CA: University of California Press.

Burke, A., Maxwell, V. and Shearer, I. (2012). *Iran*. London: Lonely Planet.

Burrin, P. (1999). Nazi antisemitism: animalization and demonization. In R.S Wistrich (ed.), *Demonizing the other: anti-Semitism, racism and xenophobia* (p.223–35). Amsterdam: Harwood Academic Publishers.

Chanes, J.A. (2004). *Antisemitism*. Santa Barbara, CA: ABC-CLIO.

Chesler, P. (2003). *The new anti-Semitism: the current crisis and what we must do about it*. San Francisco, CA: Jossey-Bass.

Christison, K. and Christison, B. (2009). *Palestine in pieces: graphic perspectives on the Israeli occupation*. London: Pluto Press.

Chryssochoou, X. (2014). Identity processes in culturally diverse societies: how is cultural diversity reflected in the self? In R. Jaspal and G.M. Breakwell (eds), *Identity process theory: Identity, social action and social change* (pp.135–54). Cambridge: Cambridge University Press.

Cinnirella, M. (2013). Think "terrorist", think "Muslim"? Social psychological mechanisms explaining anti-Islamic prejudice. In M. Helbling (ed.)

Islamophobia in the West: measuring and explaining individual attitudes (pp.179–89). Abingdon: Routledge.

Cinnirella, M. (2014). The role of perceived threat and identity in Islamophobic prejudice. In R. Jaspal and G.M. Breakwell (eds), *Identity process theory: identity, social action and social change* (pp.253–69). Cambridge: Cambridge University Press.

Clark, J.E. (2012). Engaging the Apartheid Analogy in Israel/Palestine. Athens: ATINER'S Conference Paper Series, No: MED2012-0155. http://www.atiner.gr/papers/MED2012-0155.pdf (retrieved 17 December 2013).

Cohen, F. (2009). The new Anti-Semitism Israel model: empirical tests. *Dissertation Abstracts International*, 69, 6471.

Cohen, F. (2012). Do political cartoons reflect antisemitism? *Journal for the Study of Antisemitism*, 4(1), 141–64.

Cohen, F., Jussim, L., Harber, K.D. and Bhasin, G. (2009). Modern anti-Semitism and anti-Israeli attitudes. *Journal of Personality and Social Psychology*, 97(2), 290–306.

Cohen, F., Jussim, L. Bhasin, G. and Salib, E. (2011). The modern anti-Semitism Israel model: an empirical relationship between modern anti-Semitism and opposition to Israel. *Conflict & Communication Online*, 10(1), 1–16.

Cohen, M.R. (1995). *Under crescent and cross*. Princeton, NJ: Princeton University Press.

Cohen, M.R. (2002). Medieval Jewry in the world of Islam. In M. Goodman and J. Cohen (eds), *The Oxford handbook of Jewish studies (Oxford handbooks in religion and theology)* (p.193–218). Oxford: University of Oxford.

Cohen, S.E. (2012). Israel's West Bank barrier: an impediment to peace? *Geographical Review*, 96(4), 682–95.

Cohen-Almagor, R. (2009). Holocaust denial is a form of hate speech. *Amsterdam Law Forum*, 2(1), 33–42.

Cohn, N. (1966), *Warrant for genocide: the myth of the Jewish world-conspiracy and the protocols of the elder of Zion*. New York: Harper & Row.

Corenblum, B. and Stephan, W.G. (2001). White fears and native apprehensions: an integrated threat theory approach to intergroup attitudes. *Canadian Journal of Behavioural Science*, 33(4), 251–68.

Corrigan, E.C. (2009). Is anti-Zionism anti-Semitic? Jewish critics speak out. *Middle East Policy*, 6(4) 146–59.

Costanza, W. (2012). Hizballah and its mission in Latin America. *Studies in Conflict and Terrorism*, 35(3), 193–210.

Cravatts, R. (2011). Antisemitism and the campus left. *Journal for the Study of Antisemitism*, 4(2), 407–42

Crossan, J.D. (1996). *Who killed Jesus?: exposing the roots of anti-Semitism in the gospel story of the death of Jesus*. Hammersmith: HarperOne.

Cunningham, P.A. (2010). Jews and Christians from the time of Christ to Constantine's reign. In A.S. Lindemann and R.S. Levy (eds), *Antisemitism: a history* (pp.47–62). Oxford: Oxford University Press.

D'Alessio, S.J. and Stolzenberg, L. (1991). Anti-Semitism in America: The dynamics of prejudice. *Sociological Inquiry, 61*, 359–66.

Diller, J.V. (1980). Identity rejection and reawakening in the Jewish context. *Journal of Psychology and Judaism, 5*(1), 38–47.

Dinnerstein, L. (1994). *Antisemitism in America*. New York: Oxford University Press.

Doty, R.M., Peterson, B.E. and Winter, D.G. (1991). Threat and authoritarianism in the United States, 1978–1987. *Journal of Personality and Social Psychology, 61*, 629–40.

Dunbar, E. and Simonova, L. (2003) Individual difference and social status predictors of anti-Semitism and racism US and Czech findings with the prejudice/tolerance and right wing authoritarianism scales. *International Journal of Intercultural Relations, 27*, 507–23

Dundes, A. (ed.) (1991). *The blood libel legend: a casebook in anti-Semitic folklore*. Madison, Wisconsin: University of Wisconsin Press.

Durán, K. and Hachiche, A. (2001). *Children of Abraham: an introduction to Islam for Jews*. Jersey, New Jersey: Ktav Publishing Inc.

Dyszynski, C. (2010). London Review of Books: 10 years of anti-Israel prejudice. http://justjournalism.com/reports/london-review-of-books/#fn43 (Retrieved 5 January, 2013).

Eisenberg, L.Z. and Caplan, N. (1998). *Negotiating Arab-Israeli peace: patterns, problems, possibilities*. Bloomington/Indianapolis: Indiana University Press.

Eisenberg, L.Z. and Caplan, N. (2003). The Israel-Jordan peace treaty: patterns of negotiation, problems of implementation, *Israel Affairs 9*(3), 87–110.

Elpeleg, Z. (1993). *The grand mufti: Haj Amin al-Hussaini, founder of the Palestinian national movement*. London: Frank Cass & Co.

Fein, H. (1987). Dimensions of antisemitism: attitudes, collective accusations and actions. In H. Fein (ed.), *The persisting question: sociological perspectives and social contexts of modern antisemitism, current research on antisemitism* (pp.67–85). Berlin/New York.

Feldberg, M. (ed.) (2002). *"The Massena blood libel". Blessings of freedom: chapters in American Jewish history*. New York: American Jewish Historical Society.

Fernández-Morera, D. (2003). The myth of the Andalusian paradise. *The Intercollegiate Review, 39*(1–2), 23–31.

Finlay, W.L. (2005). Pathologizing dissent: identity politics, zionism and the "self-hating Jew". *British Journal of Social Psychology, 41*, 201–22

Fischel, J.R. (2005). The new anti-Semitism. *Virginia Quarterly Review, 81*(3), 225–34.

Fisk, R. (2001). *Pity the nation: Lebanon at war*. Oxford: Oxford University Press.

Florence, R. (2004). *Blood libel: the Damascus affair of 1840*. Madison, Wisconsin: University of Wisconsin Press.

Ford, H. (1920). *Volume 1: The international Jew: The world's foremost problem*. Dearborn, MI: The Dearborn Publishing Co.

Frank, D.H. (ed.) (1993). *A People apart: chosenness and ritual in Jewish philosophical thought.* Albany, NY: SUNY Press.

Fraser, R. (2005). The academic boycott of Israel: why Britain? *Jerusalem Center for Public Affairs* 36(1). http://www.jcpa.org/phas/phas-36.htm (retrieved 18 January 2013).

Friesel, E. (2011). On the complexities of modern Jewish identity: contemporary Jews against Israel. *Israel Affairs, 17*(4), 504–19.

Frindte, W., Wettig, S. and Wammetsberger, D. (2005). Old and new anti-Semitic attitudes in the context of authoritarianism and social dominance orientation: two studies in Germany. *Peace and Conflict: Journal of Peace Psychology, 11*(3), 239–66.

Funkenstein, A. (1993). *Perceptions of Jewish history.* Berkeley and Los Angeles: University of California Press.

Gavrilis, G. (2004). Sharon's endgame for the West Bank barrier. *The Washington Quarterly, 27*(4), 7–20.

Gecas, V. (1982). The self-concept. *Annual Review of Sociology, 8*, 1–33.

Gerber, J.S. (1986). Anti-Semitism and the Muslim world. In D. Berger (ed.) *History and hate: the dimensions of anti-semitism* (pp.73–94). New York: NY: Jewish Publications Society.

Gibson, J.L. and Howard, M.M. (2007). Russian anti-Semitism and the scapegoating of Jews. *British Journal of Political Science, 7*, 193–223.

Gilbert, M. (1985). *The Holocaust.* New York: Henry Holt and Company.

Gilbert, M. (1998). *Israel: a history.* New York, NY: HarperCollins.

Goitein, S.D. (1971) *A Mediterranean society* (vol. 2). Berkeley, CA: University of California Press.

Gold, J.T. (1988). *Monsters and madonnas: the roots of christian antisemitism.* New York, NY: Syracuse.

Göller, K.H. (1987). Sir Hugh of Lincoln. From History to Nursery Rhyme. In B. Engler and Kurt Müller (eds), *Jewish life and Jewish suffering as mirrored in English and American literature* (pp. 17–31). Paderborn: Schöningh.

Golsan, R.J. (2010). Antisemitism in modern France: Dreyfus, Vichy and beyond. In A.S. Lindemann and R.S. Levy (eds), *Antisemitism: A history* (pp.136–49). Oxford: Oxford University Press.

Goodman, D.G. and Miyazawa, M. (2000). *Jews in the Japanese mind: the history and uses of a cultural stereotype.* Lanham, MA: Lexington Books.

Gorst, A. and Johnman, L. (1996). *The Suez crisis.* London: Routledge.

Graham, D. and Boyd, J. (2010). *Committed, concerned and conciliatory: the attitudes of Jews in Britain towards Israel.* London: Institute for Jewish Policy Research.

Gray, M. (2010). *Conspiracy theories in the Arab world: sources and politics.* London: Routledge.

Green, D.P., Glaser, J. and Rich, A. (1998). From lynching to gay bashing: the elusive connection between economic conditions and hate crime. *Journal of Personality and Social Psychology, 75*, 82–92.

Greenberg, J., Pyszczynski, T., Solomon, S., Roseblatt, A., Veeder, M., Kirland, S. and Lyon, D. (1990). Evidence for terror management theory II: the effects of mortality salience on reaction to those who threaten or bolster the cultural worldview. *Journal of Personality and Social Psychology*, *29*, 61–139. New York: Academic Press.

Gregory, W.E. (2001). Scapegoating. In E. Craighead and C.B. Nemeroff (eds), *The Corsini encyclopedia of psychology and behavioral science* (3rd edn, vol. 4). New York: Wiley.

Gross, J. (2006). *Fear: anti-Semitism in Poland after Auschwitz: an essay in historical interpretation*. New York: Random House.

Halmari, H. (1993). Dividing the world: The dichotomous rhetoric of Ronald Reagan. *Multilingua*, *12*(2), 143–76.

Harkin, H. (2002). The return of anti-Semitism. *Wall Street Journal*, 5 February 2002. Available at www.opinionjournal.com/forms/printThis.html?id=95001818 (retrieved 20 March 2012).

Haselton, M. G., and Buss, D.M. (2003). Biases in social judgment: design flaws or design features? In J.P. Forgas, K.D. Williams and W. von Hippel (eds), *Social judgments: implicit and explicit processes* (pp. 23–43). New York: Cambridge University Press.

Haslam, N. (2006). Dehumanization: An integrative review. *Personality and Social Psychology Review*, *10*(3), 252–64.

Herf, J. (2006). *The Jewish enemy: Nazi propaganda during World War II and the Holocaust*. Cambridge, MA: Harvard University Press.

Herzl, T. (1895/1946). *The Jewish State*. Mineola, NY: Dover Publications.

Herzog, H. (1994). The Jews as 'Others': on communicative aspects of antisemitism. *Analysis of Current Trends in Antisemitism*, *4*. Jerusalem: Hebrew University.

Hilberg, (1985). *The destruction of the European Jews*. New Haven, CT: Yale University Press.

Hiro, D. (1973). *Black British, white British*. Harmondsworth: Penguin.

Hirszowicz, L. (1966). *The Third Reich and the Arab east*. Toronto: Toronto University Press.

Hitler, A. (1925/2007). *Mein Kampf*. Delhi: Jaico Publishing House.

Hughes, G. (2010). *Political correctness: a history of semantics and culture*. Oxford: Wiley-Blackwell.

Hurwitz, H. and Medad, Y. (2011). *Peace in the making: the Menachem Begin – Anwar Sadat personal correspondence*. Jerusalem: The Menachem Begin Heritage Center.

Hussain, A.J. (2007). The media's role in a clash of misconceptions: the case of the Danish Muhammad cartoons. *The international journal of press/politics*, *18*(2), 112–30.

Iganski, P. and Kosmin, B. (eds.) (2003). *A new antisemitism? Debating Judeophobia in 21st century Britain*. London: Profile.

Imhoff, R. and Banse, R. (2009). Ongoing victim suffering increases prejudice: the case of secondary anti-semitism. *Psychological Science*, *20*(12), 1443–7.

Isaac, B. (2010). The ancient Mediterranean and the pre-Christian era. In A.S. Lindemann and R.S. Levy (eds), *Antisemitism: a history* (pp.34–46). Oxford: Oxford University Press.

Israel, J. (2010). *A revolution of the mind: radical enlightenment and the intellectual origins of modern democracy*. Princeton, NJ: Princeton University Press.

Jacobson, J. (1997). Religion and ethnicity: dual and alternative sources of identity among young British Pakistanis. *Ethnic and Racial Studies, 20*(2), 238–56.

Jahanbegloo, R. (2007). Holocaust denial in Iran and anti-Semitic discourse in the Muslim world. Paper presented at the Centre for Minority Studies, History Department, Royal Holloway University of London, Egham.

Jaher, F.C. (1994). *A scapegoat in the wilderness: the origins and rise of anti-Semitism in America*. Cambridge: Harvard University Press.

Jaspal, R. (2011a). Caste, social stigma and identity processes. *Psychology and Developing Societies, 23*(2) 27–62.

Jaspal, R. (2011b). *The construction and management of national and ethnic identities among British South Asians: an identity process theory approach*. Ph.D. dissertation, Royal Holloway, University of London, UK.

Jaspal, R. (2011c). What are the psychological motives underlying anti-Semitism and anti-Zionism? Some data from Iran, Canada and the UK. Paper presented at BPS Social Psychology Section Annual Conference, Fitzwilliam College, University of Cambridge, 6th–8th September 2011.

Jaspal, R. (2013a). Anti-Semitism and anti-Zionism in Iran. *Israel Affairs, 19*(2), 231–58.

Jaspal, R. (Chair) (2013b). *Continuities and discontinuities of anti-Jewish sentiment in societal discourse*. Symposium conducted at the 29th Annual Meeting of the Association of Israel Studies, Los Angeles, CA, 24–26 June 2013.

Jaspal, R. (2013c). Israel in the Iranian media: demonizing the "Zionist Regime". *Israel Journal of Foreign Affairs, 7*(1), 77–86.

Jaspal, R. (2013d). Social representations of Jews and the Jewish State among Iranian adolescents: a qualitative study. In R. Jaspal (Chair), *Continuities and discontinuities of anti-Jewish sentiment in societal discourse*. Symposium conducted at the 29th Annual Meeting of the Association of Israel Studies, Los Angeles, CA, 24–26 June 2013.

Jaspal, R. (2013e). British Sikh identity and the struggle for distinctiveness and continuity. *Journal of Community and Applied Social Psychology, 23*(3), 225–39.

Jaspal, R. (2014a). Delegitimizing Jews and Israel in Iran's international Holocaust cartoon contest. *Journal of Modern Jewish Studies, 2*(3), 422–42.

Jaspal, R. (2014b). Imagining "home": identity processes among Persian Israelis and Iranian Jews. Paper presented at the 30th Annual Meeting of the Association for Israel Studies, Ben Gurion University, 23–25 June 2014.

Jaspal, R. (2014c). Representing the Arab spring in the Iranian press: Islamic awakening or foreign-sponsored terror? *Politics, Groups, and Identities. 13*(2), 167–89.

Jaspal, R. (2014d). Representing the "Zionist Regime": mass communication of anti-Zionism in the English-language Iranian press. *British Journal of Middle Eastern Studies. 41*(3), 287–305.

Jaspal, R. and Breakwell, G.M. (eds) (2014). *Identity process theory: identity, Social Action and Social Change.* Cambridge: Cambridge University Press.

Jaspal, R. and Cinnirella, M. (2010a). Coping with potentially incompatible identities: accounts of religious, ethnic and sexual identities from British Pakistani men who identify as Muslim and gay. *British Journal of Social Psychology, 49*(4), 849–70.

Jaspal, R. and Cinnirella, M. (2010b). Media representations of British Muslims and hybridised threats to identity. *Contemporary Islam: Dynamics of Muslim Life, 4*(3), 289–310.

Jaspal, R. and Cinnirella, M. (2012). The construction of ethnic identity: insights from identity process theory. *Ethnicities, 12*(5), 503–30.

Jaspal, R. and Cinnirella, M. (2013). The construction of British national identity among British South Asians. *National Identities, 15*(2), 157–75.

Jaspal, R. and Cinnirella, M. (2014). Hyper-affiliation to the religious ingroup among British Pakistani Muslim gay men. *Journal of Community and Applied Social Psychology, 24*(4), 265–277.

Jaspal, R. and Coyle, A. (2014). Threat, victimhood and peace: debating the 2011 Palestinian UN state membership bid. *Digest of Middle East Studies, 23*(1), 190–214.

Jaspal, R. and Nerlich, B. (2014). When climate science became climate politics: British media representations of climate change in 1988. *Public Understanding of Science, 23*(2), 122–41.

Jaspal, R. and Sitaridou, I. (2013). Coping with stigmatised linguistic identities: identity threat and ethnolinguistic vitality among Andalusians. *Identity: An International Journal of Theory and Research, 13*(2), 95–119.

Jaspal, R. and Yampolsky, M. (2011). Social representations of the Holocaust and Jewish Israeli identity construction: insights from identity process theory. *Social Identities: Journal for the Study of Race, Nation and Culture, 17*(2), 201–24.

Jikeli, G. (2009). Antisemitism among young Muslims in London. Paper presented at the International Study Group Education and Research on Antisemitism Colloquium 1: Aspects of Antisemitism in the UK, 5.

Jikeli, G. (2010). Anti-Semitism in youth language: the pejorative use of the terms for "Jew" in German and French. *Conflict and Communication, 9*(1), 1–13.

Jikeli, G. (2013). Perceptions of the Holocaust among young Muslims in Berlin, Paris and London. In G. Jikeli and J. Allouche-Benayoun (eds), *Perceptions of the Holocaust in Europe and Muslim communities: sources, comparisons and educational changes* (pp.105–32). New York: Springer.

Jikeli, G. and Allouche-Benayoun, J. (eds). (2013). *Perceptions of the Holocaust in Europe and Muslim Communities: Sources, Comparisons and Educational Challenges*. New York: Springer.

Kaplan, E.H. and Small, C.A. (2006). Anti-Israel sentiment predicts anti-semitism in Europe. *Journal of Conflict Resolution, 50*(4), 548–61

Karl, H.G. (1987). Sir Hugh of Lincoln. From history to nursery rhyme. In B. Engler and K. Müller (eds), *Jewish life and Jewish suffering as mirrored in English and American literature* (pp.17–31). Paderborn: Schöningh.

Karsh, E. (2002). *The Arab-Israeli conflict: the Palestine war 1948*. Oxford: Osprey Publishing.

Karsh, E. (2011). Zionism and the Palestinians. *Israel Affairs, 14*(3), 355–73.

Katz, Y. and Hendel, Y. (2012). *Israel vs. Iran: the shadow war*. Dulles, VI: Potomac Books.

Kelley, H.H. (1967). Attribution theory in social psychology. In D. Levine (ed.), *Nebraska Symposium on Motivation* (vol. 15) (pp.192–238). Lincoln, NE: University of Nebraska Press.

Kelman, H.C. (1976). Violence without restraint: reflections on the dehumanization of victims and victimizers. In G.M. Kren and L.H. Rappoport (eds), *Varieties of psychohistory* (pp. 282–314). New York: Springer.

Khomeini, R. (1981). *Islam and revolution I, writings and declarations of Imam Khomeini*. United States of America: Mizan Press.

King, R.D. and Weiner, M.F. (2007). Group position, collective threat, and American anti-semitism. *Social Problems, 54*(1), 47–77.

Klaff, L. (2010) Anti-Zionist expression on the UK campus: free speech or hate speech? *Jewish Political Studies Review, 22*, 3–4.

Klein, A. (2009). Characterizing "the enemy": Zionism and Islamism in the Iranian and Israeli press. *Communication, Culture & Critique, 2*, 387–406.

Klier, J.D. and Lambroza, S. (eds) (1992). *Pogroms: anti-Jewish violence in modern Russian history*. Cambridge: Cambridge University Press.

Klug, B. (2003). The collective Jew: Israel and the new antisemitism. *Patterns of Prejudice, 37*(2), 117–38.

Kofta, M. and Sedek, G. (2005). Conspiracy stereotypes of Jews during systemic transformation in Poland. *International Journal of Sociology, 35*, 40–64.

Konig, R., Eisinga, R. and Scheepers, P. (2000). Explaining the relationship between Christian religion and anti-Semitism in the Netherlands. *Review of Religious Research, 41*(3), 373–93.

Konig, R., Scheepers, P. and Falling, A. (2001). Research on antisemitism: a review of previous findings and the case of the Netherlands in the 1990s. In K. Phalet and A. Örkény (eds), *Ethnic minorities and inter-ethnic relations in context: A Dutch Hungarian comparison*. Aldershot: Ashgate.

Kornberg, J. (1993). *Theodor Herzl: from assimilation to Zionism*. Bloomington/ Indianapolis: Indiana University Press.

Kotek, J. (2009). *Cartoons and extremism: Israel and the Jews in Arab and Western media*. Edgware: Vallentine Mitchell.

Kramer, M. (1995). *The salience of Islamic antisemitism.* London: Institute of Jewish Affairs.

Krekovičová, E. (1997). Jewishness in the eyes of others: reflection of the Jew in Slovak folklore. *Human Affairs, 7*(2), 167–83.

Kressel, N. (2003). Antisemitism, social science, and the Muslim and Arab world. *Judaism: A Quarterly Journal of Jewish Life and Thought, 52,* 3–4.

Kumaraswamy, P.R. (2010). Indian Muslims and the three js: Jews, Jerusalem and the Jewish state. In M. Ma'oz (ed.), *Muslim attitudes to Jews and Israel: the ambivalence of rejection, antagonism, tolerance and co-operation* (pp.215–29). Eastbourne: Sussex Academic Press.

Kudenko, I. and Phillips, D. (2009). Multicultural narratives and the construction of identity: the British Jewish experience. *Space and Polity, 14*(1), 65–80.

Kudenko, I. and Phillips, D. (2010). The model of integration? Social and spatial transformations in the Leeds Jewish community. *Journal of Ethnic and Migration Studies, 35*(9), 1533–49.

Küntzel, M. (2010). Iranian anti-Semitism: stepchild of German national socialism. *Israel Journal of Foreign Affairs, 4*(1) 43–51.

Laqueur, W. (2006). *The changing face of antisemitism: from ancient times to the present day.* Oxford: Oxford University Press.

Laskier, M. (1995). Egyptian Jewry under the Nasser Regime, 1956–70. *Middle Eastern Studies,* 31(3), 573–619.

Lazar, A., Litvak-Hirsch, T., and Chaitin, J. (2008). Between culture and family: Jewish Israeli young adults' relation to the Holocaust as a cultural trauma. *Traumatology, 14*(4), 93–102.

Lazarus-Yafeh, H. (1999). Jews and Christians in medieval Muslim thought. In R.S. Wistrich (ed.), *Demonizing the other: anti-Semitism, racism and xenophobia* (pp.88–107). Amsterdam: Harwood Academic Publishers.

LeCouteur, A. and Augoustinos, M. (2001). The language of prejudice and racism. In M. Augoustinos and K.J. Reynolds (eds), *Understanding prejudice, racism, and social conflict* (pp.215–30). London: Sage.

Levy, H. (1999). *Comprehensive history of the Jews of Iran* (Costa Mesa, CA: xx)

Levy, R.S. (2010). Political antisemitism in Germany and Austria, 1848–1914. In A.S. Lindemann and R.S. Levy (eds), *Antisemitism: a history* (pp.121–35). Oxford: Oxford University Press.

Lewin, K. (1948) *Resolving social conflicts: selected papers on group dynamics.* New York: Harper and Row.

Lewis, B. (1999). *Semites and antisemites: an enquiry into conflict and prejudice.* New York: W.W. Norton.

Lewis, B. (2003). *The crisis of Islam.* New York: Random House.

Lewis, B. (2004). *The Jews of Islam.* Princeton, NJ: Princeton University Press.

Lindemann, A.S. and Levy, R.S. (eds) (2010a). *Antisemitism: a history.* Oxford: Oxford University Press.

Lindemann, A.S. and Levy, R.S. (2010b). Introduction. In A.S. Lindemann and R.S. Levy (eds), *Antisemitism: a history* (pp.1–16). Oxford: Oxford University Press.

Lipstadt, D. (1993). *Denying the Holocaust: the growing assault on truth and memory*. London: Plume.

Litvak, M. (1998). The Islamicization of the Israeli-Arab conflict: the case of Hamas. *Middle Eastern Studies*, *23*(1), 148–63.

Litvak, M. (2006). The Islamic Republic of Iran and the Holocaust: anti-Semitism and anti-Zionism. *Journal of Israeli History*, *25*(1), 267–84

Litvak, M. and Webman, E. (2009). *From empathy to denial: Arab responses to the Holocaust*. New York: Columbia University Press.

Litvak, M. and Webman, E. (2010) Israel and antisemitism. In A.S. Lindemann and R.S. Levy (eds), *Antisemitism: a history* (pp.237–49). Oxford: Oxford University Press.

Liwerant, J.B. (2011). Mexico in a region under change. *Journal for the Study of Antisemitism*, *3*(1), 27–38.

Loewenthal, K.M. (2000). *Psychology of religion: a short introduction*. Oxford: One-world Publications.

Loewenthal, K.M. (2014). Religion, identity and mental health. In R. Jaspal and G.M. Breakwell (eds), *Identity process theory: identity, social action and social change* (pp.316–34). Cambridge: Cambridge University Press.

Longerich, P. (2010). *Holocaust: the Nazi persecution and murder of the Jews*. Oxford: Oxford University Press.

Louis, W.R. and Shlaim, A. (eds) (2012). *The 1967 Arab-Israeli war: origins and consequences*. Cambridge: Cambridge University Press.

Lyons, E. (1996). Coping with social change: processes of social memory in the reconstruction of identities. In G.M. Breakwell and E. Lyons (eds), *Changing European identities: socio-psychological analyses of social change* (pp. 31–40). Oxford: Butterworth- Heinemann.

Maccoby, H. (1996). *A pariah people: the anthropology of antisemitism*. London: Constable.

Macshane, D. (2008). *Globalising hatred: the new antisemitism*. London: Phoenix.

Makovsky, D. (2005). Gaza: Moving forward by pulling back. *Foreign Affairs*, *84*(3), 52–62.

Markovits, A.S. (2006). A new (or perhaps revived) "uninhibitedness" toward Jews in Germany. *Jewish Political Studies Review, 18*(1–2).

Markowe, L. (1996). *Re-defining the self: coming out as a lesbian*. London: Wiley.

Marques, J.M., Yzerbyt, V.Y. & Leyens, J-P. (1988). The "black sheep effect": Extremity of judgments towards ingroup members as a function of group identification. *European Journal of Social Psychology, 18*, 1–16.

Marques, J.M., Abrams, D., Páez, D. and Hogg, M.A. (2001). Social categorization, social identification, and rejection of deviant group members. In M.A. Hogg & R.S. Tindale (eds), *Blackwell handbook of social psychology (Vol. 3): Group processes* (pp. 400–424). Oxford, UK: Blackwell.

Marr, W. (1879). The victory of Judaism over Germanism. Bern, Rudolph Costenoble. English translation: http://www.kevinmacdonald.net/Marr-Text-English.pdf (retrieved on 7 January 2013).

Matar, I. (1981). Israeli settlements in the West Bank and Gaza Strip. *Journal of Palestine Studies, 11*(1), 93–110.

Matas, D. (2005). *Aftershock: anti-Zionism and anti-Semitism.* Hightown: Gazelle Book Services.

McAdams, D.P. (2001). The psychology of life stories. *Review of General Psychology, 5*, 100–122.

Menashri, D. (1991). The Jews of Iran: between the Shah and Khomeini. In S. Gilman and S. Katz (eds), *Anti-Semitism in times of crisis* (pp.353–71). New York: New York University Press.

Menashri, D. (2000). *Post-revolutionary politics in Iran: religion, society and power.* London: Routledge.

Menocal, M.R. (2002) *The ornament of the world: how Muslims, Jews and Christians created a culture of tolerance in medieval Spain.* USA: Little, Brown and Co.

Meyer, P.H. (1963). The attitude of the enlightenment toward the Jew. *Studies on Voltaire and the Eighteenth Century, 26*, 1177.

Milgram, S. (1963). Behavioral study of obedience. *Journal of Abnormal and Social Psychology, 67*, 371–8.

Milkewitz, A. (2011). Antisemitism in Brazil. *Journal for the Study of Antisemitism, 3*(1) 157–66.

Mishal, S. and Sela, A. (2000). *The Palestinian Hamas: vision, violence and coexistence.* New York: Columbia University Press.

Molavi, A. (2005). *The soul of Iran: a nation's struggle for freedom.* New York: W.W. Norton & Co.

Moscovici, S. (1988). Notes towards a description of social representations. *European Journal of Social Psychology, 18*, 211–50.

Moscovici, S. (2000). *Social representations: studies in social psychology.* Cambridge: Polity Press.

Moscovici, S. and Hewstone, M. (1983). Social representations and social explanations: from the 'naive' to the 'amateur' scientist. In M. Hewstone (ed.), *Attribution theory: social and functional extensions* (pp. 99–125). Oxford: Blackwell.

Mottale, M. (2011). Iran's clerical regime's "Jewish Problem". *Democracy and Security, 7*(3), 258–70.

Nelson, T. (2002). *The psychology of prejudice.* Needham Heights, MA: Allyn & Bacon.

Nerlich, B. and Jaspal, R. (2014). Images of extreme weather: symbolising human responses to climate change. *Science as Culture 23*(2), 253–76.

Nets-Zehngut, R. and Bar-Tal, D. (2007). The intractable Israeli-Palestinian conflict and possible pathways to peace. In J. Kuriansky (ed.), *Beyond bullets and bombs: grassroots peacebuilding between Palestinians and Israelis* (pp.3–13). Westport, CT: Praeger.

Newman, D. (2008). Britain and the academic boycott of Israel. *Israel Journal of Foreign Affairs*, 2(2), 45–55.

Norman, J.M. (2010). *The second Palestinian Intifada: civil resistance.* London: Routledge.

Norton, A.R. (2007). *Hezbollah: a short history.* Princeton, NJ: Princeton University Press.

Oren, N. and Bar-Tal, D. (2007). The detrimental dynamics of delegitimization in intractable conflicts: the Israeli-Palestinian case. *International Journal of Intercultural Relations, 31*, 111–26.

Oren, N. and Bar-Tal, D. (2014). Collective identity and intractable conflict. In R. Jaspal and G.M. Breakwell (eds), *Identity process theory: identity, social action and social change* (pp.222–52). Cambridge: Cambridge University Press.

Pappé, I (2006). *A history of modern Palestine: one land, two peoples.* Cambridge: Cambridge University Press.

Pappé, I. (2007). *The ethnic cleansing of Palestine.* Oxford: Oneworld.

Pardo, E.J. (2007). Race and the nuclear race: anti-semitism in Iran. In M. Korinman and J. Laughland (eds), *Shia power: next target Iran?* (pp.69–91). London: Mitchell & Co. Ltd.

Pargament, K.I., Trevino, K., Mahoney, A. and Silberman, I. (2007). They killed our Lord: the perception of Jews as desecrators of Christianity as a predictor of anti-semitism. *Journal for the Scientific Study of Religion, 46*(2), 143–58.

Parsons, N. (2005). *The politics of the Palestinian authority: from Oslo to Al-Aqsa.* London: Routledge.

Patton, M.Q. (1990). *Qualitative evaluation and research methods.* London: Sage.

Pauley, B.F. (1998). *From prejudice to persecution: a history of Austrian anti-Semitism.* Chapel Hill, NC: University of North Carolina Press.

Peach, C. (2005). Muslims in the UK. In T. Abbas (ed.), *Islamic political radicalism: a European perspective* (pp.18–30). Edinburgh: Edinburgh University Press.

Perry, M. and Schweitzer, F. (2002). *Antisemitism: myth and hate from antiquity to the present.* Basingstoke: Palgrave Macmillan.

Perry, M. and Schweitzer, F.M. (2008). *Antisemitic myths: a historical and contemporary anthology.* Bloomington/Indianapolis: Indiana University Press.

Poliakov, L. (1974). *The history of anti-Semitism.* New York: The Vanguard Press.

Porat, D. (1999). The protocols of the elders of Zion: new uses of an old myth. In R.S Wistrich (ed.), *Demonizing the other: anti-Semitism, racism and xenophobia* (p.322–34). Amsterdam: Harwood Academic Publishers.

Potter, J. and Wetherell, M. (1987). *Discourse and social psychology: beyond attitudes and behavior.* London: Sage.

Quinley, H.E. and Glock, C.Y. (1979). *Anti-Semitism in America.* New York: Free Press.

Raab, E. (1983). Anti-Semitism in the 1980s. *Midstream, 29*,11–18.

Rein, R. (2003). *Argentina, Israel and the Jews: Peron, the Eichmann capture and after.* Bethesda, MD: University Press of Maryland.

Riek, B.M., Mania, E.W. and Gaertner, S.L. (2006). Intergroup threat and outgroup attitudes: a meta-analytic review. *Personality and Social Psychology Review*, *10*(4), 336–53.

Rolef, S. H. (Ed.). (1993). *Political dictionary of the State of Israel.* Jerusalem: The Jerusalem Publishing House Ltd.

Rosenfeld. A. (2011). *The end of the Holocaust.* Bloomington: Indiana University Press.

Rosenfeld, A. (2013). *Resurgent antisemitism: global perspectives.* Bloomington, IN: Indiana University Press.

Roth, N. (2002). *Conversos, inquisition, and the expulsion of the Jews from Spain.* Madison, WI: University of Wisconsin Press.

Rothstein, R. (1986). Jews in Slavic eyes – the paremiological evidence. In *Ninth World Congress of Jewish Studies* (pp.181–188). Jerusalem.

Rubenstein, J. and Naumov, V.P (2001). *Stalin's secret pogrom: the postwar inquisition of the Jewish anti-fascist committee.* New Haven, CT: Yale University Press.

Rubenstein, R.L. (2009). Defeat, rage and Jew-hatred. *Journal for the Study of Antisemitism*, *1*(2), 95–138.

Sacks, J. (2003) A new antisemitism? In P. Iganski and B. Kosmin (eds). *A new antisemitism? Debating Judeophobia in 21ˢᵗ century Britain* (pp.38–53). London: Profile Books Ltd.

Salmons, P. (2003). Teaching or preaching? The Holocaust and intercultural education in the UK. *Intercultural Education*, *14*(2), 139–49.

Salzborn, S. (2010). The politics of antisemitism. *Journal for the Study of Antisemitism*, *2*(1), 89–114.

Samuels, S. (2009). A welcome from the chair. *Journal for the Study of Antisemitism*, *1*(1), 1–4.

Sarshar, H. (2014). Days of darkness, days of light: the unknown story of Iran's Jews. *Reform Judaism.* http://reformjudaismmag.org/PrintItem/index.cfm?id=1013&type=Articles (retrieved 1 February 2014).

Schäfer, P. (1998). *Judeophobia: attitudes toward the Jews in the ancient world.* Cambridge, MA: Harvard University Press.

Schönbach, P. (1961). *Reaktionen auf die antisemitische Welle im Winter 1959/60.* Frankfurt am Main: Europäische Verlagsanstalt.

Schvindlerman, J. (2011). Latin America and the Middle East: the political background. *Journal for the Study of Antisemitism*, *3*(1), 51–60.

Schwartz, D.R. (1999). Antisemitism and Other–isms in the Greco-Roman world. In R.S Wistrich (ed.), *Demonizing the other: anti-semitism, racism and xenophobia* (p.73–87). Amsterdam: Harwood Academic Publishers.

Segev, T. (1992). *The seventh million.* Jerusalem: Keter.

Selznick, G.J. and Steinberg, S. (1969). *The tenacity of prejudice: anti-Semitism in contemporary America.* New York: Harper and Row.

Semati, M. (2008). *Media, culture and society in Iran: living with globalization and the Islamic state*. London: Routledge.

Shafir, G. (1999). Zionism and colonialism. In I. Pappé (ed.), *The Israel/Palestinian question* (p.72–85). London: Psychology Press.

Shahvar, S. (2009). The Islamic regime in Iran and its attitude towards the Jews: the religious and political dimensions. *Immigrants & Minorities, 27*(1), 82–117.

Shapira, A. (2006). Israeli perceptions of anti-Semitism and anti-Zionism. *Journal of Israeli History: Politics, Society, Culture, 25*(1), 245–66.

Sharansky (2004). 3D test of anti-Semitism: demonization, double standards, delegitimization. *Jewish Political Studies Review, 17*(1–2). http://jcpa.org/phas/phas-sharansky-s05.htm (retrieved 6 May 2013).

Sharon, A. (2009). *Why is Israel's presence in the territories still called "occupation"?* Jerusalem: Jerusalem Center for Public Affairs. http://jcpa.org/text/Occupation-Sharon.pdf (retrieved 3 June 2013).

Shlaim, A. (2001). *The iron wall: Israel and the Arab world*. London: Penguin.

Shlaim, A. (2009). *Israel and Palestine: reappraisals, revisions, refutations*. London: Verso.

Shnell, I. and Mishal, S. (2008). Place as a source of identity in colonizing societies: Israeli settlements in Gaza. *Geographical Review, 98*(2), 242–59.

Short, G. (1994). Teaching the Holocaust: the relevance of children's perceptions of Jewish culture and identity. *British Educational Research Journal, 20*(4), 393–405.

Shulewitz, M.K. (ed.) (2001). *The forgotten millions: the modern Jewish exodus from Arab lands*. London: Continuum.

Shuval, J.T. (1998). Migration to Israel: the mythology of "uniqueness". *International Migration, 36*(1), 3–26.

Silberman, I. (2005). Religion as a meaning system: implications for the new millennium. *Journal of Social Issues, 61*, 641–63.

Simon, B. (2004). *Identity in modern society: a social psychological perspective*. Oxford: Blackwell.

Simon, R., Laskier, M. and Reguer, S. (eds) (2002). *The Jews of the Middle East and North Africa in modern times*. New York: Columbia University Press.

Simon, R.J. and Schaler, J.A. (2007). Anti-semitism the world over in the twenty-first century. *Current Psychology, 26*(3/4), 152–82.

Sinclair, J. and Milner, D. (2005) On being Jewish: a qualitative study of identity among British Jews in emerging adulthood. *Journal of Adolescent Research, 20*(1), 91–117

Smith, S.W. (2012). Cartoons and the new anti-Semitism. Unpublished M.Des. dissertation, Massey University, Wellington, New Zealand.

Smith, T.W. (1991). *What do Americans think about Jews? Working papers on contemporary anti-Semitism*. New York: American Jewish Committee.

Spencer, P. (2010) The Left, radical antisemitism, and the problem of genocide. *The Journal for the Study of Antisemitism, 2*(1), 133–51.

Spencer, P. and Di Palma, S.V. (2013). Antisemitism and the politics of Holocaust Memorial Day in the UK and Italy. In G. Jikeli and J. Allouche-Benayoun (eds), *Perceptions of the Holocaust in Europe and Muslim communities: sources, comparisons and educational changes* (pp.71–84). New York: Springer.

Stav, A. (1999). *Peace: the Arabian caricature: a study of anti-Semitic imagery.* New York: Gefen Publishing House, Ltd.

Stein, H.F. (1978). Judaism and the group-fantasy of martyrdom: The psychodynamic paradox of survival through persecution. *Journal of Psychohistory, 6,* 151–210.

Stephan, W.G. and Stephan, C.W. (2000). An integrated threat theory of prejudice. In S. Oskamp (ed.), *Reducing prejudice and discrimination* (pp.23–46). Mahwah, NJ: Erlbaum.

Stephan, W.G., Ybarra, O. and Rios Morrison, K. (2009). Intergroup threat theory. In T. Nelson (ed.), *Handbook of prejudice* (pp.43–59). Mahwah, NJ: Lawrence Erlbaum Associates.

Stern, M. (1974–1984). *Jews and Judaism in Greek and Latin literature,* 3 volumes. Jerusalem: Israel Academy of Sciences and Humanities.

Stillman, N.A. (1979). *The Jews of Arab lands: a history and source book.* Philadelphia: Jewish Publication Society.

Stillman, N.A. (2010). Anti-Judaism and antisemitism in the Arab and Islamic world prior to 1948. In A.S. Lindemann and R.S. Levy (eds), *Antisemitism: a history* (pp.212–21). Oxford: Oxford University Press.

Sutcliffe, A. (2010). The Enlightenment, French revolution and Napoleon. In A.S. Lindemann and R.S. Levy (eds), *Antisemitism: a history* (pp.107–20). Oxford: Oxford University Press.

Sweetser, K.D. and Brown, C.W. (2010). An exploration of Iranian communication to multiple target audiences. *Public Relations Review, 36,* 238–48.

Szajkowski, Z. (1972). *Jews, war and communism.* New York: KTAV.

Taguieff, P.A. (2010). *La nouvelle propagande anti-juive.* Paris: Presses Universitaires de France.

Tajfel, H. (1975). The exit of social mobility and the voice of social change: notes on the social psychology of intergroup relations. *Social Science Information, 14,* 101–18.

Tajfel, H. (1982). Social psychology of intergroup relations. *Annual Review of Psychology, 33,* 1–39.

Tajfel, H. and Turner, J.C. (1986). The social identity theory of intergroup behaviour. in S. Worchel, and W.G. Austin (eds), *Psychology of intergroup relations* (pp. 7–24). Chicago, IL: Nelson-Hall.

Takeyh, R. (2006) Iran, Israel and the politics of terrorism. *Survival, 48*(4), 83–96.

Triandafyllidou, A. (1998). National identity and the 'other'. *Ethnic and Racial Studies, 21*(4), 593–612.

Valins, O. (2003). Stubborn identities and the construction of socio-spatial boundaries: ultra-orthodox Jews living in contemporary Britain. *Transactions of the Institute of British Geographers, 28*(2), 158–75 van Dijk, T.A. (1993). Principles of critical discourse analysis. *Discourse and Society*, *4*(2), 249–83.

Vignoles, V.L., Chryssochoou, X. and Breakwell, G.M. (2000). The distinctiveness principle: identity, meaning and the bounds of cultural relativity. *Personality and Social Psychology Review*, *4*, 337–54.

Vignoles, V.L. (2014). Quantitative approaches to researching identity processes and motivational processes. In R. Jaspal and G.M. Breakwell (eds), *Identity process theory: identity, social action and social change* (pp.65–94). Cambridge: Cambridge University Press.

Vincze, Z.K. (2013). Anti-Jewish cartoons in the Eastern European press. In R. Jaspal (Chair), *Continuities and Discontinuities of Anti-Jewish Sentiment in Societal Discourse*. Symposium conducted at the 29th Annual Meeting of the Association of Israel Studies, Los Angeles, CA, 24–26 June 2013.

Voelklein, C. and Howarth, C. (2005). A review of controversies about social representations theory: a debate. *Culture & Psychology*, *11*(4), 431–54.

Webman, E. (2010). The challenge of assessing Arab/Islamic antisemitism. *Middle Eastern Studies*, *46*(5), 677–98.

Weil, F.D. (1985) The variable effects of education on liberal attitudes: a comparative-historical analysis of anti-Semitism using public opinion survey data. *American Sociological Review*, *50*(4), 458–74.

Wieviorka, M. (2005). *The renewal of anti-semitism in France today*, vol I: *occasional papers, department of European and classical languages and cultures*. College Station: Texas A&M University.

Wills, T.A. (1981). Downward comparison principles in social psychology. *Psychological Bulletin*, *90*(2), 245–71.

Wistrich, R. (1991). *Antisemitism: the longest hatred*. London: Pantheon.

Wistrich, R.S. (1999a). Introduction: the devil, the Jews and hatred of the "other". In R.S Wistrich (ed.), *Demonizing the other: Anti-semitism, racism and xenophobia* (p.1–16). Amsterdam: Harwood Academic Publishers.

Wistrich, R.S. (ed.) (1999b). *Demonizing the other: anti-semitism, racism and xenophobia*. Amsterdam: Harwood Academic Publishers.

Wistrich, R.S. (2004). Anti-Zionism and anti-Semitism. *Jewish Political Studies Review*, *16*(3–4). http://jcpa.org/phas/phas-wistrich-f04.htm (retrieved 10 May 2013).

Wistrich, R.S. (2005). *European anti-Semitism reinvents itself*. New York: The American Jewish Committee.

Wistrich, R.S. (2008). Waging war on Judeophobes old and new. *Haaretz*. February 24, 2008.

Wistrich, R.S. (2010). *A lethal obsession: antisemitism – from antiquity to the global jihad*. New York: Random House.

Wistrich, R.S. (2011). From blood libel to boycott: changing faces of British antisemitism. *Posen Papers in Contemporary Antisemitism*, *13*. http://sicsa.huji.ac.il/robert%20pp13.pdf (retrieved 10 May 2013).

Wistrich, R.S. (2012). *From ambivalence to betrayal: the left, the Jews, and Israel.* Lincoln, NE: University of Nebraska Press.

Wittenberg, J. (2013). Varieties of anti-Semitism in pre-war and interwar Poland. In R. Jaspal (Chair), *Continuities and discontinuities of anti-Jewish sentiment in societal discourse.* Symposium conducted at the 29th Annual Meeting of the Association of Israel Studies, Los Angeles, CA, 24–26 June 2013.

Yadlin, R. (1999). Anti-Jewish imagery in the contemporary Arab-Muslim world. In R.S. Wistrich (ed.), *Demonizing the other: antisemitism, racism and zenophobia* (pp.309–21). Amsterdam: Harwood Academic Publishers.

Yahil, L. (1990). *The Holocaust.* Oxford: Oxford University Press.

Yeroushalmi, D. (ed.) (2013). *Light and shadows: the story of Iranian Jews.* Seattle, WA: University of Washington Press.

Zimbardo, P. (2008). *The Lucifer effect: the psychology of evil.* New York: Random House.

Index